# MICHAEL J. WEISS

# Latitudes & Attitudes

**From Abilene, Texas, to Zanesville, Ohio**

**An Atlas of American Tastes, Trends, Politics, and Passions**

## LITTLE, BROWN AND COMPANY

Boston   New York   Toronto   London

*This book is dedicated to my family —*
*Phyllis, Elizabeth, and Jonathan — for their love, support, and joy.*

First Edition

Library of Congress Cataloging-in-Publication Data
Weiss, Michael J.
      Latitudes & attitudes : an atlas of American tastes, trends, politics, and passions / by Michael J. Weiss. — 1st ed.
            p.      cm.
      ISBN 0-316-92915-8 (hc)
      ISBN 0-316-92908-5 (pb)
      1. United States — Social life and customs — 1971–
2. Consumers — United States — Attitudes.   3. Consumers —
United States — Attitudes — Maps.   4. National characteristics,
American.   5. National characteristics, American — Maps.
I. Title.
E169.04.W45   1994
306.4'0973 — dc20                                        94-16003

10  9  8  7  6  5  4  3  2

RRD-OH

*Designed by Barbara Werden*

Published simultaneously in Canada by
Little, Brown & Company (Canada) Limited

Printed in the United States of America

*Latitudes & Attitudes* is based on 1992 survey-generated maps, market profiles, and demographic statistics provided exclusively by Claritas Inc. (1525 Wilson Boulevard, Suite 1000, Arlington, VA 22209 800-284-4868). The survey data were collected by the Simmons Market Research Bureau, Mediamark Research Inc., R. L. Polk & Co., Yankelovich Partners Inc., and the U.S. Bureau of the Census, and were then adjusted using the PRIZM segmentation system to create nationwide maps and local market profiles; all rights reserved. Used with permission under an agreement with Claritas Inc.

Three of the captioned maps in this book appeared in similar form in the *Atlantic Monthly:* "Lemon-Lime Latitudes" (May 1991), "Japanese and American Cars" (August 1990), and "Bookworms and Couch Potatoes" (May 1991). In addition, *Time* printed a series of maps from this book between December 1993 and October 1994. Reprinted with permission.

# Contents

# Introduction

## An Atlas of American Life

FORGET the Rand McNally view of the United States.

The real America is a nation of consumer states, of communities defined less by their geography than by the passions of their populace. Be it pizza or personal computers, classical music or conservative politics, our marketplace choices determine the true boundaries of our pluralistic society. Just as churning highs and lows cause weather maps to shift daily, the interplay of local demographics, history, and lifestyle create varying contours of American taste. This new cartography reveals the nation's true cultural diversity — why some of us enjoy croissants, sailing, and *Vanity Fair* while others have a fondness for Pop Tarts, bass fishing, and "The Oprah Winfrey Show."

Welcome to the world of consumer mapping, where Americans speak a language composed not of words but of personal choices in food, media, home furnishings, and cultural values. As much as our jobs, educations, or places of origin, consuming has become one of our defining characteristics. Through our preferences for products and ideas, we assert our identity and form bonds with others nearby and across the nation. We seek out kindred spirits who share our love of bowling or racquetball,

our concern for privacy or gay rights, our obsession with "Star Trek" or C-SPAN.

America in the 1990s is less a melting pot than a simmering stew, spiced with the distinct tastes and influences of its 260 million residents. At a time when social critics worry that the country is homogenizing into one huge neon sprawl of look-alike shopping malls, fast-food joints, and hotel chains, consumer mapping offers fresh evidence of the continuing fragmentation of society. Americans are divided not just according to rich or poor, black or white, city folk or country cousin. The nation has splintered into diverse factions of baby boomers and retirees, frequent-flying executives and pink-collar workers, mobile Westerners and settled Southerners.

Each year, high-tech pollsters and market researchers survey more than 50 million people to understand better these myriad population segments and predict what they'll do (and buy) next. Yet the answers often remain unpublicized, the province of number-crunching analysts. As a result, few of us know how our neighbors live — why some prefer Buicks to Hondas, rock to Rachmaninoff, school prayer to sex education. Aside from Peeping Toms and possibly our hairdressers, We-the-People really don't know too much about each other.

*Latitudes & Attitudes* examines the American experience by revealing the nation's diverse subdivisions of tastes, trends, politics, and passions. As a consumer atlas, the book offers 88 color-coded maps depicting our preferences for a wide range of products, activities, and issues. Fleshing out these nationwide portraits are local highlights of the nation's 211 consumer markets — the basic units upon which these maps are built — which share similar media and retail outlets, values and idiosyncracies. From Abilene, Texas, to Zanesville, Ohio, these markets form the boundaries that businesses and the media commonly use to dissect the population and speak to their prime audiences with the right drawl.

By graphically charting market preferences, consumer maps document the rise and fall of the latest fads and the persistence of major social trends. While one map shows how the oat bran revolution has collapsed, another illustrates why the abortion debate is so intractable. Some maps are counterintuitive, depicting, for example, the link between condom sales and working women. Still others, spotlighting such products as white bread, Twinkies, mobile homes, and Cadillacs, prove that what's status to some is déclassé to others.

But consumer maps are more than snapshots of a society in motion: they change with time, demographic fluctuations, and the introduction of new products. Mouthwash, instant mashed potatoes, and video games, all launched in coastal metro areas, now find their most devoted fans in heartland communities. Baking from scratch, by contrast, has evolved from a downscale necessity to an upscale hobby, as affluent consumers now find satisfaction in creating loaves of homemade walnut bread. Some map patterns are the result of external forces, like the concentration of Japanese-car dealers near the nation's coastal ports. But customs, once established, tend to endure. The popularity of lemon-lime soda in the Upper Midwest coincides with the century-old settlement of Northern European immigrants, whose relatively bland diet is complemented by tart beverages.

Consumer maps show us at a glance our communities' preferences for everything from Barcaloungers to the death penalty, graphically displaying the nation's essential diversity. If nothing else, these maps serve as a reality check on contemporary culture. To wit, more Americans go hunting than invest in the stock market; more work on their cars than pursue gourmet cooking; more go to the bowling alley than the health club. Turn down the glare of the national media and you'll see it emerge: the true shape of American society, in all our variety and contradictions.

Studying America through its consumption patterns is nothing new, especially for the business community. As early as the 1930s, Sears knew from catalog orders that factory workers loved decorative plants, while Southern women bought yard goods because they preferred to sew their own dresses rather than buy them. After the postwar economic boom gave Americans more disposable income and leisure time, researchers turned to measures of standard demographics — age, sex, and income — to classify consumers and monitor their marketplace behavior. Computers then revolutionized the ability of businesses to target consumer groups accurately. By the 1970s, marketers were creating segmentation systems like PRIZM (Potential Rating Index for Zip Markets) that married census data with product information to sort consumers into lifestyle types, such as Money & Brains (affluent city enclaves filled with educated couples and singles) and Norma Rae–ville (lower-middle-class mill towns home to racially diverse families). Today, with the click of a computer mouse, businesses can pinpoint the one neighborhood within three miles of a store where they'll find the highest number of college-educated, Toyota-owning camera buffs between the ages of 25 and 34 who live in $175,000 homes.

Increasingly, consumer maps and market profiles are helping marketers in their tireless efforts to give consumers what they want even before they know they want it. Calico Corners, the fabric retail chain, uses consumer maps to decide the best locations for opening new stores. The Postal Service has developed maps of consumer types to decide which commemorative stamps to stock in its 400 philatelic centers around the country. From the maps they know that the serious collectors are found in markets like San Francisco and Washington, D.C., while casual collectors live in smaller cities like Lincoln, Neb., and Fargo, N.D. When a company called Direct Image Concepts, Inc., produced a national map of Elvis Presley fan-club members, officials in Yuba City, Calif., were so impressed to learn that their farming community was one of the hot markets that they threw a festival for the King, complete with a skydiving appearance by the Flying Elvises.

Knowing the preferences of communities today can give businesses a good idea of what consumers will buy tomorrow. In 1990, after Buick transformed its dated Park Avenue into a sleeker, Jaguaresque coupe, it turned to survey-based maps to find the best markets to roll out the new model. Concentrating on communities in the Northeast and on the West Coast, Buick boosted Park Avenue sales by 20 percent using

specific magazines and TV shows to reach its target audience. In New York City, Saatchi and Saatchi is just one of many advertising agencies that employ consumer maps combined with lifestyle surveys to develop customized appeals for everything from Hollywood movies to health care.

To be sure, computerized marketing techniques have raised concerns among some sociologists who fear the fallout of a consumption-crazed society. Fresh in their memories are the excesses of the 1980s, which spawned a savings and loan crisis, the highest federal debt in history, and a generation of Americans addicted to credit. The Media Foundation, a consumer watchdog group that uses satiric ads to condemn the ethic of wasteful consumption, maintains that too many Americans care for little beyond their next purchase and that we should all learn to live with less. In one magazine ad, the group derides the materialism of a well-dressed young man who stands above the slogan: "I buy. Therefore I am."

In their defense, marketers maintain that their efforts actually help consumers focus only on the goods and services they really want. Every year, Americans are confronted with 25,000 new products. Each day, we're bombarded with an estimated 1,500 messages. Target-marketing attempts not only to steer selected products toward selected people — say, baby formula toward expectant families in suburban homes — but to keep the same products away from those who aren't interested, such as childless couples living in urban apartments. The goal, say marketers, is to eliminate waste for businesses and reduce information clutter for consumers.

But in their attempts to refine consumer data, target-marketers are coming under increasing attack by privacy rights advocates. These activists are not disturbed merely by dinnertime phone calls from telemarketers trying to push vinyl siding — annoying as they may be. Privacy advocates warn that by swapping consumer data among themselves, companies can create detailed profiles of individual households, right down to which political parties a family supports, what medicines they buy, and whether they've contributed to Planned Parenthood or the Moral Majority.

To quiet these concerns, more companies are turning to survey-based consumer maps like the ones in this book to predict marketplace behavior. These maps — more formally known as market potential index maps — can calculate a product's sales potential in a community without exploiting individual household data. And they're becoming increasingly important as Americans spend more time working and shopping from the privacy of their homes. Whereas catalogs were once the only means of purchasing for isolated consumers, by the year 2000 an estimated 20 percent of all goods and services will be purchased directly from the homes of Americans via interactive computer, phone, and television. The global village is fast becoming a global shopping mall.

Already many businesses rely on consumer maps that recast the nation as 211 markets whose borders are defined by audience-measuring companies, such as the Arbitron Ratings Co. or the A. C. Nielsen Co. Unlike state and county units, these communities (which, in this book, follow the borders defined by Arbitron's Areas of Dominant Influence) better reflect the media and retail forces that influence consumer buying decisions. Encompassing a city as well as its outlying suburbs, each consumer market is home to residents who shop at the same malls, root for the same sports teams, see the same TV commercials, and wear the same T-shirts that often display slogans that capture the flavor of a community, like Detroit's "Where the weak are killed and eaten" or Madison, Wisconsin's "The Alternative to Reality."

But not all consumer markets are created equal. The nation's largest, New York, N.Y., represents 18.7 million people sprawling across Connecticut, New Jersey, and Long Island. The smallest consumer market, Alpena, Mich., is made up of only 41,000 people living in a remote resort along Thunder Bay. Within these market extremes are state capitals and factory towns, farming communities and midsize cities — each with its own values, lifestyles, and consuming patterns. Viewed as a whole, the market profiles illustrate each community's square of the great American patchwork: how it compares to other markets around the country, whether it's a proletarian island in a sea of upscale consumers.

In this age of virtual reality, consumer maps are how business researchers see every U.S. community, often from faraway offices overflowing with computer-generated charts and printouts of local consuming patterns. You may disagree with the picture that emerges of your town — at least as it reflects your own personal tastes — but be assured that the business community believes in the reality of these portraits. And whenever they make decisions based on the data — to expand a business, adjust inventory distribution, open a new store, or close one down — they reinforce these portrayals. Market profiles have a way of becoming self-fulfilling prophecies.

Against this backdrop, *Latitudes & Attitudes* is designed as a guide to consumer tastes as well as a reference for anyone interested in

America's markets. Within its three parts, the book strives to make sense of the American experience. The first section of the book is devoted to consumer maps, revealing patterns of behavior and ideology that crisscross the landscape. The second part of the book, presenting capsule profiles of every consumer market, serves as a popular encyclopedia of American marketplace behavior: the products we buy, the activities we pursue, the attitudes we hold dear at the local level. In the last section, a chart ranks the popularity of all the lifestyle interests featured throughout the book within all 211 markets. It allows readers to learn at a glance how products, interests, and ideas play out in each community.

As for me, my interest in consumer mapping began six years ago when I was researching my book *The Clustering of America,* which examines the nation not as 50 states but as 40 lifestyle types based on Claritas's PRIZM clusters. Over the course of a year, I visited neighborhoods in every cluster to discover how residents spend their time and money. But as I traveled to communities around the country, it became apparent that there were local and regional differences that influenced why some Americans drove Dodge pickups while others preferred Nissan flatbeds. No one had tapped the deep reservoir of survey data, available on everything from who plays racquetball to who supports environmental activists, to create a popular work that explored the character — and consumer passions — of the American people. Becoming a survey surfer, I rode the crest of current consumer databases to discover who does what around the country, in search of the big picture through small insights.

For *Latitudes & Attitudes,* my expedition brought me to the latest market and polling research. The computer-generated maps for this book were developed using PRIZM and COMPASS software by Claritas Inc., one of the nation's oldest and largest target marketing companies. The map captions were gleaned from nearly 3,000 reports from product and activity surveys conducted by Simmons Market Research Bureau and Mediamark Research Inc., two of the nation's most widely used syndicated research firms, which conduct annual surveys of 20,000 adults. Car and truck data came from R. L. Polk & Co., the market information firm known for its huge database of automobile registration listings. Demographic statistics originated with the U.S. Bureau of Census. And the political and social issues information began as survey questions in the Yankelovich Monitor, a nationwide 2,500-person poll that has tracked trends for more than 20 years. To explain the influences underlying the maps, I turned to more than 100 experts in the fields of marketing, sociology, history, and psychology for their analysis as well as their anecdotes.

Ultimately, this book offers proof that where we live affects our attitudes toward what we buy — and buy into. As much as we like to think of American society as a great equalizer, we remain a diverse consumer nation, united and divided by how we spend our time and money. By illustrating our subcultures of "green" consumers and Nintendo lovers, aging folkies and fans of "The Simpsons," consumer maps help us appreciate who we are, how we got here, and where we are going. Those results, on display in the following pages, act as a window, giving us a glimpse of the way our community fits into the national whole.

Rand McNally, say hello to the real America.

# Let Them Eat Bread

## People Who Eat Fresh Croissants vs. White Bread

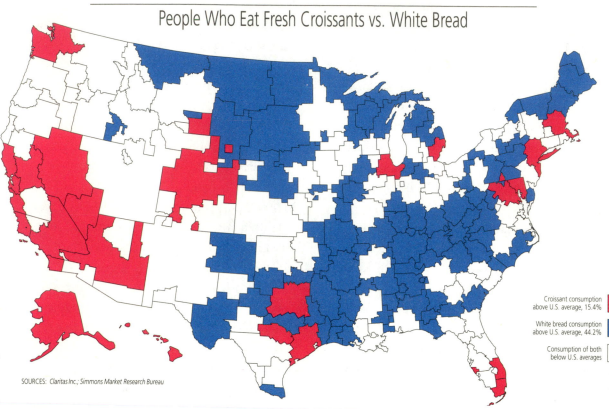

Croissant consumption
above U.S. average, 15.4%

White bread consumption
above U.S. average, 44.2%

Consumption of both
below U.S. averages

SOURCES: *Claritas Inc.; Simmons Market Research Bureau*

I N AMERICA, the cut of your bread says much about your class — though for reasons that have little to do with crust. Eating fresh croissants — buttery, flaky, hot from the oven at the local coffee shop — is one of the telltale signs that you are a person of distinction. The chief consumers of croissants tend to be frequent-flying executives from cities like New York, Washington, and San Francisco who earn over $100,000 a year. They enjoy sports like sailing and skiing, and such epicurean magazines as *Gourmet* and *Food and Wine*. At a lunchtime restaurant, they're the first to ask for a wine list, if there is any Grey Poupon mustard, whether the ice cream is Häagen-Dazs.

The heavy consumers of white bread are the stalwarts of small towns in Arkansas, Tennessee, and Mississippi, living in lower-income households with lots of singles, retirees, and children. When the Wheat Industry Council developed profiles of white-bread customers, the two biggest users were dubbed Overweight Snackers and Unconcerned Food Lovers. These are the folks who smoke, snack on doughnuts, eat at fried-chicken joints, and couldn't care less about exercise. When the fitness and whole-grain revolutions swept the country, they were too busy watching TV soaps — and munching on white bread smeared with peanut butter and jelly or Kraft Miracle Whip Salad Dressing straight — to notice.

In many respects, white bread is the bottom of the food chain; even Hostess Twinkies has a more upscale consumer profile. Although you can find croissant lovers who share a taste with white-bread fans for, say, cheese and tea, they draw the line at actually eating a slice of bleached bread. In fact, there are no markets with above-average buying rates for croissants and white bread. And yet, from a nutritional standpoint, white bread is healthier than high-cholesterol croissants. Bonnie Liebman, nutrition director for the Center for Science in the Public Interest, observes that croissants are marketed like "nouveau junk food. They're sold in health food stores and restaurants like quiche and high-fat yogurt," she says, "but they clearly aren't good for you." Indeed, the popularity of croissants among certain markets simply has more to do with snob appeal than nutrition.

# Pizza People

## People Who Buy Fast-Food Pizza

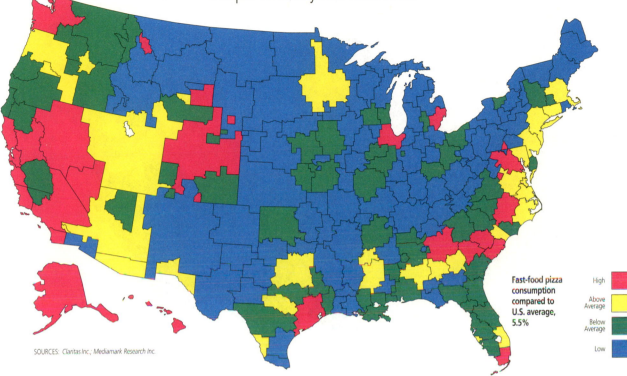

Fast-food pizza
consumption
compared to
U.S. average,
5.5%

High
Above Average
Below Average
Low

SOURCES: *Claritas Inc.; Mediamark Research Inc.*

ALMOST a century has passed since Gennaro Lombardi opened the first pizzeria in New York's Little Italy neighborhood, and he'd no doubt be amazed at what his concoction has spawned. With toppings ranging from trendy spinach and crabmeat to the more classic pepperoni and mushroom, pizza has become the nation's favorite snack food as well as one of our more popular dinner entrees. Americans consumed nearly two billion pizza pies in 1992, accounting for one in twenty meals at home, double the rate of only a decade ago.

Behind this passion for pizza, economic necessity and social pressures have helped create the hot markets along the nation's coasts. Out West, the consumers tend to be dual-income couples who have gone to college, work at white-collar jobs, and are of the baby boom generation. In the Southeast, they include a disproportionate number of households with young children and twenty-something working mothers who hold downscale factory jobs. Both groups have turned to fast-food pizza because of the decrease in time available to prepare traditional meals. Despite the stampede of women into the labor force, they still shoulder the burden for preparing meals in eight out of ten households. And what could be easier for dinner than a call to the nearest Domino's, Pizza Hut, or Shakey's?

Another factor that distinguishes pie people, especially men, is their passion for sports. Compared to average Americans, pizza lovers are more likely to watch professional basketball, boxing, and golf on television, listen to professional and college football on radio, and read magazines like *Ski* and *Golf Digest*.

Marketing statistics indicate this pizza connection with men is a holdover from adolescence, when boys are twice as likely as girls to eat pizza because it's portable, messy, and doesn't require silverware to consume.

Naturally, there are regional preferences for pizza toppings. In the South, hamburger is preferred while New Englanders favor cheese. Midwestern residents like sausage, and those on the West Coast go for the works, with a small group requesting esoteric variations such as pineapple and goat cheese. The most popular topping in the country is pepperoni, which may explain why pizza lovers also share a fondness for fruity soda pop, table wine, and cocktails made with rum and vodka. People who eat spicy foods, according to flavor experts, also prefer sweeter drinks.

# North of the Nut Line

## People Who Buy Snack Nuts

Snack nuts consumption compared to U.S. average, 45.6%

High
Above Average
Below Average
Low

SOURCES: *Claritas Inc.; Simmons Market Research Bureau*

FORGET the Mason-Dixon Line. In America, a kind of nut line bisects the nation's midriff, separating the nut-happy areas in the North from the less-nutty zones of the South. Part of the reason is the cold weather. "A fatty food like nuts makes you feel warm," explains Carol Cutler, a cookbook writer and syndicated columnist. "Nuts have a rich taste in your mouth and, even subconsciously, attract Americans in the north when they want to snack."

But another factor is alcohol. Communities in the northern part of the country tend to throw more cocktail parties, where nuts are served as a complement to mixed drinks. Surveys show markets with high nut consumption also sell a lot of vodka, rum, beer, and brandy. Nut lovers tend to be educated, affluent married couples with children, whose interests include politics, film, and college sports; one can easily imagine the cocktail-party chatter that goes with a handful of nuts. There's also a concentration of those over 65 in heartland communities who regard nuts as a more age-appropriate snack food than, say, greasy potato chips or pork rinds. Nutritionists note that nuts like filberts and cashews are an older person's acquired taste.

The areas in the South with the lowest consumption rates of snack nuts also happen to coincide with the nation's Bible Belt — the home of conservative Baptists, who abstain from hard liquor. Demographically speaking, these areas have higher-than-average numbers of poor, elderly widows, not unlike the old-fashioned image of nut consumers in the past: grandmas who used to put out nuts in serving dishes before Sunday dinners. But with a greater preference for herbal tea than "Long Island tea" cocktails, these folks have less need for snack nuts and instead munch on corn chips and potato chips.

To geographically underscore the fundamental difference between these two groups, a map of Americans who enjoy listening to religious radio is the reverse image of this nut map. Apparently, mixed nuts and church mixers don't mix.

# Meat and Potatoes

## People Who Eat Beef vs. Instant Mashed Potatoes

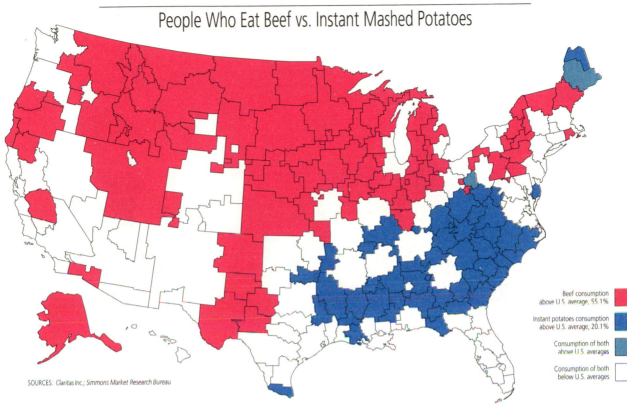

Beef consumption above U.S. average, 55.1%

Instant potatoes consumption above U.S. average, 20.1%

Consumption of both above U.S. averages

Consumption of both below U.S. averages

SOURCES: Claritas Inc.; Simmons Market Research Bureau

FORGET the fish, pesto salad, or those precious grilled baby-vegetable dishes foisted on us by nouveau cuisine's celebrity chefs. Americans have always had a special place in their bellies for comfort foods like meat and potatoes. Granted, the decline of the nation's industrial base and the rise of the health movement dealt body blows to U.S. meat consumption — dropping from 80 to 65 pounds per person per year between 1970 and 1990. Young, affluent, cholesterol-conscious consumers now order leaner poultry and fish.

Still, there remains a strong contingent of politically incorrect carnivores who like to see red on their plates. Though they cross socioeconomic lines, most beef hounds are small-town consumers, over-50 married couples who have high school diplomas, hold blue-collar jobs, and have lived at the same address for decades. They're widely scattered across the Midwest and West as well as what's left of the industrial Northeast. On average, beef eaters are more likely to enjoy working-class pursuits such as hunting, needlework crafts, and bowling. But they also exhibit more urbane tastes befitting a middle-class lifestyle. They belong to business clubs, own computers, and invest in mutual funds — all at high rates. Their political views are middle-of-the-road, supporting a conservative cause like the death penalty as well as a more liberal issue like nuclear waste disposal.

While the fans of instant mashed potatoes share the beef eaters' taste in country music and light trucks, they're more inclined to listen to gospel music, chew tobacco, and watch professional wrestling. In part, this occurs because processed foods generally appeal to markets that are more Southern, African American, older, and downscale than average Americans. Another factor is that well-off beef eaters with a hankering for spuds may order a baked potato alongside a two-inch flame-charred Porterhouse. In one area, however, instant-mashed-potato lovers do surpass beef eaters: conservatism. The devotees of spontaneous spuds want to ban abortion and return prayer to the schools.

Interestingly, for all the vitriol nutritionists have heaped on beef lovers, the diets of carnivores are healthier than those of instant-mashed-potato lovers. Beef eaters also relish salads, fish, fresh fruit, and oat bran. Synthesized-potato fans have higher rates for enjoying fried chicken, candy bars, and other processed foods. In only two markets — Bangor, Maine, and Wheeling, W. Va. — are meat and instant potatoes both eaten at above-average rates, reflecting similar concentrations of rural, rightist retirees.

# Ice Cream Spooners: Fat and Thin

## Consumers of Ben & Jerry's Ice Cream vs. Weight Watchers Frozen Desserts

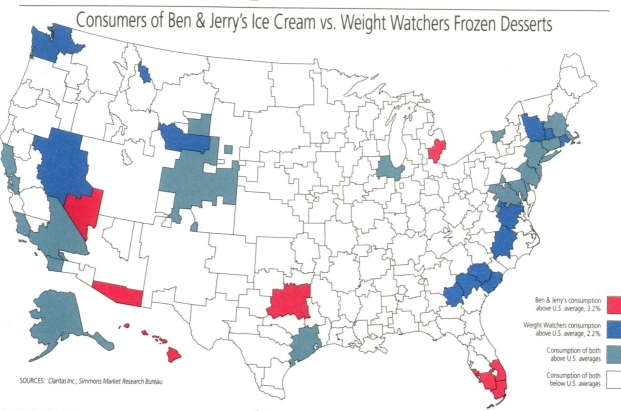

Ben & Jerry's consumption above U.S. average, 3.2%

Weight Watchers consumption above U.S. average, 2.2%

Consumption of both above U.S. averages

Consumption of both below U.S. averages

SOURCES: *Claritas Inc.; Simmons Market Research Bureau*

FOR those who've had more than a passing acquaintance with love handles, one of medicine's great mysteries is why dieting never succeeds. The above map proves we don't have a chance. The markets with strong sales of Weight Watchers low-fat ice cream — especially along the Northeastern and California coasts — are the same as those purchasing high rates of Ben & Jerry's fat-rich ice cream. In other words, many Americans follow a binge-and-diet cycle, shifting between sensible and splurge-worthy ice cream in a dubious attempt at thinness. Medical researchers call this yo-yo dieting. Ice cream experts call this good business.

"What happens when a product loses fat is that it also loses flavor," says Ed Marks, editor of *The Ice Screamer* industry newsletter. "So when people get tired of blandness they indulge themselves a little bit."

Resisting ice cream in any form is difficult for any segment of society, but especially educated, upscale, over-40-year-olds, who are the prime scoopers of both kinds of ice cream. Many fans of each brand share similar lifestyles: reading books, seeing movies, joining health clubs, and attending rock concerts. But ice cream enthusiasts draw the line when it comes to ideological attitudes. Ben & Jerry's, which has been coming out of Vermont for 16 years, appeals to younger baby boomers, who are more liberal, socially responsible, and hip enough to appreciate a flavor named Cherry Garcia — though not necessarily interested in settling in mostly rural, downscale Vermont. Attitude surveys find these consumers concerned about the environment, protecting a woman's right to an abortion, and gay rights. They're more urban-based because that's where the

more leftist media are located, observes Marks.

The devotees of Weight Watchers frozen desserts, a brand created by a Brooklyn homemaker in 1963, tend to be a bit older, have more children, and be markedly more conservative — and brand loyal. They try to avoid temptations, whether it's shunning risky convertibles and gambling casinos or avoiding trendy lifestyle magazines in favor of the more staid *Forbes* and *Business Week*. (*Weight Watchers* magazine, surprisingly, is not one of their favorites.) When it comes to issues, these ice cream customers worry about family values and reverence for the elderly. Indeed, one of the few concerns on which the fans of Ben & Jerry's and Weight Watchers agree is their desire for more ice cream. One food poll found they both share the same second- and third-favorite foods: Frusen Gladje and Häagen-Dazs ice cream.

# The Cholesterol Map

## Consumers of Oat Bran vs. Bacon

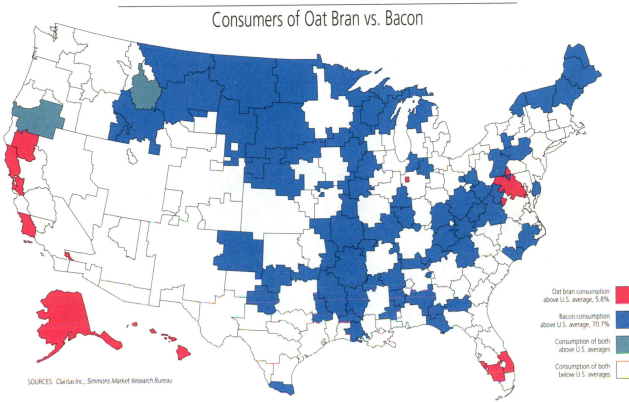

Oat bran consumption above U.S. average, 5.8%

Bacon consumption above U.S. average, 70.7%

Consumption of both above U.S. averages

Consumption of both below U.S. averages

SOURCES: *Claritas Inc., Simmons Market Research Bureau*

IN the battle of the bulge, cholesterol has taken up a stronghold and refuses to budge. As this map shows, bland, good-for-you oat bran is no match for the saliva-inducing sizzle of bacon. While the food police have helped ban bacon from most urban kitchens, the sentence has not been carried out in the countryside, where breakfast still means six strips on a plateful of eggs.

Bacon, long a staple of pan-fried cuisine, remains a favorite throughout the American heartland, where hog-raising is an ingrained part of the culture. Some 70 percent of U.S. households eat bacon, the largest segment of which includes older, more working-class, more family-oriented, and less educated consumers. Bacon fans also boast above-average rates for driving trucks, listening to country music,

gardening, and watching TV — a significant fact when it comes to nutrition. The better-educated get their health messages from print media, while the less-educated get their nutritional information from TV ads. Indeed, bacon fans also consume sausage, fried chicken, and cold cuts at high rates. And while these folks aren't big on alcoholic beverages — one health risk they do avoid — smoking cigarettes and chewing tobacco are common.

The dozen areas where marketers have been most effective in selling cholesterol-cutting oat bran tend to be the nation's wealthiest and most educated markets, such as Washington, San Francisco, and West Palm Beach. Oat bran consumers tend to be over 35 years old, earn more than $50,000 a year, and, thanks to their high rate of reading scientific magazines, follow

the latest health trends. Although these consumers are more likely than average Americans to buy fish, salads, and skim milk, you'd hardly classify them as nutritional purists, given their fondness for fatty cheeses, nuts, and ice cream. Indeed, polls indicate that the oat bran revolution fizzled because consumers in the 1990s simply aren't ready to completely trade taste for low-fat foods. In supermarkets throughout upscale metro areas, both healthy and high-fat foods remain big sellers.

As for the two markets with high consumption rates of oat bran and bacon — Butte, Mont., and Medford, Oreg. — both are rugged, exurban areas where educated, back-to-the-land residents see no inconsistency in going hunting, shopping at organic food stores, and indulging in savory slabs of bacon.

# Bagelmania

## People Who Buy Bagels

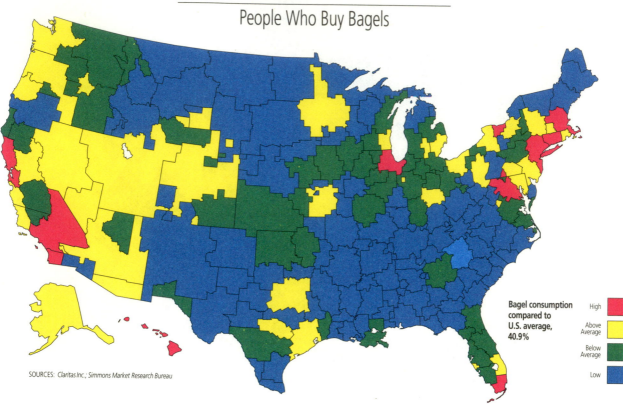

Bagel consumption compared to U.S. average, 40.9%

High
Above Average
Below Average
Low

SOURCES: *Claritas Inc.; Simmons Market Research Bureau*

**S**O you were expecting maybe a map of where you can find a great bagel — a big, crusty-on-the-outside, chewy-on-the-inside, hot-from-the-oven bagel designed for a *schmear* of cream cheese? Get a local map of New York City and forget the rest of the country.

Most bagels today bear only a faint resemblance to the original invented by a Jewish Viennese baker in 1683 and brought to America by East European immigrants in the early 20th century. More than five million bagels were sold last year in all sorts of strange mutations: Sara Lee's frozen bagels, fast-food versions à la Burger King, garden-herb bagel chips, and oddball flavors like banana nut, blueberry, and cheddar cheese. Once likened to "a doughnut dipped in cement," the bagel has become as American as pizza and can be found at any mall worth its food court.

But for all this bagel diaspora, the biggest fans continue to be residents of cities with comparatively high Jewish populations: New York, Boston, Washington, Chicago, and Miami. Bagel consumers are educated, upscale Americans of European descent who like to read books, attend the theater, support leftist politicians, and travel abroad — very often to the Old Country. Bagel crumbs can often be found in the publications they read at above-average rates, like the *Wall Street Journal,* the *New Yorker,* and *Scientific American.* At other meals, you'll spot the bagel lovers with a glass of imported red wine, a plate of Gouda cheese, and a bowl of Weight Watchers ice cream. Opinion polls show that these con-

sumers long to spend more time entertaining friends and relatives — perhaps with a bagel *nosh.*

But you don't have to be Jewish to love bagels; indeed, bagelmania is growing, especially along the West Coast and in some surprising secondary markets like Seattle and Salt Lake City. Industry executives ascribe this phenomenon to the bagel's healthful, low-fat, high-carbohydrate appeal; bagel junkies are also into aerobic exercise, hiking, and tennis. Alas, popularity has not been kind to the bagel. More and more bagels are now mass-produced, using a bake-and-steam process rather than the boiling method used for centuries. The result is a squishier California-style bagel, perfect for a sandwich of bean sprouts and tofu spread that would make lox-loving purists blanch.

# Twinkies

## People Who Eat Hostess Twinkies

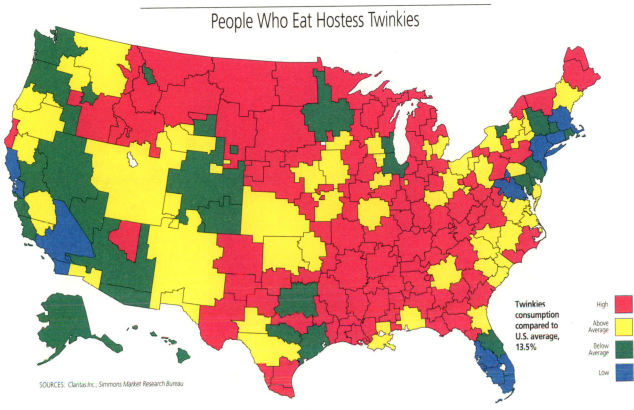

Twinkies consumption compared to U.S. average, 13.5%

High
Above Average
Below Average
Low

SOURCES: Claritas Inc., Simmons Market Research Bureau

FEW creations of food technology have achieved the — how shall we say? — *stature* of the Hostess Twinkie. Invented in 1930 by a baker who was inspired by a billboard advertising Twinkle Toe Shoes, those cream-filled sponge cake torpedoes have become, in the words of food writers Jane and Michael Stern, a piece of "edible Americana." Twinkies have been favored by TV stars ranging from Howdy Doody to Archie Bunker, and they were used to help celebrate the fiftieth birthday of another American icon, Superman. Of course, the darker side of the squishy snack cakes is often raised by nutritionists, who note that a diet consisting solely of Twinkies — whose main ingredients are sugar and enriched flour — can lead to cancer, heart disease, and perhaps insanity. In 1978, former San Francisco Supervisor Dan White was convicted of manslaughter rather than murder because of "diminished mental capacity" due to a diet of Twinkies and candy bars — the so-called "Twinkies defense." However, the residents of the San Francisco Bay area ironically rank low on Twinkies consumption.

So where are the Americans today flirting with insanity and death for a sticky golden tube? Out in the country, according to the above map. The highest concentration of Twinkies consumers lives in downscale rural communities filled with blue-collar workers, children under the age of 17, and African Americans. As a group, they're more likely than average Americans to enjoy gardening, chewing tobacco, professional wrestling, and country music. Unlike Dan White, most Twinkies aficionados supplement their diet with more than candy bars, though survey results would hardly allow nutritionists to sleep easier. Among their favorite foods: bacon, aerosol cheese, peanut butter, and corn chips, all washed down with milk, cola, Kool-Aid, or malt liquor.

Knowing such facts, representatives of Twinkies-maker Continental Baking Co. of St. Louis rarely promote their creation's nutritional value. And a wise move, that. Opinion polls show most Twinkies lovers are oblivious to health foods and the fitness boom. They come across as staunch conservatives who advocate a return to the traditional family, with women in the kitchen and Twinkies served with a glass of whole milk.

# Juicy Fruits

## People Who Buy Apples vs. Oranges

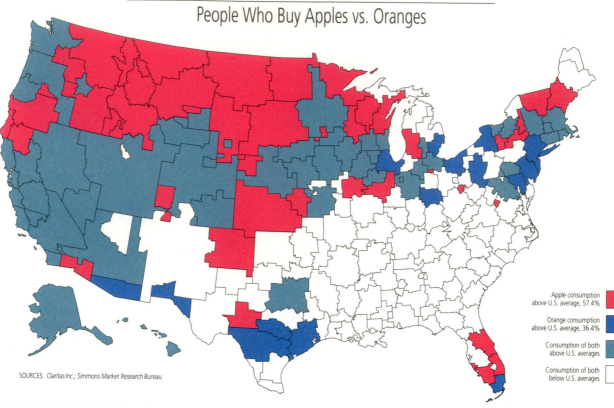

Apple consumption
above U.S. average, 57.4%

Orange consumption
above U.S. average, 36.4%

Consumption of both
above U.S. averages

Consumption of both
below U.S. averages

SOURCES: *Claritas Inc.; Simmons Market Research Bureau*

COMPARING apples to oranges makes perfect sense when the subject is food consumption. Both fruits appeal to similar groups — white, college-educated, and affluent — who are found disproportionately in the northern tier of the U.S. In fact, Americans may best be divided into fruit lovers and everyone else, since fans of many fruits share a comparable profile. Among the few distinctions: banana lovers include more downscale families with children, while grapefruit devotees include a greater number of wealthy senior citizens.

America's fondness for fresh fruit has been fueled by the growing health consciousness of consumers, especially among baby boomer and upscale households that are concentrated outside the South. Between 1980 and 1992, demand for fresh fruit grew by 13 percent to 99 pounds per person annually. But fruit fans don't subsist on Valencias and Granny Smiths alone. They're big buyers of many unprocessed foods — fresh vegetables, unbleached breads, spring water, and natural cheeses — and relatively weak consumers of beef stew, chili, baked beans, and, significantly, canned fruit and frozen fruit juices. Fruit fans tend to stock their kitchens with time-saving appliances like food processors and woks to slice, dice, and sauté their fresh ingredients into quick and healthy entrees.

To be sure, some differences exist between those who prefer apples and those who prefer oranges. As the world's best-known temperate fruit, the apple claims its chief fans in small-town and rural communities throughout the Upper Midwest and the Northwest, where apple orchards predominate. And apple fanciers are more old-fashioned than orange enthusiasts, more supportive of issues involving family values and school prayer. Orange fans are slightly more urban, upscale, and liberal, politically and socially, and more concerned about nuclear waste, endangered animals, and gay rights. Consistent with a long-held belief that citrus is a powerful aphrodisiac, orange lovers buy condoms at high rates. Maybe that apple in the Garden of Eden was really an orange.

# 60-Second Gourmets

## People Who Eat TV Dinners vs. Fast Food

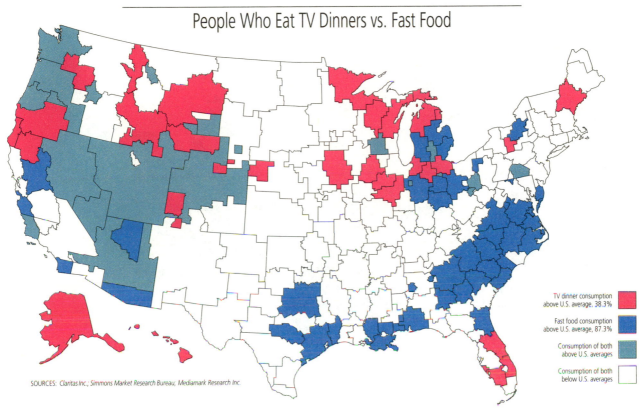

TV dinner consumption above U.S. average, 38.3%

Fast food consumption above U.S. average, 87.3%

Consumption of both above U.S. averages

Consumption of both below U.S. averages

SOURCES: *Claritas Inc.; Simmons Market Research Bureau, Mediamark Research Inc.*

CHAOTIC schedules, two-career couples, and frequent snacking have helped turn the conventional sit-down dinner into a casualty of modern America. But choosing among the alternatives, nuking a Lean Cuisine or hitting the closest McDonald's, results in a map of two entirely different kinds of people.

Those who eat frozen meals tend to be upper-middle-class, 18-to-34-year-old singles who live in the West and Midwest. They're more likely than average Americans to jog, work out at a health club, frequent dance clubs, and — most important — eat meals at odd hours. They choose frozen entrees over fast-food partly out of geographic necessity: many are apartment-dwellers who face a major commute to reach widely dispersed drive-ins. In their solo households, they'll heat up an enchilada to eat while watching an MTV video or an HBO movie. Social historian Margaret Visser has observed that, like the frozen entrees packaged in single containers, these consumers are self-sufficient. "We do not cling, stick or mingle," she's written archly of TV dinner devotees. "We do not need to share, to talk, to interrelate."

An even easier route to preparing a meal is having someone else do it. But most fast-food fans, many of them middle-class two-career couples who live in the West, South, and Mid-Atlantic states with their children, can't afford a live-in chef. Although they may not be gathering around a dining-room table for a meal, they do place value on the family unit. Besides eating together at drive-ins — their favorite chains are McDonald's, Pizza Hut, Taco Bell, and Dairy Queen — they're more likely than average Americans to rent videos, visit campgrounds, swim, and work on home-renovation projects together. These households are big subscribers to magazines like *Family Handyman, Better Homes & Gardens,* and *Popular Mechanics.* And fast-food fans are more conservative than microwave-dinner devotees, supporting a return to traditional women's roles, sexual relations, and family meals. Unfortunately, the push of women into the workforce has also moved dinner conversations to the drive-in.

# Lemon-Lime Latitudes

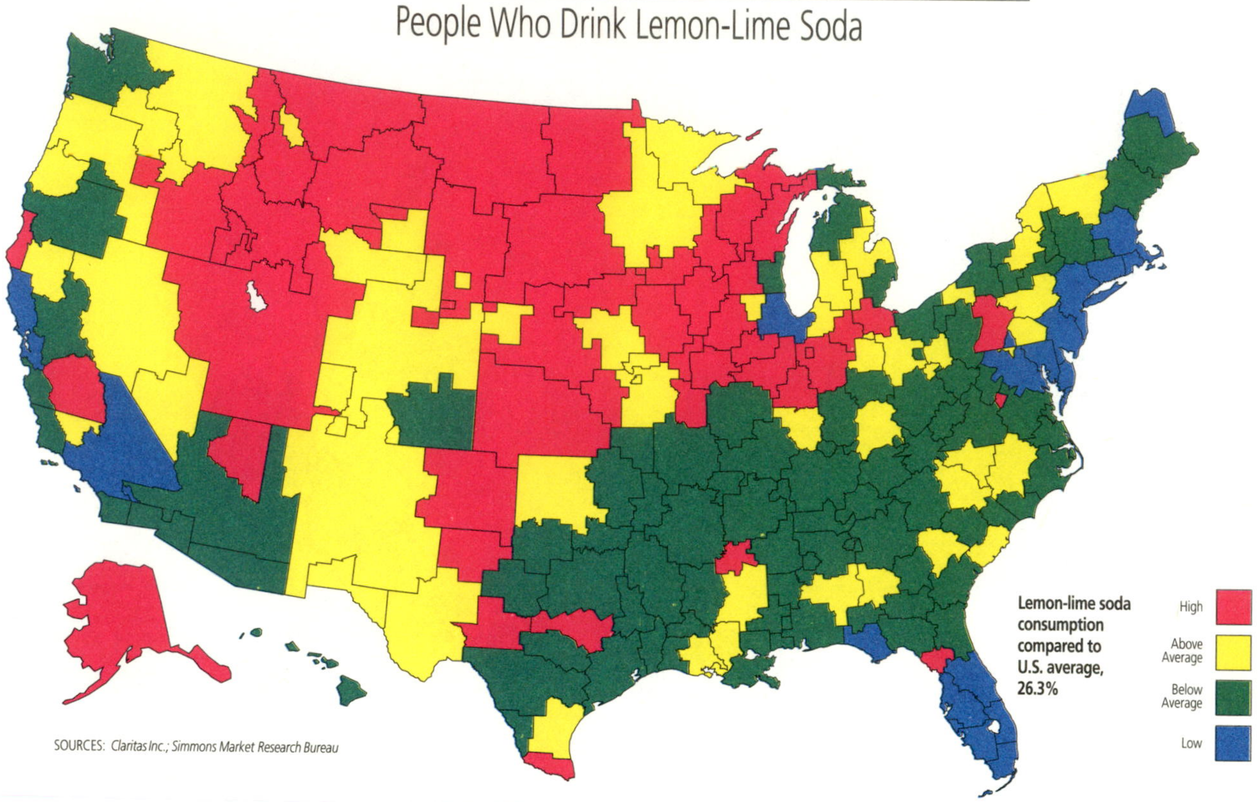

## People Who Drink Lemon-Lime Soda

Lemon-lime soda consumption compared to U.S. average, 26.3%

High
Above Average
Below Average
Low

SOURCES: *Claritas Inc.; Simmons Market Research Bureau*

THEY say there's no accounting for taste, but soft-drink consumption patterns reveal the strong influence of demographics, culture, and class. Serving as a useful marker for a more general taste for tartness, mapping consumption of lemon-lime soft drinks reveals areas where people prefer a sourness or sharpness of taste in their food and drink over sweetness. Overall, the lemon-lime soda data suggest that one-quarter of all households in America prefer tart to sweet.

Who are the people who like to pucker up? One group includes affluent, white-collar, suburban college graduates who read epicurean magazines and travel abroad. They're the sorts of people who've educated their palates to be receptive to sensations other than sweetness (a powerful craving we're all born with). Another group with similar tastes consists of blue-collar residents of northern small towns and rural areas — markets heavily populated by people of European extraction. Northern European tastes have long made room for tartness, in such forms as relishes, pickles, and vinegar-based sauces, as a counterpoint to a relatively bland diet that is heavy in meat and other animal products. "The higher you go into a meat cuisine, the lower the seasoning profile," says culinary authority Elisabeth Rozin.

By contrast, tart drinks hold less appeal in areas with a disproportionate concentration of people who are African American or foreign-born (Hispanic, for the most part) — that is, the southern and coastal states. The popularity of sweet comestibles among African Americans may have roots, food historians say, in the plantations of the Old South, where sugarcane, a "slave crop," was a source of cheap calories in the form of cane syrup, molasses, and jams. For its part, Hispanic-American cuisine, which features many spicy bean-, rice-, and corn-based dishes, is in some respects the exact opposite of Northern European cuisine and demands a different complement: sweeter (or blander) flavors. Residents of America's untart tier favor colas, fruity soft drinks, and fruit juices to wash down their empanadas, jambalayas, and BBQ.

The relatively few tart fans in the Northeast can be explained by several unusual factors that depress sales of lemon-lime sodas in that region. These include the cola companies' powerful distribution networks along the eastern seaboard and the strong preference among Jews, who are heavily represented in the Northeast, for ginger ale.

# Bag People and Caf-Fiends

## Consumers of Herbal Tea vs. Ground Caffeinated Coffee

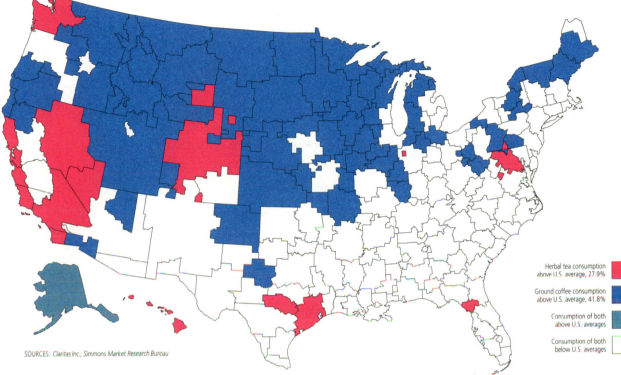

Herbal tea consumption above U.S. average, 27.9%

Ground coffee consumption above U.S. average, 41.8%

Consumption of both above U.S. averages

Consumption of both below U.S. averages

SOURCES: *Claritas Inc.; Simmons Market Research Bureau*

DRINKING coffee and tea are among the most common of tribal rituals. But preferring one or the other is a matter of attitude as much as geography, the hot beverages being consumed at higher rates in the northern, chillier climes of the U.S.

Herbal tea, once confined to health food stores, rolled into mainstream supermarkets about a decade ago, trying to shed its hippie image along the way. Today the beverage's biggest fans are college-educated, white-collar workers — women outnumbering men by a ratio of three to two — who want an all-natural alternative to caffeinated coffee and sugar-filled, artificially flavored sodas. With their concentration along the Left Coast, many herbal-tea drinkers are aging boomers who haven't lost their counterculture roots. They're more likely than average Americans to enjoy New Age music, backpack-

ing, and magazines like *Omni* and *Rolling Stone*. While herbal-tea manufacturers sometimes trumpet the therapeutic aspects of their products, herbal-tea drinkers are hardly health fanatics. Food surveys show they're also big on TV dinners, ice cream, and restaurant chains like Denny's and Sizzler. Furthermore, they're not even averse to caffeine, viewing herbal tea as a better late-night choice than a hot stimulant. During the day, herbal-tea drinkers have above-average rates for drinking coffee and cola — regular and decaffeinated.

Ground-coffee drinkers are a few rungs down the status ladder, though they're not to be confused with the gourmet-coffee lovers of the big cities who frequent Starbuck's and speak with authority about Jamaican Blue Mountain beans. The more pedestrian ground-coffee fans include a mix of affluent suburbanites and working-

class folk from small towns and rural areas throughout the Upper Midwest. As a group they're into skiing, classical music, and country clubs, as well as woodworking, bowling, and hunting. Because of their preponderance in the heartland, ground-coffee drinkers are also more likely than average consumers to sit down to Betty Crocker–style meals that feature biscuits, baked beans, and beef. And if there's no coffee available, they'll make do with almost anything else: cocoa, draft beer, or Diet Coke — but not herbal tea.

Perhaps the biggest gulf separating ground coffee from herbal tea is the political views of their imbibers. The fruity herbal-tea fans are liberals tolerant of gay marriages, sex education in the schools, and nude beaches. Coffee drinkers are right-of-center, more supportive of traditional women's roles, sexual relations, and religious values.

# Red, White, and Wine

## Consumers of Imported Red Wine vs. Imported White Wine

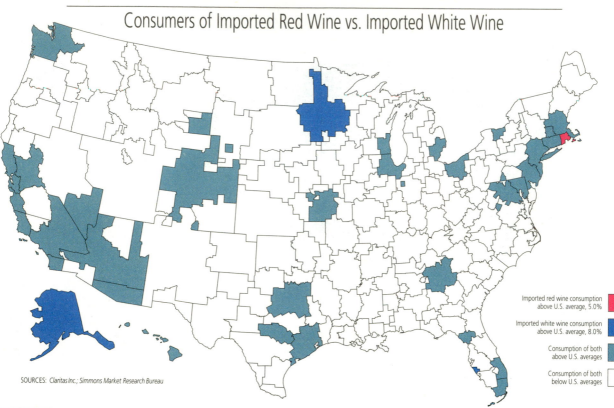

Imported red wine consumption
above U.S. average, 5.0%

Imported white wine consumption
above U.S. average, 8.0%

Consumption of both
above U.S. averages

Consumption of both
below U.S. averages

SOURCES: *Claritas Inc.; Simmons Market Research Bureau*

WINE is usually associated with gracious living — excepting, of course, the subgenres of wine coolers, jug wines, or skid-row rotgut. The connoisseurs of imported wine, however, have the most refined taste and the fattest pocketbooks of nearly all U.S. consumers, including those wine buffs who buy prestigious domestic labels. Imported-wine enthusiasts — and the overlapping markets above indicate their fondness for both white and red bouquets — exhibit high rates of six-figure incomes, expensive homes, and executive jobs. They're more likely than average Americans to drive luxury imports, belong to country clubs, and travel abroad.

But in the debate over which wine is more sophisticated — a concern for all the upwardly striving — red is stuffier by a nose. Preferred disproportionately in upscale Hartford, Conn., imported red wine tends to appeal to consumers who are a bit older, more affluent, and slightly more educated than imported–white wine connoisseurs. Red fans have higher rates for visiting Europe, listening to classical music, and attending the theater. Politically, most imported-wine consumers support gay rights and environmental concerns, but the fans of red are a bit more self-centered, less willing to volunteer their time to fight pollution, more likely to agree with the statement "I try to have as much fun as I can now and let the future take care of itself."

Imported–white wine buffs, by contrast, more closely resemble the typical literate party animal: many are liberal, cheese-eating supporters of consumer and environmental causes. With more children around the house, it's not surprising that they tend to drive more minivans, see more movies, and frequent more ice cream parlors than their red-drinking counterparts. They're also more likely to wear their political correctness on their sleeves: They work for gun control, reduced military spending, and sex education in the schools. Especially prevalent in the Minneapolis and Alaska markets, they are less insistent on refined cuisine. Compared to imported-red fans, white-wine lovers consume a lot more TV dinners, mashed potatoes, and pork and beans.

# Joe Sixpacks

## People Who Drink Budweiser vs. Coors vs. Miller

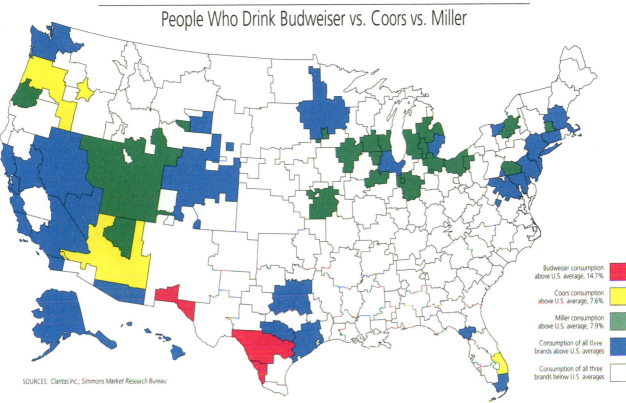

Budweiser consumption above U.S. average, 14.7%

Coors consumption above U.S. average, 7.6%

Miller consumption above U.S. average, 7.9%

Consumption of all three brands above U.S. averages

Consumption of all three brands below U.S. averages

SOURCES: *Claritas Inc.; Simmons Market Research Bureau*

IT'S tempting to imagine a consumption map of America's top three beer brands depicting lots of coastal towns where brew-happy college students gather over spring break. In fact, this map of brand loyalty rather than gross swillage — on average, men in their twenties drink about 3½ beers *each day* — shows that the best markets for domestic beer include blue-collar industrial towns as well as white-collar cities with lots of young singles. And the brewer with the most loyal fans turns out to be Miller, with three times as many hot markets compared to Bud and Coors combined.

Before this statement ends up in some trash-the-competition commercial, a few caveats are in order: Budweiser's 15 percent penetration of the market is about twice the individual rates of Coors and Miller,

so Bud drinkers tend to guzzle other brands as well throughout the country (the blue and white areas on the map). Actually, they tend to drink anything alcoholic: wine, imported beer, scotch, rum, and probably even Fuzzy Pink Navels if that's the only booze around. Bud fans, generally upper-middle-class singles in their early twenties, keep their beer gut in check by working out a lot. They're more likely than average Americans to jog, exercise, lift weights, and play racquetball.

As for Coors drinkers, they tend to be a bit more educated, affluent, and more likely to be married. They show a fondness for light beer, vodka, and domestic wine, but they're also as likely to sit down with a glass of diet soda or skim milk. Their favorite pastimes include reading books, watching movies, and working

on political campaigns (typically liberal).

Compared to the other beer drinkers, Miller fans are more urban, less educated, and slightly older — in their thirties and forties — consistent with other brand-loyal consumers. They drink a lot of alcohol and enjoy racquet sports, not to mention rock concerts, movies, and travel. But Miller fans, typically found in the nation's Rust Belt, are more into radio than reading — listening particularly to pro football, baseball, and classical music.

Given this passion for all kinds of alcohol, it's no wonder that the blue areas represent the largest portion of the map: domestic-beer lovers who have little brand loyalty. No doubt America's conglomerate breweries and their interchangeable commercials are to blame.

# Bookworms vs. Couch Potatoes

## Heavy Book Buying vs. Heavy TV Viewing

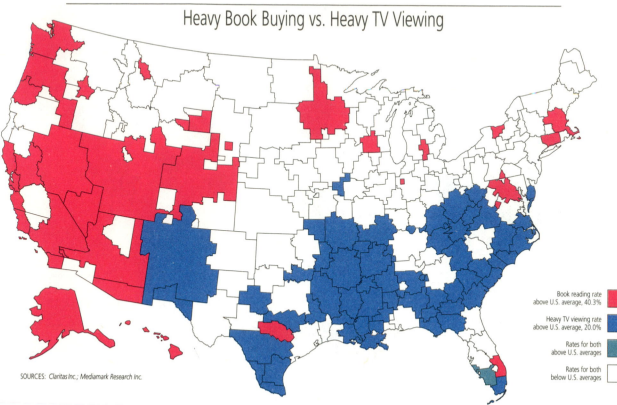

Book reading rate
above U.S. average, 40.3%

Heavy TV viewing rate
above U.S. average, 20.0%

Rates for both
above U.S. averages

Rates for both
below U.S. averages

SOURCES: *Claritas Inc.; Mediamark Research Inc.*

THERE may be people who read lots of books *and* watch lots of television, but divide the nation by people who do one or the other and the geography seems to form two distinct archipelagoes. To the west and in scattered eastern metros are those who read books at above-average rates. In the South and other rural areas live people who watch exorbitant amounts of TV (35 or more hours a week). South Florida, the one area where big book buyers and heavy television viewers overlap, demographic disparities are among the most extreme in the nation: old and young, rich and poor, educated and academically challenged.

Not surprisingly, the key factor separating the bookworms from the couch potatoes is the average level of education. People who read books tend disproportionately to have college degrees, expensive homes, and substantial incomes; when they're not reading, they are more likely than average Americans to participate in such activities as skiing, sailing, and playing racquetball. Because well-educated people have been more likely than most other Americans to join the migration to the high-tech boomtowns of the West, book-reading in the western states is relatively heavy. Also, the amount of time spent watching TV in the West is depressed by the fact that women there are likely to work outside the home.

The people who log the most time in front of the television set are located disproportionately in the South and are more likely than other Americans never to have finished high school. They are a sedentary bunch in other respects, too. Even though heavy TV viewers are more likely than other Americans to live in mobile homes, they also are among the Americans who change their address least frequently. Heavy viewers also have high rates of smoking cigarettes, eating high-fat diets, drinking significant amounts of domestic wine and malt liquor, and entertaining at home. When they flip on their sets they like to watch soaps, game shows, sitcoms such as "Fresh Prince of Bel Air," and melodramas like "Beverly Hills, 90210."

"We're not a nation of 'Masterpiece Theatre' viewers," observes John Robinson, director of the Americans' Use of Time Project at the University of Maryland. "The more education you have, the less TV you watch and the more you do of almost everything else." In one survey, Robinson found that, while Americans spend more free time watching TV than doing anything else, they rated the activity as less enjoyable than most other activities — including reading books. "TV," he says, "is an easy way to suspend your animation."

# Fantasyland

## People Who Attend Theme Parks

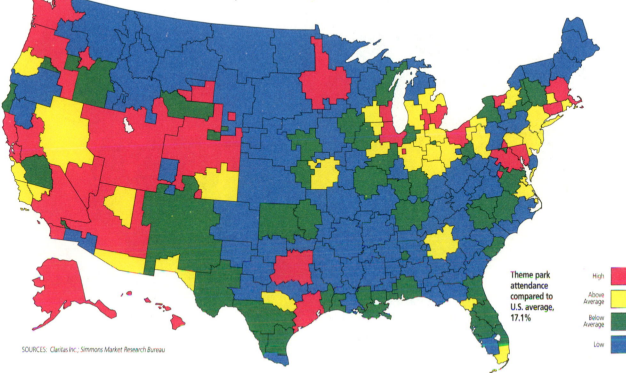

Theme park attendance compared to U.S. average, 17.1%

High
Above Average
Below Average
Low

SOURCES: *Claritas Inc.; Simmons Market Research Bureau*

To say that theme parks are popular is like saying Elvis Presley used to make records. Disney World draws more than 14 million people a year — surpassed only by Mecca, Kyoto, and the Vatican. Not simply overgrown carnivals, theme parks are corporate fairylands big enough to have their own zip codes. In these sanitized playgrounds, visitors can experience everything from terrifying alligators at Gatorland and King Kong gone berserk at Universal Studios to European villages (minus those rude foreigners, of course) at Busch Gardens — all from the strapped-in safety of their seats.

Given this pure escapism, you'd think that protective parents and their youngsters would be the biggest fans of these make-believe worlds. However, the popularity of theme parks among communities filled with kids under the age of 17 is below the national average. In fact, the highest concentration of theme park visitors is found among childless couples (married or single) between the ages of 35 and 54; in other words, baby boomers who grew up on Mickey Mouse and graduated to Donald Trump. Theme park patrons are found most often in the Northeast and in the rapidly growing communities west of Denver. They tend to be college-educated, white-collar, $50,000-plus earners with enough time and money to fork over $100 for a four-day admission ticket. And more unmarried people go to theme parks because they tend to have more free time than married couples with children.

In lifestyle terms, theme park fans aren't homebodies. They're not interested in working under their cars or doing their own renovation projects. Many would rather pour their energy into social and physical activities, such as downhill skiing, tennis, swimming, and aerobics. They like to go out at night to take adult-education classes, attend political activities, and meet colleagues at business clubs. And they're big on eating dinner out, frequenting theme restaurant chains like Red Lobster and Taco Bell. Hardly the hot dog and cotton candy crowd, they'd be much more likely to stop at a kiosk selling croissants, fresh fruit, and Ben & Jerry's ice cream.

# Mall Walkers

## People Who Shop at Malls

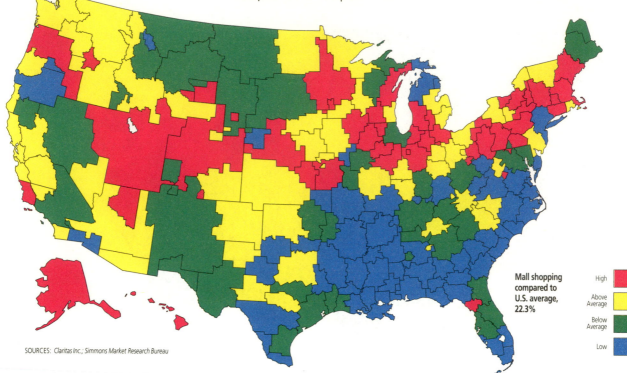

**Mall shopping compared to U.S. average, 22.3%**

High
Above Average
Below Average
Low

SOURCES: *Claritas Inc.; Simmons Market Research Bureau*

B Y MOST ACCOUNTS, the malling of America is complete. Shopping malls, which first popped up like crocuses on the rural landscape in the 1960s, have become the village squares of contemporary society, where Americans go to shop, eat, exercise, be entertained, and romance each other. We go to malls more often than we show up in church. Their burgeoning popularity has prompted developers to build bigger and flashier centers: the giant Mall of America near Minneapolis is 4.2 million square feet — the size of 34 average American shopping centers.

But even the smaller malls manage to lure average Americans to spend a half day each month shopping 'til they drop. Those who get the most pleasure from the mall — the consumer hedonists who confess to enjoying shopping more than sex — tend to be white married couples over 45 years old. Although many of the nation's largest malls are located on the urban fringe in what writer Joel Garreau has termed "edge cities," America's biggest mall fans live in small towns and rural areas far from the corner grocer of metropolitan America. They're educated, upper-middle-class, and have the taste to match: they enjoy movies, computers, golf, and classical music, most of which can be satisfied by mall stores. And they're big on travel beyond the nearest mall: they take ski trips, domestic flights, and vacation trips to Canada, the Caribbean, and Europe. Indeed, the highest concentration live in the nation's northern states, originally settled by Europeans who pushed across the country to settle the American frontier.

In some respects, mall shoppers are contemporary explorers of a different sort, graying thrill-seekers who consider malls adult theme parks. Mall shoppers claim they like to try new foods, explore new vacation spots, and do things on the spur of the moment, which may explain why so many confess they like shopping more than sex. These Americans fill their wallets not with condoms but with multiple credit cards.

# Cows, Corn Dogs, and Karaoke

## Those Who Attend State Fairs

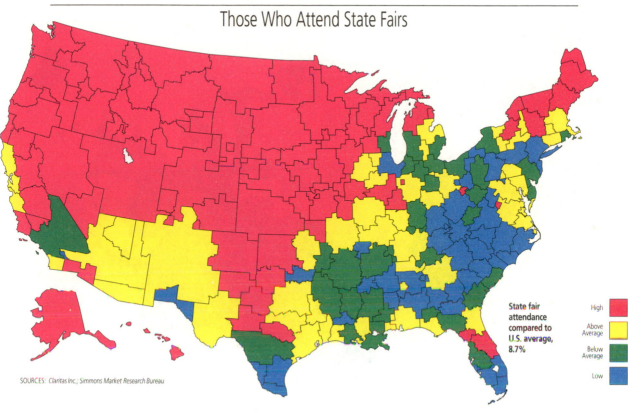

State fair attendance compared to U.S. average, 8.7%

High
Above Average
Below Average
Low

SOURCES: Claritas Inc.; Simmons Market Research Bureau

ONCE the gathering place to admire a hefty heifer or a prize pumpkin, state fairs have become magnets for bungee-jumping and karaoke singing. On today's midway, cotton candy and corn dogs have been replaced by nachos and frozen yogurt. Carnival rides now feature likenesses of public television kiddie celebs like Barney the dinosaur and Thomas the Tank Engine. Evening entertainment is no longer a square dance but more often a concert by a faded pop star like Neil Sedaka or Bobby Vee.

Behind this gussying up is a demographic tale: State fairs have moved uptown, or at least expanded their audiences from the Farm Belt to suburban markets with high rates of young, mobile Americans, especially across the Western boom states. Today's fairgoers represent two very different kinds of people. One group includes young farm families with modest incomes and lots of kids who attend to celebrate their way of life; they're the folks with the John Deere caps who truck in the pigs and pies for display. Surveys show they're big on woodworking, baking from scratch, country music, and powerboating.

Mingling with the country folk are baby boom suburbanites with white-collar jobs, $75,000-plus incomes, and, also, lots of kids. They show up at state fairs for the family entertainment as well as the educational exposure to a rapidly disappearing way of life. Culturally curious, they spend their leisure time also reading books, taking adult education classes, and attending movies, plays, and concerts (pop, rock, and classical). Their top-rated TV show is "Siskel & Ebert at the Movies."

Together, this schizophrenic demographic profile produces a map whose top markets range from rural New England to the cosmopolitan Pacific Northwest. Yet because both groups tend to include married couples with children, their lifestyles overlap. Fairgoers from both country and suburb share a fondness for Nintendo, TV dinners, mall shopping, and musical instruments. At a state fair, their respective cultures collide in the karaoke booth.

# The Call of the Moose

## Members of Fraternal Orders

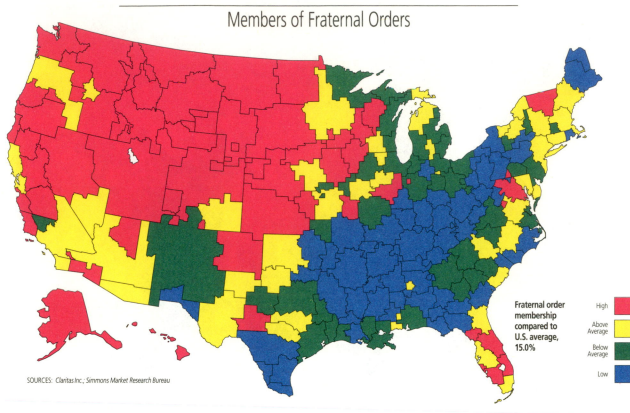

Fraternal order membership compared to U.S. average, 15.0%

High
Above Average
Below Average
Low

SOURCES: Claritas Inc.; Simmons Market Research Bureau

FRATERNAL orders were a venerated American institution long before Ralph Kramden immortalized them in "The Honeymooners." Known for their ritual inductions and wacko hats as well as their civic projects and parade appearances, fraternal orders at one time were the centers of community life in many small towns. The lodges of Moose, Elks, Eagles, and Shriners served as rural oases for entertainment and camaraderie. Their exalted rulers were the local business and political leaders. Learning the secret handshake was a big deal.

But like the spotted owl, many fraternal orders seem headed for extinction. Relatively few under-35-year-olds have joined the ranks, partly because, having grown up

with the women's movement, they no longer think it's cool to hang out with the boys at the lodge. Demographic surveys show that fraternal orders have an aging membership — most joiners are over 65 years old — and a shrinking population base — the top markets include retirement havens like Sarasota, Fla., Sioux City, Iowa, and North Platte, Neb. Although a higher-than-average percentage have lived in their homes for more than 20 years, they're not poor people. Having built up their nest egg over the years, many are upper-middle-class with the money to travel widely, invest in stocks, and own camcorders and other expensive camera equipment.

Still, fraternal orders continue to exist in the wide-open West

because residents living relatively isolated lives appreciate the social value of such organizations — an impulse Alexis de Tocqueville described in *Democracy in America* in 1835. Like the rural attendees of state fairs who gather to celebrate their society (and whose map is nearly identical to the one above), fraternal order members have rejected hectic cosmopolitan cities, preferring to join smaller groups of like-minded souls for camaraderie. Surveys show that they're more likely than average Americans to belong to country clubs, business clubs, veterans clubs, religious clubs, and even book clubs. Lucky for them, not all these groups require secret handshakes.

# Movie Buffs and Videophiles

## Moviegoers vs. Video Renters

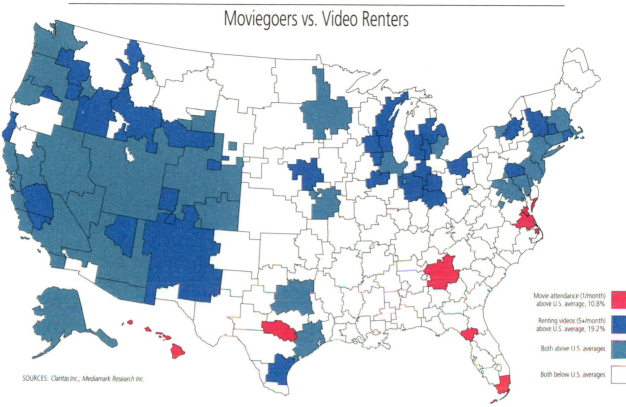

Movie attendance (1/month)
above U.S. average, 10.8%

Renting videos (5+/month)
above U.S. average, 19.2%

Both above U.S. averages

Both below U.S. averages

SOURCES: *Claritas Inc.; Mediamark Research Inc.*

HOLLYWOOD, beware: In the debate over whether to go out to a movie or rent a video, more Americans are opting for their couches. True, both movie ticket sales and video rentals have declined in recent years as Americans devote more time to television viewing and a few healthier pursuits like jogging and swimming. But as the map above indicates, nearly twice as many people spend their entertainment budget on video rentals than on movie tickets, and more Americans do both than only watch films.

What separates filmgoers from video-renters? Mostly, a desire to be on the cutting edge of culture. Hardcore moviegoers tend to attend plays, classical concerts, and art openings regularly, and to read business, epicurean, and science magazines spotlighting the latest trends. You can see their fondness for the new and the chic in other

lifestyle patterns: they're more likely than average Americans to own a fax, cook with a wok, and watch "Saturday Night Live." Even their homes, found more often along the nation's borders, have the best geographic chance of exposure to multicultural influences. The highest concentration of movie buffs is found among college students, young singles, and middle-aged married couples living in the suburbs of cities like Austin, Atlanta, and Miami.

As for the biggest video fans, they're slightly less affluent, a bit less educated, and certainly more conservative — the kind of people who invest in savings bonds rather than stocks. They're more likely than average Americans to live in midsize and rural areas — markets such as Boise, Flagstaff, and Dayton — and to care more about sports like golf, baseball, and football than being up on the latest trends in

film, art, and music. With more kids at home than movie buffs, video renters opt for the easier and cheaper alternative of staying at home and whipping up their own popcorn. In addition, they make use of videos as electronic baby-sitters while only occasionally wishing they could flee the house with their childless neighbors for the nearest vanguard cinema.

But seven-dollar movie tickets aren't the only reason video fans are staying at home. They tell pollsters they advocate a return to traditional standards of family life, including quality time spent together watching a TV screen. Typically watching more than seven hours of TV on a weekday, video renters admit that they tune in to sports, talk shows, and sitcoms in a big way. But when it comes to romance and mystery entertainment, the usual TV wasteland sends them off to the video store.

# Scratch and Bake

## Those Who Bake from Scratch

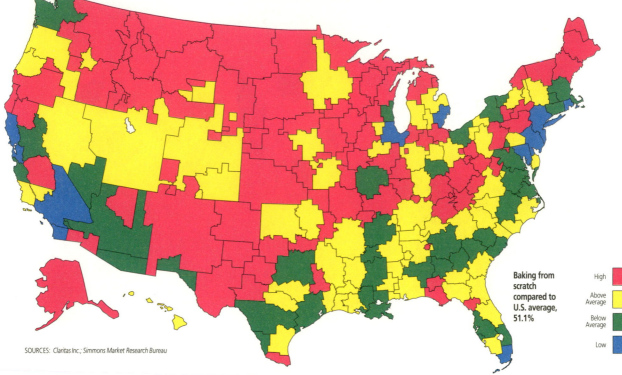

**Baking from scratch compared to U.S. average, 51.1%**

High
Above Average
Below Average
Low

SOURCES: *Claritas Inc.; Simmons Market Research Bureau*

A half-century ago, most American households baked from scratch, spending four to six hours kneading and punching enough dough for bread to last the week. But the rise in working women, microwaves, and frozen food signaled the decline in home-baked breads, rolls, and sweet goods. By 1980, those willing to bake from scratch were mostly downscale homemakers more interested in saving money than time. "Old white people and young black people," is how John Yurkis of the Denver-based Home Baking Association summed them up. "They baked to save money."

Today from-scratch baking occurs in about half of all households, and the highest rate is centered in rural and small-town America, especially markets throughout the North Central states and the Ohio Valley. These home bakers are over 45 years old, never finished high school, hold blue-collar jobs, and live in homes valued at under $75,000. Because a disproportionate number of bakers are in the labor force, they're mostly concocting cookies, muffins, and quick-loaf breads that save both time and money.

But lately, the image of home bakers has turned upscale. With the advent of bread machines and healthier foods, baking has begun to attract other demographic segments such as affluent couples — men and women — who hold post-graduate degrees. No longer needing to save money, they regard baking as a creative hobby that allows a certain self-expression in their olive-and-walnut-rye masterpieces. Men seem particularly drawn to bread-making, which has a more manly appeal than other culinary specialties. Aptly, today's hottest-selling bread machines have names like "Mr. Loaf" and "Breadman."

Given this unlikely pair of demographic groups, the lifestyle of America's bakers is a mishmash. They range from tobacco-chewing, rodeo-loving, truck-driving, country music fans to globe-trotting, golf-loving, minivan-driving, classical music enthusiasts. In this age of inconspicuous consumption — a hangover from the '80s — it's likely that baking from scratch will increase among upscale consumers. The Yankelovich Monitor reports the percentage of Americans who view owning an expensive car as a sign of success at its lowest point in more than two decades, while more personal signs of accomplishment continue to thrive. Thus the Beemer owners of the '80s now boast of growing their own herbs for their home-baked loaves of bread.

# Waiting for the Payoff

## Owners of $10,000+ in Stocks vs. Heavy Lottery Players

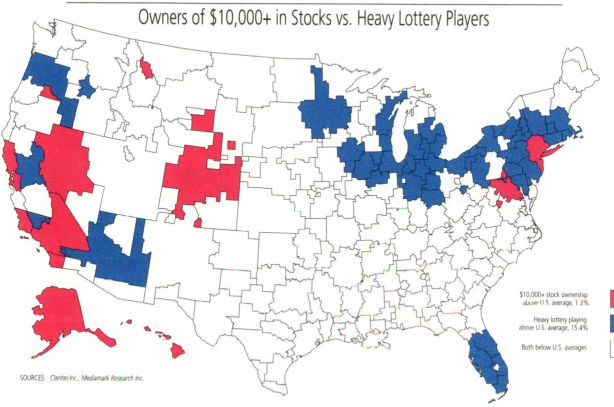

$10,000+ stock ownership above U.S. average, 1.3%

Heavy lottery playing above U.S. average, 15.4%

Both below U.S. averages

SOURCES: *Claritas Inc.; Mediamark Research Inc.*

IN America, one of the biggest differences between the rich and the poor is their perspective on the future. The most affluent households, which are concentrated around the nation's big cities, are many times more likely than the poorest to buy insurance, establish long-term savings accounts, and hold more than $10,000 in stocks. Having deeper pockets is only one factor, however; the more critical quality is patience — the ability to sit tight while awaiting big returns on their investment.

Though playing the stock market requires shrewdness and smarts, most of all it demands the faith to let your money ride out shifting business fortunes. Those who take the long view generally are educated, white-collar executives living in the suburbs of New York, Washington, D.C., and San Francisco. With their financial cushion, there's nothing slow about their lifestyle:

they enjoy skiing and tennis as well as traveling at home and abroad. Yet they shy away from the more immediate gratification of buying lottery tickets, gambling at casinos, and watching TV entertainment in favor of more circumspect activities, such as reading books and attending the theater. In surveys they admit that they "like to plan five to ten years ahead" and have "respect for age and experience."

Lottery games, by contrast, offer instant prizes, quick cash, and daily payouts — although most of the big jackpots are paid out over many years. And the biggest dabblers in what's been called "the poor man's stock market" tend to be middle-class, high school–educated blue-collar workers living, disproportionately, in the Rust Belt and Northeast. Surveys show that they're big on bowling, gambling casinos, and TV sports, and lottery officials know this. In many states,

instant-scratch tickets revolve around gambling or sports themes to create the illusion that the player is participating in a game. The real prize isn't the thrill of victory, however, but the quick buck. According to polls, lottery players agree with statements like "I like to do things on the spur of the moment."

There's little appreciation for the reality of a lottery drawing: A player has only a 1,000-to-1 chance of hitting a three-digit jackpot — and a better chance of getting hit by lightning.

The one anomaly to the rule about future-thinking rich Americans is the group of devoted lottery players living in affluent retirement communities throughout Florida and California. Although they have the money to buy stocks, at their advanced age they're less interested in the long haul of the stock market than the short-term action of a lottery ticket.

# La-Z-Folks

## Buyers of Recliners

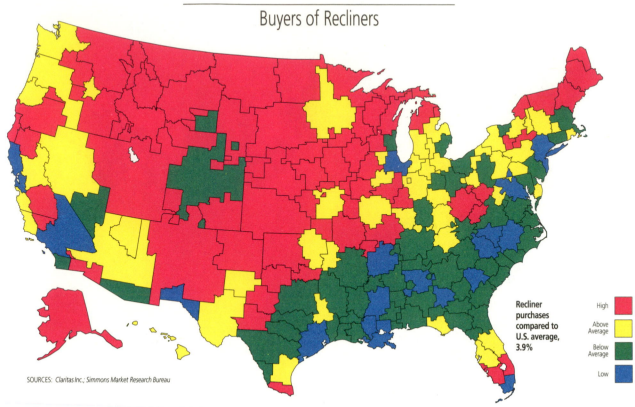

Recliner purchases compared to U.S. average, 3.9%

High
Above Average
Below Average
Low

SOURCES: Claritas Inc.; Simmons Market Research Bureau

THE pursuit of comfort in America has recorded few achievements to surpass the invention of the reclining chair. Created in 1928 as a comfortable place to loaf, recliners were once the sole province of men, who'd sink into the padded mechanized chairs like potato chips into onion dip. Today, motion furniture, as the recliner is known in the industry, has been sexually liberated, and it even features model names like Lydia and Daphne after characters from romance novels. Recliners are fixtures in one-quarter of the nation's homes, typically located in the living room with an unobstructed view of the television set and within arm's reach of a remote control–equipped snack tray.

Squint at the above map and you'll have the visual equivalent of onomatopoeia: the yellow area resembles a reclining chair, opened to its full-loaf position. The concentration of recliners in the northern part of the country is due to a combination of factors, chief among them being the cold weather. "If

> *During harsh winters, Northerners sink into recliners like potato chips into onion dip.*

you're housebound for part of the year, you want a comfortable chair to watch TV or read a book," says Richard Micka, vice president of the La-Z-Boy Chair Company.

But demographics also play a role. Recliners are bought most often by married couples of European ancestry who tend to live in small, middle-class towns where informality dominates. Surveys show that these residents have a low tendency to attend theaters, concerts, and health clubs. Curled up in their padded Herculon recliners, they're more likely to watch TV baseball, football, and golf, or to read magazines such as *Reader's Digest, Popular Science,* and *Better Homes & Gardens*. True, when they're upright, recliner owners are handy around the house — engaging in gardening, grass cutting, or ceiling-fan installation — all at rates higher than those who don't own recliners. But after a long day's tinkering, the zen of the Barcalounger draws them into serene meditation — or a nap.

# Wok Wonks

## Wok Users

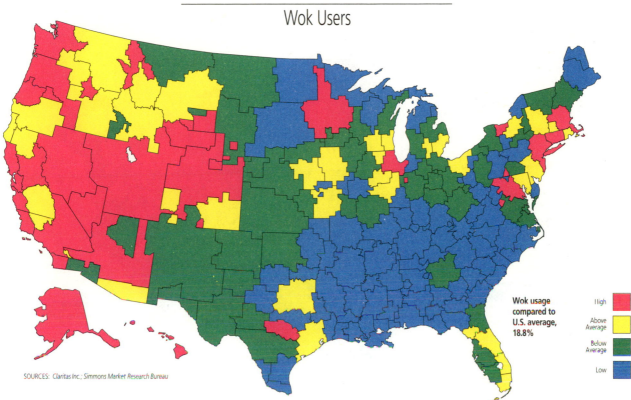

**Wok usage compared to U.S. average, 18.8%**

High
Above Average
Below Average
Low

SOURCES: *Claritas Inc.; Simmons Market Research Bureau*

THERE'S nothing complicated about woks: they're basic concave skillets developed by the Chinese for efficient stir-frying. Asian immigrants brought wok cookery with them when they came to America and, in many respects, the above portrait of wok users is similar to a map of where Asians settled at rates above the national average (about 3 percent nationwide). The top markets for Asian-Americans include San Francisco, San Diego, New York, and Hawaii — where 62 percent of the 1.1 million residents call themselves Asian — and woks naturally sizzle in these areas.

But ever since the health food revolution of the '70s, woks have been adopted by most cosmopolitan communities where residents tend to be educated, affluent, and well traveled. Attitude surveys show a relatively high percentage are gay, buy "green" products, and worry about endangered animals.

*Baby-boom families use woks like low-tech microwave ovens: a source for meals on the run.*

Wok owners like to read business and science magazines along with epicurean publications like *Gourmet, Bon Appetit,* and *Food and Wine.*

Mapping the popularity of woks is useful in illustrating what social commentator Paul Fussell calls "proletarian drift," the movement of trendy products into the American mainstream. Already woks have made inroads into the American heartland, moving eastward from California into Colorado, and in a dozen yellow-shaded metro areas, such as Milwaukee and Kansas City. These are communities with lots of baby boomers, kids, and working mothers — the kind who use woks as they would microwave ovens to whip up meals in a hurry. They're less affluent and educated than the gourmet-cooking wok owners, but they're receptive to trying new foods and specialty products once unheard of in heartland America. They see woks not as an expression of status but as a source of convenience to create stress-free, stir-fried meals.

# This Old Spouse

## Owners of Stationary Power Tools

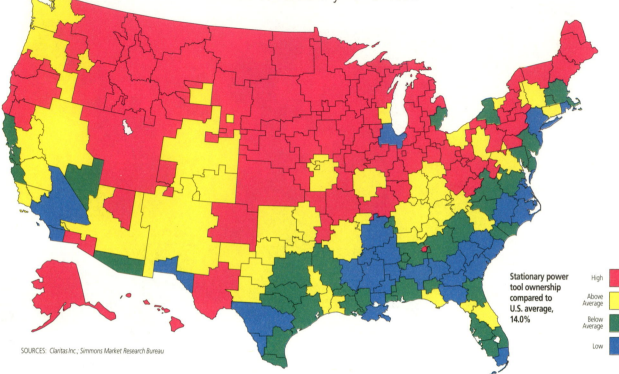

Stationary power tool ownership compared to U.S. average, 14.0%

High — Above Average — Below Average — Low

SOURCES: *Claritas Inc.; Simmons Market Research Bureau*

HOME IMPROVEMENT, like chocolate, can be addictive. You begin painting the trim and replacing the storm windows and before you know it you're remodeling the bathroom, paneling the basement, and retrofitting the fireplace. With baby boomers now several years into their first homes, the number of do-it-yourselfers — and concomitant power-tool sales — is going up as fast as skylights. Nowhere is this more evident than in the northern tier of the country, where the nexus of severe weather, aging housing, and affluent homeowners all combine to increase the rate of owning stationary power tools (those big-ticket items like band saws and drill presses) that find

their way into basements and garages.

The majority of power-tool owners are married men with children, middle-class and middle-aged guys living in homes throughout small-town and rural America. These Bob Vila disciples not only own power tools but also garden tillers, chain saws, lawn mowers, and, to haul everything around, the compact pickup truck. Like small-town consumers everywhere, they tend to be belongers, joining bowling leagues, business groups, fraternal orders, and veterans clubs, perhaps to corral buddies into lending a hand with their latest projects. Power-tool owners generally have some college education and are more likely than average Americans to

own computers, take adult-education courses, and read books (though poetry typically takes a backseat to tips on wallpapering). Among their bibles are *Family Handyman, Popular Science,* and *Home Mechanix.*

Renters and condo owners may be tempted to dismiss power-tool freaks as obsessive-compulsives who can't live without a project in the works. Yet opinion surveys paint a far different portrait, that of brave homeowners who enjoy the challenge of hiking, skiing, traveling abroad, and discovering new ways to invest their money at home. With drill press and buzz saw, they look for new additions to conquer as well.

# Computer Culture

## Owners of Personal Computers

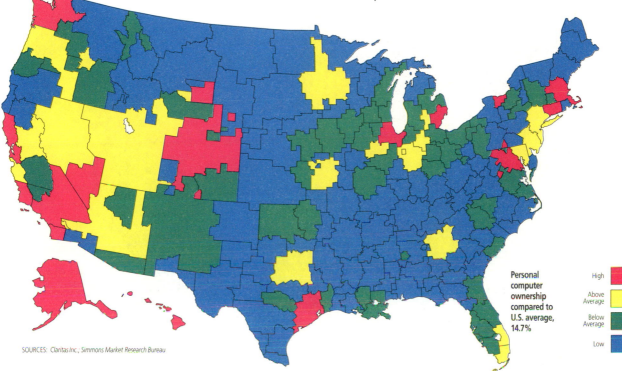

Personal computer ownership compared to U.S. average, 14.7%

High

Above Average

Below Average

Low

SOURCES: *Claritas Inc.; Simmons Market Research Bureau*

IT is patently untrue that the personal computer was invented so freelance writers could work at home in their underwear. Nevertheless, in the 15 years since the development of the microprocessor sparked the mass production of low-cost but powerful small computers, PCs have encouraged the explosion of home offices, especially in the largest metros, where workers are exhausted from commuting. Today, an estimated 40 million people work at home, and about half rely on personal computers to do all or part of their paid work. The hottest markets are cities like Chicago, Los Angeles, and Boston, where PCs — and fax machines — make it easier to move information rather than people across the urban sprawl. (By contrast, the map of America's mobile home owners, who have low mobility rates, is nearly an exact opposite of the map above.)

But population density is only one important predictor of PC ownership; sex and affluence are even more critical. PC owners tend to be men — women are the primary users in only one-quarter of the homes — have incomes over $75,000, homes valued at over $250,000, and college degrees displayed on the wall. Active away from their video monitors, PC owners are more likely than average Americans to belong to health clubs, attend cultural events, enjoy gourmet restaurants, and collect art and antiques. Contrary to their nerdy image, PC owners enjoy a surprisingly eclectic lifestyle. They enjoy science fiction as well as business journals; they enjoy sailing as much as bowling; around the house, you're as likely to find them doing a crossword puzzle as working on their cars. And they're television's diehard sports fans, preferring to watch a basketball or football game over a news or entertainment special.

When they're not hitching rides on the information superhighway, PC owners can be found traveling the country's more concrete roads, having high rates for business trips, domestic flights, and traveling abroad. Scratch a computer owner and you'll find a frequent flyer.

# Plastic Borders

## People Who Spend $10+ at Tupperware Parties

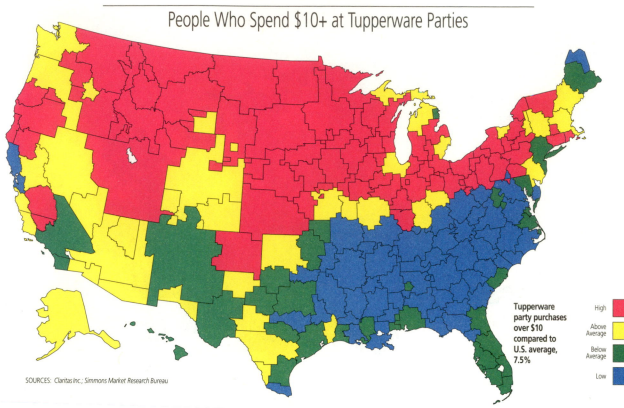

Tupperware party purchases over $10 compared to U.S. average, 7.5%

High
Above Average
Below Average
Low

SOURCES: Claritas Inc.; Simmons Market Research Bureau

NO, the northern tier of the United States has not been invaded by June Cleaver and Donna Reed clones. But this map showing where people spend more than ten dollars at a Tupperware party may lead you to believe otherwise.

Since the 1950s, Tupperware parties have been Major Social Events throughout small-town and rural America, where women gathered around a molded Jell-O salad and were schooled in the virtues of "burping" the famous seal. If you believe Premark International of Deerfield, Ill., the company that makes Tupperware, those gatherings have gone upscale. Tupperware parties now are often held in office conference rooms and daycare centers, and the product's rel-

atively high price has earned it the nickname "Yupperware." Today's designer line comes in neon colors, with acrylic models suitable for microwave ovens and smaller containers just right for singles and one-parent families. And it's true that almost 90 percent of all U.S. households have at least one piece of Tupperware lurking in a cabinet.

Nevertheless, surveys show that Tupperware's biggest collectors are still traditional homemakers, women who clip coupons while listening to golden oldie radio stations, and whose husbands enjoy camping and fishing at higher than average rates — and no doubt sneak off with a couple of containers to store their bait. That more of these women live in the North than the South is a

function less of climate than demographics: these areas have a higher concentration of heartland families that are white, middle-class, and residents of the same address for decades. They look at Tupperware as a miracle of modern science, the only way to store leftover Hamburger Helper safely.

Still, it would be incorrect to mistake Tupperware partygoers for wild and crazy party animals. They consume beer, wine, and cocktails at below-average rates, and they're not into dancing, gambling, or foreign travel. A large segment like to hang around the house and watch television or bake from scratch; their most reckless activity is trying out a new dessert recipe on the family.

# Reigning Cats and Dogs

## Owners of Cats vs. Dogs

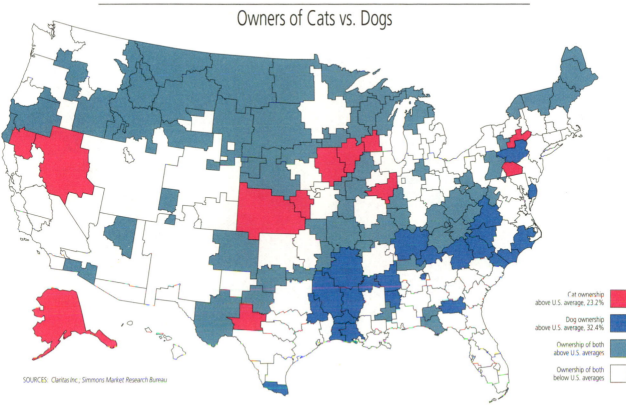

Cat ownership above U.S. average, 23.2%

Dog ownership above U.S. average, 32.4%

Ownership of both above U.S. averages

Ownership of both below U.S. averages

SOURCES: *Claritas Inc.; Simmons Market Research Bureau*

AMERICA is home to more pets than children, but that doesn't mean they're treated with any less affection — the pets, that is. Each year pet owners shower their furry friends with more than $2 billion worth of leashes, treats, toys, and specialty products — 165 new ones were introduced in 1990 alone — and serve up some $7 billion in food. American voters mistrust Presidents who don't like animals and typically elect dog lovers, although the current First Pet, Socks the cat, is scarcely as unconventional as the sheep Woodrow Wilson kept on the White House lawn.

According to tradition, dogs and cats don't get along. But the map above indicates that great stretches of America's wide-open countryside are home to both animals at high rates. Indeed, one-third of all dog owners have cats or, put another way, one-half of all cat owners have dogs.

While the owners of dogs and cats often debate the superiority of their respective animals — and thus, themselves — survey results show cat owners sit higher on the status ladder, but only by a whisker. Both groups include a disproportionate number of working-class married couples with children under the age of 17; in fact, having a baby is a reliable harbinger of pet acquisition. Dog and cat owners share a fondness for heartland activities like gardening, camping, fishing, and attending rodeos. They're above-average consumers of pickups, power tools, and recliners. And all describe themselves as political moderates.

But cat owners, who include more educated, affluent females, have a higher rate of buying books, seeing movies, and using computers. They're more likely than dog owners to read *National Geographic* and *U.S. News and World Report* than the *National Enquirer* and the *Star*. And they're even slightly more politically centrist than the more conservative dog devotees, who tend to favor the death penalty, school prayer, and the pro-life movement. Cat fanciers are more individualistic, more daring about new foods and new vacation spots, and more likely to pick up their pets as strays or from friends. By contrast, dog owners are more akin to pack animals, congregating at kennel clubs and dog shows, acquiring their pets from professional breeders.

As for the children of dog and cat owners, animal love can take on zoolike qualities: besides keeping cats and dogs, they're just as likely to accumulate fish, birds, and other animals before they grow up.

# Downwardly Mobile

## Owners of Mobile Homes

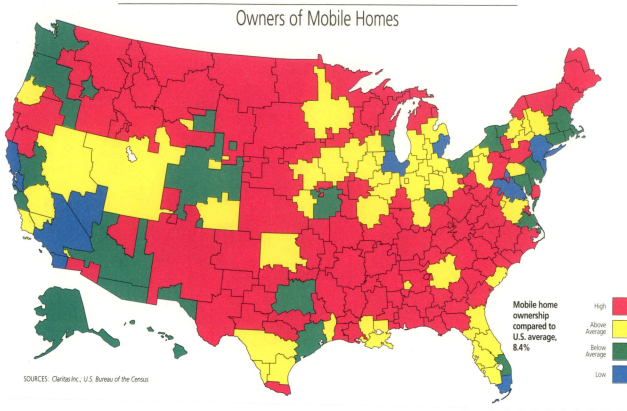

Mobile home ownership compared to U.S. average, 8.4%

High · Above Average · Below Average · Low

SOURCES: Claritas Inc.; U.S. Bureau of the Census

I T'S one of life's little ironies that virtually the only traveling a mobile home does is from the factory to the new owner's parking space — unless you count displacement due to hurricanes or tornadoes. Given all the news footage of mobile homes floating down swollen rivers, flattened like pancakes, or leaning crazily against a tree, you'd think mobile homes are most popular in the nation's stormy regions, acting like magnets for Toto-tossing twisters.

But mobile homes actually are a widespread phenomenon, serving as the primary residence for one in every sixteen Americans. Manufactured housing units — as they're known in the trade — are especially fashionable in the nation's Southern and Western states; in

Wyoming and South Carolina, one in six housing units is a mobile home. By contrast, they're as rare as courteous taxi drivers in the nation's largest metros and, in routinely hurricane-ravaged Hawaii, only one residence in a thousand is a mobile home.

The image of mobile homeowners often takes a beating in the media. True, they're more likely than average Americans to have low income and education levels — not to mention a fondness for the *National Enquirer,* pro wrestling, tobacco products, and Kool-Aid over imported wine. But people who take pride in their double-wides are not lowlifes or losers. The late Sam Walton, founder of the Wal-Mart retail chain, lived in a mobile home for years — even after

he made his first billion. In fact, mobile-home owners are as likely as average Americans to have children at home and more likely to be between the ages of 18 and 34 years.

No doubt, the difficulty for this segment of the population to attain the American Dream of traditional home ownership makes mobile homes attractive. The average mobile home in 1990 cost $27,800 compared to $149,000 for a new single-family dwelling, according to the Manufactured Housing Institute. But the newest mobile homes cost upwards of $75,000 and boast porches, picture windows, and pitched roofs. And demographers confirm that mobile homes are increasingly upwardly mobile, and not just during storms.

# Junk Mail Junkies

## Direct-Mail Respondents

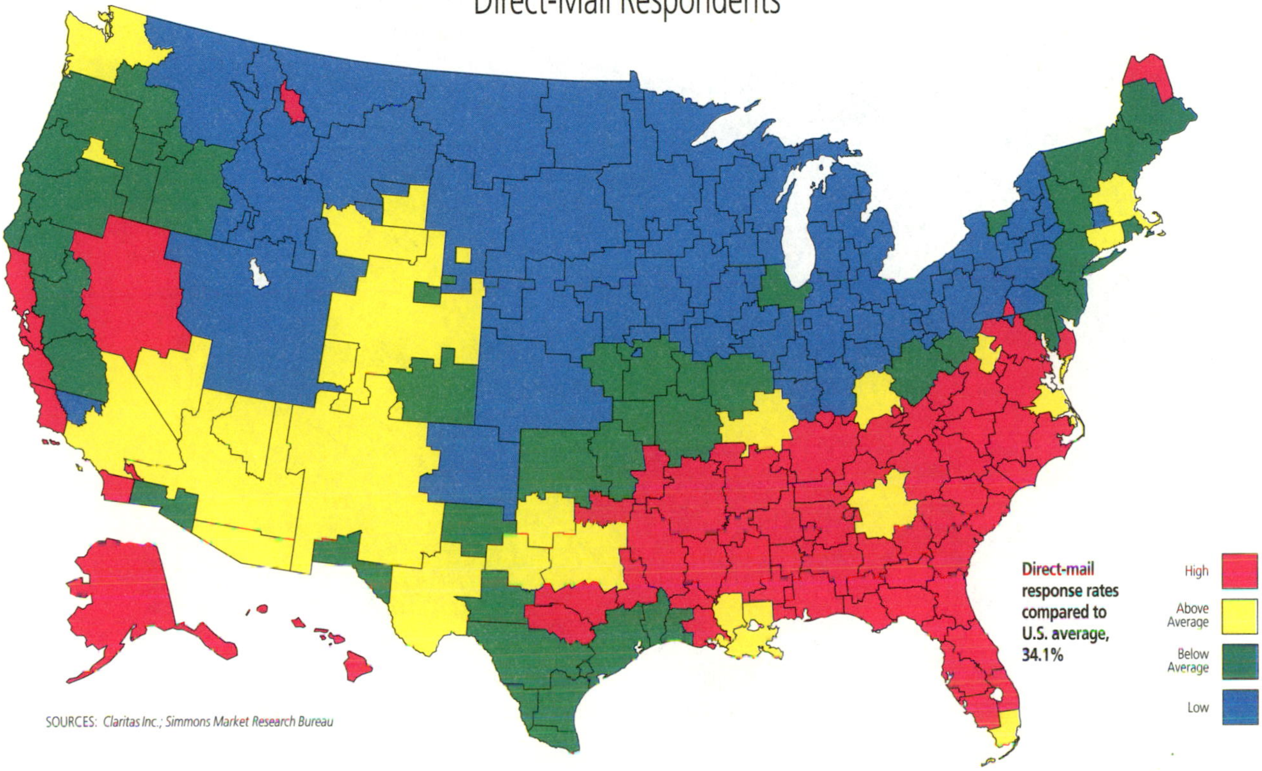

**Direct-mail response rates compared to U.S. average, 34.1%**

High
Above Average
Below Average
Low

SOURCES: *Claritas Inc.; Simmons Market Research Bureau*

THE industry calls it direct mail, but most of us know it as junk. While many Americans claim they hate the flotsam that arrives each day in the mail — the fund-raising pitches, the pet catalogs, the upper-cased exhortations for a "21-DAY FREE TRIAL MEMBERSHIP" — don't believe their protestations. Surveys show that 78 percent of Americans open and read junk mail, and more than half respond to catalog pitches at least once every six months. In 1993, that love-hate relationship resulted in upwards of $200 billion in mail-order purchases and donations — enough to keep direct-mail marketers pushing the postal onslaught to the tune of 70 billion pieces of third-class mail every year.

But the 100 million Americans who shop each year by mail or phone don't fall into any single consumer type, Ed McMahon's peculiar appeal notwithstanding. You've got your young Honda-driving, gold card–carrying, time-pressed shoppers getting their underwear from Victoria's Secret or their outerwear from J. Crew. And you've got your downscale, elderly *Southern Living*–subscribing residents of retirement communities buying hard-to-find Elvis plates from the Franklin Mint. A high concentration of both live in the South in part because of the dearth of upscale specialty shops (notice that fewer people buy by mail in major metros like Atlanta, New Orleans, and Miami). And another pocket of junk-mail buyers live out West

along the California coast, where mobile baby boomers like to mail away for hard-to-find fashions and gadgets offered in East Coast catalogs. "People who've recently relocated always need products but may not know the lay of the land," explains Chet Dalzell of the Direct Marketing Association. "So they have their mailbox."

The people who are most likely to throw out their junk mail without opening it tend to be middle-aged, high-income professionals from the nation's largest cities. They're the folks in the designer suits who will tell you that they've been there, done that, and own one already. Forty-odd pounds of junk mail and several trees are wasted on them annually.

# The Fax Empire

## People Who Own Home Facsimile Machines

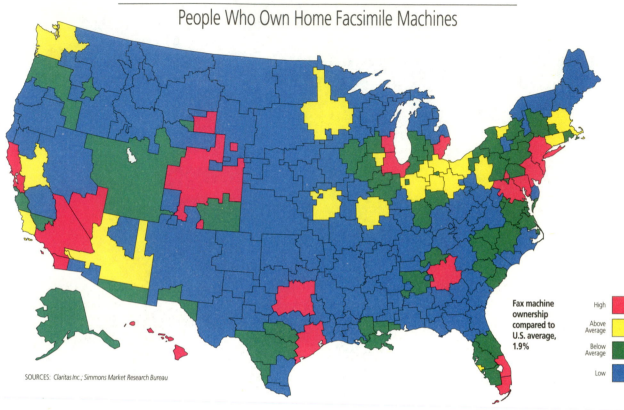

Fax machine ownership compared to U.S. average, 1.9%

High

Above Average

Below Average

Low

SOURCES: *Claritas Inc.; Simmons Market Research Bureau*

IN today's information age, where telecommunicating and E-mail have blurred the boundaries of the nation's power centers, there's an easy way to determine where the real action is. Just chart the flow of information and ideas transported between home- and office facsimile machines — the Fax Empire. By that measure, the map above reveals the nation's true centers of power to be 18 markets across the country, word-dependent places that control the nation's information flow.

Not surprisingly, these power centers coincide with the nation's largest metropolitan areas, places like New York, Washington, Los Angeles, and Chicago, which are home to the highest concentration of white-collar workers. Compared to average Americans, the nation's power elite are more likely to be older (45 years old and up), richer (earning over $100,000), and better educated (a higher percentage holding an advanced degree). They live in a fast-paced world where the next best thing to faxing is FedExing. (The map above is virtually identical to Federal Express's prime territories for overnight deliveries.) But contrary to the workaholic stereotype, these hot markets have large numbers of working women and married couples with children. When they're not exporting information, fax owners tend to have stable family lives.

Indeed, if the fax machine was designed to reduce the white-collar workload, it seems to be succeeding. Fax owners have higher-than-average rates for attending movies and concerts (rock as well as classical), playing golf and tennis, and traveling to Europe and the Caribbean. They're insatiable techies who also tend to own computers, CD players, expensive cameras, and other high-end electronic playthings. And they like to indulge their taste for wine, imported cheese, fancy ice cream, and gourmet cooking.

But in one aspect of their lives, they don't kid around: money. One survey of 95 financial products found that fax owners invested in 85 financial instruments at higher-than-average rates — everything from stocks and mutual funds to IRAs and medical insurance. In the Fax Empire, information is power is money.

# Electronic Boomers

## People Who Buy Boom Boxes

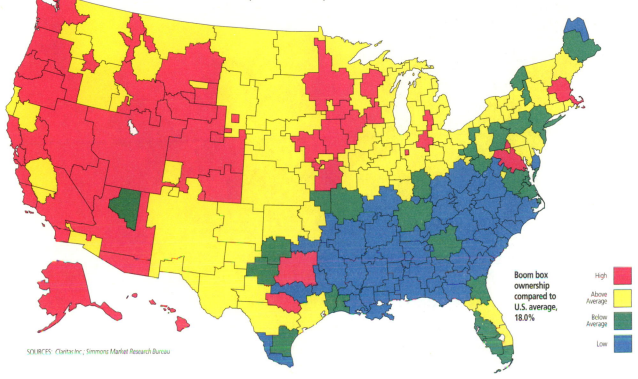

Boom box ownership compared to U.S. average, 18.0%

High
Above Average
Below Average
Low

SOURCES: *Claritas Inc.; Simmons Market Research Bureau*

O NCE inner-city annoyances known as "ghetto blasters," today's boom boxes have fled the city for the 'burbs — taking along upmarket price tags. The latest generation of "portable stereo systems" can cost more than $500 depending on the features, which can include dual tape decks, radio, compact disc player, and detachable speakers. Boom boxes are now de rigueur in most teenage bedrooms and college dormitories, and though not many owners actually lug around the monster boxes, you're sure to find yourself occasionally within ear-splitting shot of the few who believe it's their right to broadcast their favorite noise over as wide a radius as possible.

In the '90s, the biggest boom-box fans are white, upper-middle-class teenagers who live in midsize cities and towns in the West — markets like San Diego, Denver, and Reno. Conversely, low incomes hold down consumption rates in the South. While their 50-year-old parents may be tuning in to pop and easy listening music stations, boom-box owners favor classic rock, jazz, or punkier contemporary bands. These members of the so-called Generation X — sandwiched between baby boomers and their children — are active outdoorsy types who ski, swim, hike, and play racquetball at high rates. And they're big on other electronic goods, such as stereos, CD players, camcorders, and PCs. But this fascination with gadgets does not extend to kitchen appliances. Boom-box owners are more likely than average Americans to frequent fast-food drive-ins like Wendy's and Taco Bell.

Opinion surveys reveal boom-box owners to be more self-centered than other Americans, expressing little respect or trust in senior citizens, religious leaders, consumer advocates, or news reporters. They're more interested in getting enough exercise than reading, more supportive of teaching sex education than family values in the schools. In a Yankelovich poll of 100 opinion questions, the issue uppermost in their minds was finding new vacation spots — surely to offend ever more unsuspecting vacationers with their beach blaster or boom-box car.

# Babes in Toyland

## People Who Buy Plush Dolls/Animals vs. Nintendo

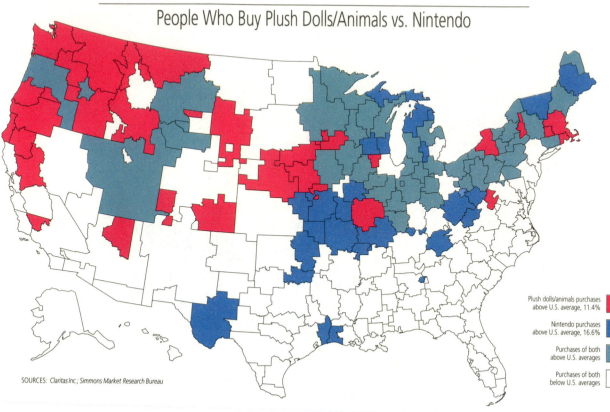

Plush dolls/animals purchases above U.S. average, 11.4%

Nintendo purchases above U.S. average, 16.6%

Purchases of both above U.S. averages

Purchases of both below U.S. averages

SOURCES: *Claritas Inc.; Simmons Market Research Bureau*

THIS map addresses one of the great conundrums of our time: whether to be a hip parent of the '90s and buy a youngster a hyper-popular video game, thereby encouraging their descent into the Land of Lost Game Boys, or admit you're a sentimental fool and present a cuddly stuffed animal that's about as cool as Barney. This is no trifling matter, given that the toy industry generates some $15 billion in retail sales. And as the overlapping areas of the map indicate, parents and grandparents tend to buy both kinds of toys at steep rates. Nearly one in three households has purchased a Nintendo game or squishy doll in the last year.

But who's buying what for whom? Nintendo, the Japanese company that burst onto the market in 1985, has made its home video games almost as ubiquitous as comic books were in the '50s. Nintendo games are now found in more than 30 million U.S. households, especially in suburban and rural fringe markets where buyers tend to be under-45-year-old married couples who've parlayed blue-collar jobs into middle-class comfort. These folks place a premium on adult toys such as powerboats, RVs, and motorcycles, and don't mind dropping $100 for a video-game machine and another $50 for game cartridges. Good with their hands — Nintendo buyers are big on home repair — more than a few equate video-game competency with real-world computer skills. Others view video games as a form of interactive television, TV being one of their biggest passions.

Plush dolls and animals generally cost a fraction of the Nintendo package — unless, of course, you're talking about investing in virtual-reality dolls that shiver, burp, cry, or speak several Romance languages. But compared to Nintendo buyers, the Americans who lean toward old-fashioned dolls and animals are wealthier, older, more racially diverse, and more often childless — not to mention less aware of the video invasion. The better-educated Americans prevalent in the West are less likely to watch TV — and to be influenced by numerous video-game commercials — when selecting toys. They're prone to buying the kinds of toys they grew up with, such as stuffed animals.

Ideologically, there are some stark differences between these toy consumers. The stuffed-animal fans are more concerned about issues like education, personal creativity, and getting enough exercise. Not so the Nintendo fans, though they should be. One study showed that schoolchildren underwent a 10 percent decline in cardiovascular fitness in the '80s, and cited Nintendo as a chief culprit.

# Condomania

## People Who Use Condoms

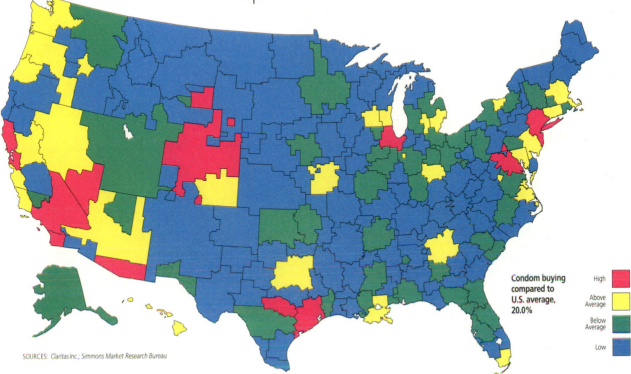

Condom buying compared to U.S. average, 20.0%

High · Above Average · Below Average · Low

SOURCES: Claritas Inc.; Simmons Market Research Bureau

IT should have been obvious when condoms with names like Trojan and Ramses began being edged out by brands with names like Kimono, Lady Protex, Touch, and Arouse ("For Her"): the most important factor influencing condom sales in this country has nothing to do with men. With an estimated two-thirds of all condoms purchased by women, the hottest markets for condom sales all feature a strikingly high rate of women in the labor force. True, condom usage is typically high in big-city metros with concentrations of young singles — rich and poor, white and black, gay and straight — who've gotten the message about practicing safe sex. But beyond the audience of sexually active young people, the red-hot areas for condom usage — cities like New York, Houston, Denver, and Los Angeles — are filled with working

*Not just for him anymore, condoms are hot items in cities filled with working women.*

women concerned about intimacy in the age of AIDS.

This is not to say that condom consumers are in general risk-averse, the Volvo owners of America's lovers. They tend to be active in ways other than sex, like jogging, foreign travel, water sports, and going to gambling casinos; indeed, Las Vegas is the nation's top market for condom usage. In terms of their social attitudes, Yankelovich surveys also found that condom users are pretty liberal, supporting nude beaches, homosexual marriages, and sex education on television. Their favorite magazines include *GQ, Self, Esquire,* and *New Woman.*

But when it comes to adventure, folks in these markets apparently don't want to play sexual roulette. In fact, demand has never been higher among women buyers, who acknowledge in product surveys that the biggest advantage of condoms is "peace of mind."

# Desperately Seeking Soothing

## People Who Buy Headache Remedies

Headache remedy purchases compared to U.S. average, 89.6%

High
Above Average
Below Average
Low

SOURCES: *Claritas Inc.; Simmons Market Research Bureau*

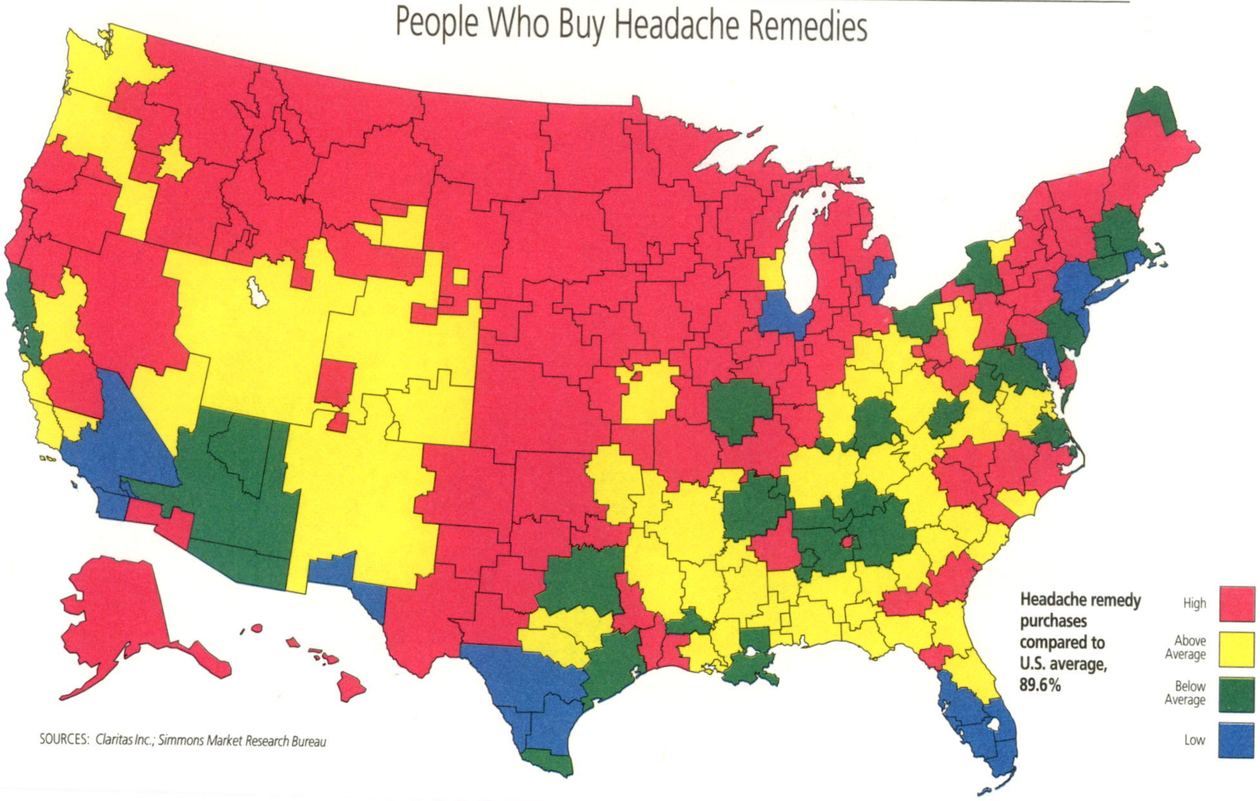

WHO gets the biggest headaches in America? The stressed-out urban executive coping with million-dollar decisions and thousands of employees? The suburban homemaker juggling crying infants, mounds of dirty laundry, and the hassles of carpooling? In fact, surveys reveal what physicians and marketers call a "flat profile," that is, people from virtually all backgrounds get headaches at about the same rate.

However, access to treatments influences what kinds of people purchase over-the-counter medication. Dr. Seymour Diamond, executive director of the National Headache Foundation, observes that the most common headaches are tension- or depression-related, and most often strike white-collar workers. Yet these people don't always head right for a drugstore. "The higher the income bracket," says Diamond, "the greater the likelihood an individual will seek professional treatment," thereby reducing over-the-counter sales in densely populated metros.

The top groups for buying nonprescription headache remedies are middle-aged blue-collar parents in small towns (coping with noisy, repetitious jobs) and elderly residents of farm areas (dealing with the aches of aging). Widely dispersed from New England across the Midwest to California, these communities share no single lifestyle: their consumers are more likely than average Americans to like gospel as well as classical music, bus travel as well as luxury cars, *Parade* as well as the *New Yorker*. These markets simply share fewer doctors than metropolitan areas, and they have a greater incidence of self-treaters.

What's striking about the Americans least likely to buy headache remedies is that they tend to be single city-dwellers who have upper-middle-class incomes and homes. Marriage, kids, and the worries associated with extreme poverty or wealth all seem to contribute to the need for headache remedies. And contrary to surveys that find married men happier and longer-living than their single brethren, the above map indicates that such satisfaction comes with a price: more headaches than average folks. Then what's the real way to spell relief? S-T-A-Y S-I-N-G-L-E.

# The Scent of a Man

## People Who Buy Obsession for Men vs. Old Spice

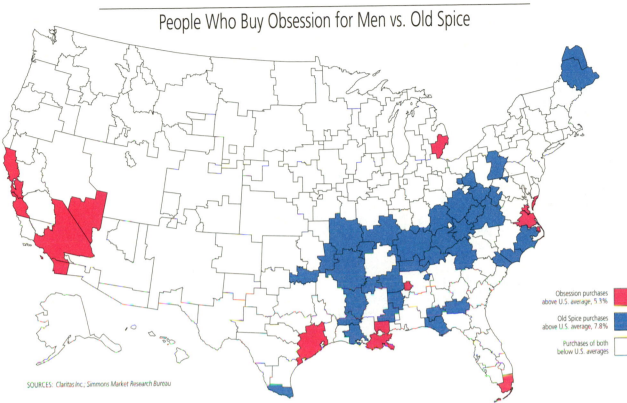

Obsession purchases above U.S. average, 5.3%

Old Spice purchases above U.S. average, 7.8%

Purchases of both below U.S. averages

SOURCES: *Claritas Inc.; Simmons Market Research Bureau*

FEW products are more advertising-driven than perfume, mainly because the image precedes the product. And few tap into the attitude-sensitive soul of men more than cologne. Half of all men under the age of 50 regularly use cologne or aftershave, all hoping to evoke the smell of a Stetson hat, a rum toddy, or a horse's saddle. They've turned the men's fragrance market into a $1.5-billion-a-year industry, an astonishing figure considering that many men's colognes cost a relatively modest $5 to $15 an ounce. Women, by contrast, may spend $225 an ounce on perfume, which may explain why they buy roughly half of all men's cologne.

Still, men have their favorites. Their top-selling cologne, Old Spice, has been around since 1937 and was particularly popular among GIs during World War II. Classified in the lighter citrus family of colognes, Old Spice costs less than ten dollars a bottle, a particularly important selling point to consumers, the greatest proportion of whom are older married men of modest means from working-class communities throughout the South. They spend their free time pursuing activities such as hunting, woodworking, and fishing. This portrait of an old-fashioned American male is completed, according to polls, by findings that Old Spice is often passed down from father to son. Aptly, Old Spice fans remark that they wish Americans would show the elderly more respect.

Obsession for Men, one of the heavy Oriental cologne types that mixes mandarin, amber, and oak moss, arrived in 1986 with a flourish of homoerotic advertising that depicted well-muscled naked men cavorting with naked, lifeless women. The message was kinky, which apparently has touched the hot buttons of a racially mixed crowd of under-35-year-old singles and single parents living in cities. Surveys show they appear to be active in the dating scene — fond of alcohol, health clubs, and live music — and are less traditional in their sexual mores (read: gay or bisexual).

"Young men looking to make a statement as swingers wear a heavier scent like Obsession," says Annette Green, director of The Fragrance Foundation. "Old Spice is for a man who can wear it around other men and not worry about the statement he's making."

Is marketing really able to create two so diametrically different audiences: the old shoe versus the young stud, the quiet married man versus the partying sex fiend? Well, let's put it this way: compared to average Americans, the highest-rated lifestyle activity for Old Spice users is chewing tobacco. Among Obsession buyers, it's buying condoms.

# Pregnancy Testers

## Users of Home Pregnancy-Test Kits

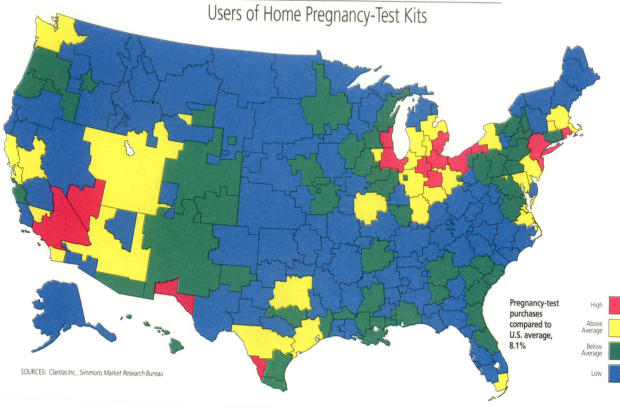

Pregnancy-test purchases compared to U.S. average, 8.1%

| High | Above Average | Below Average | Low |

SOURCES: *Claritas Inc.; Simmons Market Research Bureau*

MAYBE it's the inevitable outgrowth of the sexual revolution that home pregnancy tests today are the fastest-growing segment of the family-planning market. While pregnancy used to be something to share privately, today it is brazenly celebrated on magazine covers and shamelessly featured in pregnancy-test kit commercials with real people discussing their sex lives. At a cost of $10 to $25, home tests are a relatively cheap and cheerful way of determining whether a woman is a mother-to-be. And sales keep rising — they now top $150 million — because time-pressed women don't want to wait or pay for a doctor's visit.

But just as all pregnancy tests are not created equal, pregnancy-test markets are not uniformly distributed across the country. The highest concentration of users lives in the fast-paced big cities as well as second-tier markets in the nation's Rust Belt. These consumers tend to be 18-to-34-year-old singles and divorcées who live in apartments, have blue-collar and low-level white-collar jobs, and earn from $10,000 to $20,000 annually. They work hard and play hard, and are night owls who like TV dinners, dance clubs, and late-night talk-show hosts David Letterman and Arsenio Hall. They're more likely to watch TV than read books — though they wish they spent more time reading — and compromise by picking up magazines like *Cosmopolitan, Glamour,* and *Mademoiselle.*

Having been on the market less than 20 years, pregnancy-test kits have still not gained widespread acceptance in heartland America, the rural, blue areas shown above.

Women there and in more cosmopolitan cities still go to their physicians to find out if they're pregnant — the final word for 75 percent of all U.S. women. (A curious 12 percent of women tell pollsters they don't know how they learn they're pregnant.)

While pregnancy-test users may not necessarily be more sexually active than other U.S. women, they're certainly more daring than average Americans. In surveys, kit users claim to support gay rights, nude beaches, and broad concepts such as sensuousness and hedonism. They're also big on gambling, more likely to buy lottery tickets, visit gambling casinos, and agree with the statement "I like to live for today." Most important, only about half of all pregnancy-test users hope for positive results; the rest seem to be playing pregnancy roulette.

# Smokers

## People Who Smoke Cigarettes

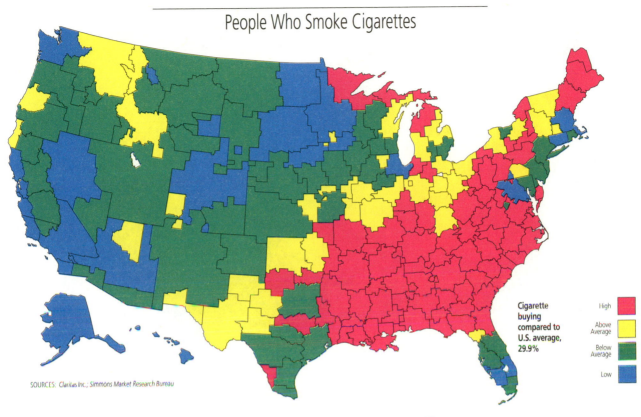

Cigarette buying compared to U.S. average, 29.9%

High
Above Average
Below Average
Low

SOURCES: Claritas Inc.; Simmons Market Research Bureau

AMERICA'S cigarette belt encompasses many of the rural areas in the country where tobacco is grown. But it also has the dubious distinction of reflecting the areas where Americans have the highest rates of stroke and lung cancer — the two leading causes of death in the U.S.

Contrary to the old image of glamorous, well-heeled sophisticates, today's smokers tend to be downscale and poorly educated blue-collar residents of farms and inner cities — "people who have a difficulty in understanding long-term risks, whether it's smoking, cholesterol, or high blood pressure," says John Banzhaf III, director of Action on Smoking and Health. Befitting a group that's failed to respond to the message that cigarettes are hazardous to your health, smokers include a higher-than-average rate of senior citizens, recent immigrants, and men (out-numbering women by a ratio of 5 to 4) who became addicted to cigarettes in their teens.

As a group, smokers are a relatively sedentary lot who consume high rates of heavily sugared, high-fat foods such as sausage, candy, powdered soft drinks, and fried chicken. Smokers are more likely than average Americans to enjoy pro wrestling, listen to rhythm & blues, and watch television for hours each day. It's not unexpected that researchers report an inverse relationship between unhealthy behavior and consumption of media that convey health warnings, and smokers follow the trend. In cigarette-crazy communities, the most popular magazines are soft-news titles like the *Star,* the *National Enquirer,* and *True Story.*

While U.S. cigarette consumption has dropped over the years thanks to public-health campaigns, warning labels, and restrictive advertising, the downscale smokers in these hot markets have thus far resisted antismoking efforts. When tobacco company R. J. Reynolds Tobacco proposed a new cigarette brand, Dakota, to be targeted to young, blue-collar females, the marketing plan mentioned heavy advertising at one of their favorite spectator sports: tractor pulls.

That campaign was pulled after a public outcry, but tobacco companies have found a way to increase consumption with a strategy more powerful than slick and cynical marketing: drop the price of cigarettes. Clinton Administration tax writers know that affordability is the most important element in tobacco consumption and continue to debate whether a tax of 50 cents or a dollar will snuff out a few butts. In the '90s, smoking a cigarette remains one of the nation's cheapest of cheap thrills.

# Floss and Rinse

## Users of Dental Floss vs. Mouthwash

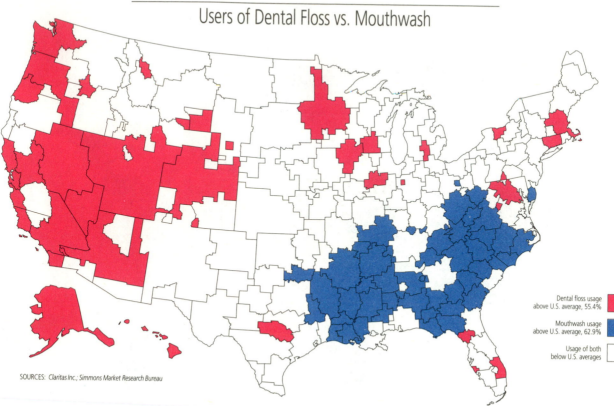

SOURCES: *Claritas Inc.; Simmons Market Research Bureau*

Dental floss usage
above U.S. average, 55.4%

Mouthwash usage
above U.S. average, 62.9%

Usage of both
below U.S. averages

IN the 35 years since that boy in the Crest commercial declared, "Look, Mom, no cavities," dental care has changed dramatically. Researchers discovered the link between plaque and gum disease, and companies responded by creating shelves full of toothpastes, flosses, and mouthwashes designed to eliminate the groaty film. Then Madison Avenue stepped in, trumpeting these products' abilities to not only fight plaque but also promote a sexy, close-up, fresh smile.

If the formula is so simple, why, as the map above indicates, is the bathroom behavior of Southerners so different from Westerners? Class is a big factor. Flossers are generally upscale, educated consumers from big cities and college towns who've gotten the message that a thin thread may be the best tool for holding on to their teeth. "Those are the cities where the dental schools and periodontists are

located," notes Dr. Linda Niessen, chairwoman of the Department of Public Health Sciences for Baylor College of Dentistry.

In addition, flossers are found in abundance in the West because mobile Americans most often settle there, and mobility is a function of education. More health conscious than average Americans, flossers join health clubs at high rates, worry about getting enough exercise, and support public service ads about birth control and drug abuse. When it comes to food, they eat preventively, especially low-cholesterol foods like oat bran, popcorn, and rice cakes. "They're part of a health model that says, 'Your activities can make a difference,'" says Niessen.

As for the nation's mouthwash users, they're more concerned about the odors caused by food, bacteria, and gum disease — or, in the euphemism of advertisers, "morning breath." Although nothing

is completely effective against bad breath, that hasn't stopped the engine of American industry from promoting mouthwash as the only salvation for those worried about their social life, job promotion, or first kiss in the morning. Southerners are particularly sensitive to those pitches because of two factors: tobacco and poor health care. Smoking and chewing tobacco are two major sources of bacteria that cause halitosis, and Southerners indulge in them at the highest rate in the nation.

Moreover, mouthwash consumers — who tend to be older, more downscale, and less educated than average Americans — typically treat themselves instead of seeing a dentist for problems. Rather than brush, floss, or seek professional care, mouthwash users simply take a swig from their favorite green or yellow bottle and go on their merry way.

# Runners Up

## People Who Go Jogging

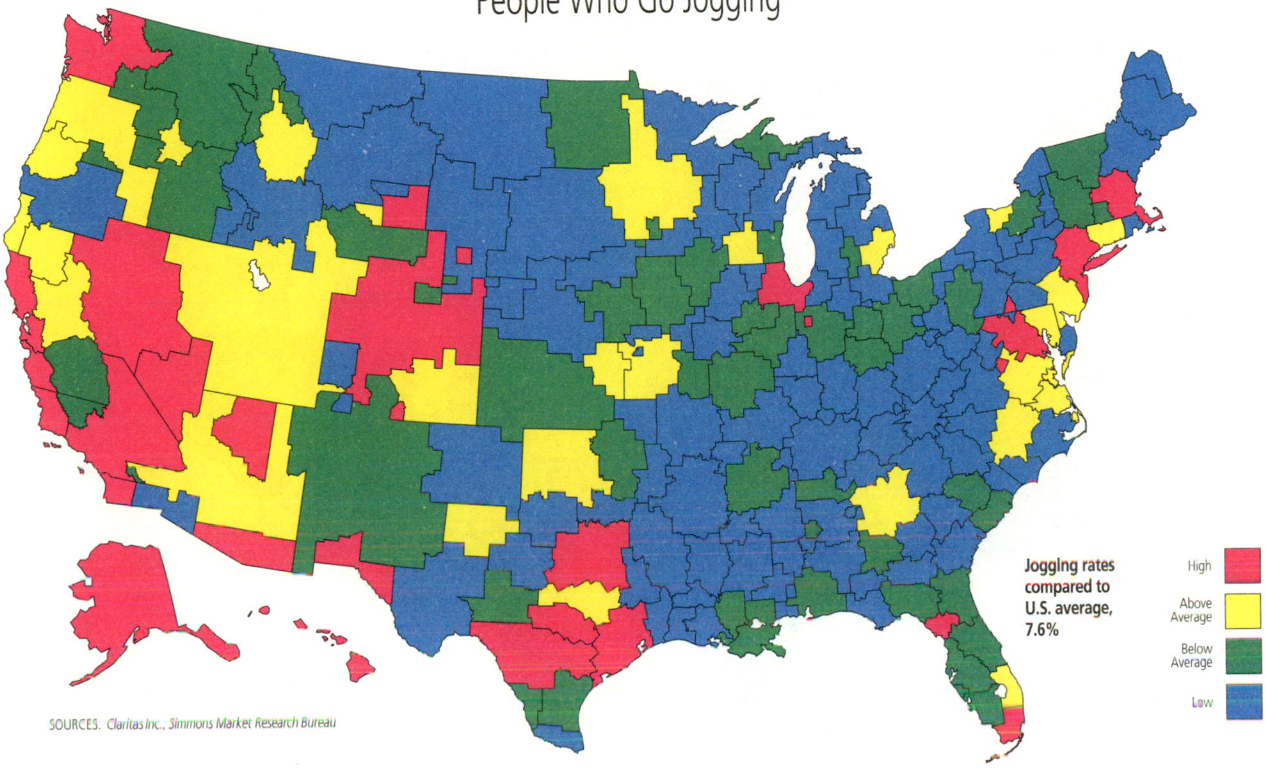

**Jogging rates compared to U.S. average, 7.6%**

High
Above Average
Below Average
Low

SOURCES. *Claritas Inc., Simmons Market Research Bureau*

THE running revolution that erupted in the 1970s today has slowed to a walk as bad-kneed baby boomers have settled into middle age and cellulite. But a hearty corps of Americans still lace up their Nikes to jog along streets, ravines, and school tracks, and not all are brawny jocks or student athletes, cutting class for an afternoon jaunt. In fact, there's plenty of evidence that the majority of the nation's joggers are workaholic professionals who want a quick, high-aerobic form of exercise that can be squeezed into their time-compressed schedules.

As the map above shows, joggers tend to live in areas where they can run year-round, either outdoors in Sunbelt communities — like Houston or San Diego—or in the nation's big cities, where abundant health clubs and Ys offer indoor tracks. The highest proportion are college-educated singles in their twenties and thirties who hold well-paying jobs in business, finance, or entertainment services.

Although jogging does not carry the same cachet as, say, sailing or skiing — writer Alison Lurie defined a high-status sport as one "that requires a great deal of expensive equipment or an expensive setting or both" — joggers are more likely to play upper-middle-class sports like tennis and racquetball rather than pursue such proletariat activities as bowling and billiards. Indeed, when they're not doing laps after work, joggers are a fairly

civilized lot, enjoying jazz, theater, and gourmet cooking. By contrast, the nation's sedentary souls in the map's blue areas spend more of their time watching TV; their idea of exercise is gardening or fishing.

While jogging critics may think that all that roadwork is excessive if not downright obsessive, joggers counter that they run to maintain their equilibrium. One poll found that their favorite food was not popcorn or yogurt, as one might expect, but high-fat, artery-hardening ice cream. Joggers are heavy consumers of Ben & Jerry's, Häagen-Dazs, and Frusen Gladje, reflecting their ethic: Work hard, run hard, eat guilt-free.

# They Shoot Ducks, Don't They?

## People Who Own Hunting Rifles

Hunting rifle ownership compared to U.S. average, 9.7%

High
Above Average
Below Average
Low

SOURCES: *Claritas Inc.; Simmons Market Research Bureau*

IN the court of public opinion, few sports are more politically incorrect than hunting. One recent poll found that fully one-third of all Americans believe hunting should be outlawed, and the figure is even higher among urban residents. But as the map above indicates, hunters have hardly been harassed into oblivion and can be found in every region of the country. Some 17 million Americans continue to take aim at whatever quacks or bounds through the woods, a fact influenced by both history and geography. Hunters are most prevalent in rural markets where residents have a tradition for hunting as well as access to land where killing game is permitted.

For rifle manufacturers, however, the demographic news about hunters isn't as encouraging as, say, the growing population of white-tailed deer. While the number of hunters is steadily dropping, their average age is constantly rising. A disproportionate number of hunting rifle owners are over 55, earn less than $35,000 at blue-collar jobs, and live in homes worth less than $50,000. Contrary to their media image as Yahoos with firearms — fueled partly by their fondness for chewing tobacco and pickups — most hunters are solidly middle class. They're more likely than average Americans to belong to business clubs, enjoy photography, and own investment property. And the high cost of hunting trips — guides, lodging, and licenses can cost more than $250 — is moving the sport upscale. Politically, hunters tend to be centrists who support the death penalty, oppose gun control, and describe themselves as game when it comes to trying new foods to eat — typically the prey they kill.

But how to explain the antihunting sentiment in the nation's big cities, where, after all, meat eaters simply pay someone else to do what hunters do for sport? Slaton L. White, assistant managing editor for *Field & Stream,* cites the breakup of the traditional family for the disappearance of urban hunters. "Hunting is very much an activity that's passed down generationally," he says. "And too often a breakup in the family causes problems in continuing that tradition."

Then there's another school of thought that contends bleeding-heart urbanites have been seduced by too many movies in the vein of *Bambi* — arguably the most powerful antihunting movie ever made. Many city-dwellers raise animals to the same evolutionary plane as humans, contrary to rural-based hunters who raise animals for slaughter. As White explains, "It's a fundamentally different view of how the universe is ordered."

# Two If By Sea

## People Who Go Sailing vs. Powerboating

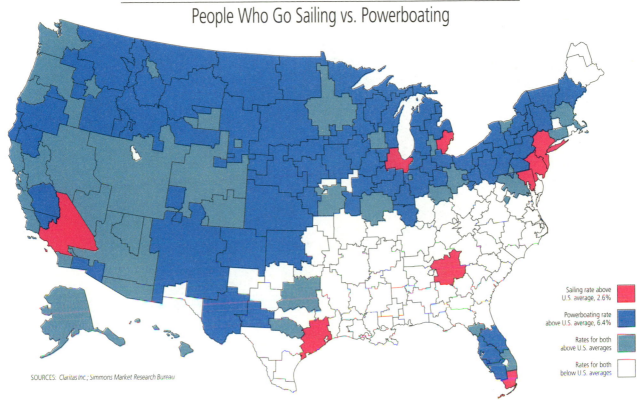

Sailing rate above
U.S. average, 2.6%

Powerboating rate
above U.S. average, 6.4%

Rates for both
above U.S. averages

Rates for both
below U.S. averages

SOURCES: *Claritas Inc.; Simmons Market Research Bureau*

MOST Americans' ancestors came here by boat, and to this day the water retains an allure for many. But our preference for sail versus motorized transport is divided as much by class as geography, those lovers of sailboats typically drawn to coastal waters while powerboats ply inland lakes.

Sailing remains the more upscale of the two, a perfect example of "prep" culture according to *The Official Preppy Handbook*. As writer Lisa Birnbach observed, "It offers fresh air, physical and intellectual challenge, and the thrill of being financially frivolous . . . like standing in a cold shower while tearing up $100 bills." Not that the nation's sailors can't afford it. Demographically speaking, these over-45-year-olds tend to earn more than $100,000 a year and hold executive jobs in business, education, or finance. They have

upscale tastes to match their boating style: a passion for hanging out at the country club, traveling abroad, and investing in stocks. In their well-furnished galleys you'll find plenty of scotch, imported beer, and wine (red and white). When the weather turns cold and the seas too choppy, they head for the ski slopes — another sport that requires sun, wind, exotic locales, cumbersome equipment, and a hefty bank account.

With more than twice as many devotees as sailing, powerboating is more a bread-and-butter sport. Fans still tend to be well off, white-collar, and college-educated, but a higher percentage are younger, middle class, and more rural than the suburban sailors. Powerboaters are more likely to belong to a business club than a country club, see movies than plays, own mutual funds than stocks. They're fonder of TV than of most magazines, pre-

ferring to watch tournaments of golf, figure skating, auto racing, and, one of the few contests sleepier than baseball, sport fishing. Being water-borne techie freaks who equip their powerboats with marine radios, fish-finders, and depth-finders, it's no surprise that they also like land-based gadgets like radar detectors, computers, and tape decks.

But what most separates sailors from boaters is ideology. The motor heads are moderates, supporters of privacy rights and environmental protections, opposed to gay rights and legalizing drugs. Sailors, William F. Buckley Jr. notwithstanding, are polo shirt–wearing liberals, strong backers of abortion rights, gay marriages, and consumerism. And, shocker of all shockers, they support social pluralism, perhaps even allowing powerboaters into their waters — as long as they don't make waves.

# Fairways to Heaven

## People Who Golf 20+ Times a Year

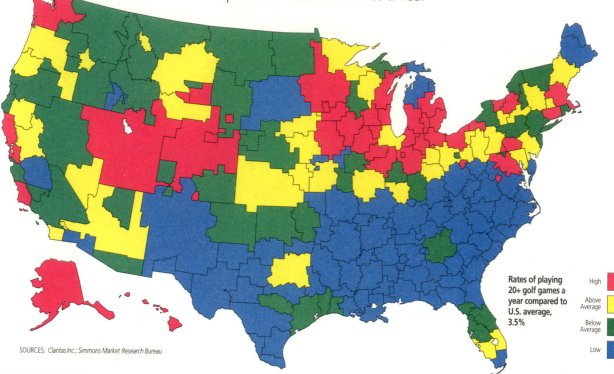

Rates of playing 20+ golf games a year compared to U.S. average, 3.5%

High

Above Average

Below Average

Low

SOURCES: *Claritas Inc.; Simmons Market Research Bureau*

THINK of the map above as a guide to where you're most likely to find five irons wrapped around tree trunks. Actually, the areas in red represent markets where residents are most likely to have played golf more than 20 times a year and, thus, have had more opportunity to create those sculptures of sports frustration.

What's striking is how few of these markets are the Sunbelt home of the Palm This or Pebble That country club, where major tournaments are usually played. In fact, the highest concentrations of avid golfers are found in the nation's major metros, along with some Rust Belt cities like Rockford, Ill., Pittsburgh, Pa., and Toledo, Ohio. A contributing factor is that many of these cities and bedroom suburbs offer easy access to inexpensive municipal courses, attracting more than the country-club set to the sport. Surveys confirm that golfers, while upscale, are no

---

*No longer limited to blue bloods in loud pants, today's golfers include backpackers and rock fans.*

---

longer simply blue bloods in go-to-hell plaid pants. Today's fans also go backpacking, listen to rock music, and take adult-education courses at above-average rates.

This profile of baby boomer golfers is confirmed by experts on the game. Author Alan Green notes the sport's growing popularity among fortysomething men whose knees are too banged up to play basketball. "They can't hack it at hoops anymore," he says. "So they turn to golf, an intense game where you play against yourself, and it makes them feel like athletes again."

That, at least, is the logical explanation. Another is a fad in some northern states described by Green: playing golf in the snow using a black or fluorescent pink ball. This allows golfers to challenge the public courses year-round, trying to avoid trees as well as snow traps.

# Stationary Bikes and Campsites

## People Who Buy Home-Gym Equipment vs. Go Overnight Camping

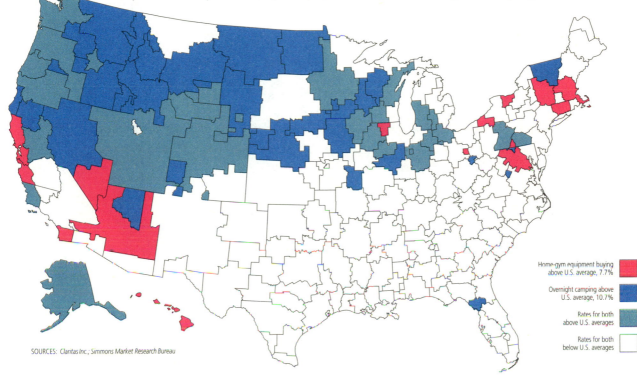

Home-gym equipment buying above U.S. average, 7.7%

Overnight camping above U.S. average, 10.7%

Rates for both above U.S. averages

Rates for both below U.S. averages

SOURCES: *Claritas Inc.; Simmons Market Research Bureau*

WE live in a paradoxical world: our leisure time is expanding but we feel more time-pressed than ever before. We watch increasing amounts of TV but rate that activity with decreasing satisfaction. And when we have free time, the way we spend it has much to do with how we spend our work time.

Consider the white-collar professionals who constitute the nation's biggest market for home-gym equipment. The largest segment is upscale, educated couples over 45 years old, fighting their spreading waistlines in the privacy of their suburban and exurban homes. They typically lead hard-driving lives, are workaholics who also travel a great deal, do volunteer work, and frequently go out to dinner. Although most fitness regimens require exercise in conjunction with moderating calories, these home gymnasts like to reward

themselves after their workouts: they take regular trips to Dunkin' Donuts, Friendly's, and TGIF's. Personal-gym owners consider their homes retreats where their workouts recharge them for the next day's grind. As Yankelovich pollster Watts Wacker observes, "Fast-track people love the pace and things that help them maintain it."

Those into camping are more likely to be blue-collar thirtysomethings from small towns who like to get away from their modest homes and workday routines for family camping trips. Typically owners of RVs, campers, and trailers, they're also big on outdoorsy activities like fishing, waterskiing, and hiking — in other words, everything you'd expect to do on a camping trip. Around the house, they'd just as soon veg out with the kids in front of the TV. With their strikingly high rate for owning recliners, they regard their homes

as restful sanctuaries from their physical jobs.

As the overlapping markets indicate, fans of home exercise and outdoor sports aren't mutually exclusive. On the other hand, neither group is found at high rates in southern climes, where residents find it too hot to camp and too costly to spend several thousand dollars on a Stairmaster. But these Americans are fundamentally different from each other in mind-set: the gym rats are inner-directed souls who feel the need to fulfill their own expectations and wish they spent more time home with their kids. The camping fans feel no such angst: constantly surrounded by children at home and co-workers on the job, they consider camping an opportunity to get away from it all — even if their favorite campground is as crowded as Times Square.

# Of Courts and Alleys

## Racquetball Players vs. Bowlers

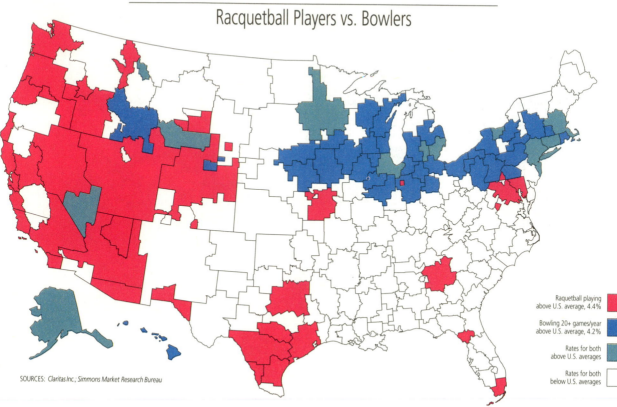

Raquetball playing
above U.S. average, 4.4%

Bowling 20+ games/year
above U.S. average, 4.2%

Rates for both
above U.S. averages

Rates for both
below U.S. averages

SOURCES: *Claritas Inc.; Simmons Market Research Bureau*

IT'S like the difference between draft beer and Mouton Cadet. Racquetball is an upper-crust sport — costly for a club membership, court time, and racquet gear — while bowling is a game for proles who wear street clothes, rent numbered shoes, and play ten frames for less than the price of a burger. But this map also reveals that the two sports are divided by more than shoe leather: Racquetball is the sport of America's booming Western states, following the migration of young white-collar workers to the West during the 1980s. Meanwhile, bowling's core audience is centered in the aging Rust Belt, a game of union workers who like the camaraderie of boys' nights out and ladies' leagues.

Having exploded onto the sporting scene in the late 1960s, racquetball now attracts an estimated six million fans nationwide. Clubs sprang up in major metro areas where YMCAs and JCCs had handball courts that could double as racquetball courts with little renovation. The sport's first national champion, a San Diego dentist, is typical of today's players: young professionals who get a good, quick aerobic workout, burning 600 calories in an hour. These mobile, under-44-year-olds tend to be accepting of the newest ideas, the trendiest products, and most progressive political views. Racquetball fans are more likely to catch the just-released movie than to wait for the video.

Bowling, by contrast, has been around forever — or at least since 5200 B.C., according to British archaeologists who found bowling-like gear in an Egyptian tomb. The postwar suburban boom in this country popularized the game among families, as shopping-center alleys offered a sport that could be enjoyed in air-conditioned comfort. Today's bowlers tend to be high school–educated, middle-aged players who also enjoy lotteries, gambling casinos, and television; the passion for TV and gambling dates to the '50s, when flattopped guys tried to win $100,000 prizes on shows like "Jackpot Bowling." Indeed, bowlers' values seem locked in the Eisenhower era: they worry about nudity in movies and nontraditional roles for women.

Still, the fans of racquetball aren't completely removed from those of bowling; in a handful of major metros, both sports are enjoyed at above-average rates. This may be the result of bowling's recent efforts to lure adult boomers and their boomlet families to alleys with kid leagues, on-site nurseries, and alley bumpers to prevent impressionable youths from becoming scarred by rolling gutter balls. While fans of both games share a fondness for golf and tennis, you can tell them apart by their dress code.

# TV Bleacher Bums

## People Who Watch TV Baseball

Baseball viewership compared to U.S. average, 35.6%

High — Above Average — Below Average — Low

SOURCES: Claritas Inc.; Simmons Market Research Bureau

ASTROTURF, designated hitters, and greedy free agents have all conspired to kill our drowsy national pastime. But baseball still has its fans, especially among TV viewers in small-town America who faithfully watch the game between beer commercials and reruns of "Happy Days."

Although baseball's core constituency used to be young, working-class, white men — among whose ranks came most major-league players — today's TV baseball aficionados tend to be older and more affluent, though still white and male. Their favorite magazines include *Sunset, Forbes,* and *Money.* They like to travel, drive a luxury car, and maintain a brokerage account, and they prefer meals not of hot dogs and beer but of baked chicken and Diet Coke.

The move of many baseball games from free to cable TV in part explains baseball's draw among well-off retirees, though TV spectators also tend to enjoy radio baseball.

The absence of African-American baseball fans — due to the sport's past racist policies on the field and in the front office — helps explain the sport's unpopularity among markets in the Old South and the nation's major metros. "The image of the kid growing up with Mickey Mantle's picture on his dresser was never sold to blacks," observes Paul Dickson, author of *The Dickson Baseball Dictionary.* "And some ballparks, like Fenway Park, traditionally were inhospitable to black fans and even some players." Experts today estimate that African Americans represent less than 7 percent of big-

league baseball attendance totals, and that figure isn't appreciably higher for televised game viewership.

The weak showing of TV baseball in big cities also can be explained partly by the nature of the game. Compared to up-tempo basketball, baseball is languid: guys in baggy pants playing in the pasture. In addition, the presence of two or more teams in markets like New York and Chicago contributes to the relative lack of TV baseball fans in those metros. Simply put, locals can usually take themselves out to a ball game rather than plant themselves in front of the small-screen version — an abundance of riches not lost on Washingtonians still longing for a single baseball team in the nation's capital.

# Football Fanatics

## People Who Watch TV Pro Football

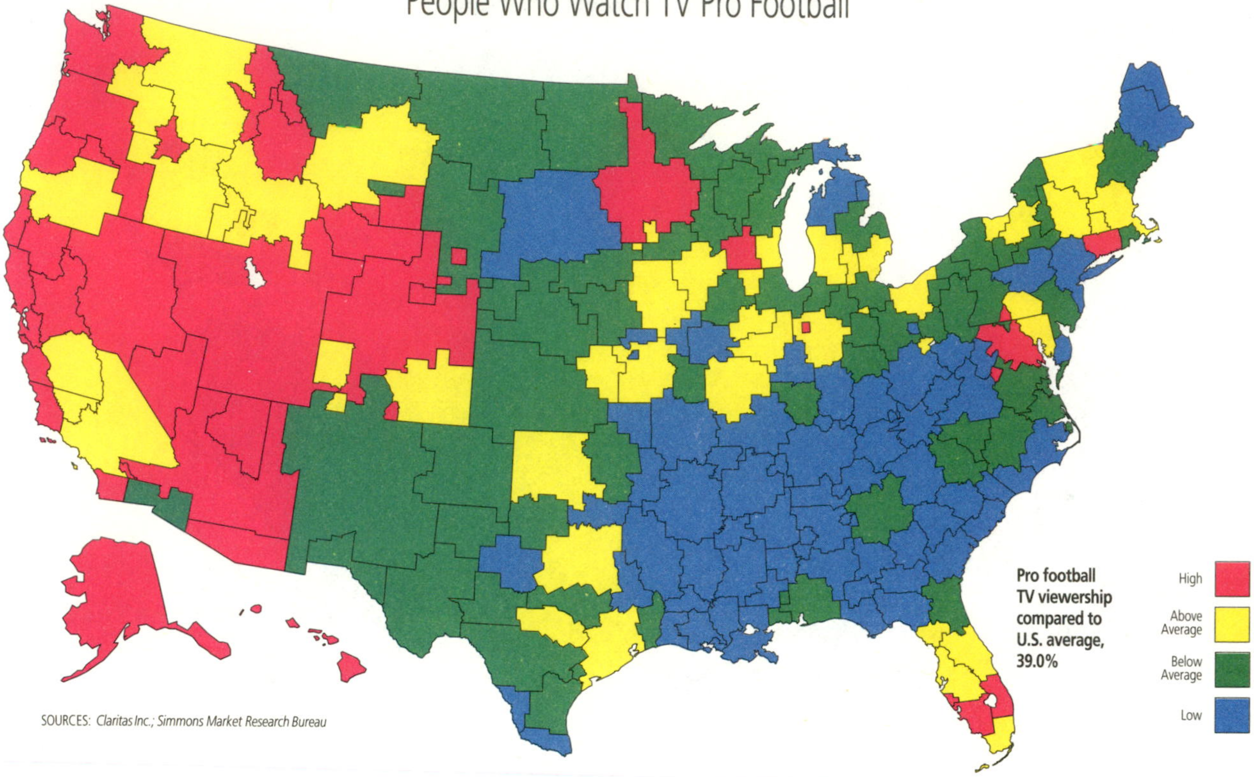

Pro football
TV viewership
compared to
U.S. average,
39.0%

High
Above Average
Below Average
Low

SOURCES: *Claritas Inc.; Simmons Market Research Bureau*

FACE IT: professional football is a sport of barbarians, a violent contest of huge men without necks smashing into each other's chests to keep one guy from moving a pigskin one yard down the turf. Sure, the game has changed over time: the salaries skyrocketing, the coaching more corporate, and the players less rowdy off the field. But football remains a rough-and-tumble sport where brutish players and vicious hitters continue to star in highlights films.

Fans of televised pro football, on the other hand, are shown in surveys to be refined, even cultured souls. They're more likely than average Americans to enjoy classical music, books, theater, and movies as well as athletic activities like tennis, skiing, and sailing. They tend to be active investors of stocks, mutual funds, and tax-sheltered annuities, no doubt sharing some of their insights at the local country club or business group, which they belong to at high rates. According to demographic profiles, football fans tend to be college-educated men earning over $50,000 annually and living in small towns — far from an NFL franchise they can cheer from the stands.

Education and mobility help explain the gap between pro football fans in the West and South. Southerners, who have low rates of mobility and college attendance, tend to follow high school football and local college teams with which they feel a geographic connection. In their book *Atlas of American Sport,* authors John F. Rooney Jr. and Richard Pillsbury even name the Dixie region "Pigskin Cult." Westerners, whose mobility and education patterns are reversed, tend to be bigger fans of the pro teams because of their less parochial interests. When they're not watching the Hogs or the Monsters of the Midway, they can be found tuning in to the Learning Channel or reading *Smithsonian* or the *Wall Street Journal.*

But if there's anything that shatters the old rabid-fan image, it's what these football viewers drink while screaming for a sack. Compared to the U.S. average, they prefer imported white wine to Bud, Pabst, or even Heineken. Perhaps in halftime commercials should be depicting not battling beer bottles, but ex-linemen tipping glasses of Soave Bolla or Macon Village.

# Hoopsters

## People Who Watch Professional vs. College Basketball on TV

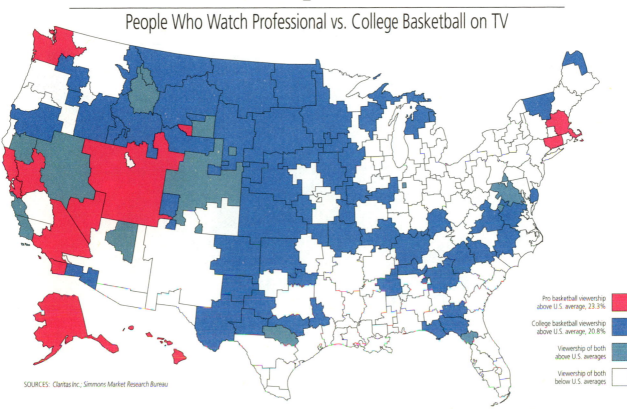

Pro basketball viewership above U.S. average, 23.3%

College basketball viewership above U.S. average, 20.8%

Viewership of both above U.S. averages

Viewership of both below U.S. averages

SOURCES: Claritas Inc.; Simmons Market Research Bureau

IT began in 1891 when a Massachusetts phys-ed teacher named Dr. James Naismith invented a game to help his students exercise between football and baseball seasons. Today it's a national obsession marked by televised slam-dunk contests, the March madness of the NCAA college tournament, and daily pickup games on city lots and suburban courts. Some 40 million people shoot hoops each year, and twice as many tune in to pro and college games on TV.

But different regions of the country prefer one level over the other: the looser, half-court college game or the high-scoring, physical-inside pro game. Although basketball evolved on the asphalt playgrounds of Northeastern cities, today's biggest fans of the professional version are concentrated in a handful of West Coast metros that tend to have NBA franchises. Many pro fans, it seems, are married baby boom men who have moved up in the world: they're white and black, mobile and individualistic. Having fled to the suburbs out West, they've been rewarded more for their competitive drive than their cooperative spirit. As they watch pro basketball, they concentrate on star-gazing rather than admiring the teamwork. "Pro ball has become a form of celebrity entertainment," says Wayne Patterson, a research specialist with the Basketball Hall of Fame. "People go to watch Shaquille O'Neal, not the Orlando Magic."

The TV fans of college basketball, however, are more group-oriented, typically loyal alumni or residents of college towns who follow each year's new squad more closely than their own children. Because college fans are a bit older and more affluent than their pro counterparts, their lifestyles are a bit more sedate as well. They're more likely than average Americans to belong to veteran groups and fraternal orders. Through it all, their allegiance to their alma mater remains firm: besides college hoops, they watch college football and listen to college basketball and football on the radio as well.

While pro basketball fans also enjoy the college game — especially in university towns like Austin, Gainesville, and Charlottesville — pro hoopsters are more health conscious, as seen in their preference for fresh fruit, oat bran, and spring water. And they're more nonconformist in their social attitudes. While college fans place their trust in religious leaders, pro fans would rather listen to environmental critics and consumer advocates. Opinion polls show they also value personal expression — especially in the form of a tomahawk jam.

# Rim Shot

## Buyers of Japanese vs. American Cars and Trucks

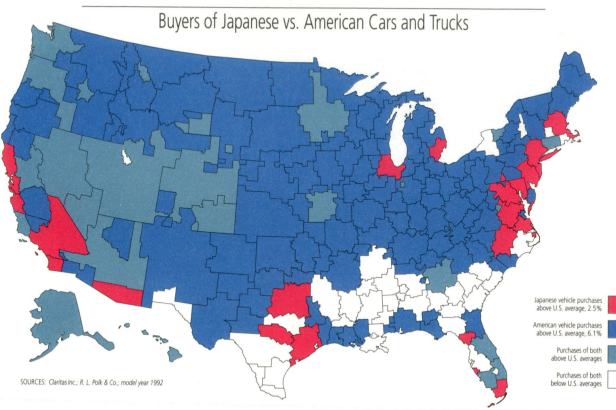

Japanese vehicle purchases above U.S. average, 2.5%

American vehicle purchases above U.S. average, 6.1%

Purchases of both above U.S. averages

Purchases of both below U.S. averages

SOURCES: Claritas Inc.; R. L. Polk & Co.; model year 1992

IN an era of mass communications and glib evocations of a "global village," it's sometimes easy to overlook the imperative of geography and logistics. The relative popularity of Japanese cars and trucks in America's coastal areas has much to do with the fact that most vehicles still arrive from Japan by boat, and are then off-loaded in ports such as Seattle, Long Beach, and Newark. To minimize overland freight costs, Japanese auto makers at first opened dealerships near these port cities. Advertising campaigns then focused on these local markets, reinforcing local preferences for Japanese models along the East, West, and Gulf coasts. In fact, marketers nicknamed this geographic pattern "the Japanese smile."

The split between Japanese and American automotive consumers also reflects the broad demographic disparity between America's coasts and interior. Japanese-car buyers tend disproportionately to have six-figure incomes, college degrees, white-collar jobs, and a receptivity to foreign-made products. Cosmopolitan in their outlook, they are more likely than the average American to travel abroad, listen to all-news radio stations, and read business magazines. These educated consumers respond positively to Japanese claims that their cars are of superior quality and believe that Japanese cars represent "smart buys."

Those who buy American-made cars and trucks are more likely to live in small towns and rural communities where residents share traditional beliefs and value the "Made in the USA" label. These consumers tend disproportionately to have some college education, earn between $35,000 and $75,000 a year, live in middle-class neighborhoods, and work in factories. They're group-oriented, more likely than the general population to belong to religious clubs, join bowling leagues, frequent veterans halls (the men), and throw Tupperware parties (the women). As consumers, they tend to be loyalists who invest in their companies' stock, listen to golden-oldie radio stations, and patronize local car dealers who traditionally sell Big Three nameplates.

The two dozen areas of overlap on the map represent locations where the confluence of upscale suburbanites and middle-class townies results in blurred tastes and confusion over automotive origins. With the recent opening of Japanese-car and -truck factories in inland America, many consumers no longer regard Japanese vehicles as rare exotics. By contrast, the unshaded areas represent markets where residents can't afford to buy any new car — Japanese or American — or where imports from other countries are preferred.

# Land Yachts

## Owners of BMWs vs. Cadillacs

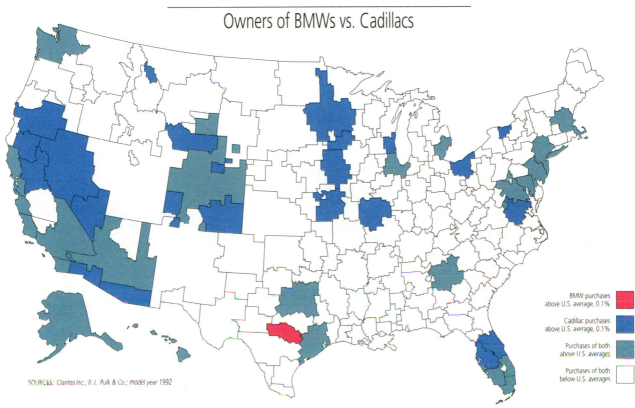

BMW purchases
above U.S. average, 0.1%

Cadillac purchases
above U.S. average, 0.1%

Purchases of both
above U.S. averages

Purchases of both
below U.S. averages

SOURCES: *Claritas Inc., R. L. Polk & Co.; model year 1992*

ALL cars carry messages of status, though most of us are limited in what our cars can say by what our wallets will bear. But what if price were no object? That's the reality for the typical owners of BMWs and Cadillacs who, as the top 1 percent of all U.S. car buyers, can afford the $30,000-plus average price tags these makes command. Despite the perception of BMW owners as being as different from Cadillac drivers as Rolex watches are from pinky rings, the above map shows they share many of the same communities filled with wealthy suburbanites — the kind of people who've arrived even before they drive up in their cars.

Still, age and attitude separate these car owners in many communities. Beemers appeal to younger, more liberal, and wealthier drivers — the yuppies of Houston, for instance. BMW owners are 50 per-cent more likely than average Americans to have six-figure incomes. They're 25 percent more likely to enjoy European travel, classical music, tennis, and the theater. And as younger consumers — their median age is about 40 — they're more likely to go jogging and dancing, buy condoms and flowers, and watch "Saturday Night Live" and "Murphy Brown." Progressive in their politics, they exhibit high rates of buying "green" products, supporting gay marriages, and donating time to fight pollution. They believe that buying a well-engineered Beemer reflects an enlightened consumer choice as much as subscribing to the *New York Times,* their favorite publication.

Cadillacs tend to be the preferred mode of transportation for over-55 staid Midwesterners who love boulevard barges with cushy interiors and limo-style lengths. These well-heeled motorists are into beef and bacon, domestic wine and Cold Duck, gardening and woodworking. Although both groups describe themselves as political liberals, Cadillac owners come from the more centrist wing. They support school prayer, oppose nudity in movies, and feel guilty about buying foreign goods — the exact opposite of BMW buyers. And yet there's a flashy, gold-chain air about Cadillac owners. They're always looking for new investment opportunities and new vacation destinations.

As was demonstrated with the disastrous introduction of its Cimarron in the 1980s, Cadillac probably will have trouble cracking the younger BMW market. For one thing, dealers can smell Cadillac owners a mile away; they're the ones reeking of Old Spice. BMW owners, by contrast, are seriously into Obsession.

# Cheap Seats

## People Who Buy Ford Escorts

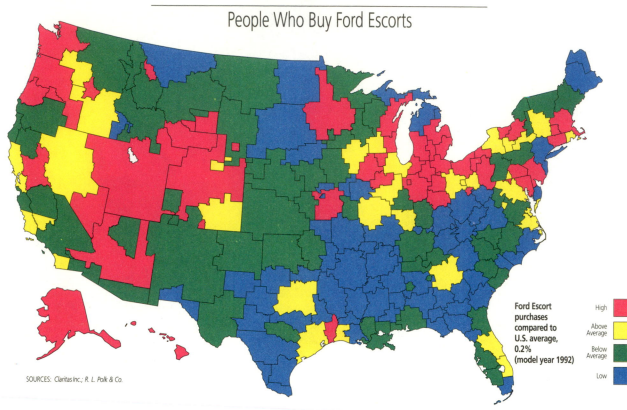

Ford Escort purchases compared to U.S. average, 0.2% (model year 1992)

High

Above Average

Below Average

Low

SOURCES: *Claritas Inc.; R. L. Polk & Co.*

W E'RE talking no-frills basic transportation: four wheels, an engine, backseats, and a steering wheel. In the economy-car class, the Ford Escort stands out as America's best-selling compact, with a $10,000 sticker price and an all-purpose reputation; in the words of *Car and Driver,* it's an automotive Swiss Army Knife. Over the years, the Escort has managed to rack up impressive sales —nearly 200,000 were bought in 1992 — by being not necessarily all things to all people but by appealing to at least three different kinds of motorists.

The first group is women under the age of 35 who are single, work in entry-level jobs or are still in school, and live on the suburban fringe — especially in the Great Lakes area. Typically, the Escort is their first car, essential wheels to get them from home to work, shopping mall, the health club, and

back. From their cars' tape decks you'll usually hear modern rock groups. Under the seats you'll likely find the crumpled remnants of munchies runs to fast-food joints.

The second group of Escort owners is boomer families who need a second car for Mom or Dad to commute to work on weekdays and to the golf course on weekends. These owners tend to have upper-middle-class incomes, college degrees, and spacious homes in the nation's larger metros. In these Escort households, popular activities include skiing, attending the theater, and taking foreign trips. Interestingly, their primary car is likely to be an import; favorites include Acuras, Volkswagens, and Toyotas.

Finally, the Ford Escort is a car of choice for people over 55 years old, especially widows and retirees, who want a no-fuss vehicle for short trips to the shopping center. These owners tend to live in rural areas and

retirement resorts in the Sunbelt, where they like to spend their time woodworking, gardening, and, for a splurge, going to gambling casinos. Inside their homes, they own recliners, power tools, and stereos at above-average rates. And they're big on print media — reading books, subscribing to travel magazines, and belonging to book clubs all at high rates.

Although crude demographic surveys indicate that the Ford Escort's target audience likely would be a boomer family from suburbia, these lifestyle profiles indicate three distinct target groups that marketers can't ignore. "To go after an Escort owner, you should be advertising in *Ms., Time,* and the AARP magazine," says Jim Dries, R. L. Polk's manager for automotive marketing information services. "As with most cars, the Escort means different things to different people."

# The Swede Smell of Success

## Owners of Volvos

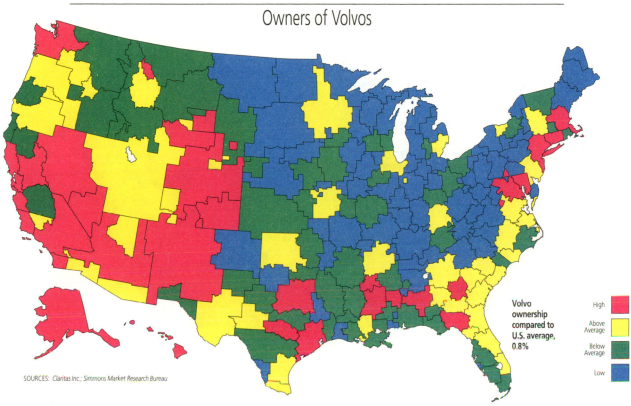

Volvo ownership compared to U.S. average, 0.8%

High
Above Average
Below Average
Low

SOURCES: *Claritas Inc.; Simmons Market Research Bureau*

UNTIL RECENTLY, a long-held maxim in the automotive industry was "safety doesn't sell." That's changed now thanks to increased car safety information and public outrage over highway deaths. But while many manufacturers now extol the virtues of their airbags and anti-lock brakes, no car maker has been selling safety longer or with as much consistency as Volvo. Forget styling. Year in and year out, models like the 940 and 240 look as stodgy and old-fashioned as a dowager. But all Volvos offer the Swedish company's steel–safety-cage construction, air bags, three-point seat belts, anti-lock brakes, and a reputation for longevity. Such features appeal to a loyal following of educated, upscale motorists who are blasé about sleek looks, gas mileage, and cost (most price tags top $20,000).

"These are people who think they're making a smart choice because they are not swayed by style," says Jack Gillis, author of *The Car Book*. "They buy a Volvo to fulfill their image of themselves as careful people."

The popularity of Volvos among educated consumers helps explain the hot markets along the nation's coastal metros like Washington, Boston, and San Francisco. But other factors influence the map. Affluent retirees are drawn to Volvos in the Southwest; the 940 and 960 models have twice as many owners over the age of 55 as under the age of 35. In addition, owners can be found clustering in some more elderly downscale markets in the South that have access to dealers selling used Volvos. The weak penetration of Volvos into the Midwest is a function of distribution; Volvos arrive in the U.S. in New Jersey, Florida, and California, and few dealers are found in the heartland.

Ironically, those safety-conscious conservative drivers drawn to Volvos also tend to be politically liberal Americans. Opinion polls show they have high rates for supporting abortion rights, gay rights, "green" products, and ecological concerns. The environmental watchdog group Greenpeace has even found success targeting its fund-raising appeals to Volvo owners in upscale city neighborhoods.

Apart from that liberal streak, Volvo owners tend to pursue activities designed to ensure them a long life with their cars. They are health conscious and have white-collar jobs that come with good benefits. Even their approach to food is preventive: if they drink milk, it's skim; if they drink beer, it's light. So it figures that when it comes to cars, they drive the automotive equivalent of a high-fiber diet.

# Muscle Cars

## Buyers of Ford Mustangs, Chevrolet Camaros, and Pontiac Firebirds

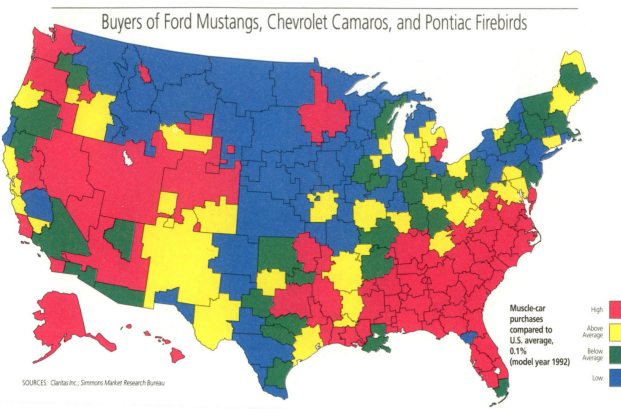

Muscle-car purchases compared to U.S. average, 0.1% (model year 1992)

High — (red)
Above Average — (yellow)
Below Average — (green)
Low — (blue)

SOURCES: Claritas Inc.; Simmons Market Research Bureau

IT wasn't so long ago that muscle cars were nearly obsolete. In the 1970s era of fuel economy and the oil embargo, many Americans ignored gas guzzling, horsepower-heavy sporty compacts — like the Ford Mustang, Chevy Camaro, and Pontiac Firebird — in favor of sensible, fuel-efficient subcompacts like Datsuns, Toyotas, and Hondas.

But muscle cars never really disappeared in the South, where driving a jacked-up hot rod suitable for stock-car racing has always been a status symbol among the good-ol'-boys who still speak kindly of moonshine-running and resistance to New South Liberalism. And in recent years, as the median age of new-car buyers has topped 40, hot-rod sales have revved up in the West, where baby boomers and affluent empty-nesters want to recapture some of their wild youth with a car that's got plenty of horses under the hood. Today, the hottest muscle car markets include Charlotte, N.C., and Tuscaloosa, Ala., as well as Phoenix, Ariz., and Palm Springs, Calif.

Not surprisingly, the lifestyle of muscle-car owners is a bit schizophrenic. Among the Southerners, who tend to be young, blue-collar high school graduates, popular pastimes include hunting, fishing, listening to heavy metal music, and watching TV auto racing. In the West, drivers generally are upper-middle-class, college-educated retirees or white-collar bureaucrats who enjoy skiing, movies, rock 'n' roll, and TV golf. There is common ground: most muscle-car owners are married, have multiple cars, and are big on auto sound systems and college sports.

Of course, you may wonder why anyone would need a hopped-up muscle car capable of 120 miles per hour when speed limits remain 55 throughout most states. In fact, surveys show that most owners are not rebels without causes; they're really mild-mannered, sensitive guys at heart. When all the survey numbers are crunched, the tough guys you'd imagine behind the wheel of a muscle car actually display a fondness for wok-cooking, home fax machines, oat bran cereal, and buying flowers for special occasions.

# Bronco Busters from the 'Burbs

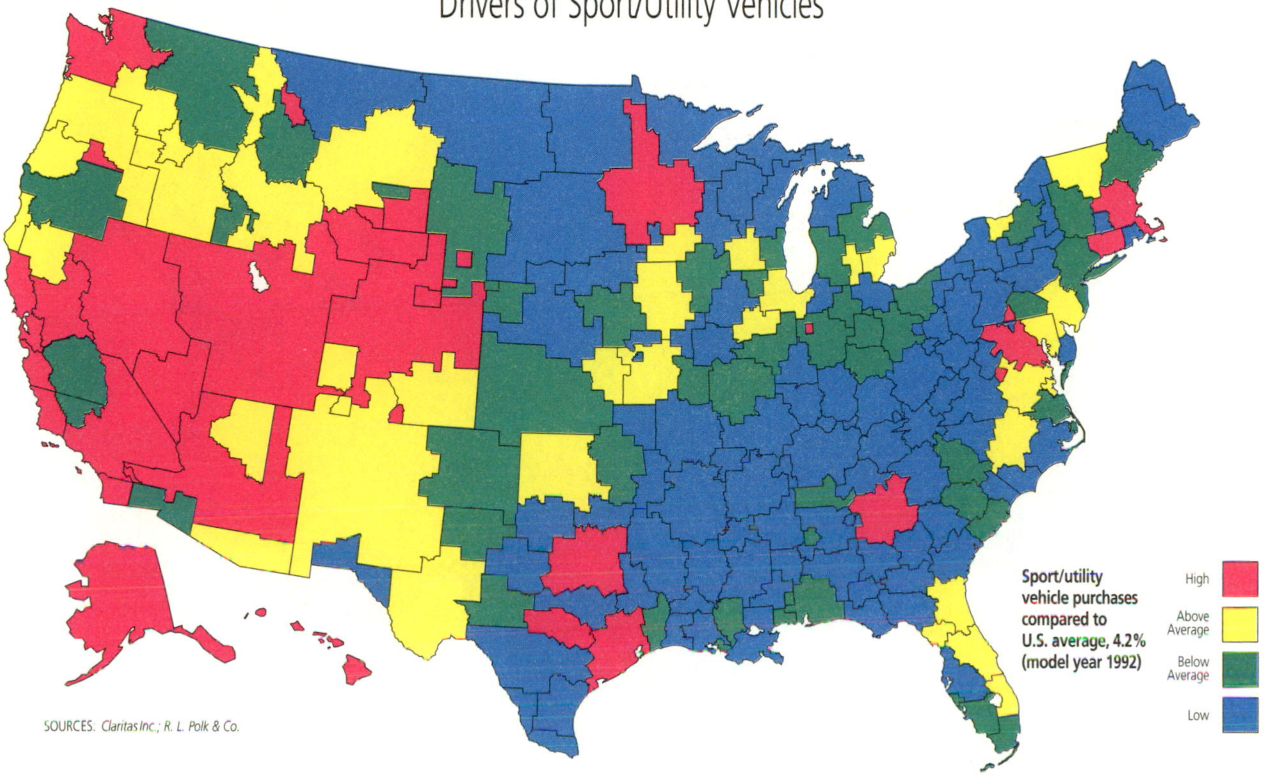

## Drivers of Sport/Utility Vehicles

Sport/utility vehicle purchases compared to U.S. average, 4.2% (model year 1992)

High
Above Average
Below Average
Low

ONCE UPON A TIME, Westerners considered themselves free spirits and adventurers who helped settle a wide-open country. But that hardly explains the popularity of sport/utility vehicles west of the Mississippi today. Although these rugged, four-wheel-drive vehicles — like Blazers, Explorers, Cherokees, Broncos, and Range Rovers — are built to tackle the roughest terrain, the most challenging trip most of them take is to a video store or pee-wee football game. Their biggest fans are married, upscale suburbanites who appreciate what the vehicles are not: boring sedans, clunky station wagons, or run-of-the-mill minivans. Literally and figuratively, the sport/utility driver looks down on all the common folk of the road.

Some armchair psychologists have speculated that driving sport/utility vehicles serves as an outlet for aggressive feelings spawned by the daily rat race of commuting. Indeed, these drivers, whose average age is 38, tend to be highly paid business professionals with college degrees and homes worth more than $250,000 located in a handful of Eastern metros and Western boom states. But sport/utility vehicles represent only one outlet for pent-up tensions: their owners are also into skiing, tennis, racquetball, and swimming. And they have a rich cultural life as well, more likely than average Americans to enjoy the theater, classical music, imported wine, and magazines like *Smithsonian* and *Architectural Digest*.

What surveys reveal is an individualist's streak among these Walter Mittys of the highway. Sport/utility-vehicle owners are more likely than average Americans to work out in home gyms, spend their free time doing volunteer work, and invest their money in self-directed mutual funds. They just know their limits. While they enjoy driving a conventional sport/utility vehicle, they haven't taken to the ultimate outdoorsy, off-road contraption: the Humvee. The military vehicle made famous during Desert Storm is now sold to civilians willing to pay $39,500 to $75,000. But sales are flat and low consumer interest is causing manufacturing layoffs. Even Walter Mitty has to draw the line somewhere in the suburban desert.

# Shotguns and Pickups

## Buyers of Domestic Light Trucks

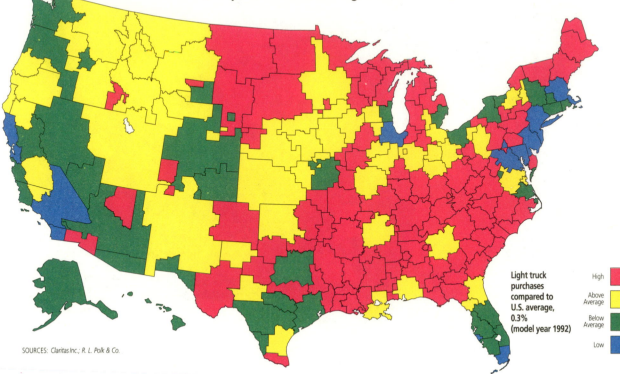

SOURCES: *Claritas Inc.; R. L. Polk & Co.*

Light truck purchases compared to U.S. average, 0.3% (model year 1992)

High — Above Average — Below Average — Low

THE answer on the "Jeopardy" board would read: "Light trucks, light trucks, and light trucks." And the correct question: "What are the three hottest automotive trends in the 1990s?"

At least that's the gospel according to industry experts, who note that light trucks, which include compact and full-sized pickups, constitute almost one-third of all vehicle sales, a 50 percent increase over a decade ago. Because pickups are simpler and cheaper to build than sedans — and don't have to meet sedans' tougher safety and gas-mileage standards — they've become popular entry-level cars for young people interested in sitting tall in the driver's saddle for under $10,000. They offer a decent ride, an increasingly spiffier interior, and plenty of room in the back for ice

chests, sleeping bags, and over-sized Elvis posters.

That, at least, is how industry analysts describe the nouveau light-truck driver. But as the map above shows, light trucks have been and always will be the pack mules of rural America, particularly in the South. The highest concentration of buyers are married, blue-collar workers with high school degrees, lower-middle-class incomes, and homes valued at under $75,000. These folks are the nation's do-it-yourselfers, who frequently stuff their flatbeds with power tools and car parts. In these households, the men bond during hunting trips, the women at Tupperware parties, and everyone plops into a Barcalounger to watch television; they typically watch more than seven hours a day.

In an age when popular culture

pushes the envelope toward the hip, slick, and nouvelle, light trucks represent a throwback to the past. Owners tell surveyors of their support for traditional values — stability, home, and family — and their food-buying habits seem right out of the '50s. They're more likely than average Americans to eat pork and beans, beef stew, American cheese, and canned vegetables. Despite Madison Avenue's attempts to erase the *Easy Rider* link between pickup trucks and shotgun racks, truck owners have a remarkably high rate for owning hunting rifles — a fact not lost on the executives at Claritas Inc., when they set out to name the nation's 40 archetypical lifestyle types in the early 1970s. Perhaps the most vivid nickname — applied to small crossroads villages throughout the countryside — was Shotguns & Pickups.

# From Cream Puffs to Lemons

## Buyers of Used Cars

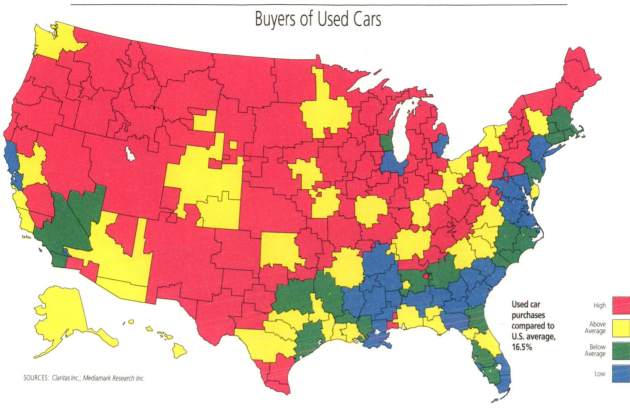

Used car purchases compared to U.S. average, 16.5%

High
Above Average
Below Average
Low

SOURCES: *Claritas Inc.; Mediamark Research Inc.*

AMERICANS love to look at spanking new cars but usually buy shiny *used* ones. There's no mystery to the reason: cost. The average 1993 model had a suggested retail price of more than $17,000, while the average used car went for $8,000. That 112 percent spread helps explain why nearly three times as many used cars as new ones were bought in the last year, about 30 million recycled vehicles.

Although used cars are for sale from Maine to California, their appeal isn't universal. The highest concentration of buyers are working-class Americans whose modest incomes force them to scale back their visions of a dream machine. These motorists tend to be high school–educated married couples with children living in older homes. They're big on home improvement and car repair, much more likely than average Americans to install their own plugs, shocks, and mufflers and to read magazines like *Home Mechanix* and *Popular Science*. A disproportionate number have borrowed money from the bank for life insurance, a home improvement project, and, not surprisingly, a car.

As for the markets where Americans are least likely to buy used cars, they're found most often at the extremes of the socioeconomic ladder. Affluent Americans in cities like New York and Chicago would rather buy new cars as expressions of their lofty status and to keep up with the latest styles. The poor, living in inner cities as well as country towns like Tupelo, Miss., and Monroe, La., simply can't afford the cost of most cars — new or used. For transportation, they either walk or ride the bus.

Indeed, used-car dealers sell the most vehicles in small-town America where residents have unpretentious tastes in lifestyle as well as cars. In these communities — among the best used-car markets are Zanesville, Ohio, Johnstown, Pa., and Mankato, Minn. — the women like to garden, make crafts, and bake from scratch. The men are into woodworking, camping, and powerboating at high rates. When pollsters asked them to list their biggest concerns, the top one out of 100 was respect for the elderly. Apparently, that applies to old cars as well.

# Suckers for "The Simpsons"

## Viewers of "The Simpsons"

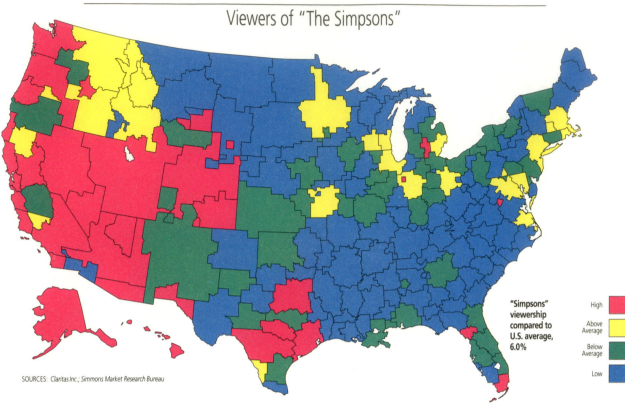

"Simpsons" viewership compared to U.S. average, 6.0%

- High
- Above Average
- Below Average
- Low

SOURCES: *Claritas Inc.; Simmons Market Research Bureau*

**W**HAT is it about the American West that makes residents wacky for the cracked portrait of blue-collar family life shown in "The Simpsons"? There's nothing in viewer surveys that indicates any particular personal fondness for Marge's blue beehive hairdos or for working at a nuclear power plant like Homer. And sociologists have yet to report the appearance of a generation of Bart-alecks who cheat at Scrabble, break into movies, and watch TV while hanging upside down on the couch.

Yet the nation's western states are home to the highest concentration of mobile, educated baby boomers. And like the animated sitcom family, the most fanatical followers of "The Simpsons" appear to be living their own warped version of the idealized Ozzie & Harriet family: their households are filled with young, non-white, divorced, or single parents.

"Simpsons" fans are more likely than average Americans to be college-educated service workers who have recently moved into new apartments. They typically have more than three children who, in this era of high divorce rates, money problems, and family flux, can surely relate to Bart's anarchic, kid's-eye perspective. As creator Matt Groening has observed, "A lot of people identify with being kicked around."

Still, it would be a stretch to say the program's fans have Simpsonesque lifestyles. Most viewers are heavily into outdoor sports, such as tennis, skiing, jogging, and bicycling, as well as music, ranging from jazz and classical to rock and pop. They're still in the dating scene, spending time at movies, rock concerts, health clubs, and adult education courses — the '90s version of the singles bar. These are parents whose idea of quality

time is watching TV with their kids. More educated and white-collar than "Roseanne" fans, "Simpsons" viewers are appreciative of the animated show's parodies of other parodies, such as takeoffs of Garrison Keillor's Lake Wobegon world.

"People watch 'The Simpsons' so they can recite lines the next morning in the office and relish the revolutionary rhetoric," says TV critic Joanne Ostrow of the *Denver Post.* "It's radical in the old-fashioned sense of the word."

Indeed, former President George Bush knew he was risking few votes when he once promised to make America more like "The Waltons" and less like "The Simpsons." Fans of "The Simpsons" describe themselves as liberal and share the leftist views of a generation ago. In one opinion poll of 100 issues, the most important concern among "Simpsons" viewers was legalizing drugs.

# Tabloid TV

## Viewers of "A Current Affair"

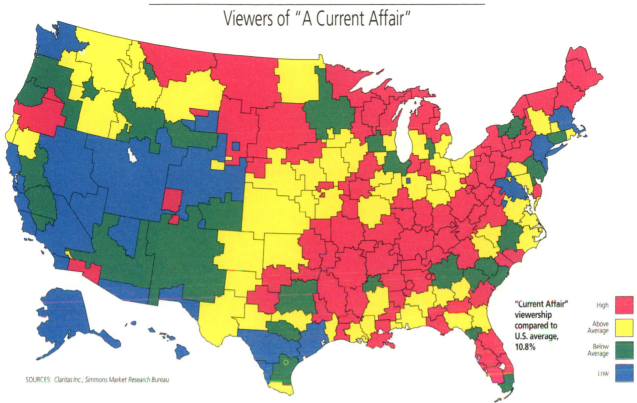

**"Current Affair" viewership compared to U.S. average, 10.8%**

High — Above Average — Below Average — Low

SOURCES: *Claritas Inc.; Simmons Market Research Bureau*

AS the granddaddy of tabloid television, "A Current Affair" is responsible for spawning a slew of low-road news shows, such as "Hard Copy," "Inside Edition," and "American Journal." But this syndicated program distributed by Fox remains arguably the most popular, serving as many as 20 million viewers a gut-grabbing diet of sex, scandal, crime, and ordinary people in extraordinary situations. As hostess Maureen O'Boyle presents each story with her squeaky-clean girl-next-door smile, viewers feel no guilt as they wade through the muck. "If we do a story about a sex case," says senior program producer Dick McWilliams, "it's from the viewpoint of someone looking down and frowning."

While critics won't confuse "A Current Affair" with the "MacNeil-Lehrer Newshour," a racially mixed group of older, downscale, rural viewers lap up Fox's juicier stories. Many of the show's best markets have fewer than 100,000 residents — communities where locals drive trucks, chew tobacco, listen to gospel music, and still believe that pro wrestling is for real. These are the consumers who have grits and "Co'-Cola" for breakfast, beef stew and biscuits for dinner, and "American Gladiators" — their top-rated game show — for dessert. Their favorite reading matter includes *True Story, Jet,* and those "Current Affair" cousins, the *National Enquirer* and the *Star.* Politically conservative — phone polls found that they voted for Bush over Clinton by a margin of 9-to-1 in 1992 —

they're pro-life, anti–big business, and in favor of family values.

Why are country folk drawn to "A Current Affair"? For the most part, viewers in these small towns with little nightlife and violent crime can find pleasure in knowing that the shocking stories on the show happen to other people in other places. With front-row seats for the nightly spectacle of human folly, they feel absolutely rich in their modest homes surrounded by old-fashioned traditions. "A large part of our appeal is having Joe Sixpack and the Missus realize that their lives aren't so bad after all," observes McWilliams. "There's always some poor bastard who's worse off, some guy whose wife just tried to kill him."

# Political Junkies

## C-SPAN Viewers

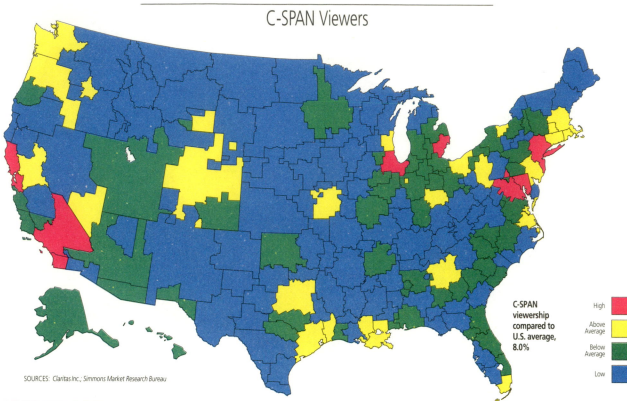

C-SPAN viewership compared to U.S. average, 8.0%

High
Above Average
Below Average
Low

SOURCES: Claritas Inc.; Simmons Market Research Bureau

DON'T look for fancy sets or 20-second sound bites. C-SPAN, the Cable Satellite Public Affairs Network, offers the *sound meal,* unedited coverage of the nation's public affairs without ads, spin doctors, or blow-dried anchorpeople. The daily fare — a video vérité of speeches, debates, and uncut congressional hearings — is sometimes only slightly more fascinating than a test pattern.

Still, C-SPAN has thousands of devotees from all political stripes. And because the network has no concern for ratings, advertisers, or underwriters (its $16.2 million annual budget comes entirely from local cable companies offering C-SPAN as a public service), the map above provides an unadulter-ated view of where America's hard-est-core political junkies live. Not surprisingly, power centers like Washington, New York, and Los Angeles figure prominently on the map. What these communities have

*In Washington, D.C., women complain of men who make love by the light of C-SPAN broadcasts.*

in common is a preponderance of residents who are single, 25-to-34-year-old, lower-level white-collar workers — the classic portrait of the Capitol Hill staffer.

When they're not watching C-SPAN, these viewers lead active political lives, and are twice as likely as nonviewers to contact a member of Congress, make a political contribution, or volunteer for a campaign. C-SPAN's fans tend to be fond of cable TV in general, channel surfing among other stations, such as HBO, VH-1, ESPN, and even the Weather Channel. And their culinary tastes reinforce their couch potatoism: favorite mealtime activities include ordering take-out food, calling Domino's Pizza, and making a run to Dunkin' Donuts — all the ingredients for a scintillating evening watching a C-SPAN quorum call. Indeed, when *Washingtonian* magazine surveyed sex in the nation's capital, some women complained of men who made love by the unromantic light of a flickering C-SPAN broadcast.

# Where Talk Is Cheap

## Viewers of "Oprah" vs. "Donahue"

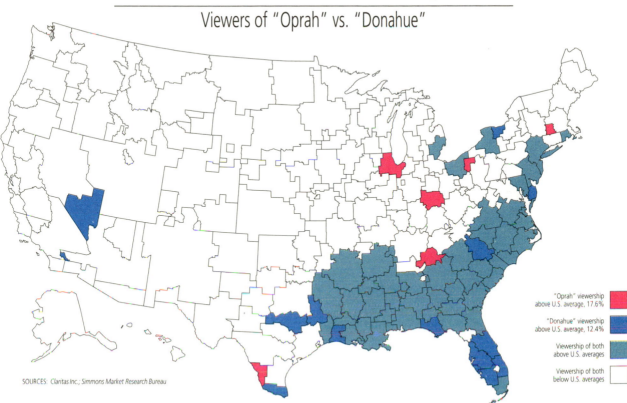

"Oprah" viewership
above U.S. average, 17.6%

"Donahue" viewership
above U.S. average, 12.4%

Viewership of both
above U.S. averages

Viewership of both
below U.S. averages

SOURCES: *Claritas Inc.; Simmons Market Research Bureau*

WHEN Jack Paar left "The Tonight Show" in 1962, his explanation was succinct: "There's nobody left to talk to." Little did he know how many current TV gabmeisters would prove him wrong. As veteran hosts Oprah Winfrey and Phil Donahue have proven year in and year out, talk is cheap, and audiences are insatiable when it comes to the voyeuristic thrill of eavesdropping on the pains, problems, and perversions of others. This appeal crosses over to fans of both shows who share many of the same markets throughout the South. That's understandable, given the region's dubious distinction as having the lowest high school completion rate in the nation. What's surprising is that many of the talk-show voyeurs are Bible Belt females with a strong conservative streak.

Because personality sells talk shows, Oprah is probably her own best guest. In her eighth year as one of the few syndicated African-American hosts, she appeals most to black audiences of modest means, educations, and home values. As consumers, they're big on bus travel, lotteries, and minority-oriented media: BET cable, magazines like *Jet* and *Ebony,* as well as radio stations that play gospel music. In opinion surveys, they express a kind of sexual schizophrenia, supporting traditional religious and family values while also expressing tolerance for a woman's right to an abortion and nudity in movies. No doubt this helps explain the popularity of Oprah, herself a religious person, as she forays into tabloid territory interviewing unapologetic vixens. As she's so rightly observed, "I consider myself a surrogate viewer."

Phil Donahue, who helped pioneer the talk-show format 26 years ago, appeals to the same audience as Oprah, except for attracting a slightly higher percentage of senior citizens, especially widows. The result, in lifestyle terms, is a higher rate of residents taking Canadian vacations, buying new dining room furniture, and subscribing to publications like *Harper's Bazaar* and *Southern Living.* On the other hand, they're a less strident group when it comes to religious and social concerns, and are more interested in news and current affairs than Oprah's loyalists. Phil's fans support legalizing drugs and oppose a return to traditional sexual standards. Oprah's minions are the reverse.

Fortunately, devotees of both programs share a strong belief in being nonjudgmental about other people's lives and have a high tolerance for sex education on TV. Phil and Oprah would never have thrived without them.

# Late-Night Laffs vs. Prime-Time Gaffes

## Viewers of "Saturday Night Live" vs. "America's Funniest Home Videos"

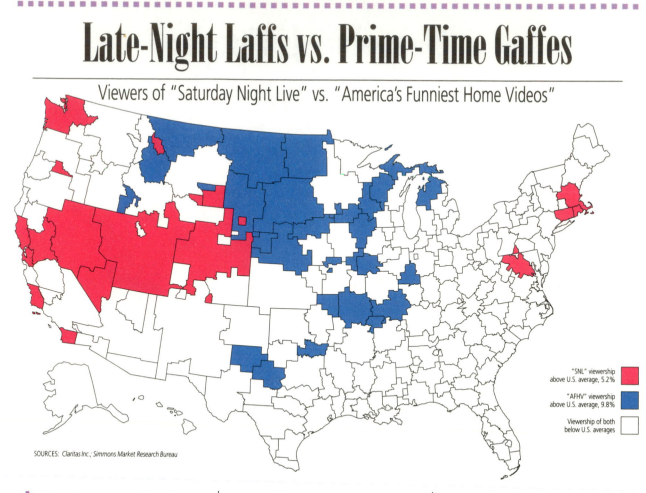

"SNL" viewership
above U.S. average, 5.2%

"AFHV" viewership
above U.S. average, 9.8%

Viewership of both
below U.S. averages

SOURCES: *Claritas Inc.; Simmons Market Research Bureau*

AMERICANS are addicted to live comedy, whether it's the viewer-submitted videos of pratfalls and stupid pet tricks on "America's Funniest Home Videos" or the stand-up comics, new music, and political satire of "Saturday Night Live." But as the above map indicates, different folks like different jokes.

"Saturday Night Live," whose 19-year mainstay is cutting-edge comedy, appeals most to an audience of young, educated baby boomers — the counterculture kids of the Woodstock generation. Living in a handful of big East Coast cities and fast-growing markets in the West, they tend to be trendsetters who try to see the latest plays and films, hear the newest progressive and contemporary rock groups, and buy the most up-to-date consumer electronics. They're big on

current affairs, more likely than average Americans to read newspapers, listen to all-news radio, and subscribe to publications like the *New York Times, Vanity Fair,* and *Scientific American.* They tune in to "Saturday Night Live" as much to catch the latest band and see the newest Hollywood starlet as to watch satirists mock the newsmakers and public figures with whom they're so preoccupied.

The biggest fans of "America's Funniest Home Videos" are of a different generation: Depression-era babies. A disproportionate number are older rural folks whose children are grown, whose incomes are modest, and whose preferred pastimes include listening to country music, sitting on their porches, and puttering around their garden or workshop. Many aren't rich enough

to own their own camcorder, and they describe themselves as conservative churchgoers who guard their privacy. In other words, watching someone else's misadventures on "America's Funniest Home Videos" is about the wildest thing they do on a Sunday.

Such disparities help explain why no U.S. markets have high rates of viewership for both shows. "SNL" fans support liberal causes: gay marriages, social pluralism, and consumerism. "AFHV" viewers are self-described conservatives who trust religious leaders, want the return of prayer to the schools, and support traditional family roles. And yet they all could take comfort in recognizing their commonality: the viewers of both programs hate talk shows like "Oprah" and "Donahue."

# Roseanne's Fans

## "Roseanne" Viewers

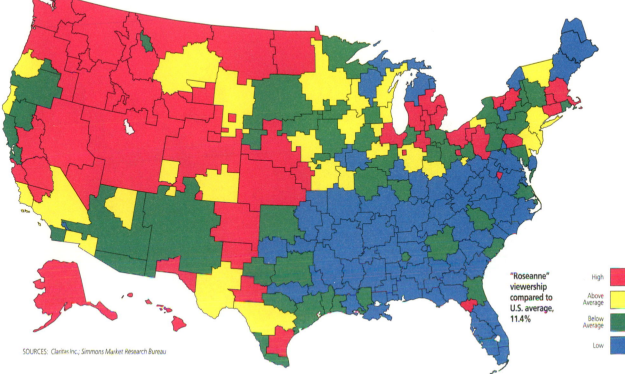

"Roseanne" viewership compared to U.S. average, 11.4%

High
Above Average
Below Average
Low

SOURCES: *Claritas Inc.; Simmons Market Research Bureau*

NOT since Archie Bunker first bellowed for Edith to bring him a beer have Americans so warmly embraced a blue-collar family. "Roseanne," the nation's top-rated television program over the last five years, has found success by trashing TV's usually idealized portrait of the American family. In the Connors household, the kids are disrespectful, a family meal often means take-out pizza, and conversation drips with sarcasm like a Sloppy Joe. Yet the family interaction masks an overstuffed couchful of real affection and solidarity, and therein lies the appeal. From kitchen to diner job to local bar, Roseanne Arnold cheerfully mocks the June Cleaver image of the nurturing guardian of the hearth. "They're all mine," she says of her three kids during one Thanksgiving episode. "Of course,

I'd trade any one of them for a dishwasher."

Most all of America happily tunes in to this domestic reality check, except the rural South, where wholesome TV moms are still venerated. "Roseanne" fans tend to resemble the fictional Connors, that is, middle-class families with several children, a working mom, and a blue-collar dad. According to surveys, viewers' lifestyles imitate TV art: meals revolve around spaghetti, BBQ, and Domino's delivery; favorite activities include bowling, camping, and riding motorcycles; and cultural interests range from movies to the occasional rock concert. Although loyal households typically earn more than $50,000 annually, these folks still devote their weekends to doing home-improvement projects and working on their cars, and a major-

ity tell pollsters they wish they spent more time on household chores. TV takes up a big chunk of their leisure time, but they prefer gentle sitcoms like "Coach" and "The Wonder Years" to comedies with more satiric bite like "Seinfeld" and "In Living Color."

Perhaps surprisingly, "Roseanne" fans are political middle-of-the-roaders. Despite supporting gay and abortion rights, they see themselves as more conservative than liberal, and are more likely to place their trust in religious rather than community leaders. Like Dan and Roseanne, these midscale Americans are liberal in their social views until the issue affects the kids. In fact, they're more strongly opposed to legalizing drugs than any other issue.

# Soap Zones

## People Who Watch Daytime Soaps

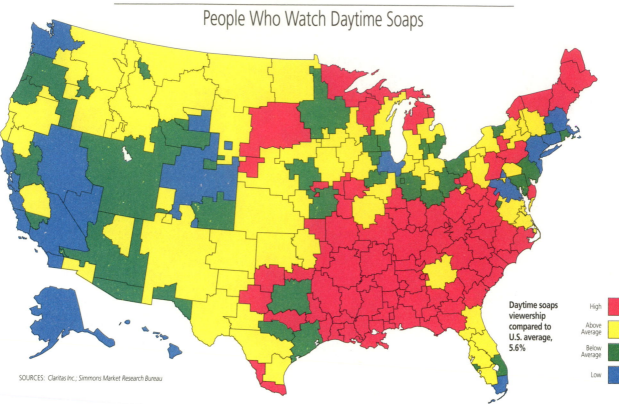

Daytime soaps viewership compared to U.S. average, 5.6%

High
Above Average
Below Average
Low

SOURCES: *Claritas Inc.; Simmons Market Research Bureau*

EVIL twins and unnatural deaths, lovers' quarrels and shocking pregnancies, overly dramatic music and brilliantly bad acting: TV's soap operas can never be accused of messing with a successful formula. But for years they've thrived: 50 million households watch "All My Children," "As the World Turns," and the other daytime soaps. And the reason is no mystery, especially among downscale viewers, daytime soaps' biggest fans. Americans have a somewhat perverse fascination for the lives of the idle rich, at least the soaped-up version — those who wear gaudy jewelry, sleep around, bear children, disappear, then end up on a desert island with amnesia about the whole affair.

Although most TV shows are written and produced in New York or Los Angeles, the largest audience for soaps is in nonmetropolitan areas, particularly throughout the South. These markets are characterized by low educational and income levels. A disproportionate number of soap fans are lower-class homemakers and unemployed

---

*Shameless women, improbable amnesiacs, and long-lost relatives attract Southerners in droves to daytime soaps.*

---

residents who have time in the afternoon to sit in front of the tube to catch up on the day's exploits between the sheets. There's also a number of markets along the Southeast coast with a high per-

centage of female factory workers whose dirty secret is that they videotape their favorite soaps to watch at night.

Indeed, many of the best soap markets — like Greenwood, Miss., Jackson, Tenn., and Albany, Ga. — are rural, racially mixed communities with few entertainment options, such as cinemas and theaters. Soap fans are more likely than average Americans to watch a lot of TV and less likely to read newspapers, books, and magazines. And their favorite titles — such as the *Star,* the *National Enquirer,* and *True Story* — indicate a peculiar distaste for the hard-core reality of news and current events. They watch soaps to escape their ordinariness and glimpse the lifestyles of the rich and shameless.

# MTV Maniacs

## People Who Watch MTV

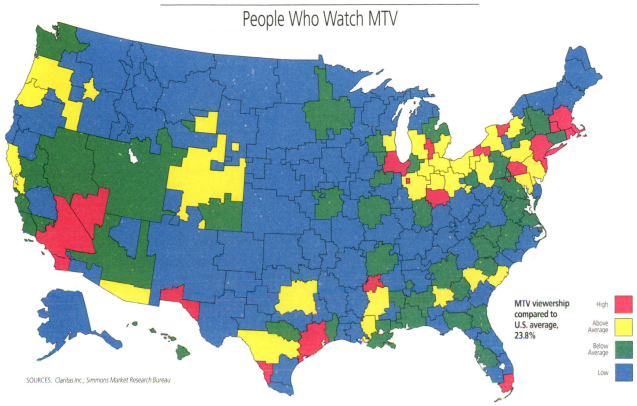

MTV viewership compared to U.S. average, 23.8%

High
Above Average
Below Average
Low

SOURCES: Claritas Inc.; Simmons Market Research Bureau

PERHAPS you've wondered where the cult of young grooviness thrives, where Americans are hooked on rock videos and surfer dudes interviewing the hip new hip-hop act. If TV is chewing gum for the mind, MTV is laced with acid. And the map above shows that the hardest-core fans are city-dwellers in the Northeast. These viewers are more accustomed than, say, Midwest ranch-dwellers, to stumbling onto a cool party and hangin' — as MTV so often does with its camera crews. Then again, you have to wonder what aspect of metropolitan life can make otherwise conservative youths believe that baggy pants, bad haircuts, and phony air-guitarists are cool.

But the top 20 markets of MTV viewers also include some small to midsize cities, like El Paso, Tex., Erie, Pa., and Lafayette, Ind. And while some viewers may be interested only in vicariously living the life of a music-video star, MTV's success in these areas has more to do with advertising dollars. When MTV debuted in 1981, it set out to deliver the difficult-to-reach 14-to-34-year-old demographic segment to record companies, beer manufacturers, and purveyors of acne creams. A decade later, the network has become wildly successful. MTV's red-hot markets have high concentrations of young singles, African Americans, and apartment-dwellers. And all share

tendencies to sample teen- and twentysomething-oriented offerings: cola, milk, beer, TV dinners, CD players, pregnancy-test kits, liberal politics, and, of course, albums, tapes, and CDs.

By the time Americans reach the age of 35, they begin to regard MTV as, in the words of writer Frank Owen, "the craven worship of image over content, noise over meaning." They soon retire to the nation's calm blue midsection, small-town and rural markets crawling with couples aged 45-plus living in homes for more than a decade. With a heavy sigh, they recall the good old days of rock 'n' roll and tune instead to VH-1.

# Armchair Vigilantes

## People Who Watch "Cops"

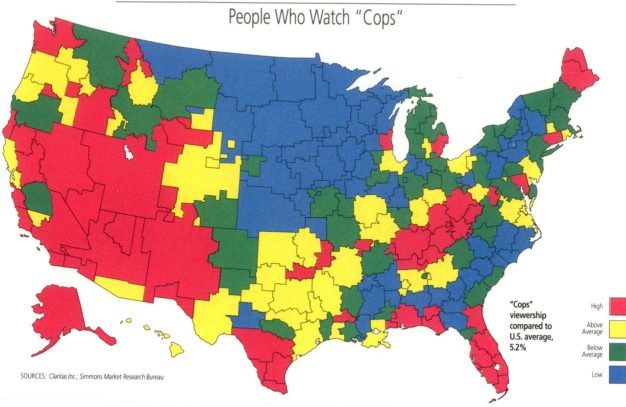

"Cops" viewership compared to U.S. average, 5.2%

High
Above Average
Below Average
Low

SOURCES: *Claritas Inc.; Simmons Market Research Bureau*

THE premise behind "Cops" couldn't be simpler: a handheld minicam rides shotgun in a police car as it cruises rough neighborhoods. Yet what emerges — raw, spontaneous emotions from real crime fighters and real perpetrators — is often undeniably gripping. In four years, Fox's "Cops" has featured hostage dramas, drug buys, and domestic disputes with an in-your-face coarseness. "Cops" cameras have been known to arrive while a burglary is still being committed. Even with the alleged criminals signing releases to appear on TV, few come off looking like saints. In their trash-filled homes the subjects, typically drunken, doped-up, or armed to the teeth, will never be confused with family members on "Full House."

But what of the armchair vigilantes who enjoy bringing this view of society into their living rooms? H. L. Mencken once observed that Americans have a libido for the ugly, and "Cops" preys on that desire among a certain segment of the populace. Those voyeurs who most enjoy watching cops catch crooks tend to be blue-collar workers living in downscale neighborhoods on the urban fringe. They include a disproportionate number of high school dropouts, single parents, Hispanics, and unemployed citizens. And they're most likely found in the nation's mountain areas, along the Rockies and the Alleghenies. Florida is filled with fans, in part because the show originated in the state's Broward County before moving on to other crime scenes. Conversely, "Cops" devotees are least likely to be found in affluent suburban areas where TV-viewing rates in general are low, and in Midwestern farm communities, where residents prefer to think of the crimes linked to drugs and poverty as a bad dream.

As a group, "Cops" fans have some of the same consuming patterns associated with the petty criminals captured on the show. They're more likely than average Americans to drive muscle cars, listen to rap, gamble at casinos, and drink a lot of alcohol. On the other hand, opinion polls indicate the show's viewers are God-fearing and law abiding. They support school prayer and antipornography legislation, and they're strongly religious. They prove the TV programmer's maxim that Americans like to watch people on TV they wouldn't normally invite into their homes. Besides being fans of "Cops," they have high rates for watching a number of similar shows that specialize in America's criminal-justice system: "Rescue 911," "America's Most Wanted," "Unsolved Mysteries," and — after an arrest has been made — "The People's Court."

# Tchaikovsky and Twang

## People Who Buy Classical Music vs. Country Records, Tapes, or CDs

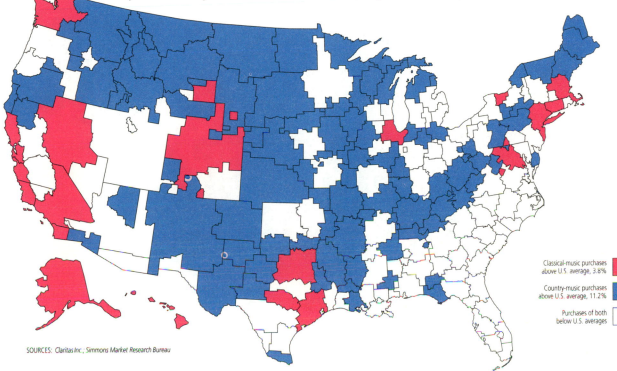

Classical-music purchases
above U.S. average, 3.8%

Country-music purchases
above U.S. average, 11.2%

Purchases of both
below U.S. averages

SOURCES: *Claritas Inc.; Simmons Market Research Bureau*

**F**OR MANY YEARS, classical music has had what could diplomatically be called an Audience Problem: the rich white people who traditionally support highbrow music are steadily dying off with no young people to take their place. Industry executives have tried to expand their audience by featuring sexy couples on the covers of classical albums and even promoting certain classical pieces as heavy-metal music. An EMI CD called "Heavy Classix" offers "fifteen head-banging compositions" including the "1812 Overture" and Wagner's "Valkyrie."

But the map above indicates that classical music still has some ways to go before Metallica groupies discover the "rock" in Rachmaninoff. The 4 percent of the populace who buy classical music remain America's moneyed urban class: college-educated white-collars who pull down six-figure incomes. Although

some 1,500 symphony orchestras are in residence throughout the U.S., classical music's biggest audiences live in cities like New York, Chicago, and Houston, which boast grand symphony halls. Away from the concerts, classical lovers typically play tennis, travel abroad, and support their local NPR station. These are people who relax with a croissant and the *Times* on Sundays with Mozart wafting from their CD players.

The audience for country music, by contrast, is roughly three times larger, an indication that country's appeal has crossed over into the mainstream. No longer just the music choice of dropouts and hayseed rodeo fans who chew tobacco, country-music lovers are high school–educated blue-collar folk with incomes ranging from lower- to upper-middle class. They are more likely than average Americans to take adult education courses,

belong to business clubs, and invest in mutual funds. Indeed, millions of upscale baby boomers who grew up imitating Mick Jagger's swagger are now finding favor with Garth Brooks's guitar-smashing concerts.

While there are Americans who no doubt are passionate about both classical and country music — down-home Reba McEntire, for one, was trained as a classical violinist — there are no markets where consumers buy both genres at above-average rates. Attitudinal differences between the lovers of Chopin and Mary Chapin-Carpenter apparently keep these audiences apart. Classical lovers, for instance, are liberal supporters of gay rights, environmental issues, and consumerism. Country fans support traditional family values, the death penalty, and privacy rights. The highbrows hate most TV fare. Their country cousins tend to watch more than fifty hours of TV every week.

# Classic Rockers

## People Who Buy Classic Rock Records, Tapes, and CDs

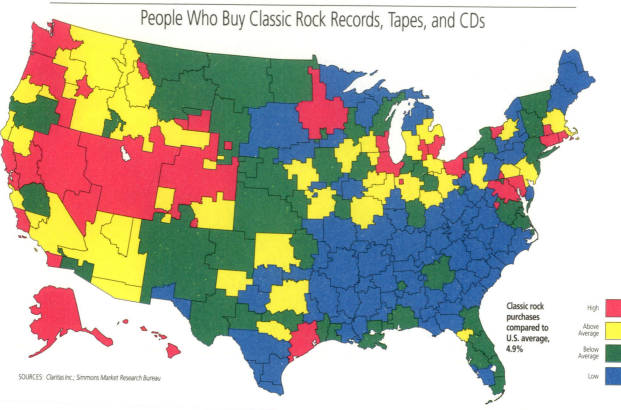

Classic rock purchases compared to U.S. average, 4.9%

High
Above Average
Below Average
Low

SOURCES: *Claritas Inc.; Simmons Market Research Bureau*

A GENERATION AGO, they tuned in, turned on, and dropped out. Today, they're over 40, married, settled behind a white picket fence, and content to talk about the counterculture as if it were a historical event somewhere between the Korean War and Watergate. But the 1960s music that accompanied their youth has survived intact, and the baby boomers who grew up celebrating the pleasures of sex, drugs, and rock 'n' roll have maintained most of their musical allegiances. They tune in to classic rock stations and replace their worn vinyl records with tapes and CDs by the Beatles, Rolling Stones, Beach Boys, and Motown groups.

Unlike the classic rock performers, many working-class toughs thumbing their screaming guitars at establishment moms and dads, today's classic rock fans have bought into the system, at least judging by the variety of credit cards they carry: Visa, MasterCard, and American Express, as well as bank and gasoline credit cards. These listeners tend to be 35-to-54-year-old suburbanites with white-collar jobs and upper-middle-class homes (with elaborate CD systems) concentrated in the nation's largest metros and growing western markets. Rummage around on their coffee tables and you'll likely find movie ticket stubs mixed in with magazines like *U.S. News & World Report, Time,* and *National Geographic*. Open the fridge and there's a good chance you'll find skim milk, light beer, and domestic white wine. Interestingly, classic rock fans are only lukewarm on the issue of legalizing drugs, and it's likely they're not indulging in too many mind-altering addictions, given their fondness for health clubs, jogging, and weight training. Apparently, they'd rather drop pounds than acid.

It should also be noted that these aging rockers are not the same people as MTV fans, those irreverent twentysomethings with shrinking attention spans. Despite some overlap in tastes and geography — all are concentrated in the nation's coastal metro areas — these boomers tend to be older, wealthier, and just plain more settled. They still own ripped jeans, tie-dyed shirts, and beat-up guitars, but they're likely hidden in a closet along with other mementos of their far-out years.

# Folkies

## People Who Buy Folk Music Records, Tapes, or CDs

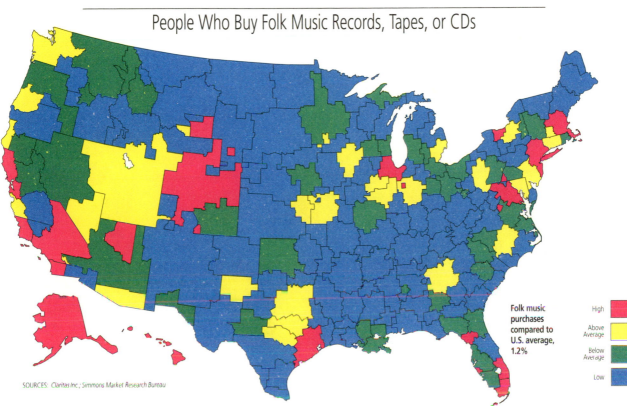

Folk music purchases compared to U.S. average, 1.2%

High
Above Average
Below Average
Low

SOURCES: *Claritas Inc.; Simmons Market Research Bureau*

WHERE have all the folkies gone? Gone to the nation's big cities and a handful of college towns, according to the above map. Folk music's raw and passionate sound has all but disappeared from the American heartland except in that rare natural-food store, Birkenstock outlet, or leftist bookshop. But stop inside the beltways of major metros and you'll still hear the strains of Joan Baez or Phil Ochs filtering through coffeehouses and find street singers strumming their Martins to "Blowin' in the Wind" or "City of New Orleans."

Naturally, today's folk fans have aged since the days of "Kumbaya" and "Puff, the Magic Dragon." They've also broken a lot of their one-time antimaterialistic tenets and are doing quite well financially. They're 50 percent more likely than average Americans to have six-figure incomes and own $250,000-plus homes. The highest proportion are college-educated baby boomers with jobs in business, a fondness for tennis, and a well-stocked liquor cabinet. And yet despite their wealth, these aging folkies haven't forgotten their liberal roots. They're likely to engage in nonpolitical volunteer work and to support causes ranging from gay and abortion rights to social pluralism and environmental concerns. They've even retained a taste for organic foods, consuming rice cakes, herbal tea, natural cheese, and fresh vegetables at high rates.

While folk revivalism in America seems to blossom at regular intervals, the map above indicates folk music is currently experiencing a national remission. For one thing, most Americans who buy tapes and CDs have made country and rock their mainstream music and wouldn't know Pete Seeger from Peter Yarrow. For another, folkies have grown content with other genres — notably jazz, classical, and reggae — or, like Joni Mitchell, have moved toward a fusion of folk, pop, and jazz. And those genres, like folk music, are popular in only a few dozen cities and college towns. If you're a folkie, this land is no longer your land.

# From Bop to Hip-Hop

## Buyers of Jazz vs. Rap Records, Tapes, or CDs

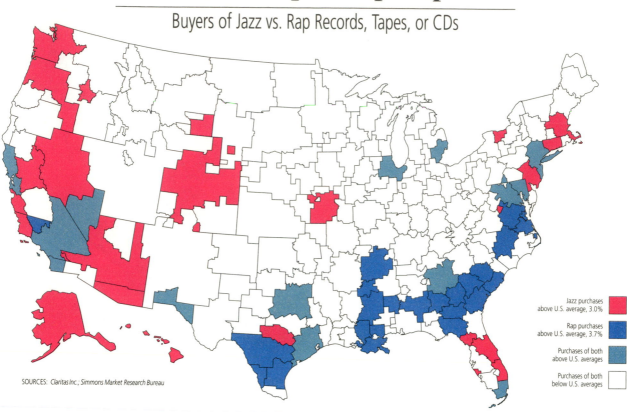

Jazz purchases
above U.S. average, 3.0%

Rap purchases
above U.S. average, 3.7%

Purchases of both
above U.S. averages

Purchases of both
below U.S. averages

SOURCES: *Claritas Inc.; Simmons Market Research Bureau*

IMPROVISATION, the struggle for wider acceptance, deep African-American roots: the same traits characterize both jazz and rap in this country. Born in the nightlife of cities with substantial minority populations, both genres grew up as music showcased on the street, in downtown clubs, and inside crowded dance halls. Over time, they developed their strongest followings among single city-dwellers in many of the same urban markets.

But since its origins a century ago, jazz has moved uptown, becoming less a music for spirited dancing and more a music for serious listening. Today its biggest fans include white, white-collar yuppies, thirtysomething and up, living well on the urban fringe of cities like Boston, Denver, and Portland. Jazz buffs are big on all the arts — theater, film, and literature — as well as individualist sports like jogging

and aerobics. And they're about as politically correct as Americans can be, telling pollsters of their concern for gay rights, consumerism, and environmental issues. You'll find these folks in their $250,000 town houses sipping a glass of Chivas with a Wynton Marsalis CD playing in the background.

Blasting from a boom box or club sound system, rap has always been an abrasive, foreground music. Despite the increasing number of hip-hop artists who are white, female, or suburban, rap has remained an inner-city sound. With lyrics ranging from sex-and-gun fantasies to black self-help to "gangsta" violence, rap has found its audience among downscale, 18-to-24-year-old singles and divorced men and women. Many now live beyond the big cities in southern mill towns, south Texas, and small metro areas, like Richmond and Memphis. Surveys show that rap fans are partial

to pro basketball, TV movies, Japanese cars, and fast food. And while they're not much on the visual arts, they're passionate about sound. They buy not only rap recordings, but also modern rock, rhythm & blues, gospel, comedy, *and* jazz.

Beyond demographics, the biggest difference between jazz and rap fans is not just generational but one of mind-set. Jazz buffs are into history — they tell pollsters, "I wish I lived in an earlier age" — and appreciate jazz's evolution from Dixieland to bop to fusion. The rap fans of Public Enemy and Sister Souljah couldn't care less about the past, admitting that they live for today. Ripping apart history, rappers mix sound bites from Malcolm X speeches with James Brown riffs to create ghetto-centric sounds protesting an establishment of which many jazz fans are happily a part.

# Modern Rockers

## People Who Buy Modern Rock Records, CDs, or Tapes

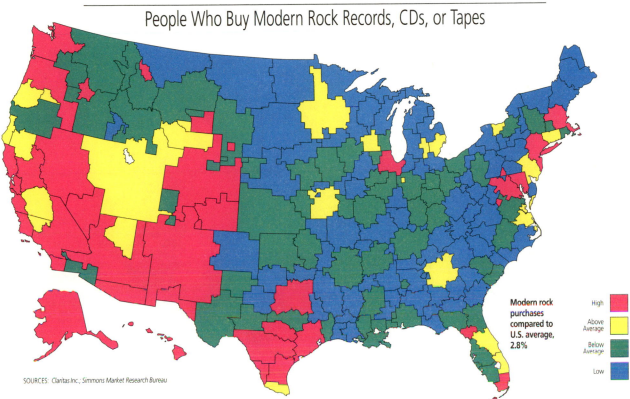

Modern rock purchases compared to U.S. average, 2.8%

High

Above Average

Below Average

Low

SOURCES: *Claritas Inc.; Simmons Market Research Bureau*

**M**USICAL TASTE, experts know, is largely a function of age: The music you fall in love with as a teenager often determines your favorite sound for the rest of your life. "Many people just close their mind to new music after they hit forty," observes musical archivist Eric Kulberg. "That's why people listen to the same Doobie Brothers albums for twenty years."

So it is that the biggest fans of modern rockers like the B-52s, Fine Young Cannibals, XTC, and Depeche Mode came of age in the 1980s — the so-called baby-bust generation born at the end of the baby boom. Also known as Generation X, these twentysomethings tend to be cynical, single city-dwellers who have low-level white-collar jobs and some college but no degrees. They're in their prime years of music fandom — people start cutting back their music purchases at age 40 — and they're big on having fun. They like to go clubbing, attend concerts, and buy tapes and CDs of jazz artists, reggae groups, and rock bands from the '70s, such as Aerosmith, Yes, Lynyrd Skynyrd, and Fleetwood Mac. They spend the highest percentage of their entertainment budget on televisions, radios, and sound equipment, such as CD and cassette players. Having logged some 23,000 hours in front of their TVs before the age of 20, it's no surprise that they're among the nation's biggest consumers of Domino's pizza and take-out from Taco Bell or Wendy's. With their feet propped up on a coffee table scattered with *Rolling Stone, Shape,* and *People,* they fall asleep with the cable TV tuned to MTV or VH-1.

Although baby busters generally have a reputation for being apathetic, the ones who listen to modern rock are relatively tuned in. Compared to average Americans they're more likely to be liberal-party activists. In opinion polls, they express a belief in consumer power, a concern about military spending, and a fear for ozone depletion. On the other hand, they're also a libidinous bunch who buy a lot of condoms, like nude beaches, and support legalizing drugs.

# From Satanic Depths to Spiritual Heights

## People Who Buy Heavy Metal vs. Gospel Records, Tapes, or CDs

**Heavy metal-music purchases** above U.S. average, 6.2%

**Gospel-music purchases** above U.S. average, 2.6%

**Purchases of both** above U.S. averages

**Purchases of both** below U.S. averages

SOURCES: *Claritas Inc.; Simmons Market Research Bureau*

ONE genre is the devil's music, the other developed in Protestant churches during the 19th century. Accordingly, no one should be surprised that the metal fans of Guns N' Roses, Metallica, and Mötley Crüe would be different from those who appreciate the sacred sounds of the Mighty Clouds of Joy, Sister Rosetta Tharpe, and the Dixie Hummingbirds.

Heavy metal gained popularity in the '70s on the backs of black leather–clad singers who offered squealing guitars, gross stage antics and bombastic vocals. A mind-numbing stepchild of rock 'n' roll, metal appealed to disenchanted teens drawn to the dirgelike tempos and Gothic black magic imagery, biblical allusions, and doomsday scenarios — in other words, your basic adolescent's anarchistic world. Today, heavy metal is approaching middle age and survives mainly in America's

blue-collar towns — especially out West and along the Great Lakes — filled with married, high school–educated factory workers apparently used to industrial-strength noise. Heavy-metal fans are big on owning motorcycles, pickups, and powerboats.

But the values inside heavy-metal households should not be confused with the rebellious sentiments expressed in most heavy-metal fanzines. Concerns about religion, faith, and morality top one recent poll. The parents of heavy metal listeners are more likely than average Americans to advocate traditional sexual roles, watch the Christian Broadcasting Network, and support school prayer.

Gospel music, whose fans share a belief in the importance of religion and school prayer, has its roots in the call-and-response singing of African-American preachers and their congregations. The

concentration of gospel in the South can be explained by the spreading of the music by rural Pentecostal churches. Today's gospel fans tend to live in rural communities throughout the Bible Belt with high concentrations of African Americans of modest means and educations. Besides gospel, they frequently listen to rap and rhythm & blues, especially gospel-influenced artists like Aretha Franklin and Ray Charles.

But gospel enthusiasts aren't into dancing or nightclubbing; indeed, most are homebodies and teetotalers. Their vices are cigarettes, junk food and television, especially game shows, soaps, and talk shows. Perhaps their biggest sin is that, in contrast to the love-thy-neighbor message of so many gospel songs, these Americans have a passion for bash-thy-opponent TV pro wrestling.

# Highbrows vs. Enquiring Minds

## Readers of the *New Yorker* vs. the *National Enquirer*

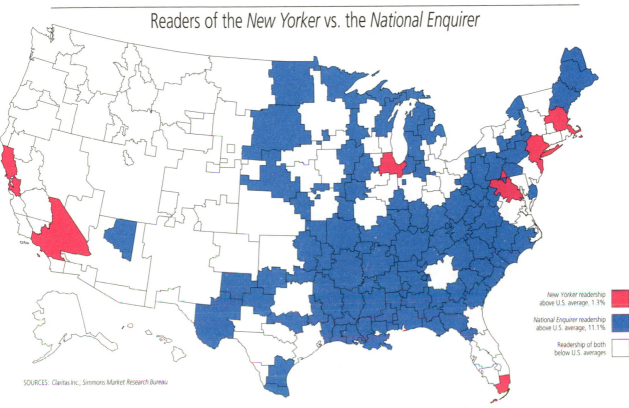

New Yorker readership
above U.S. average, 1.3%

National Enquirer readership
above U.S. average, 11.1%

Readership of both
below U.S. averages

SOURCES: *Claritas Inc.; Simmons Market Research Bureau*

AMERICA lacks an accepted way to distinguish among the social classes, unlike the snobby Brits who make things easy with inherited titles, royal honors, or silly ranks. But one convenient way to observe the yawning gap between highbrow and lowbrow status in the U.S. is to map areas where residents prefer the *New Yorker* versus the *National Enquirer*.

The *New Yorker,* presenting a blend of literate reporting, distinctive fiction, and tart criticism, has moved more toward topical irreverence since the arrival of editor Tina Brown in 1992. Still to many longstanding subscribers, it remains the journal of record for urbane society. When editor Harold Ross launched the magazine some 60 years ago he declared in the prospectus, *"The New Yorker* will be the magazine which is not edited for the old lady in Dubuque." His prediction still holds true. Today the glossy is read

at rates above the U.S. average in only eight metropolitan markets — and all are a far cry from Iowa.

According to demographic profiles, the *New Yorker's* fortysomething readers make up the nation's top quartile, with a higher-than-average percentage earning six-figure incomes, living in million-dollar homes. In lifestyle terms, they're more likely than average Americans to travel abroad, attend the theater, read books, play tennis, and drink imported wine — no surprise here. However, among their more prosaic tastes, *New Yorker* readers also enjoy gambling casinos, rock concerts, and lifting weights.

These folks draw the line at tales of alien spacecraft, Hollywood dirt, and people with miraculous healing powers. Those subjects — the weird, the gruesome, and the bizarre twists of current events — are for the readers of the *National Enquirer*. With low incomes, home values, and

education levels — a significant proportion never finished elementary school — the nation's enquiring minds care more about escapism and entertainment than real news.

When the *National Enquirer's* editor Ian Calder was once asked about the typical reader, he responded, "Mrs. Smith from Kansas City." He, too, was right, although the highest concentration of readers is found farther south, where there are larger families, more homemakers, and less interest in current affairs and literary magazines. Interestingly, there is not a single U.S. market where both the *New Yorker* and the *National Enquirer* are read at above-average rates, though that may change as the line between serious and tabloid journalism blurs. Already, both publications have seen fit to run articles on pederastic priests, sleazy motel murders, Heidi Fleiss, and Lorena Bobbitt.

# Too Many Cooks

## Readers of *Gourmet* vs. *Family Circle*

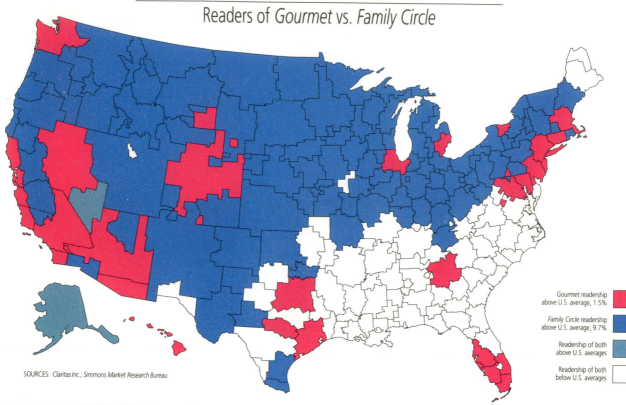

Gourmet readership
above U.S. average, 1.5%

Family Circle readership
above U.S. average, 9.7%

Readership of both
above U.S. averages

Readership of both
below U.S. averages

SOURCES: *Claritas Inc.; Simmons Market Research Bureau*

WHEN it comes to the nightly ritual of asking what's for dinner, there's an easy way to predict whether the answer will be continental cuisine or family-style fare. Reading extravagant *Gourmet* or frumpy *Family Circle* is one indicator of whether the family cook is preparing escalope de poulet à l'orange or tuna patty melt.

*Gourmet,* the self-proclaimed "magazine of good living," finds its biggest fans in the markets with the nation's highest median incomes; one in seven readers is a millionaire. They're most often childless urbanites who use *Gourmet*'s fancy recipes to create drop-dead chic dinner parties, the kind of folks who don't have to worry about little mouths demanding catsup with every meal. *Gourmet* readers like wine — more domestics than imports, more white than red — along with healthy ingredients, such as chicken, yogurt, and fruit. But all that wholesome stuff can send a body into shock, so that's why you'll occasionally find these people slumming it at Dunkin' Donuts.

*Family Circle,* which calls itself "the world's largest-selling women's magazine," is read more often (5 million readers versus *Gourmet*'s 900,000), and its subscribers hail from farm and factory communities across America's northern tier. Here, middle-class homemakers and working mothers need to whip up something in a hurry for hungry kids, and they look to *Family Circle*'s cheap-meal planners. Not coincidentally, these readers are the nation's prime consumers of packaged goods, such as hot dogs, macaroni, cookies, and ice cream — all the ingredients for a backyard cookout. Indeed, *Family Circle*'s biggest fans are outdoorsy family people into fishing, camping, and gardening.

As for the South's lack of readers for both magazines, one historic reason concerns the business practices of Madison Avenue ad agencies that, prior to the late '60s, gave magazines no credit for their circulation in the South. "Their reasoning was basically that Southerners were rednecks who still lived in huts," recalls Richard Lepere, a Washington-based publications consultant. "Magazines basically wrote off the South." That changed after the birth of *Southern Living* in 1965, which grew prosperous targeting readers in 13 southern states.

By a strange convergence of socioeconomically diverse singles and couples, the Las Vegas and Alaska markets have high rates of reading both magazines. Both areas stand out as aberrations on the American landscape, a mishmash of tastes and attitudes on the exurban frontier. Both are areas that report heavy consumption of lobster as well as canned chili.

# The Fairest of Them All

## Readers of *Vanity Fair*

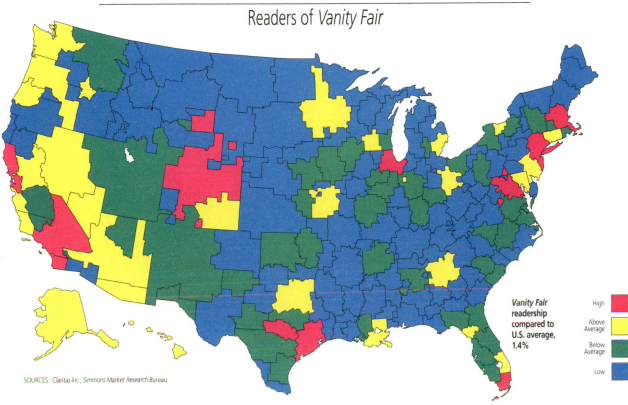

*Vanity Fair* readership compared to U.S. average, 1.4%

High
Above Average
Below Average
Low

SOURCES: *Claritas Inc., Simmons Market Research Bureau*

A CASE can be made that the glossiest magazine in America — the one with "the most buzz," in the words of industry analysts — is *Vanity Fair*. Ever since Condé Nast revived the magazine in 1981, the publication has ridden a wave of popularity — and sometimes vulgarity — for its recipe of spotlighting naughty debutantes and semi-celebrities mixed in with investigative reports and purple-prosed commentary. Its unconventional covers alone, including photos of a nude, pregnant Demi Moore and model Cindy Crawford shaving bisexual singer k. d. lang, have generated a sea of ink. The result is "buzz," which may be measured by the number of issues stolen from gym bags and condo mailboxes.

The highest percentage of *Vanity Fair* copies are disappearing in a handful of the nation's largest cities, the nexus of urban America, where culture vultures care about cutting-edge trends (whether it's Vidalia onions or Bosnian rape victim relief). There, readers fall into two distinct groups, the first composed of the young and the hip, apartment-dwelling recent college grads without much money who want to keep abreast of the latest attitudes and literary trash — the kind who turn first to articles like "Rich Kids, Dead Parents." Their lives are filled with jogging, racquetball, seeing movies, and attending rock concerts. When they watch TV, which is rarely, it's to tune in sports or comedy favorites like "David Letterman," "In Living Color," and "The Simpsons."

The core of *Vanity Fair* readers, however, are the people of society — "those who glitter with the glory of the hummingbird," as T. S. Eliot put it, "who sit in the sty of contentment." They're more likely than average Americans to belong to country clubs, travel abroad, ski, sail, drink scotch, and frequent classical concerts. They're also the ones with high rates for reading books and other magazines, like *Forbes, Bon Appetit, GQ,* and *Travel & Leisure*. These are America's limousine liberals, who support decriminalizing marijuana, gay marriages, and gun control, while opposing the pro-life movement, school prayer, and traditional women's roles.

What all of *Vanity Fair*'s readers have in common is a longing for longer days. In lifestyle surveys, they yearn to spend more time working, exercising, and entertaining friends — though not reading magazines. For *Vanity Fair*'s fans, the days are too short and the gossipy articles long enough.

# McPaper People

## People Who Read *USA Today*

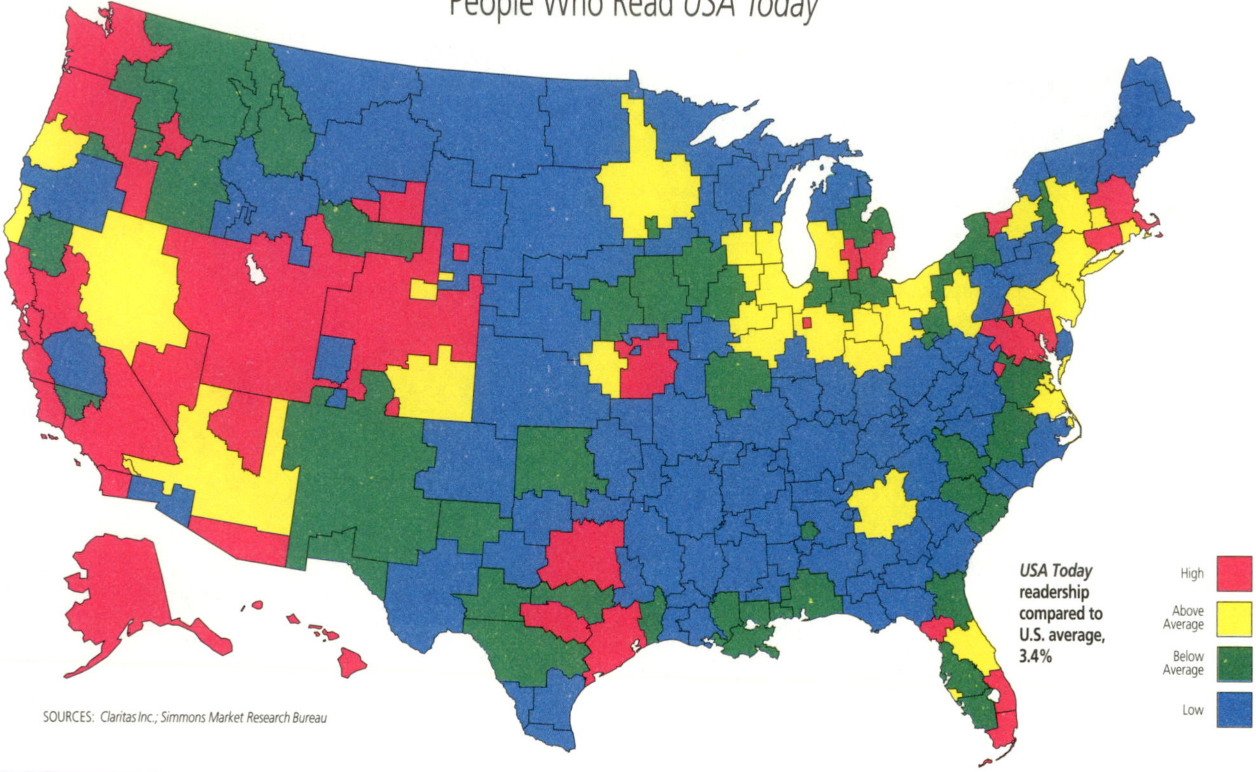

*USA Today* readership compared to U.S. average, 3.4%

High
Above Average
Below Average
Low

SOURCES: *Claritas Inc.; Simmons Market Research Bureau*

IT was dismissed as "McPaper" when it debuted in 1982 for its short stories, chirpy optimism, and flashy format that read like fast food for the mind. But *USA Today* managed to survive, its circulation now more than 1.8 million and its light-and-lively format copied by dozens of papers across the USA. Never a money-making venture — *USA Today* has lost more than $800 million since its founding — the presses keep rolling despite the paper's reputation as a creation more concerned with packaging than substance.

Still *USA Today* has found a niche among the nation's traveling class: white-collar salespeople and rootless Americans who go wherever the best-paying jobs can be found and read *USA Today* in addition to their local paper. These mobile readers tend to live in the nation's metros and second-tier cities — like Kansas City, Seattle, and Austin — with high concentrations of upper-middle-class adults holding jobs in business, finance, and education. They boast some of the nation's highest rates for driving a rented car, traveling by plane, and taking domestic business trips. Not surprisingly, they're more interested in business media than anything else; in a survey of 100 publications, their favorite titles were the *Wall Street Journal* and *Barron's*.

*USA Today* fans, however, are not the CEOs who have already made it to the top: they're more likely to belong to health clubs than country clubs, more interested in movies than theater, bigger fans of modern rock and jazz than classical music. *USA Today*'s video-age graphics appeal to them partly because they have definite couch-potato tendencies: they watch more than five hours of TV on a typical day, mostly sports, movies, and cable's CNBC and VH-1.

Perhaps their fondness for TV explains the acceptance of sound bite–sized stories, news summaries, and catchy trend charts that are *USA Today* mainstays. Core readers are basically not newshounds. In a Yankelovich survey, they admit that they place greater trust in car salesmen and corporate PR types than print journalists. And while *USA Today* trumpets coverage of all-American trends and breaking stories, its politically liberal readers feel no commitment to Buying American. As a *USA Today* headline might read: "Our Readers Turn Backs on USA (see chart)."

# Bunny Habitats

## Readers of *Playboy*

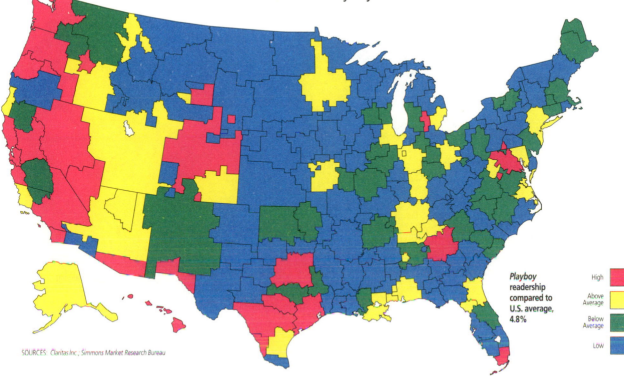

*Playboy* readership compared to U.S. average, 4.8%

High
Above Average
Below Average
Low

SOURCES: *Claritas Inc.; Simmons Market Research Bureau*

PICTURES of naked women titillated men long before Hugh Hefner printed bare-chested photographs of Marilyn Monroe in 1953. But it was his creation, *Playboy* magazine, that turned every man's buxom fantasies into an empire. At its peak, *Playboy*'s circulation reached nearly 7 million readers, mostly guys who loved seeing overdeveloped starlets and topless pictorials of Girls of the Big Eight Conference. Since then, the circulation has dropped by over half to 3.4 million readers — of whom nearly 20 percent are women. The reasons for the decline are many: competition from more sexually explicit magazines and videotapes, the decision by some convenience store chains to drop skin rags, and the number of men who are finally "getting it," that is, men who exhibit a more enlightened attitude toward women.

However, *Playboy* still thrives in the red-hot markets pictured above. Except for a scattering of metro areas east of the Mississippi, the heaviest concentration of these fans live along the West Coast, where Americans are generally younger, politically more liberal, and wear fewer tailored suits to the office. Surveys show that readers are a mixed lot, ranging from the residents of exclusive subdivisions to those in housing projects. Compared to the national average, they're more likely to be college-educated, unmarried, Hispanic, and African American. As consumers, they're into cars, clothes, consumer electronics, and fern bars like TGIF's, where they enjoy downing bottles of Budweiser and Heineken. Oh, yes: *Playboy*'s fans are sexually active, if the number of condoms and home pregnancy-test kits they buy is any indication.

Since reading *Playboy* is typically a solitary experience, it's perhaps no surprise that the magazine's fans avoid group activities like bowling or belonging to social clubs. On the other hand, many of the bunny-less blue markets above turn out to be blue-collar communities where residents tend to join veterans groups, fraternal orders, and religious organizations.

# Left Field

## Political Liberals

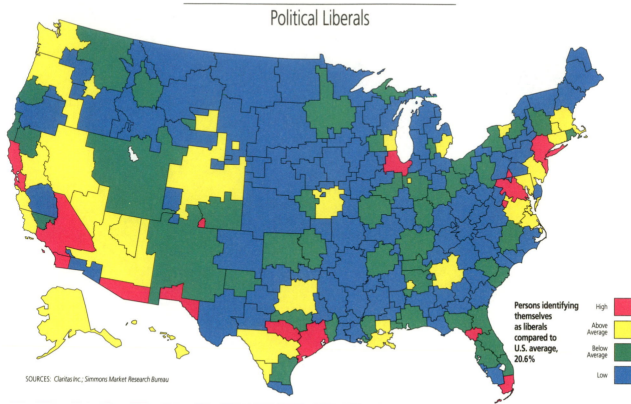

Persons identifying themselves as liberals compared to U.S. average, 20.6%

High
Above Average
Below Average
Low

SOURCES: Claritas Inc.; Simmons Market Research Bureau

TODAY's voters identify with a variety of political orientations depending on the issue, their cultural roots, and demographic realities. The Americans who identify themselves as liberals are concentrated, not unexpectedly, in the Northeastern corridor, the Left Coast, and a handful of yupscale markets, like Houston, Chicago, and Miami. Surveys reveal that the nation's liberals constitute a coalition of diversity: affluent suburbanites with a progressive social agenda; young, single city-dwellers who back more radical leftist causes; older, blue-collar ethnics who support family values; and younger, downscale minorities who are patriotic and religious.

With these disparate groups, it's no surprise that the typical liberal suffers from multiple-personality disorder. Some liberals worry about jobs, others worry about getting enough exercise. Opinion polls show that core liberal issues include women's rights, environmental protection, consumer affairs, and gay rights. Otherwise, liberals are moving toward the political center. No longer closely linked to the labor movement, liberals claim they would not pay more to buy products made in the USA (though they do feel guilty about it). Meanwhile, their concern about traditional family values is growing, with many expressing a strong interest in spending more time with their children. Still, it's not yet time to draft Pat Buchanan as a spokesman for liberals: they list legalizing drugs as one of their key issues.

As for the lifestyles of America's liberals, they're not the dull models of political correctness you might imagine them to be. As a group, they enjoy drinking, dancing, and watching R-rated movies at high rates. They're also more health conscious than average Americans, more likely to jog and belong to health clubs, more likely to fill their grocery carts with yogurt, whole-grain products, and spring water. Though they're not big on TV viewing, they will tune in to satiric comedies like "Saturday Night Live," "The Simpsons," and "In Living Color."

Although only one in five Americans admits to calling him- or herself the "L" word, liberals may exert more power than their apparent numbers and geographic concentration suggest. Part of the reason is their political activism, far above that of conservatives and moderates. Another factor is the mood of the 1990s, when the liberal agenda has distanced itself from radical-fringe elements. During the 1992 election, Bill Clinton was able to capitalize on this recasting of the Democratic Party by appealing to voters with a core concept of liberalism: a receptivity to change.

# The Right Stuff

## Political Conservatives

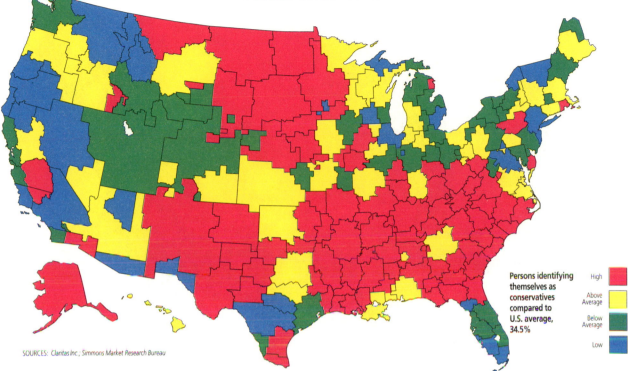

Persons identifying themselves as conservatives compared to U.S. average, 34.5%

High — Above Average — Below Average — Low

SOURCES: Claritas Inc.; Simmons Market Research Bureau

THE 12-year reign of Reagan-Bush conservativism may have ended with the 1992 election, but a solid third of the electorate still identify themselves as political conservatives. Like liberals, they are of several minds: upscale, metropolitan couples who are pro-business and anti-government; young, suburban families whose overriding concern is economics; and older, downscale small-town and rural voters who believe in hard work, family stability, and religious values. Unlike more left-leaning Americans, high concentrations of conservatives are widely scattered across the country, especially in the South and Midwest, from Texas to the Dakotas. Political scientist Daniel Elazar has traced America's traditionalists to post–Civil War Southerners who carried their conservative ideology with them as they migrated across the nation's southern tier to Califor-

nia. In fact, many of the counties that voted for George Wallace in 1972 reflect those immigration patterns in the map pattern above.

How different is the lifestyle of conservatives from that of liberals? Let me count the ways. Concentrated in the nation's hinterlands, they're more likely than average Americans to hunt, fish, camp, and drive pickup trucks. Around the house, the men enjoy woodworking, the women gardening, and everyone snuggles into their recliners to watch TV. In part because of their fondness for TV, only a dozen magazines are read at above-average rates. Interestingly, these conservative voters support typically liberal consumer advocates and have above-average rates for watching CNBC and reading *Consumer's Digest*.

Given this portrait out of a "Morning in America" spot, it's no surprise that these voters believe in

God, country, and respect for their elders — Ronald Reagan, especially. On the issues, they're for school prayer, family values, and the death penalty, pro-life and against gun control. And, contrary to the image of the BMW-driving yuppie Republican, the Americans who call themselves conservatives are patriotic protectionists who worry about increasing sales of foreign goods — and their attendant loss of U.S. jobs. Indeed, political analysts trace George Bush's 1992 loss to his weak performance on domestic affairs.

Because conservatives generally have a low rate for voting — only 20 percent of the Americans who describe themselves as conservatives vote — it takes a strong candidate to galvanize the rank-and-file. Judging from the last presidential election, neither party nominee lured them from their recliners and into the voting booth.

# Return to Center

## Political Moderates

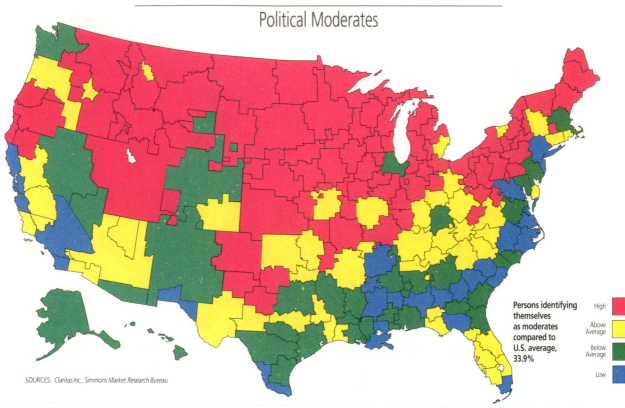

Persons identifying themselves as moderates compared to U.S. average, 33.9%

High — Above Average — Below Average — Low

SOURCES: Claritas Inc.; Simmons Market Research Bureau

NEARLY one in three Americans eschews the labels on either end of the political spectrum, inhabiting instead an amorphous centrist terrain, the middle of the road. Although it's tempting to think of moderates as apathetic voters — contemptuous of both politicians and government — they are nothing of the sort. In that great American tradition of voting like your parents, the nation's moderates can be traced to the New England Puritans whose descendants migrated westward and settled much of the northern tier of the country. These middle-of-the-roaders have very high voting patterns and consider themselves economic liberals and social conservatives. With the largest segment composed of white families and elderly couples with blue-collar jobs, they're concentrated in small towns and rural villages ideologically and geographically bridging the more liberal cities and conservative farm towns.

As a group, middle-of-the-roaders tend to lead lives of quiet moderation, avoiding solo pursuits, such as painting or jogging, in favor of group activities. The men like to bond on fishing junkets, the women enjoy bowling leagues, and everyone attends political rallies. They're somewhat traditional in their media tastes, enjoying radio stations that play golden oldies, baseball games, and nostalgia programs. But their preferences in magazines are more eclectic than the conservatives' fare, enjoying *Working Mother* and *Popular Science* in addition to *Good Housekeeping* and *Colonial Homes*.

Despite their fondness for stable middling pursuits, political moderates hold views across the ideological spectrum. Like liberals, they worry about environmental threats. Aligning with conservatives, they prefer a rightist social agenda, backing the pro-life movement, traditional religion, and school prayer. Mostly, though, surveys show they're open-minded Americans who, seated firmly on the fence, wait to be convinced by one side or the other. Moderates are the nation's swing voters that both liberals and conservatives must court in every election to win.

"Moderates are comfortable people, members of the Chamber of Commerce and involved in the church," observes Kenneth Martis, a political geography professor at West Virginia University. "They're straight out of the moralist tradition of the Puritans who thought of the state and society first. And they've carried that cultural baggage for generations."

# Abortion Banners

## People Who Advocate Banning Abortions

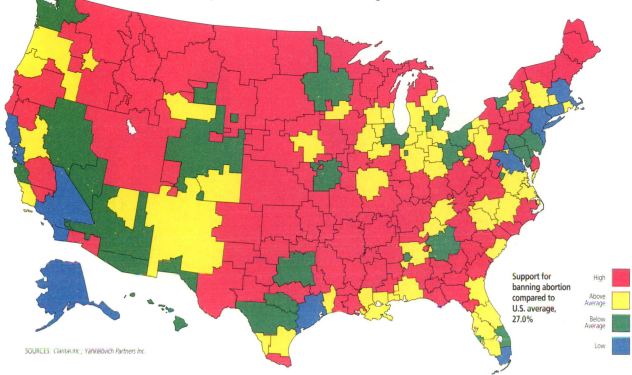

Support for banning abortion compared to U.S. average, 27.0%

High · Above Average · Below Average · Low

SOURCES: Claritas Inc.; Yankelovich Partners Inc.

OPINION polls consistently show a majority of Americans support abortion rights in some form, but it's hard to believe that looking at this map. Because abortion opponents are strongest in America's most sparsely settled areas, they seem to blanket much of the nation. In these wide-empty markets, particularly throughout the North Central states, they've been successful in getting legislatures to pass restrictive abortion laws that shut down abortion clinics and force women to travel increasingly longer distances to find available services.

That power encourages abortion opponents who, demographically speaking, resemble proletarian hayseeds. They're more likely than average Americans to have failed to finish high school, earn less than $20,000 annually (typically at factory and farm jobs), and live in relatively cheap housing. In their homes, they like to read the Bible, watch religious TV shows, and listen to gospel music. Outside, they enjoy activities that can only be described as contemporary blood sports: hunting, fishing, and watching pro wrestling. Although in their rhetoric, abortion opponents will describe a clinic as a "kill center" and defend their role as lifesavers, the map above is nearly identical to the map of those who support the death penalty. In other words, the staunchest pro-lifers also happen to be pro-executioners.

That irony isn't lost on the nation's abortion rights supporters, concentrated in America's densely populated upscale metropolitan areas. Compared to the U.S. average, they're more likely to have six-figure incomes, live in homes worth more than $500,000, and have completed post-graduate schooling. And their lifestyle tends to include tennis and travel, books and plays, newspapers like the *New York Times*, and magazines like *Forbes*.

This difference between abortion rights supporters and opponents helps explain why the debate has failed to produce a compromise: there's little common ground — in terms of geography, ideology, or lifestyle — to bridge the two sides. One group supports school prayer and traditional sexual roles, the other believes in environmentalism and women in the workforce. One drinks Kool-Aid at dinner, the other serves dry white wine.

# Shades of Gay

## Those in Favor of Gay Rights

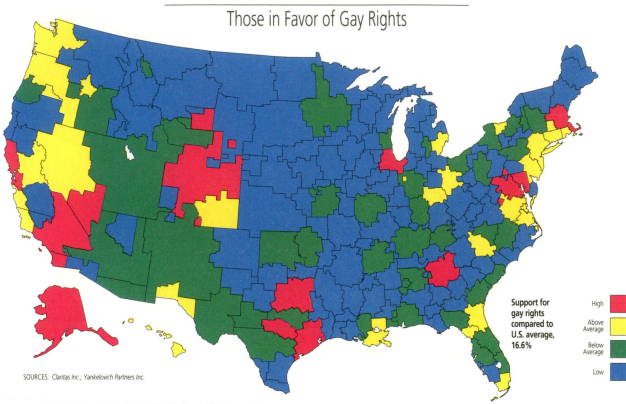

Support for gay rights compared to U.S. average, 16.6%

High
Above Average
Below Average
Low

SOURCES: *Claritas Inc.; Yankelovich Partners Inc.*

HERE'S one of the peculiar ironies of American life: While homosexual behavior is fairly widespread in the United States — some studies show as many as 20 percent of Americans have had a gay or lesbian experience — tolerance toward gays is not. Residents in only a handful of communities claim they favor gay rights, and many of those markets are located in states with tough anti-gay sodomy laws (such as Texas, Georgia, Maryland, and Nevada). Indeed, there's no correlation between the percentage of residents who back gay rights and the presence of laws sanctioning nontraditional families or banning discrimination against gays and lesbians.

The biggest factor behind a community's support for gay rights is proximity to other gays. The most tolerant markets are a mix of large metros and college towns that boast high concentrations of gay or lesbian residents. Demographically speaking, these folks tend to be urban singles who are mobile, under 34 years old, and hold white-collar jobs. "The freedom of the city allows the gay and lesbian community to live openly and to have a sense of community with their own bookstores, bars, and recreation centers," says Robin Kane, spokesperson for the National Gay and Lesbian Task Force. "And the visibility of the community allows it to grow exponentially."

The flip side, those Americans most opposed to gay rights, are more likely to be rural, married parents who are over 55 years old and have lived at the same address for years. They worry about protecting family values and advocate a return to traditional religious values and sexual relations. They prefer to keep their distance — literally and ideologically — from the nation's gays and lesbians.

What do lifestyle surveys show about America's gay-rights supporters? They seem to be fans of nightlife as well. They drink a lot (scotch, rum, cognac, wine, and beer) and like going out (to concerts, plays, and gambling casinos) as well as working out (jogging, racquetball, and exercise). They're also very accepting of other progressive social issues: they support a woman's right to an abortion, permit sex education on TV, and accept nudity in magazines (among their favorite titles: *GQ, Playboy,* and *Bon Appetit*).

Perhaps most important to the gay rights movement is that supporters come out of the closet. According to surveys, the backers of gay rights tend to be political activists determined to push for their agenda. But as the map shows, they'll need to push into America's heartland to be successful.

# Private Lives

## Those Concerned About Privacy

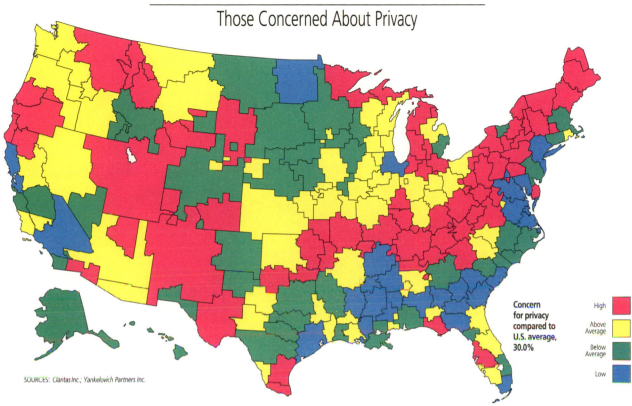

Concern for privacy compared to U.S. average, 30.0%

High
Above Average
Below Average
Low

SOURCES: Claritas Inc.; Yankelovich Partners Inc.

IT'S a decade after 1984, and Big Brother has settled into American homes like a nosy houseguest. Through credit bureaus, warranty cards, and shoppers clubs, he keeps track of what we buy and how we live in the nation's 95 million households. He captures our names, addresses, and lifestyle activities using Caller ID technology whenever we dial an 800 or 900 number. And thanks to a revolution in computer technology over the last decade, he can easily sell and swap files, building ever more detailed portraits of what credit cards we use, what soup we eat, what magazines we read, and what causes open our checkbooks. It's enough to make a private citizen head for the hills.

Which is exactly where you'll find those Americans who are most concerned about privacy. They live in some of the nation's most desolate areas: in the Appalachian, Ozark, and Rocky mountains as well as the Desert Southwest and the wilderness areas of Maine, Michigan's Upper Peninsula, and northern Idaho. Private people tend to be one of two kinds: downscale singles under 25 years old who work at blue-collar jobs and have a fondness for heavy metal music and hunting; or over-65 retirees who've lived in the same modest home for decades and enjoy country music and woodworking. All share a strong streak of independence, doing their own home improvements, fixing their own cars, preferring solitary fishing to gang bowling. Comparatively few read a daily newspaper — too much worldly news, no doubt — but a higher-than-average percentage pick up magazines like the *National Enquirer, True Story, Playboy,*

and — the epitome of an inward focus — *Self.*

Fortunately for direct marketers, the Americans most likely to be bombarded by junk mail and telemarketing intrusions — upscale city-dwellers — are the least concerned about privacy. Apparently for these people who've chosen to live cheek by jowl in dense metropolitan areas, there's no room for privacy. And while many vocal Americans have complained about invasions of privacy — 3.5 million have asked the Direct Marketing Association to delete their names from databases — they're a small minority. As former Oklahoma congressman Glenn English has so rightly observed, "Privacy is an issue in which public concern and interest is a mile wide and an inch deep."

# Chargers and Savers

## People with High Credit-Card Balances vs. Large Savings Accounts

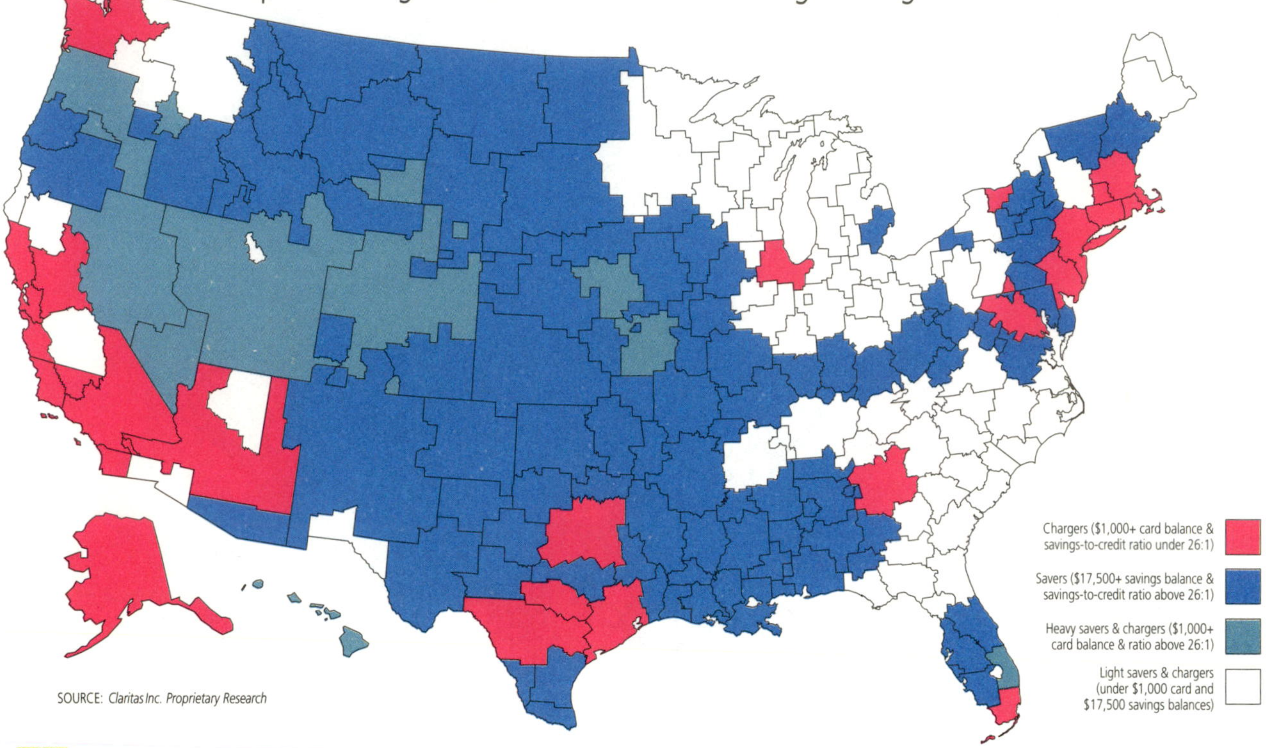

Chargers ($1,000+ card balance & savings-to-credit ratio under 26:1)

Savers ($17,500+ savings balance & savings-to-credit ratio above 26:1)

Heavy savers & chargers ($1,000+ card balance & ratio above 26:1)

Light savers & chargers (under $1,000 card and $17,500 savings balances)

SOURCE: *Claritas Inc. Proprietary Research*

HOW you handle your finances may be nobody's business but your own. But your tendency to save money rather than run up credit-card debt is as plain as the above map. Because the well-to-do have the resources to run up both balances, this map adjusts for their deep pockets by depicting areas where the *ratio* of an average household's savings account balance to its outstanding credit-card balance — that is, the impulse to use cash or credit — is above the national average.

Take America's savers, the 34 percent of all householders who, on average, have $22,964 socked away in passbook, checking, and money-market accounts. Demographically speaking, the nation's biggest savers tend disproportionately to be elderly, modestly educated, and downscale. Conservative in their outlook, they'll place what extra cash they have in insurance policies rather than gamble on

stocks. They avoid charge cards in part because they live on fixed incomes and want to avoid 18 percent credit-card interest charges.

But geography also plays a role. A significant percentage of savers live in sparsely populated towns throughout the Midwest where there are relatively few upscale stores. Residents here aren't pro-saving so much as anti-plastic; when they go shopping, they head for cash-and-carry stores. Moreover, savers' areas also mirror the heartland regions hardest hit by the mid-'80s recession. "These folks did their big-time charging earlier and are now trying to save their money to pay off their debt," says Paul Richard, a director of the National Center for Financial Education.

To find the nation's plastic people, the other 46 percent of U.S. households that maintain relatively high credit-card balances, look for two demographic groups. The first consists of young, urban singles

who rely on their charge cards to support the spiraling cost of living in cities like Boston and Los Angeles. These are the free spenders who visit gambling casinos, take cruises, and buy audio equipment. The second group of chargers consists of upscale, white-collar suburbanites who use their credit cards to maintain a sophisticated lifestyle. Rather than stashing their cash, they're more likely to blow their money on restaurants, theater tickets, and skiing trips.

One other factor separates heavy savers from heavy chargers: mobility. Chargers tend to rent their residences, lease their cars, and travel abroad at above-average rates. Savers are more likely to live at the same residence for decades, avoid airplanes, and prefer camping trips. When credit-card marketers tell them "Don't leave home without it," these people simply stay put.

# Green Consumers

## Those Willing to Pay 10% More for "Green" Products

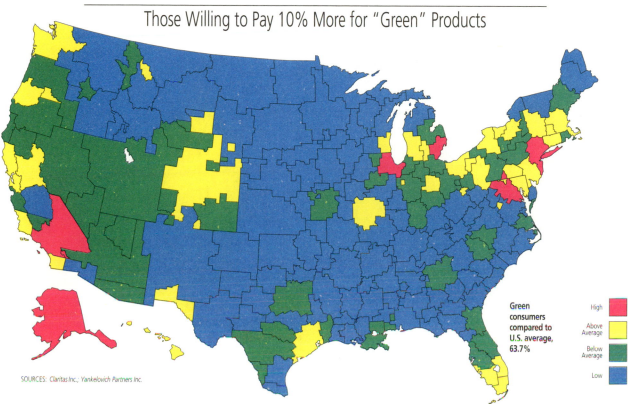

Green consumers compared to U.S. average, 63.7%

High
Above Average
Below Average
Low

SOURCES: *Claritas Inc.; Yankelovich Partners Inc.*

WHEN it comes to ecology, Americans seem to fall over their Birkenstocks claiming they're environmentalists. Once a fringe group, today nearly two-thirds of U.S. citizens tell pollsters that they're willing to pay 10 percent more to buy environmentally friendly "green" products. But market researchers also report only a small percentage of eco-sensitive consumers are willing to act on their beliefs. And the map above indicates that a disproportionate number live in only a handful of big-city markets — areas home to nearly one-quarter of all households — revealing a gap between word and deed throughout much of the nation west of Chicago.

Surprisingly, America's green consumers aren't the upscale politically correct who traditionally belong to environmental groups and believe that buying green products will improve the planet. The largest segment are predominantly single, lower-middle-class urbanites who equate green products with other trendy, specialty goods. They're politically liberal, musically hip — their favorite genres are jazz and modern rock — and they enjoy sports like tennis, skiing, racquetball, and aerobic exercise. Interestingly, they're not particularly big on the great outdoors, caring little for activities like camping, fishing, and hiking. They seem much more comfortable relaxing on their futons made from recycled materials, thumbing through a copy of *Rolling Stone,* and indulging in a bowl of Ben & Jerry's Rain Forest Crunch ice cream. At the supermarket these folks go for the status boost that comes with premium brand-name products.

Are green consumers merely another example of the MacNeil-Lehrer Syndrome — that curious phenomenon that occurs when people tell market surveyors they're watching a "serious" news program on PBS when in reality they're glued to "Three Stooges" reruns? In their defense, some Americans who want to be environmentally correct consumers don't have many friends in the marketplace. Many eco-sounding products actually do nothing for the environment. Still, the bottom line etched by this map is that a lot of Americans who say they'd pay more for green in their products are actually more concerned about the green in their wallets.

# Chicken Littles

## People Concerned About Ozone Depletion

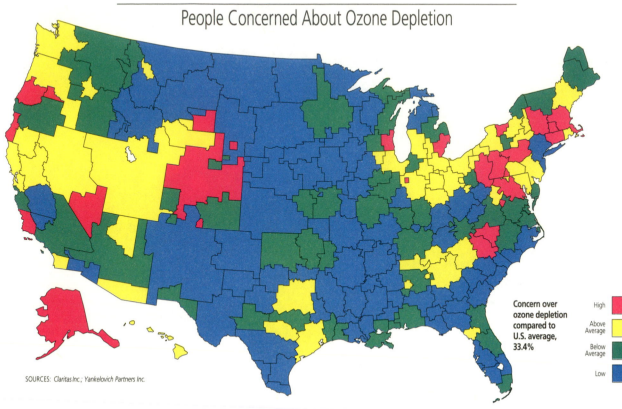

Concern over ozone depletion compared to U.S. average, 33.4%

High
Above Average
Below Average
Low

SOURCES: *Claritas Inc.; Yankelovich Partners Inc.*

THE ozone layer, the thin atmospheric shell that protects Earth's inhabitants from the sun's harshest ultraviolet rays, has been under attack by man-made chemicals since the start of the Industrial Revolution. But it's only since 1979 that scientists have been warning the public of danger-ously thinning ozone. Their big fear is that too much ozone will disap-pear, allowing hazardous sunlight to reach the earth, causing dramatic climate shifts, skin cancers, and early deaths. Already Australians, who experience a seasonal "ozone hole," cope with the harsh sunshine by donning shirts, hats, and plenty of sunscreen — a process nick-named "slip, slap, and slop."

But because ozone depletion is not well understood — or as palpa-ble as such other environmental threats as toxic dumps or water pollution — those alarmed about the condition generally are not the typical weekend Greenpeace war-riors. In fact, the largest group are sun-worshipers who hail from col-lege towns — like Eugene, Oreg., and Lafayette, Ind. — and Rust Belt city-dwellers who know firsthand what belching smokestacks can do to the environment. They're more likely than average Americans to hike, camp, sail, cycle, and fish, as well as vacation on Caribbean beaches and the Colorado ski slopes. They favor magazines that offer science news in a nontechni-cal style: *Discover* and *Popular Sci-ence* rather than *Scientific American* and *Psychology Today.* And attitude polls indicate that their concern about ozone has more to do with how the environmental threat will affect their leisure time and tan lines. Indeed, they're less worried about nuclear waste and endangered animals than about preserving nude beaches and dis-covering new vacation spots.

Demographically speaking, ozone alarmists are not the richest or smartest Americans: They tend to have some college experience, earn upper-middle-class incomes, and be in their twenties and thirties — folks who came of age after the first Earth Day in 1970. But if the above map is any indica-tion, those concerned markets should be growing. Surveys show that they're liberal, active in civic affairs, and like to host gatherings to spread the word about the prob-lem. "Issues like ozone depletion have become cocktail party conver-sation," observes Doug Moss, edi-tor and publisher of *E-Magazine.* "Even nightclub comedians are now making jokes about ozone."

# Giving a Hoot

## People Concerned About Endangered Animals

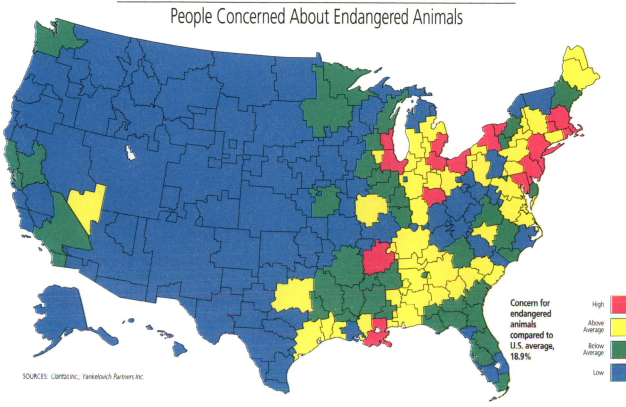

Concern for endangered animals compared to U.S. average, 18.9%

High
Above Average
Below Average
Low

SOURCES: Claritas Inc.; Yankelovich Partners Inc.

FEW maps reveal a more polarized American populace than this one, spotlighting the jobs-versus–endangered animals debate. The people who care most about the spotted owl and the gnatcatcher live in the nation's big cities east of the Mississippi — areas where asphalt began replacing animal life long ago. But most of the flashpoints of the controversy occur in rugged areas of the West where residents care little about saving wild animals except, perhaps, to get them in the crosshairs of their rifles. In both ideology and geography, the country is split down the middle when it comes to concern about endangered animals.

Moreover, other factors separate animal welfarists from their opponents. Supporters of endangered animals tend to be middle-class, twentysomething singles who read magazines like *GQ* and *Glamour.* Although they may have seen

endangered animals only in zoos, they've been sensitized to the issue in large part by environmental advocates. "Most of the major groups have their membership and fund-raising activities concentrated in the East and in larger metropolitan areas," says John Behm, director of the urban wildlife program division for the National Wildlife Federation. "The number of supporters in the cities just wipe out the number in rural areas."

Their opponents are more likely to be twice as old married couples living in small town and rural communities. The largest group is blue-collar workers who hold jobs in fishing, forestry, and mining — the very occupations that are often most affected by species-protection laws. These folks are big on outdoor activities like fishing, skiing, and target shooting; significantly, their numbers include residents of

the top ten markets for hunting. Their favorite reading matter includes *Field & Stream, Mother Earth News,* and local newspapers that, in Behm's words, "would present endangered animals as a human issue and not a global environmental one."

Still, the issue straddles both class and political lines. The yellow areas in the South represent a number of downscale mill towns with above-average rates of animal welfarists, reflecting in part a spiritual conviction that all God's creatures have rights. So it is that Americans who care about endangered animals — Northerners and Southerners, liberals and conservatives — include fans of jogging *and* pro wrestling, rap dancing *and* Broadway musicals. No doubt, the one fact that unites them is that few have ever been personally endangered by an animal.

# Capital Punishers

## Supporters of the Death Penalty

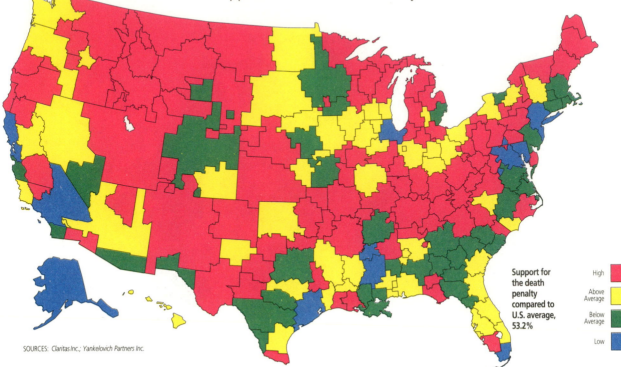

Support for the death penalty compared to U.S. average, 53.2%

High — Above Average — Below Average — Low

SOURCES: *Claritas Inc.; Yankelovich Partners Inc.*

FRONTIER justice isn't dead in America, if you read between the lines of this map. Although violent crimes resulting in capital punishment are concentrated in America's inner cities, residents in those communities are *least* likely to support the death penalty. Outside the nation's metros, however, an eye-for-an-eye doctrine reigns. Support for the death penalty is widespread across the country, especially in the most isolated communities. As civil libertarian Henry Schwarschild recently observed, "Our culture seems to be in a very bad mood."

What kind of Americans support a punishment that's been banned in Canada, Mexico, and throughout Western Europe? Traditionalists, mainly. Proponents tend to be high school–educated blue-collar factory and farm workers. They're big fans of country music, fishing, and rodeos — the kind of folks who buy American cars (Chevys, Fords, and Dodges are big among them) and read magazines like *1001 Home Ideas, Colonial Homes,* and *Outdoor Life.* Although they describe themselves as middle-of-the-roaders, their political attitudes are decidedly right of center. Polls find that those who support the death penalty also oppose abortion rights, gay rights, and the environmental movement.

In some respects, their tough stance on criminals can be explained by other factors, most prominently their uncertain economic status: While death penalty proponents have middle-class incomes, many have taken out bank loans and are working hard to keep up their payments for mortgages, personal loans, auto loans, and home-improvement loans. Then again, there may be a link between their approach to capital punishment and their personal attitudes toward killing in general. Many of the hot markets for death penalty support are identical to the ones where Americans enjoy hunting game for support. Proponents of the you-are-what-you-eat nutrition theory also may see a correlation between hard-hearted philosophy and their artery-hardening diets. One marketing poll found their four most popular foods are, in descending order, bacon, frankfurters, sausage, and ham.

# Praise the Lord and Pass the Joint

## Supporters of Legalizing Drugs vs. School Prayer

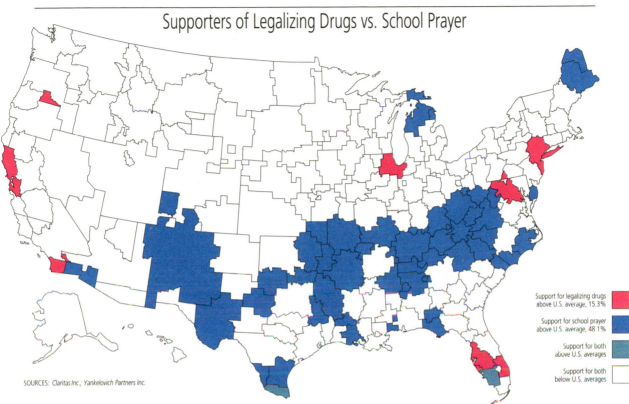

Support for legalizing drugs
above U.S. average, 15.3%

Support for school prayer
above U.S. average, 48.1%

Support for both
above U.S. averages

Support for both
below U.S. averages

SOURCES: *Claritas Inc.; Yankelovich Partners Inc.*

AMERICANS are basically a patriotic people, but that doesn't mean everyone agrees with the law of the land. This map highlights areas where citizens from both ends of the political spectrum want public prohibitions ended: from the left, the ban on drugs, from the right, the outlawing of school prayer.

Take the grassroots movement supporting legalized drugs, composed, it seems, of energetic hedonists. Most are young, single urbanites who cite attending rock concerts as their favorite activity and support greater acceptance of nude beaches as one of their pet political causes. Tending to work in business or entertainment services, they're big on drinking and crazy about recordings — from rock and jazz to comedy and Broadway musicals. Interestingly, they have relatively few financial investments (perhaps their money goes up in smoke) and they seem averse to life insurance. While they may be fiscally unfit, physically they're quite healthy. They're much more likely than average Americans to be joggers and to belong to health clubs.

In contrast, there's a small-town, Southern bias among those who want to see prayer returned to the classroom, but the most defining characteristic is kids. These conservative families are big on minivans, the Disney Channel, *Seventeen* magazine, and junk food. Many of the adults are traditionalists in other areas besides prayer: they support the death penalty, traditional women's roles, and respect for the elderly. When they're not working at blue-collar jobs, they like to spend their time in old-fashioned pursuits like fishing, hunting, and gardening. Oddly enough, teenagers in these areas also buy a lot of heavy metal music, perhaps one reason that their parents are so adamant about getting prayer back into their children's lives.

Given the sharp, liberal-conservative split on these issues, it's no surprise that few markets have above-average support for both legalizing drugs and returning prayer to the schools. Still, there are two unusual markets where both issues play well: McAllen-Brownsville, Tex., whose population is 75 percent Hispanic, and Ft. Myers–Naples, Fla., where the median age is 57. While both communities are otherwise conservative on social issues, the Texas border residents are accepting of drug smuggling from Mexico while the elderly Florida residents believe it's okay to take any kind of medication to alleviate the ailments of old age. As on many maps, defining the borders of these support groups is an exercise in human as well as geographical distinctions.

# The Markets

## What's Hot / What's Not Across the USA

THIS SECTION offers profiles of the nation's 209 consumer markets as defined by Arbitron's Areas of Dominant Influence (ADIs), plus the Alaska and Hawaii markets not relegated to any ADI. Each capsule portrait includes demographic data and lifestyle information divided into lists of What's Hot and What's Not compared to national averages. Eleven categories of interests are presented in these lists in the following order:

- Lifestyle Highlights
- Sports/Leisure
- Household Products
- Television
- Music/Radio
- Periodicals
- Food
- Drink
- Cars/Trucks
- Financial
- Politics/Issues

## Abilene-Sweetwater, Texas

| What's Hot | What's Not |
|---|---|
| Grandchildren, sweepstakes, rodeos, crafts | Foreign travel, books, wine, real estate |
| Fishing, hunting, sewing, gardening | Tennis, jogging, racquetball, bowling, golf |
| Garden tillers, recliners, video games | PCs, CD players, faxes, radar detectors |
| "Price Is Right," "Major Dad," "Sally" | C-SPAN, "Joan Rivers," "In Living Color" |
| Spanish radio, gospel, country | All-news radio, classical music, jazz, rock |
| *Field & Stream, Ladies' Home Journal, Cycle* | *Fortune, Food & Wine, Money, Ski* |
| Ham, hot dogs, canned soup, Fritos, candy | Frusen Gladje, spaghetti, yogurt, Grey Poupon |
| Tea, Kool-Aid, light beer, Diet 7-Up | Imported and draft beer, ale, skim milk |
| Chevy pickups, Dodge Omnis, Ford Crown Victorias | Peugeots, Infinitis, Acuras, VWs |
| Mail-order medical insurance, money orders | Mutual funds, IRAs, AmEx cards |
| Conservatives, pro-lifers, less government | Liberals, endangered animals, ocean dumping |

IF THE ADS FOR denture cleansers and hair color products don't give it away, the demographics will: the Abilene-Sweetwater market is crawling with grandparents. Nearly 40 percent of the residents are over 55 years old and, coupled with the fact that marriage and children are popular in this part of Texas, the lifestyle is dominated by retirees who like to dote on their grandkids. Local consumers buy home video games, make craft trinkets, and attend rodeos all at above-average rates. In addition, Abilene-Sweetwater's rustic origins — the area was settled in the late 19th century by ranchers and buffalo hunters — make outdoor activities like hunting and horseback riding popular. But with relatively low education and income levels, there's an insular quality to their adventurism. Compared to the general population, the local citizenry travel little, not to foreign countries, gambling casinos, or ski resorts. Many would just as soon relax around a backyard grill — preferably with a grandchild bouncing on their knee.

| Downscale rural area | Racially diverse couples and families | Less than high school educations | Farming and industrial jobs |
|---|---|---|---|

### Key Demographics

| | | | |
|---|---|---|---|
| Total Population: | 284,337 | Primary Ages of Adults: | 55+ |
| Median Household Income: | $23,096 | Median Home Value: | $39,145 |

# Albany, Georgia

| What's Hot | What's Not |
|---|---|
| Home improvement, pest control, the Bible | Unions, health clubs, casinos, theater |
| Fishing, college basketball, pro wrestling | Golf, bowling, racquetball, sailing |
| Pickups, chain saws, cable TV, mobile homes | Sofa beds, lawn furniture, VCRs |
| Game shows, BET, "Fresh Prince," "Family Feud" | "Letterman," VH-1, "Married with Children" |
| Urban contemporary, country, rap, gospel | Modern rock, classical, easy listening |
| *National Enquirer, Southern Living, Ebony* | *Omni, Ski, Self, Forbes, Bon Appetit* |
| Sausage, peanut butter, BBQ sauce, Twinkies | Beef, tuna, Taco Bell, rice cakes, pretzels |
| Colas, orange juice, malt liquor, whole milk | Imported wine, ale, Diet Slice, herbal tea |
| Dodge Rams, Ford 350s, Olds 98s, Chevy Camaros | Porsche 928s, Infinitis, Saab 9000s, Ferraris |
| Loans, Medicare, whole-life insurance | $10,000+ in stocks, money-market accounts |
| Conservatives, traditional family values | Liberals, gay rights, military cutbacks |

WHAT CAN YOU SAY about a community where the *National Enquirer* and the *Star* are two of the hottest publications? For one thing, education isn't a high priority. Indeed, more than half of the adults in Albany failed to graduate from high school and less than 10 percent made it through college. Like other industrial cities in the Southeast, Albany is a pocket of conservative values, where the Bible may be the only book in the house, ethnic foods are rarely eaten, and veterans clubs are a lot more popular than health clubs. Modest incomes and home values — half of the residences are valued at under $50,000 — make home-improvement projects popular: residents install their own carpets, kitchen cabinets, and car batteries at above-average rates. But the South's infamous bugs present problems too massive for these do-it-yourselfers: termite- and pest-control services are used at some of the highest rates in the nation.

| *Working-class industrial city* | *Racially diverse families* | *Less than high school educations* | *Blue-collar manufacturing jobs* |
|---|---|---|---|

| **Key Demographics** | Total Population: | 371,786 | Primary Ages of Adults: | 25–44 |
|---|---|---|---|---|
| | Median Household Income: | $23,517 | Median Home Value: | $51,848 |

# Albany-Schenectady-Troy, New York

| What's Hot | What's Not |
|---|---|
| TV bowling, fraternal orders, coupon clipping | Theme parks, health clubs, sweepstakes |
| Golf, knitting, skiing, gardening, boating | Tennis, racquetball, jogging, sailing |
| Power tools, 35mm cameras, thermal windows | CD players, sofa beds, PCs, bicycles |
| "Evening Shade," "Coach," Lifetime, TV golf | Disney, "American Gladiators," "Family Matters" |
| Broadway and pop music, radio baseball | Jazz, classical, rap, rhythm & blues |
| *American Health, Golf Digest, Colonial Homes* | *Barron's, Vogue, Playboy, GQ, Tennis* |
| Pasta, pork & beans, Shake 'N Bake, nuts | Mexican food, canned chicken, rice, jam, gum |
| Diet Coke, skim milk, Pabst, ground coffee | Malt liquor, regular cola, rum, spring water |
| Subarus, Dodges, GMC Sierras, Chevy 4x4s | Porsches, Mercedes-Benzes, Jaguars, convertibles |
| Savings bonds, mutual funds, car loans | $50,000+ in stocks, gold cards, Keoghs |
| Moderates, nuclear waste, less government | Liberals, gun control, legalizing drugs |

ALBANY MAY BE the capital of one of the nation's biggest states, but its lifestyle resembles that of a coastal retirement resort. That's because the Albany-Schenectady-Troy market is filled with a mature population, housing stock, and approach to leisure. Most of the area's popular sports — bowling, fishing, and sailing — can be accomplished without working up an aerobic sweat. Even leisure activities can be done without leaving a reclining chair: reading books, collecting coins, doing crossword puzzles, and knitting are popular at rates above the national average. Because area consumers are comfortably fixed — with upper-middle-class incomes, midscale home values and above-average rates for college degrees — they have the time to stop and smell the gourmet cooking. Living in the shadow of the capitol building, it's no wonder they're more involved in civic activities than the general population. Contrary to most political trends that draw a direct link between age and conservative values, these folks are moderate, environmentally minded, and consumer-conscious. In Albany, chablis-and-conservation lovers thrive.

| *Middle-class state capital* | *Predominantly white singles and couples* | *High school educations* | *Manufacturing and service jobs* |
|---|---|---|---|

| **Key Demographics** | Total Population: | 1,345,711 | Primary Ages of Adults: | 25–44 |
|---|---|---|---|---|
| | Median Household Income: | $35,751 | Median Home Value: | $107,861 |

# Albuquerque, New Mexico

| What's Hot | What's Not |
|---|---|
| Rodeos, RVs, PCs, science fiction, fine art | Book clubs, foreign travel, casinos, coupons |
| Camping, skiing, running, woodworking | Boating, tennis, golf, bowling, gardening |
| Cameras, smoke detectors, recliners, grills | Home gyms, toaster ovens, faxes |
| "Primetime Live," "Tonight Show," "Cops" | "Seinfeld," "I Love Lucy," "General Hospital" |
| Spanish radio, country, golden oldies | News-talk radio, gospel, rhythm & blues |
| *Country Living, Sunset, Cycle World, McCall's* | *Money, Mademoiselle, GQ, New Yorker* |
| Chili, pudding, dried fruit, beef | Raisin bread, yogurt, TV dinners, Popeye's |
| Diet Pepsi, Coke, 7-Up, decaf coffee | Wine, ale, Sangria, malt liquor, cognac |
| Subarus, Chevy Geos, Mercury Grand Marquises | Alfa Romeos, BMWs, Volvo 940s, Acuras |
| Investment property, tax-sheltered annuities | IRAs, precious metals, stocks, savings bonds |
| Conservatives, school prayer, toxic waste | Liberals, ERA, gun control, gay TV themes |

IN *THE RIGHT STUFF*, Tom Wolfe described postwar Albuquerque as a "dirty red sod-hut tortilla highway desert city," but locals have never minded its woeful reputation. Compared to other Americans who travel hither and yon at the drop of a frequent flyer card, folks around here rarely travel by plane, train, or even bus for a weekend getaway. Having settled in this sprawling, car-dependent city bordered by mountains, they take full advantage of the ancient pueblos and wide-open landscape nearby. They camp, hike, ski, and hunt at rates far above the national average. Among their favorite magazines are *Outdoor Life, Sports Afield*, and *Field & Stream*. Although the median household income and home value are nothing to brag about, residents have gone to college at greater than average rates, and they share plenty of "good-life" activities. Many attend political and cultural events — as long as they're close to home. Even hot air balloonists come to Albuquerque when they gather for their annual festival.

| *Lower-middle-class urban area* | *Ethnically diverse singles and families* | *Some college educations* | *White-collar professionals* |
|---|---|---|---|

**Key Demographics**

| Total Population: | 1,502,251 | Primary Ages of Adults: | 25–44 |
|---|---|---|---|
| Median Household Income: | $26,605 | Median Home Value: | $74,866 |

# Alexandria, Louisiana

| What's Hot | What's Not |
|---|---|
| Veterans clubs, video games, the Bible, RVs | Movies, dancing, real estate investments |
| Fishing, hunting, running, sewing, bowling | Tennis, skiing, golf, sailing, exercise |
| Cable TV, RVs, mobile homes, chain saws | Food processors, radios, lawn furniture |
| "Classic Concentration," "Donahue," soaps | "Wonder Years," "Face the Nation," C-SPAN |
| Country, religious radio, urban contemporary | All-news radio, modern rock, radio football |
| *True Story, Southern Living, Ebony* | *Fortune, Scientific American, Self* |
| Bacon, seafood, rice, brownies, Church's | Sour cream, popcorn, rye, Trix, TGIF's |
| Cola, malt liquor, powdered drinks | Cocktails, Heineken, wine, skim milk |
| Pontiacs, Chryslers, Chevrolets, Ford F350s | Infinitis, Acuras, Hondas, Peugeots, VWs |
| Money orders, Medicare, mail-order insurance | Credit cards, stocks, mutual funds, annuities |
| Conservatives, school prayer, family values | Liberals, consumerism, abortion rights |

IN MANY WAYS, Alexandria is a city lost in a bygone era — before computers, before women joined the workforce, before folks realized that it takes a college degree to climb the socioeconomic ladder. As it is, Alexandria remains a downscale backwater in central Louisiana with only 10 percent of its adults holding college degrees and 21 percent describing themselves as homemakers — much higher than the national average. Given the relatively low incomes — 45 percent of area households earn less than $20,000 a year — many residents lead self-sufficient lives: fishing, hunting, sewing, and gardening all at above-average rates. There's little time spent on art, fashion, or the latest in gourmet cooking. Alexandria residents would rather read the Bible than most books and magazines, relax at a veterans club as opposed to a health club, and work on their car rather than attend a cultural event. Not that residents don't realize that money is the root of their downscale lifestyles: one of the most popular domestic activities is entering sweepstakes.

| *Small, downscale industrial city* | *Racially diverse families* | *High school educations* | *Farm, clerical, and manufacturing jobs* |
|---|---|---|---|

**Key Demographics**

| Total Population: | 255,100 | Primary Ages of Adults: | 18–34 |
|---|---|---|---|
| Median Household Income: | $20,993 | Median Home Value: | $50,194 |

# Alpena, Michigan

### What's Hot

Rodeos, tobacco products, baking, sewing
Hunting, waterskiing, horseback riding
Recliners, ceiling fans, power tools, rifles
"Guiding Light," "Major Dad," "Full House"
Country music, golden oldies, gospel
*Reader's Digest, Family Handyman, Woman's Day*
Ham, crackers, pizza, snack cakes, Jell-O
Tea, Countrytime, vegetable juice, Pepsi-Cola
Olds, Dodge 4x4 pickups, Ford Crown Victorias
Mail-order life and medical insurance
Moderates, death penalty, pro-lifers

### What's Not

Rock concerts, fashion, politics, casinos
Jogging, downhill skiing, racquetball
Radar detectors, PCs, sofa beds, stereos
"Simpsons," "Doogie Howser," "Honeymooners"
Soft rock, classical, news-talk radio
*Travel & Leisure, Inc., Architectural Digest*
Chicken, rice, take-out, Wheaties, chocolates
Wine, ale, imported beer, malt liquor
Toyotas, Nissans, Mazdas, Mitsubishi minivans
Credit cards, brokerage accounts, bonds
Liberals, gay TV themes, oil drilling

RODEOS, chewing tobacco, hunting, and horseback riding: at first glance, the consumer surveys draw the profile of a classic Old West cow town. But the distinct lack of Japanese cars is one clue that Alpena is a century-old resort town located on northern Michigan's Thunder Bay. What gives this market its rustic flavor is its rural setting, its large percentage of retirees — half the residents are over 53 years old — and its 19th-century housing stock. In Alpena, which could double as a set for *On Golden Pond,* residents go boating, hiking, and fishing at above-average rates. At home, their favorite domestic activities include the three C's of retirement living: crafts, collectibles, and crossword puzzles. Household incomes are low, but these residents have the time if not the money to maintain a quality lifestyle. Nearly one-third have home workshops, the better to work on their cars, renovate their kitchens, and tend their elaborate gardens — all at rates above the U.S. average.

| *Downscale retirement resort* | *Predominantly white couples and families* | *High school educations* | *Blue-collar farm, craft, and labor jobs* |
| --- | --- | --- | --- |

## Key Demographics

| | | | | |
| --- | --- | --- | --- | --- |
| Total Population: | 41,286 | | Primary Ages of Adults: | 55+ |
| Median Household Income: | $23,078 | | Median Home Value: | $46,268 |

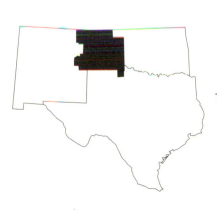

# Amarillo, Texas

### What's Hot

CNN, auto racing, country clubs, dogs
Bowling, boating, camping, woodworking
Tupperware, cameras, video games, motorcycles
ESPN, "Coach," "Family Matters," "Top Cops"
Country music, adult contemporary radio
*Popular Mechanics, Good Housekeeping, Cycle*
Sausage, tortilla chips, canned soup, candy
Kool-Aid, Diet Coke, coffee, light beer
Mercurys, Subarus, Chevy Geos and pickups
Auto loans, mutual funds, CDs
Moderates, death penalty, family values

### What's Not

Foreign travel, books, wine, theme parks
Weight training, racquetball, sailing
Toaster ovens, home gyms, sofa beds, PCs
"Hard Copy," "Joan Rivers," "Star Trek," "Loving"
Rap, soft rock, classical music, news radio
*Esquire, Cosmopolitan, Scientific American*
Chicken, tuna, spaghetti sauce, Ponderosa
Milk, orange juice, Coca-Cola, ale, scotch
Infinitis, Volvos, Alfa Romeos, Lexus ES300s
Gold cards, stocks, Christmas clubs
Liberals, abortion rights, ozone depletion

IN AMARILLO, TEXAS, a billboard might read: "Kids Welcome." Within this former oil boomtown turned world-class cattle market, more than half the households have at least one child still home — and, not surprisingly, a fondness for home video games, cameras, pets, and crafts. This group-oriented market influences the leisure time of Amarillo's citizens: they're more likely than average Americans to belong to veterans clubs, fraternal orders, and country clubs. For women, the idea of a night out is attending a Tupperware party; for men it's meeting over a Lone Star at the bowling alley or the weekly livestock auction. And yet, for all their fondness for belonging, union membership is still below average — and residents express little commitment to the buy-American ethic. In this part of the country, local allegiances are to the Texas Panhandle first and the rest of the world afterwards.

| *Lower-middle-class industrial city* | *Ethnically diverse families* | *High school educations* | *Farm, labor, and construction jobs* |
| --- | --- | --- | --- |

## Key Demographics

| | | | | |
| --- | --- | --- | --- | --- |
| Total Population: | 450,796 | | Primary Ages of Adults: | 18–34 |
| Median Household Income: | $25,386 | | Median Home Value: | $47,841 |

# Anniston, Alabama

## What's Hot

Home decorating, video games, the Bible
Gardening, fishing, hunting, jogging
Used cars, mobile homes, charcoal grills
"Oprah," "Today," "Major Dad"
Religious radio, college football, country
*Star, Soap Opera Digest, Southern Living*
Beef stew, American cheese, Fritos, brownies
Cola, powdered drinks, tea, milk, cocoa
Pontiacs, Dodge Omnis, Chevy Camaros
Home-improvement loans, Christmas clubs
Conservatives, nuclear waste, death penalty

## What's Not

Dancing, pregnancy-test kits, movies, gambling
Camping, skiing, golf, bicycling, boating
Cameras, comedy records, VCRs, microwaves
TV golf, "Siskel & Ebert," "Golden Girls"
Soft rock, middle-of-the-road, news-talk radio
*Discover, Business Week, Gourmet, Self*
Beef, TV dinners, raisin bread, Denny's
Diet RC Cola, Slice, 7-Up, wine, beer
Audis, Acuras, Volvos, Saab 9000s, BMW 6s
Brokerage accounts, bonds, gold cards
Liberals, oil drilling, consumerism

IT'S EASY TO DIVIDE Americans into fans of print or electronic media, and Anniston is firmly in the latter camp. With a higher-than-average percentage of women describing themselves as homemakers, Anniston's TV sets are tuned to soaps and game shows during the day, flicked to the early-evening news when the men come home from industrial jobs, and on to prime-time drama and professional wrestling at night — all told, upwards of seven hours of TV viewing each day. Of course, the weekends are reserved for sports, whether it's auto racing on TV or college sports on the radio. Surveys confirm that Anniston residents have relatively low rates for reading newspapers — even those devoted to sports or entertainment — and rarely pick up a magazine devoted to business, fashion, or science. Politically, like many Dixie districts, this is a conservative Democratic area where voters support school prayer and the death penalty while opposing abortion and consumerism.

| Working-class mill town | Racially diverse singles and couples | Less than high school educations | Blue-collar mining and manufacturing jobs |
| --- | --- | --- | --- |

**Key Demographics**

| | | | |
| --- | --- | --- | --- |
| Total Population: | 115,901 | Primary Ages of Adults: | 35–54 |
| Median Household Income: | $26,397 | Median Home Value: | $55,302 |

# Ardmore-Ada, Oklahoma

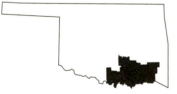

## What's Hot

Mobile homes, denture cleansers, sewing, dogs
Target shooting, fishing, pro wrestling
Compact pickups, shocks, washing machines
"Current Affair," "Murder, She Wrote"
Country, religious radio, heavy metal
*TV Guide, Woman's World, Outdoor Life*
Baked beans, pie, sausage, American cheese
Tea, tomato juice, ground coffee
Dodge Omnis, Ford Festivas, GMC pickups
Medicare, money orders, $50,000+ in stocks
Conservatives, school prayer, toxic waste

## What's Not

Newspapers, wine, lawn furniture, movies
Sailing, swimming, bicycling, bowling
Cameras, PCs, home gyms, books, toaster ovens
TV tennis, "Sisters," "Joan Rivers," HBO
Rock 'n' roll, jazz, classical, all-news radio
*Smithsonian, Mademoiselle, Food & Wine*
Tuna, pasta, waffles, TV dinners, Red Lobster
Imported beer, Diet Coke, Diet 7-Up
VWs, Volvos, Mazda RX-7s, Saturn SCs
IRAs, mutual funds, credit cards, bonds
Liberals, gay rights, green consumerism

ARDMORE-ADA is a throwback to the time when Americans were rugged individualists. Here, residents still ride horses, smoke nonfilter cigarettes, and provide food on the table by fishing and hunting. According to surveys, you won't find these folks wearing tennis togs, playing a round of golf, or joining a health club. They're people of faith — they tune in to religious radio stations and read the Bible twice as often as average Americans — and they rarely pick up anything as sophisticated as *Rolling Stone, Vogue,* or *Gourmet*. There are plenty of traditional women in Ardmore-Ada, thank-you very much, including a higher-than-average percentage of widows and women who describe themselves as homemakers. In opinion surveys, these residents wish for a return to traditional values in religion, family, and sexual relations; unlike urban women, they express no desire for more time during the day to spend on housework.

| Downscale rural area | Predominantly white couples and families | Less than high school educations | Farm, labor, and manufacturing jobs |
| --- | --- | --- | --- |

**Key Demographics**

| | | | |
| --- | --- | --- | --- |
| Total Population: | 184,612 | Primary Ages of Adults: | 55+ |
| Median Household Income: | $19,127 | Median Home Value: | $37,714 |

# Atlanta, Georgia

| What's Hot | What's Not |
|---|---|
| Politics, home furnishing, frequent flying | Car repair, veterans clubs, crafts, dancing |
| Exercise, racquetball, tennis, jogging | Bowling, hunting, knitting, boating, golf |
| Cable TV, PCs, VCRs, video games | Motorcycles, puzzles, food processors |
| "Fresh Prince," "Seinfeld," "Oprah" | TV bowling, "Northern Exposure," "Letterman" |
| Jazz, gospel, rap, pop, classical | Golden oldies, middle-of-the-road, radio baseball |
| *Jet, Essence, GQ, Gourmet, Fortune, Us* | *Mechanix Illustrated, Self, Parents, McCall's* |
| Take-out, grits, beef stew, BBQ sauce, Trix | Beef, English muffins, cheese, canned fruit |
| Cola, diet soft drinks, malt liquor, rum | Draft beer, ground coffee, tomato juice |
| Mazdas, Infinitis, BMWs, Nissan 300ZXs | Buicks, Mercurys, Olds Cierras, Subaru Justys |
| Gold cards, real estate investments, stocks | Savings bonds, CDs, money-market accounts |
| Liberals, school prayer, abortion rights | Moderates, military cutbacks, death penalty |

TALK ABOUT ECLECTIC. In Atlanta, residents like to listen to everything from jazz and classical music to gospel, modern rock, and rap. Their favorite magazines run the gamut from *Gourmet* and *Us* to the *Wall Street Journal* and the *National Enquirer*. Compared to most of the slow and easygoing South, the bright lights of "Hotlanta" seem to have attracted a populace of overachievers. While Atlantans as a whole have middle-class incomes and working-class educational levels — 76 percent of all adults never completed college — many of their tastes are decidedly upscale. They possess gold cards, attend cultural events, buy designer fashions, and invest in real estate all at above-average rates. The most popular cars include luxury imports like BMWs, Porsches, Volvos, and Ferraris. Contrary to Atlanta's semi-official motto, "the city too busy to hate," this is still a Southern city that remains socially segregated. Not so in diners, however, where patrons — white and black, yuppie and laborer — can order croissants side by side with grits.

| *Middle-class metropolitan sprawl* | *Racially diverse families* | *High school educations* | *Professional, administrative, and sales jobs* |
|---|---|---|---|

| **Key Demographics** | Total Population: | 4,013,824 | Primary Ages of Adults: | 25–44 |
|---|---|---|---|---|
| | Median Household Income: | $37,847 | Median Home Value: | $92,036 |

# Augusta, Georgia

| What's Hot | What's Not |
|---|---|
| Bus travel, cable TV, crafts, fried chicken | Finance magazines, fashion, the arts, unions |
| Walking, fishing, dancing, gardening | Exercise, camping, sailing, golf, skiing |
| Microwaves, pickups, dining room furniture | Toaster ovens, food processors, power tools |
| TV soaps, "Blossom," "Golden Girls," Disney | "Face the Nation," "Beverly Hills, 90210" |
| Gospel, rhythm & blues, rap | Easy listening, rock, radio baseball |
| *Ebony, Jet, Soap Opera Digest, Health* | *Sunset, Omni, Changing Times, Bon Appetit* |
| Peanut butter, beef stew, rice, Church's | Chicken, pasta, nuts, Ponderosa Steak House |
| Cola, tea, diet sodas, whole milk | Beer, wine, tomato juice, lemon-lime sodas |
| Nissans, Isuzus, Mazda 929s, Dodge Rams | Saabs, Jaguars, Subarus, VW Golfs |
| Whole life insurance, money orders, loans | Investment property, annuities, savings bonds |
| Conservatives, school prayer, toxic waste | Moderates, gay rights, legalizing drugs |

IF YOU ARE WHAT YOU EAT, Augusta's citizenry ought to be clucking. Residents frequent Church's, Popeye's, and Kentucky Fried Chicken outlets at higher rates than almost any other U.S. market. And yet area shoppers buy fresh chicken and coatings like Shake 'N Bake at below-average rates — clearly these consumers don't have bake-from-scratch lifestyles. In fact, many of Augusta's residents are laborers and assembly-line workers — including women who work outside the home at high rates. It's a noisy existence, and not just in the clanking textile mills: locals buy rhythm & blues and rap music at above-average rates. But with money tight, Augusta citizens have to make their own entertainment; they're big on daytime soaps, cable sitcom reruns, and talk shows hosted by Oprah and Donahue. Indeed, except for churches and nightclubs, the most popular meeting places seem to be fried-chicken joints.

| *Working-class industrial city* | *Racially diverse families* | *Less than high school educations* | *Manufacturing and administrative jobs* |
|---|---|---|---|

| **Key Demographics** | Total Population: | 603,146 | Primary Ages of Adults: | 25–44 |
|---|---|---|---|---|
| | Median Household Income: | $29,046 | Median Home Value: | $63,337 |

# Austin, Texas

| What's Hot | What's Not |
|---|---|
| Music clubs, movies, dancing, job seminars | Religious clubs, lotteries, home improvement |
| Skiing, hiking, weight training, exercise | Fishing, walking, target shooting, bowling |
| PCs, musical instruments, condoms, books | Pregnancy-test kits, ceiling fans, 35mm cameras |
| "Simpsons," "Letterman," NCAA Basketball | "Love Connection," "Sally," "Hard Copy" |
| Country, rhythm & blues, rock, swing, folk | Gospel music, urban contemporary, news radio |
| *Scientific American, Ski, Cycle World, Self* | *Star, Popular Mechanics, Prevention, Inc.* |
| Pizza, health food, corn chips, cheese, gum | Cold cuts, doughnuts, beef stew, Pop Tarts |
| Imported beer, domestic wine, spring water | Whole milk, tea, orange juice, Pabst |
| Ferraris, Saabs, Audis, VWs, Subarus, BMWs | Buicks, Dodges, Oldsmobiles, Chevy Luminas |
| Savings accounts, mutual funds, auto tellers | Life insurance, credit cards, CDs, Medicare |
| Liberals, gay rights, less government | Moderates, endangered animals, ocean dumping |

MUSICIANS FROM ACROSS the country settled in this state capital for its eclectic club scene — a melting pot of country, rock, folk, and blues — and supportive college community. The relatively young populace, two-thirds of whom are under 44, seem in perpetual motion: jogging, skiing, and hiking out-of-doors, exercising, lifting weights, and dancing in the nightclubs indoors. Those associated with government have a more sedentary if sophisticated lifestyle: many Austin residents read books, listen to classical music, and belong to country clubs all at rates above the national average. This split personality becomes readily apparent in the most popular magazines, which include science journals as well as motorcycle rags. As for Austin's common ground, residents of all stripes are drawn to the local cultural scene; the city has attracted musicians, artists, and writers since the 1960s. Austin is one of the few Texas cities where residents are more likely to attend an arts event than work on their cars.

| Middle-class state capital | Ethnically diverse singles and couples | College educations | White-collar professionals |
|---|---|---|---|

## Key Demographics

| | | | |
|---|---|---|---|
| Total Population: | 1,013,774 | Primary Ages of Adults: | 18–34 |
| Median Household Income: | $30,666 | Median Home Value: | $80,164 |

# Bakersfield, California

| What's Hot | What's Not |
|---|---|
| Baking, casinos, RVs, theme parks, dogs | Gourmet cooking, convertibles, book clubs |
| Powerboating, bowling, waterskiing, sewing | Sailing, jogging, golf, tennis, lottery |
| Tupperware, motorcycles, minivans, recliners | CD players, faxes, microwaves |
| "Roseanne," "Coach," "60 Minutes," ESPN | Game shows, "Regis & Kathie Lee," Cinemax |
| Country, heavy metal, pop | Jazz, classical, soft rock, religious radio |
| *1001 Home Ideas, TV Guide, Home Mechanix* | Newspapers, *Barron's, Ski, Self, GQ, Gourmet* |
| Mexican food, beef, canned chicken, Taco Bell | Pasta, jam, candy, rice cakes, French bread |
| Countrytime, ground coffee, Diet 7-Up, Tab | Imported wine, Diet Coke, TGIF's |
| Chevys, Pontiacs, Ford Aerostars, Saturn SCs | Mazdas, Peugeots, Volvos, Acura Legends |
| Auto and home-improvement loans, mutual funds | Education loans, Keoghs, stocks, IRAs |
| Conservatives, pro-lifers, privacy rights | Liberals, legalizing drugs, gun control |

IMAGINE THE PERFECT community for preppies, a place where people love fashion, fine wine, tennis, and European travel. That's not Bakersfield. In this California community known for producing oil and shipping farm products, residents favor bowling over golf, powerboating over sailing, playing the lottery over the stock market. Bakersfield has a lively country music scene dating to the Depression, when Midwestern farmers arrived with their hillbilly instruments and songs. Among the least popular pastimes are intellectual pursuits, such as reading books, attending the theater, or visiting museums. With a high percentage of homes filled with children, retirees, and homemakers, the Bakersfield lifestyle is strikingly family-centered. Residents acquire pets, video games, and bicycles at above-average rates. True, preppies aren't completely extinct: about 10 percent of Bakersfield residents have college degrees and earn over $75,000 a year. But you'll likely find a lot more of them pursuing the "good life" on the other side of the rocky peaks in Los Angeles.

| Middle-class commercial center | Ethnically diverse families | Less than high school educations | Labor, farming, and transportation jobs |
|---|---|---|---|

## Key Demographics

| | | | |
|---|---|---|---|
| Total Population: | 484,049 | Primary Ages of Adults: | 25–44 |
| Median Household Income: | $29,703 | Median Home Value: | $86,596 |

# Baltimore, Maryland

## What's Hot   What's Not

| What's Hot | What's Not |
|---|---|
| Health clubs, the arts, travel, books | Baking, sweepstakes, garden tillers, pets |
| Bowling, tennis, boating, jogging | Golf, camping, fishing, hunting, sewing |
| Stereos, PCs, VCRs, 35mm cameras, home gyms | Power tools, 126/110 cameras, microwaves |
| BET, C-SPAN, "Geraldo," "In Living Color" | "Family Feud," "Evening Shade," "Daytona 500" |
| Jazz, classical, easy-listening music | Religious radio, pro football, country |
| *Food & Wine, Essence, Wall Street Journal, GQ* | *Field & Stream, McCall's, TV Guide, Parents* |
| TV dinners, fish, spaghetti, croissants | Ham, peanut butter, macaroni, beef stew, pie |
| Wine, ale, spring water, Heineken, Miller | Kool-Aid, tea, lemon-lime soda, ground coffee |
| Hondas, Infinitis, Lexuses, Ferraris, Jaguars | Pontiacs, Dodges, Chevrolets, Oldsmobile 98s |
| $200,000+ homeowner's insurance, gold cards | Loans, Medicare, mail-order medical insurance |
| Liberals, abortion rights, ecological issues | Moderates, privacy rights, less government |

TO THE OLD-TIMERS, it's still a proud blue-collar town pronounced "Bawlmer": home to Babe Ruth and cigar-chomping H. L. Mencken, crab cakes and Corned Beef Row. The reality of Baltimore is a bit different, a burgeoning upscale market where residents enjoy theater, classical music, and art far more often than average Americans. Thanks to a median income of over $41,000, Baltimoreans have the money to take vacations to Europe and the Caribbean. They drive fancy imports made by Jaguar and Ferrari at above-average rates. On their coffee tables are magazines like *Money, Gourmet,* and *Architectural Digest.* While the majority of citizens boast an urban-sophisticate lifestyle, Charm City hasn't completely erased its past as a gritty working-class port. Compared to the general population, locals are still more likely to go bowling, travel by bus, and drink beer — though not at the hoity-toity Orioles Park at Camden Yards. It's the kind of quirky sensibility that's inspired such local filmmakers as John Waters and Barry Levinson in movies like "Hairspray" and "Diner."

| *Upper-middle-class metropolis* | *Racially diverse singles and couples* | *College educations* | *White-collar professionals and managers* |
|---|---|---|---|

## Key Demographics

| | | | |
|---|---|---|---|
| Total Population: | 2,629,378 | Primary Ages of Adults: | 35–44 |
| Median Household Income: | $41,646 | Median Home Value: | $112,989 |

# Bangor, Maine

## What's Hot   What's Not

| What's Hot | What's Not |
|---|---|
| Home workshop, science fiction, mobile homes | Politics, concerts, theme parks, the Bible |
| Hunting, skiing, knitting, gardening, boating | Exercise, bowling, swimming, bicycling |
| Garden tillers, cameras, hot-water heaters | Cassette decks, CD players, new cars |
| "CBS This Morning," "I Love Lucy," "Coach" | VH-1, "Joan Rivers," Wimbledon, "Star Trek" |
| Country, golden oldies, radio baseball | Soft rock, jazz, folk, all-news radio |
| *Mother Earth News, Country Living, Star* | *Time, Vogue, Fortune, House and Garden, GQ* |
| Beef, potatoes, baked beans, canned vegetables | Health food, rice, waffles, raisin bread |
| Powdered soft drinks, ground coffee, Pepsi-Cola, cocoa | Diet Coke, imported beer, wine, Tab |
| Pontiacs, Chevrolets, Oldsmobiles, Dodge Omnis | Audis, Volvos, Saabs, Peugeots, BMWs |
| Mail-order insurance, home-improvement loans | Credit cards, stocks, IRAs, mutual funds |
| Moderates, toxic waste, less government | Liberals, legalizing drugs, gun control |

THE STEREOTYPICAL NEW ENGLANDER — aloof, curt, idiosyncratic — is what you'll find in Bangor. Many are independent-minded professionals, retirees, and assorted blue-collar workers who keep to themselves. Surveys show that area folks hunt, fish, camp, and ride horses at rates far above the national average. At home, they enjoy gardening, sewing, woodworking, and making crafts. Once the lumber capital of the world, Bangor today has lost much of its economic muscle, and residents report below-average incomes, education levels, and interest in "good-life" activities such as art, fashion, and travel. Bangor is also distinct from other small cities where folks have strong feelings about faith and religion. No doubt the presence of local writer Stephen King helps explain the area passion for horror and science fiction.

| *Lower-middle-class commercial city* | *Predominantly white couples and families* | *High school educations* | *Professional, labor, and retired workers* |
|---|---|---|---|

## Key Demographics

| | | | |
|---|---|---|---|
| Total Population: | 336,394 | Primary Ages of Adults: | 35–54 |
| Median Household Income: | $28,198 | Median Home Value: | $72,363 |

# Baton Rouge, Louisiana

| What's Hot | What's Not |
|---|---|
| Gourmet cooking, fashion, video games | Casinos, movies, adult ed courses, golf |
| Hunting, gardening, sewing, fishing | Skiing, bowling, sailing, hiking, tennis |
| Cable TV, compact pickups, microwaves | Motorcycles, PCs, books, power tools |
| "Fresh Prince," NCAA Basketball, "Donahue" | "America's Most Wanted," "Tonight Show" |
| Gospel, rhythm & blues, country, rap music | Rock, pop, Broadway musicals, news radio |
| *Weight Watchers, Health, Soap Opera Digest* | *Money, Mademoiselle, Inc., New Yorker* |
| Beef stew, biscuits, rice, brownies, BBQ sauce | Beef, spaghetti sauce, sour cream, Wheaties |
| Rum, Coca-Cola, orange juice, lemon-lime soda | Scotch, draft and imported beer, Diet Slice |
| Chevy S10s, Nissan Stanzas, Isuzus, Pontiacs | Saabs, Audis, Alfa Romeos, VW Cabriolets |
| Money orders, term life insurance, auto loans | Keoghs, savings bonds, CDs, annuities |
| Conservatives, school prayer, oil drilling | Moderates, ozone depletion, consumerism |

IT'S BAD ENOUGH that Baton Rouge is home to a string of chemical plants whose toxic wastes have earned the area the nickname "Cancer Alley." What's worse is that it's become a haven for that special breed of American citizen: the Southern baby boomer (AKA Bubba Junior). With half of all household heads between the ages of 25 and 44, the area's lifestyle is a peculiar mix of self-centered interests — residents express an interest in money-making opportunities, gourmet cooking, and the latest fashions — as well as downscale intellectual activities — local folks rarely attend movies, concerts, plays, or art galleries. You see this schizophrenic personality in the list of preferred magazines, ranging from *Esquire* to the *National Enquirer*. In Baton Rouge, many locals enjoy activities that have been popular for generations, like hunting, fishing, and rooting for the local college teams; it's no coincidence that Louisiana State University has had a powerhouse basketball team for years. Being a sports fan is one of the things Southern baby boomers do best.

| *Working-class state capital* | *Racially diverse families* | *High school educations* | *Professional and manufacturing jobs* |
|---|---|---|---|

### Key Demographics

| | | | |
|---|---|---|---|
| Total Population: | 748,700 | Primary Ages of Adults: | 25–44 |
| Median Household Income: | $26,721 | Median Home Value: | $65,700 |

# Beaumont–Port Arthur, Texas

| What's Hot | What's Not |
|---|---|
| Homemaking, sweepstakes, crafts, rodeos | College degrees, gambling casinos, movies, art |
| Fishing, hunting, camping, walking | Sailing, downhill skiing, tennis, bicycling |
| Garden tillers, pickups, Tupperware, vans | Toaster ovens, food processors, CD players |
| Soaps, "American Gladiators," "Blossom" | "Married with Children," "Meet the Press" |
| Urban contemporary, country, religious radio | News-talk radio, soft rock, jazz, classical |
| *Field & Stream, Southern Living, Ebony, Jet* | *Time, Harper's Bazaar, Changing Times, Ski* |
| Seafood, sausage, canned hash, potato chips | Tuna, TV dinners, yogurt, doughnuts, rye, cheese |
| Cola, malt liquor, powdered drinks | Herbal tea, scotch, cognac, wine, ale |
| Dodges, Chevys, Ford trucks, Pontiac Sunbirds | Acuras, Toyotas, VWs, Mazdas, Lexuses, Saabs |
| Christmas clubs, life insurance, loans | Keoghs, gold cards, stocks, bonds |
| Moderates, nuclear waste, pro-lifers | Liberals, legalizing drugs, gay rights |

NEARLY A CENTURY AGO, an oil gusher at nearby Spindletop transformed these Gulf Coast towns into booming cities. Today, that black gold glamour has faded, and Beaumont–Port Arthur is a relatively downscale area whose residents work in shipping, chemical plants, and rice mills. True, they've retained some of the pioneering spirit of the early wildcatters. Folks here are do-it-yourselfers who install their own carpeting, tires, spark plugs, and light fixtures. They enjoy fishing, hunting, and gardening at higher-than-average rates. In the Beaumont–Port Arthur area, relatively few attend movies or symphony concerts; a hot time is going to a rodeo, Tupperware party, or pro wrestling match. And these folks aren't belongers: they're less likely to be members of health clubs, business clubs, or country clubs than average Americans. Indeed, while they like to listen to gospel music and religious radio stations, they rarely belong to religious clubs.

| *Lower-middle-class industrial area* | *Racially diverse families* | *High school educations* | *Transportation, manufacturing, and craft jobs* |
|---|---|---|---|

### Key Demographics

| | | | |
|---|---|---|---|
| Total Population: | 431,564 | Primary Ages of Adults: | 55+ |
| Median Household Income: | $26,073 | Median Home Value: | $44,428 |

# Bend, Oregon

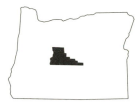

## What's Hot

Wilderness sports, pets, home workshops, RVs
Skiing, camping, fishing, hunting, bicycling
Camcorders, smoke detectors, lawn mowers, woks
"National Geographic," "Saturday Night Live"
Country, soft rock, adult contemporary
*Mother Earth News, Outdoor Life, Photography*
Chili, oat bran, pie, popcorn, nuts, Denny's
Draft beer, Kool-Aid, ground coffee, cocoa
Dodges, Lincolns, Subarus, GMC Sierras
New mortgages, loans, investment property
Moderates, legalizing drugs, toxic waste

## What's Not

Newspapers, rock concerts, health clubs
Tennis, golf, lottery, sailing, jogging
Cable TV, radar detectors, coupons, passports
MTV, "Family Feud," "Doogie Howser"
All-news radio, classical music, talk radio
*Life, GQ, Barron's, Vogue, New Yorker*
Cold cuts, spaghetti, cookies, canned hash
Spring water, ale, imported wine, diet sodas
VWs, Acuras, Cadillacs, Peugeots, Saab 9000s
AmEx cards, IRAs, stocks, mutual funds
Liberals, gay rights, gun control

WHERE DO CITY dropouts go? Well, Bend, Oregon, is one option. Although a majority of the residents have gone to college, they show remarkably little interest in newspapers, contemporary music, civic activities, the arts, and financial investments of any kind — hardly what you'd expect of a well-educated community. Befitting their location on the foot of the Cascade Range, Bend residents appear bent on returning to the wild. Compared to the general population, they're three times as likely to go skiing, twice as likely to enjoy camping, hunting, and fishing, and have above-average rates for boating, jogging, and bicycling. This passion for the out-of-doors spills over into other consuming patterns, such as their tendency to drive recreational vehicles, invest in real estate, own pets, and enjoy photography — no doubt, to capture Fido or one of the local woodland creatures. While folks here have a healthy appetite for junk food, they also purchase vitamins and health food at higher-than-average rates. Apparently, you can't completely take the city out of some people.

| *Middle-class resort area* | *Predominantly white couples and families* | *College educations* | *Farm and public administration jobs* |
|---|---|---|---|

| **Key Demographics** | Total Population: | 85,774 | Primary Ages of Adults: | 35–54 |
|---|---|---|---|---|
| | Median Household Income: | $30,434 | Median Home Value: | $81,801 |

# Billings-Hardin, Montana

## What's Hot

Photography, knitting, clubs, car repair
Horseback riding, bowling, skiing, sewing
Woks, bicycles, thermal windows, power tools
"Evening Shade," "CNN" "Tonight Show"
Country, middle-of-the-road, golden oldies
*Sports Afield, Reader's Digest, Woman's Day*
Ham, beef, soup, Jell-O, Stove Top stuffing
Powdered drinks, ground coffee, Diet Coke
Mercurys, Dodges, Pontiac 6000s, Chevy 4x4s
Medical and life insurance, CDs, Medicare
Moderates, toxic waste, family values

## What's Not

New cars, Mexican food, casinos, health clubs
Racquetball, tennis, boating, jogging
Stereos, sofa beds, coupons, radar detectors
"Seinfeld," "ABC Wide World of Sports"
Urban contemporary music, all-news radio
*Working Woman, Travel & Leisure, Forbes*
TV dinners, rice, English muffins, Popeye's
Imported beer and wine, herbal tea, Budweiser
Nissans, Toyotas, Hondas, BMWs, Acura Legends
Gold cards, money orders, stocks, IRAs
Liberals, gun control, consumerism

YOU HAVE TO WONDER at what point people began to outnumber horses in the Billings-Hardin area. Even today, many activities are still linked to our equine friends: rodeos, horseback riding, and horse racing are all enjoyed at higher-than-average rates. While Billings serves as a farm supply center and Hardin a trading center for the Crow Indian Reservation, their location near 400-foot sandstone cliffs and flat prairie encourages an outdoorsy lifestyle. Remarkably averse to television, residents are more likely than average Americans to camp, fish, hunt, and ski; inside their homes, folks tend to enjoy crafts, needlework, and baking from scratch. A couple of area colleges no doubt explain the local passion for college football and basketball. But in Billings-Hardin, which is composed of three groups of people — farmers, retirees, and baby boomers — consumer tastes run the gamut from chewing tobacco to needlepoint to heavy metal. Perhaps the only common denominator is the sugar cubes in their pockets for their horses.

| *Lower-middle-class farm supply area* | *Predominantly white families* | *High school educations* | *Farm and professional jobs* |
|---|---|---|---|

| **Key Demographics** | Total Population: | 230,596 | Primary Ages of Adults: | 35–54 |
|---|---|---|---|---|
| | Median Household Income: | $25,967 | Median Home Value: | $60,272 |

# Biloxi-Gulfport-Pascagoula, Mississippi

| What's Hot | What's Not |
|---|---|
| Veterans clubs, gambling, cable TV, the beach | Adult ed courses, movies, health clubs |
| Fishing, sewing, gardening, hunting, camping | Sailing, golf, camping, skiing, tennis |
| Washers, dryers, tires, cameras | CD players, lawn furniture, home gyms |
| "Wheel of Fortune," "Cops," "Santa Barbara" | "60 Minutes," "Siskel & Ebert," VH-1, HBO |
| Country, classical music, religious radio | Rhythm & blues, rap, soul, new wave, jazz |
| *Southern Living, Soap Opera Digest, Star* | *Gourmet, Scientific American, Money, Time* |
| Seafood, sausage, doughnuts, peanut butter | TV dinners, spaghetti sauce, French bread |
| Cola, diet sodas, milk, powdered drinks, tea | Brandy, scotch, beer, wine, decaf coffee |
| Lincolns, Chevys, Dodge Rams, Subaru Justys | Acuras, Mazdas, Hondas, Audis, VW Cabriolets |
| Home-improvement and auto loans, money orders | Mutual funds, stocks, bonds, credit cards |
| Conservatives, less government, nuclear waste | Liberals, gay rights, military cutbacks |

FIRST THINGS FIRST: they don't sing the blues in Biloxi. Nor do residents hum along to jazz, soul, rock, or classical music at above-average rates. Country and gospel music are the preferred genres, in part because of the small-town Catholic roots of many households along Mississippi's Gulf Coast. But the Biloxi-Gulfport-Pascagoula area is also home to many baby boomers of different sorts: blue-collar workers, military personnel, and beach bums. Together, they buy higher-than-average amounts of big-ticket appliances, like washers and dryers, and kid-centered items, like crafts and pets. A big night out is a trip to a pro wrestling match or dinner at a seafood restaurant, such as Long John Silver. Consistent with other small cities in the Deep South, folks around here are people of strong faith: they read the Bible, enter sweepstakes, and express an interest in money-making opportunities. Apparently, when you have faith, there's no need to sing the blues.

| *Lower-middle-class shipping and resort area* | *Racially diverse families* | *High school educations* | *Blue-collar labor and manufacturing jobs* |
|---|---|---|---|

## Key Demographics

| | | | |
|---|---|---|---|
| Total Population: | 307,324 | Primary Ages of Adults: | 25–44 |
| Median Household Income: | $25,891 | Median Home Value: | $56,087 |

# Binghamton, New York

| What's Hot | What's Not |
|---|---|
| Unions, bowling, denture cleansers, mall shopping | Gourmet cooking, travel, fine art, theme parks |
| Golf, gardening, woodworking, coin collecting | Weight training, fishing, tennis, sailing |
| Videotapes, microwaves, power tools, recliners | Books, bicycles, station wagons, CD players |
| TV bowling, "Northern Exposure," "Major Dad" | "Geraldo," "Meet the Press," "Wonder Years" |
| Golden oldies, classic rock, country | |
| *Prevention, Popular Mechanics, Woman's World* | *Fortune, House & Garden, Food & Wine, Sunset* |
| Spaghetti sauce, cold cuts, pizza, snack cakes | Mexican food, rice, yogurt, sweet rolls |
| Pepsi-Cola, ground coffee, skim milk, cocoa | Cocktails, imported wine, herbal tea |
| Chevys, Oldsmobiles, Dodge Dynastys | Toyotas, Mazdas, Acuras, Cadillac Allantes |
| Savings bonds, CDs, Medicare, Sears cards | Stocks, AmEx cards, group medical insurance |
| Moderates, death penalty, toxic waste | Liberals, oil drilling, gun control |

LIKE THE SHOE FACTORIES that once made this city famous, Binghamton is beginning to look a bit down at the heels. Nearly 40 percent of Binghamton's residents are over the age of 55, and the lifestyle has slowed to a shuffle. Among the favorite hobbies are collecting stamps and coins, making crafts, doing needlework, and completing crossword puzzles. Locals enjoy a lot of sports — like bowling and golf — that don't require working up a sweat. Although a significant portion of the area's women are home during the day, they're not spending their time in the kitchen. Many couples go out rather than cook at home, as demonstrated by the popularity of chains like Friendly's, Dunkin' Donuts, and Ponderosa Steak House. Still, not all of Binghamton should be classified as golden-agers; a significant minority are baby boom parents and younger graduate students from nearby Harper College. That may explain the local passion for modern rock, concern about the environment, and belief in consumer power. They're the ones heading for the nearby parks in hiking boots.

| *Middle-class industrial city* | *Predominantly white couples and families* | *High school educations* | *Professional, clerical, and blue-collar jobs* |
|---|---|---|---|

## Key Demographics

| | | | |
|---|---|---|---|
| Total Population: | 428,351 | Primary Ages of Adults: | 55+ |
| Median Household Income: | $30,615 | Median Home Value: | $77,243 |

# Birmingham, Alabama

## What's Hot

Home furnishing, car repair, tobacco products
Fishing, hunting, sewing, camping, gardening
Pickups, kitchen improvements, cable TV
"American Gladiators," "Blossom," "Oprah"
Gospel, country, rhythm & blues, rap
*Southern Living, Essence, Jet, True Story*
Baked beans, sausage, grits, macaroni, gum
Tea, orange juice, diet sodas, malt liquor
Dodge trucks, Chevy Camaros, Nissan Stanzas
Home-improvement loans, money orders, Medicare
Conservatives, privacy rights, pro-lifers

## What's Not

Health clubs, movies, trains, theater
Jogging, boating, bowling, skiing, bicycling
Comedy tapes, Tupperware, books, cameras
TV tennis, "Sisters," "20/20," "Empty Nest"
News radio, middle-of-the-road, golden oldies
*Cosmopolitan, National Geographic, Newsweek*
Beef, take-out, rye, cheese, canned tuna
Imported wine and beer, skim milk, vodka
Infinitis, Acuras, Saabs, Saturn SC3s
Visa cards, mutual funds, Keoghs, stocks
Liberals, consumerism, buying American

THE LARGEST CITY in Alabama was once known as the "Pittsburgh of the South" for its iron and steel works, but medical buildings have supplanted the smokestacks. Today, Birmingham's lifestyle resembles that of many Southern factory towns, still separated by class and race three decades after Bull Connor's attack dogs. Residents fish, hunt, watch TV, and read the Bible at above-average rates while displaying relatively little interest in more cosmopolitan activities, like reading books, attending cultural events, or investing in financial markets. When it comes to athletics, the aging populace would rather walk than engage in more strenuous pursuits such as running, tennis, or aerobic exercise. Owing to pockets of upscale, white-collar voters, Birmingham routinely backs Republican politicians; otherwise, this politically conservative area opposes abortion, gay rights, and consumerism. Birmingham is no place for collecting fine art, rare wine, or imported electronics.

| *Lower-middle-class industrial city* | *Racially diverse families and couples* | *High school educations* | *Manufacturing, medical, and service jobs* |
| --- | --- | --- | --- |

| **Key Demographics** | Total Population: | 1,403,383 | Primary Ages of Adults: | 55+ |
| --- | --- | --- | --- | --- |
| | Median Household Income: | $26,733 | Median Home Value: | $57,681 |

# Bluefield-Beckley—Oak Hill, West Virginia

## What's Hot

Veterans clubs, pickups, home improvement
Target shooting, horseback riding, gardening
Mobile homes, Tupperware, video games
Soaps, "Unsolved Mysteries," "Current Affair"
Country, gospel, religious radio
*Field & Stream, Star, McCall's, TV Guide*
Ham, sausage, pasta, canned chicken, Fritos
Tea, powdered drinks, milk, orange juice
Used cars, Chryslers, Mercurys, Dodge trucks
Mail-order life insurance, Medicare
Moderates, air pollution, death penalty

## What's Not

Theme parks, rock concerts, foreign travel
Tennis, racquetball, skiing, casinos
Bicycles, woks, videotapes, stereos
MTV, "David Brinkley," "Murphy Brown"
Rap, modern rock, radio baseball, jazz
*Omni, Self, Forbes, Rolling Stone, Jet*
Beef, frozen fish, rice, yogurt, rye
Draft and imported beer, wine, Diet Coke
Mazdas, Hondas, VWs, Saabs, Volvos, Audis
Mutual funds, gold cards, precious metals
Liberals, endangered animals, oil drilling

THIS PART OF West Virginia may not be the "almost heaven" John Denver sang about, but area residents don't seem to mind. In Bluefield-Beckley—Oak Hill, folks have almost an aversion to leaving their homes: they take plane, train, and bus trips at rates far lower than average Americans. And they're among the nation's citizens least likely to travel abroad. Indeed, area residents — many of whom are coal-miners, loggers, homemakers, and retirees — tend to spend their time on fix-it projects around the house: installing their own carpeting, shingles, and lighting fixtures. The extensive wilderness areas and whitewater rivers nearby do draw locals outside to hunt, fish, hike, and camp. As for the area's moonshiners of old, they've evolved into people who now spend their time mixing up batches of Kool-Aid and Countrytime lemonade.

| *Lower-class coal-mining area* | *Predominantly white families* | *Less than high school educations* | *Mining, timber, and manufacturing jobs* |
| --- | --- | --- | --- |

| **Key Demographics** | Total Population: | 362,901 | Primary Ages of Adults: | 55+ |
| --- | --- | --- | --- | --- |
| | Median Household Income: | $19,892 | Median Home Value: | $42,160 |

# Boise, Idaho

| What's Hot | What's Not |
|---|---|
| Clubs, investment property, PCs, pets | Rock concerts, theater, coupons, casinos |
| Horseback riding, fishing, camping, skiing | Tennis, swimming, sailing, golf, exercise |
| VCRs, lawn mowers, cameras, RVs, motorcycles | Radar detectors, stereos, convertibles |
| "Days of Our Lives," "Full House," "Coach" | "Loving," "Family Feud," "Married with Children" |
| Country, adult contemporary, college football | Talk radio, news radio, soft rock, jazz |
| *Ladies' Home Journal, Cycle World, Parents* | *Life, Inc., Wall Street Journal, Gourmet* |
| Pizza, chili, canned vegetables, sweet rolls | Cold cuts, waffles, canned hash, TV dinners |
| Diet Pepsi, Kool-Aid, draft beer, skim milk | Ale, imported wine, Sangria, spring water |
| Mercurys, Dodges, Fords, Subarus, Chevy Geos | Acuras, Cadillacs, Hondas, VWs, Volvo 940s |
| Mutual funds, annuities, life insurance | Savings bonds, gold cards, IRAs, stocks |
| Moderates, family values, less government | Liberals, gun control, consumerism |

IDAHO'S STATE CAPITAL is a study in contrasts: a green city surrounded by lumpy desert hills, an agricultural trading center coexisting with an urban government center. The result is an eclectic market whose residents are drawn to group activities — they join business groups, veterans clubs, and fraternal orders at high rates — as well as solitary leisure pursuits, like skiing, fishing, and hunting. No doubt, the outdoor activities are encouraged by Boise's Greenbelt, composed of ten miles of paths linking nine separate parks. Thanks to several area colleges and the state government, Boise has attracted a significant number of middle-class baby boomers to town. And yet, for all their good '60s values, Boise's boomers have forgotten their musical roots. They rarely listen to rock 'n' roll, watch VH-1 or MTV, or read publications like *Rolling Stone*. Boise is country country.

| Lower-middle-class agricultural center | Predominantly white families and couples | Some college educations | Farm, government, and construction jobs |
|---|---|---|---|

| **Key Demographics** | Total Population: | 460,906 | Primary Ages of Adults: | 25–44 |
|---|---|---|---|---|
| | Median Household Income: | $29,179 | Median Home Value: | $67,991 |

# Boston, Massachusetts

| What's Hot | What's Not |
|---|---|
| Books, foreign travel, the arts, casinos | Cheap housing, health food, crafts, the Bible |
| Skiing, tennis, sailing, golf, jogging | Camping, fishing, hunting, sewing |
| PCs, CD players, 35mm cameras, lotteries | Microwaves, washers, charcoal grills, tillers |
| "Letterman," "Doogie Howser," "Seinfeld" | Soaps, "Cops," "Sally," "Fresh Prince" |
| Classical music, modern rock, jazz | Gospel, country music, rhythm & blues, rap |
| *Scientific American, Food & Wine, Vanity Fair* | *Family Handyman, Soap Opera Digest, Star* |
| Shellfish, pasta, Italian bread, Friendly's | Beef stew, sausage, sweet rolls, Church's |
| Imported beer, wine, skim milk, decaf coffee | Tea, whole milk, Pabst, Kool-Aid, cola |
| Acuras, Hondas, Mazdas, Porsches, Saab 900s | Pontiacs, Chryslers, Ford Festivas |
| Mutual funds, savings bonds, AmEx cards | Medical insurance, money orders, loans |
| Liberals, gay rights, military cutbacks | Moderates, pro-lifers, death penalty |

IN MANY RESPECTS, Boston provides the classic portrait of the cosmopolitan American city. Although there are plenty of shot-and-beer rowhouse types, the relatively high percentage of educated, white-collar residents pursue a highbrow lifestyle characterized by attending the theater, listening to classical music, and reading up on gourmet cuisine. Compared to the general population, Boston residents are both well traveled and well informed: they see a lot of movies, enjoy several newspapers, and subscribe to magazines like *Forbes, Smithsonian,* and *Architectural Digest.* No doubt the city presence of more than 100 colleges and universities has contributed to these intellectual — not to mention liberal — interests. And yet for all these expressions of civilized taste, there's a hustler's streak not far beneath the surface: Bostonians are crazy about gambling, whether it be at casinos, racetracks, or simply the corner store's lottery machines. As local novelist George V. Higgins has observed of this spiritual tug-of-war among his neighbors: "Many of them are genuinely smart and well educated, either in the schools or in the streets."

| Upscale metropolitan area | Predominantly white singles and couples | College educations | White-collar professionals and executives |
|---|---|---|---|

| **Key Demographics** | Total Population: | 5,688,851 | Primary Ages of Adults: | 25–44 |
|---|---|---|---|---|
| | Median Household Income: | $45,278 | Median Home Value: | $182,870 |

# Bowling Green, Kentucky

| What's Hot | What's Not |
|---|---|
| Home furnishing, muscle cars, gardening, pets | The arts, foreign travel, dancing, unions |
| Horseback riding, target shooting, fishing | Bicycling, skiing, sailing, exercise |
| Microwaves, tires, washers, mobile homes | PCs, comedy records, 35mm cameras |
| Network news, "Blossom," "Family Matters" | "Wonder Years," "Simpsons," NBA Basketball |
| Country, religious radio, college sports | Jazz, rhythm & blues, Broadway musicals |
| *Sports Afield, Star, Country Living* | *Discover, Shape, Bon Appetit, Ebony* |
| Bacon, frankfurters, white bread, gum | Beef, frozen yogurt, rice cakes, chocolates |
| Tea, cola, orange juice, powdered drinks | Imported wine, draft beer, Diet 7-Up |
| Lincolns, Buicks, Plymouths, Chevy Camaros | Nissans, Toyotas, VWs, Hondas, Infiniti M30s |
| Mail-order medical and life insurance, loans | Annuities, stocks, mutual funds |
| Conservatives, privacy rights, death penalty | Liberals, school sex ed, military cutbacks |

TOURISTS KNOW IT as the only place to buy a drink between Nashville and Louisville. But Bowling Green more closely resembles other Bible Belt cities with a lifestyle steeped in tradition. Folks place their trust in God — reading the Bible and listening to religious radio are popular pastimes — and in work accomplished by their own hand. They hunt, fish, garden, and sew at rates far above the national average. And residents are skeptical of the latest trends, caring little for fashion clothing and gourmet cooking, rarely cluttering their coffee tables with publications like *GQ*, the *New Yorker*, and *Omni*. Perhaps the one area where they care about cutting-edge developments is cars: they tend to work on them, watch auto races, and take visitors to tour the local General Motors Corvette Plant. Yet even with automobiles, there's a traditional streak: Bowling Green residents tend to buy American. In one 1992 survey, nine out of ten of the most popular models were made in the U.S. while 52 of the 53 least popular had foreign name plates.

| *Lower-middle-class agricultural center* | *Predominantly white singles and families* | *Less than high school educations* | *Farm, labor, and manufacturing jobs* |
|---|---|---|---|

| **Key Demographics** | Total Population: | 125,401 | Primary Ages of Adults: | 35–54 |
|---|---|---|---|---|
| | Median Household Income: | $22,937 | Median Home Value: | $52,466 |

# Bristol, Virginia–Kingsport–Johnson City, Tennessee

| What's Hot | What's Not |
|---|---|
| Mall shopping, pro wrestling, the Bible | Adult ed courses, bus travel, fashion |
| Gardening, woodworking, coin collecting | Bowling, tennis, racquetball, weight training |
| Chain saws, cable TV, washers, motorcycles | Bicycles, home gyms, CD players, PCs |
| "CBS This Morning," "Major Dad," "Loving" | "Honeymooners," Wimbledon, "Siskel & Ebert" |
| Gospel, country, religious radio | Rap, modern rock, classical music |
| *Southern Living, 1001 Home Ideas, Star* | *Business Week, Photography, Vogue, Gourmet* |
| Ham, biscuits, brownies, pudding, breath mints | Take-out, fish, pumpernickel, cheese, Denny's |
| Tea, Pepsi-Cola, Kool-Aid, cocoa, tomato juice | Light beer, Cold Duck, imported beer and wine |
| Chevys, Pontiacs, Chryslers, Dodge Daytonas | VWs, Hondas, Mazdas, Acuras, Peugeot 505s |
| Company life insurance, first mortgages | Bonds, mutual funds, annuities, gold cards |
| Conservatives, privacy rights, buying American | Liberals, abortion rights, endangered animals |

RESIDENTS OF THIS market straddle not only two states but two lifestyles. Many activities reflect the area's agrarian past: people plant gardens, buy chain saws, and ride horses at above-average rates. But they also engage in a number of pursuits typical of industrial cities, such as working on their cars, watching pro wrestling matches, and meeting at veterans clubs more often than the U.S. average. Thanks to several area colleges, local residents support collegiate basketball and football teams. But some of the more progressive ideas on campus have yet to filter into the Tri-Cities market. Musically, for instance, rap, modern rock, and progressive jazz have yet to make it over the mountains to this area.

| *Lower-middle-class industrial area* | *Predominantly white families and couples* | *Less than high school educations* | *Farm, labor, and manufacturing jobs* |
|---|---|---|---|

| **Key Demographics** | Total Population: | 747,472 | Primary Ages of Adults: | 45–64 |
|---|---|---|---|---|
| | Median Household Income: | $23,072 | Median Home Value: | $51,610 |

# Buffalo, New York

## What's Hot

Bowling, grandchildren, TV sports, unions
Crafts, needlework, swimming, walking
Tupperware, cameras, power tools, cable TV
"Joan Rivers," "Empty Nest," "Another World"
Classic rock, middle-of-the-road, radio baseball
*Home Mechanix, Star, Self, Redbook*
Spaghetti, TV dinners, beef, pasta, oatmeal
Orange juice, ground coffee, Countrytime
Pontiacs, Chevys, Mercurys, Olds Calais
CDs, company life insurance, savings bonds
Moderates, death penalty, privacy rights

## What's Not

Business travel, books, convertibles, exercise
Waterskiing, horseback riding, jogging
Stereos, microwaves, bicycles, CD players
Wimbledon, "Family Feud," "Star Trek," MTV
Rhythm & blues, modern rock, pop music
*Ebony, House & Garden, Tennis, Gourmet*
Mexican food, yogurt, rice, BBQ sauce, Fritos
Wine, imported beer, herbal tea, diet sodas
Mazdas, Hondas, Acuras, Cadillac Sevilles
Credit lines, medical insurance, stocks
Liberals, school prayer, gay rights

IN THIS AGING INDUSTRIAL CITY, some vestiges of the old smokestack economy remain: unions, bowling leagues, and Tupperware parties to name a few. Indeed, Buffalo consumers seem to avoid more popular pursuits of the Atari generation, such as aerobic exercise, listening to modern rock over a CD player, or watching MTV. While nearly one in five women is a homemaker, not many are slaving over a stove. Indeed, Buffalo residents frequent chains like Friendly's, Ponderosa Steak House, and Dunkin' Donuts at rates above the national average. This finding may be explained by the fact that more than 40 percent of local adults are over age 55; retired couples tend to dine out rather than prepare elaborate home-cooked meals for two. And when they do cook at home, they need lots of Tupperware for storing leftovers. There's no shuffling off to Buffalo's kitchens among these active retirees.

| *Middle-class industrial center* | *Predominantly white singles and couples* | *High school educations* | *Manufacturing jobs* |
|---|---|---|---|

| **Key Demographics** | Total Population: | 1,646,213 | Primary Ages of Adults: | 55+ |
|---|---|---|---|---|
| | Median Household Income: | $30,017 | Median Home Value: | $70,670 |

# Burlington, Vermont–Plattsburgh, New York

## What's Hot

Country clubs, gourmet cooking, motorcycles
Skiing, hunting, boating, camping, knitting
Video games, power tools, pets, recliners
College basketball, "Northern Exposure," "Coach"
Country, adult contemporary, middle-of-the-road
*Reader's Digest, Working Mother, Sports Afield*
Canned soup, frankfurters, beef stew, popcorn
Diet Coke, skim milk, light beer, Pabst
Subaru, Mercurys, Plymouths, Oldsmobile 98s
Medical insurance, mutual funds, auto loans
Moderates, pro-lifers, less government

## What's Not

Movies, casinos, bowling, health food
Racquetball, weight training, lotteries
PCs, tennis racquets, station wagons
"Donahue," "American Detective," Nickelodeon
Talk radio, rap, rhythm & blues, classical
*GQ, Tennis, New York, Barron's, Star*
TV dinners, rice, canned tuna, corn on the cob
Vodka, imported beer, orange juice, rum
Toyotas, Hondas, Acuras, Jaguars, Porsches
Keoghs, money-market accounts, stocks
Liberals, endangered animals, gun control

THERE AREN'T MANY markets where you find healthy memberships in both country clubs and veterans clubs, but Burlington-Plattsburgh is one of them. Due to a higher-than-average percentage of adults either under 35 or over 65 years old — blame the University of Vermont and Plattsburg Air Force Base — the lifestyle is decidedly schizo. Area residents are into gourmet cooking, fine art, and foreign travel as well as woodworking, country music, and motorcycles. The local supermarkets are as likely to stock chewing tobacco as fine wine. And stores specializing in home furnishings do well in these parts: new homeowners are responsible for buying washers, dryers, and bedroom furniture at higher-than-average rates. Older homeowners tend to take out loans for kitchen improvements more often than the general population. Naturally, some activities are shared by members of all ages, such as attending state and county fairs. Ironically, in this market, which is home of Ben & Jerry's ice cream, locals have only mild interest in that heavenly confection; many of the area's rural, downscale residents buy less-expensive brands.

| *Middle-class commercial and university communities* | *Predominantly white families and singles* | *High school educations* | *Farm, labor, and construction jobs* |
|---|---|---|---|

| **Key Demographics** | Total Population: | 747,708 | Primary Ages of Adults: | 25–44 |
|---|---|---|---|---|
| | Median Household Income: | $32,793 | Median Home Value: | $97,320 |

# Butte, Montana

| What's Hot | What's Not |
|---|---|
| Rodeos, unions, photography, adult ed courses | Gambling, unions, CD players, theme parks |
| Jogging, hunting, skiing, horseback riding | Tennis, crossword puzzles, exercise, golf |
| Camping equipment, audiocassettes, books | PCs, food processors, stereos, coupons |
| TV horse racing, "Roseanne," "Wheel of Fortune" | "Headline News," "Hard Copy," "Seinfeld" |
| Modern rock, country, college football | Rhythm & blues, rap, jazz, classical music |
| *Mother Earth News, Cycle World, Flying* | *Fortune, Gourmet, House Beautiful, Life* |
| Ham, beef, baked beans, potatoes, raisins | Spaghetti sauce, rice, canned hash, cookies |
| Vegetable juice, draft beer, skim milk | Imported wine, orange juice, imported beer |
| Plymouths, Fords, Buicks, Dodge trucks | Cadillacs, Mazdas, Acuras, Saturns, BMWs |
| Auto loans, medical insurance, CDs | Gold cards, IRAs, precious metals, bonds |
| Moderates, pro-lifers, toxic waste | Liberals, endangered animals, consumerism |

COMPARED TO THE REST of the anti-union West, Butte stands out as a wild aberration. Founded as a pro-union mining town — first for gold, then silver, most recently copper — Butte remains inextricably tied to the rugged, treeless landscape. As a market, it ranks among the nation's top ten when it comes to skiing, camping, fishing, and hunting. And Butte is a young person's town: more than half of the adults are under the age of 44 years old, with such preferences as listening to modern rock music, buying audio- and videocassettes, and taking adult education courses. Still, for all their youth, Butte is no haven for electronic hipness: computers and CD players have yet to make it into town in a big way. And no one seems to care too much about catching the latest movie, partaking in a health-club massage, or attending a gay rights meeting. In Butte, you wear your coolness on the slopes, on the trails, or beneath a blanket of stars at the perfect campsite.

| *Lower-middle-class mining town* | *Predominantly white singles and families* | *College educations* | *Farm, education, and service jobs* |
|---|---|---|---|

## Key Demographics

| Total Population: | 132,743 | Primary Ages of Adults: | 25–44 |
|---|---|---|---|
| Median Household Income: | $24,849 | Median Home Value: | $58,078 |

# Casper-Riverton, Wyoming

| What's Hot | What's Not |
|---|---|
| Video rentals, pets, motorcycles, car repair | Talk radio, rock concerts, train travel |
| Horseback riding, fishing, hunting, camping | Tennis, walking, health clubs, lotteries |
| Washers, dryers, cameras, books, lawn mowers | Stereos, pregnancy-test kits, radar detectors |
| TV auto racing, "Tonight Show," "Coach," "Cops" | MTV, VH-1, "I Love Lucy," "Fresh Prince" |
| Country, easy listening, religious radio | Jazz, rap, news radio, folk |
| *Family Handyman, Reader's Digest, Cycle, Ski* | *Life, Esquire, Harper's Bazaar, Inc.* |
| Mexican food, beef, Shake 'N Bake, Fritos | TV dinners, cold cuts, doughnuts, bagels |
| Fruit juice, light beer, decaf coffee, cocoa | Ale, malt liquor, scotch, cola |
| Subarus, Dodges, Chryslers, GMC Sierra 4x4s | Volvos, Porsches, BMWs, Infiniti G20s |
| MasterCard, mutual funds, investment property | AmEx cards, bonds, company life insurance |
| Moderates, privacy rights, family values | Liberals, buying American, endangered animals |

NOT ALL BABY BOOMERS act alike, and the Casper-Riverton area is proof that there's a big difference between city and country cousins. In these small oil and livestock towns, where boomer families comprise 40 percent of all households, you'd be hard-pressed to find any Beemers or Volvo station wagons gracing the driveways. Many residents are more interested in the mundane aspects of setting up new households, buying washers, dryers, ceiling fans, and carpeting at above-average rates. The high concentration of young families also influences the area's fondness for fruit juice, video rentals, pets, and cameras. Yet unlike city boomers, who care about being au courant, these consumers care little about trends in the arts, music, fashion, and gourmet cooking. They're less likely than average Americans to attend rock concerts, own CD players, go jogging, or watch VH-1 on cable. Indeed, they're more interested in fast motorcycles and race horses than fast music.

| *Middle-class oil towns* | *Predominantly white families* | *Some college educations* | *Farm, mining, and construction jobs* |
|---|---|---|---|

## Key Demographics

| Total Population: | 111,797 | Primary Ages of Adults: | 25–44 |
|---|---|---|---|
| Median Household Income: | $26,594 | Median Home Value: | $53,124 |

# Cedar Rapids–Waterloo-Dubuque, Iowa

## What's Hot

Veterans clubs, mall shopping, books, baking
Fishing, hunting, golf, sewing, gardening
Charcoal grills, power tools, VCRs, radios
"CBS Evening News," "Designing Women," sports
Country, golden oldies, college football
*Field & Stream, Ladies' Home Journal, Parents*
Ham, stuffing, oatmeal, biscuits, canned soup
Diet 7-Up, light and draft beer, cocoa
Dodges, Fords, Oldsmobiles, Chevy pickups
Disability insurance, home-improvement loans
Moderates, pro-lifers, death penalty

## What's Not

Health food, theater, convertibles, the arts
Sailing, jogging, skiing, tennis, bicycling
CD players, sofa beds, woks, PCs
"Beverly Hills, 90210," "I Love Lucy," "Geraldo"
Jazz, soft rock, news radio, classical
*Cosmopolitan, Gourmet, Forbes, Sunset*
TV dinners, rice cakes, chili, chocolates
Herbal tea, Diet RC, imported beer, cocktails
Hondas, Acuras, BMWs, Peugeots, Lexus ES250s
Gold cards, stocks, Keoghs, money orders
Liberals, ocean dumping, privacy rights

THOSE WHO SAY the nation has become one giant shopping mall don't know a heartland area like Cedar Rapids–Waterloo-Dubuque. Here, at the home of Quaker Oats, the small-town American lifestyle hasn't changed much in generations. Men are still into fishing and hunting, women favor needlework and crafts, and everyone throws him- or herself into the backyard garden—no doubt, after a hearty bowl of oatmeal. You see the spirit of self-sufficiency in the higher-than-average rates for residents who do their own home renovations and work on their cars, installing thermal windows and lighting fixtures, car batteries and shocks. And like many midwestern communities close to the land, Cedar Rapids–Waterloo-Dubuque consumes a remarkable amount and variety of packaged goods, such as canned soup, pasta, and salad dressing. Not that this area qualifies as Hicksville: thanks to area colleges, a higher-than-average percentage of local adults work in education services, belong to country clubs, and read books. It's just that after a hard day behind a desk, in front of a class, or atop a tractor, most people would just as soon relax at the local Dairy Queen.

| Middle-class commercial center | Predominantly white families and singles | High school educations | Farm, education, and labor jobs |
|---|---|---|---|

### Key Demographics

| | | | |
|---|---|---|---|
| Total Population: | 822,176 | Primary Ages of Adults: | 35–54 |
| Median Household Income: | $29,193 | Median Home Value: | $52,092 |

# Charleston, South Carolina

## What's Hot

Home decorating, gourmet cooking, the arts
Bicycling, hunting, tennis, fishing
Lawn mowers, microwaves, video games
"Nightline," "Fresh Prince," "Family Matters"
Gospel music, rhythm & blues, heavy metal
*Essence, Ebony, Weight Watchers, TV Guide*
Fried chicken, seafood, rice, jam, pie
Tea, milk, malt liquor, cola, party wines
Nissans, Isuzus, GMC Jimmys
Medical insurance, money orders, auto loans
Conservatives, less government, school prayer

## What's Not

Country clubs, casinos, movies, unions
Exercise, golf, sailing, skiing, bowling
PCs, books, weights, 35mm cameras
"Tonight Show," "Face the Nation," "Doogie Howser"
Broadway musicals, modern rock, middle-of-the-road
*Smithsonian, Changing Times, Cosmopolitan*
Beef, canned tuna, rye, pretzels, yogurt
Diet Slice, imported beer, fruit juice
Acuras, Mazdas, VWs, Mercedes-Benzes, Peugeots
IRAs, mutual funds, bonds, gold cards
Liberals, ecological concerns, consumerism

THE OLDEST CITY in South Carolina has something of a split personality thanks to its racially mixed populace. There's a strong strain of the Old South in the popularity of conservative politics, maintaining the elegant, century-old homes, and collecting rare wine. But African-American influences also affect local consuming patterns in the popularity of malt liquor, rhythm & blues, and publications like *Ebony, Jet,* and *Essence.* Granted, there is some common ground: religion is big in both cultures — Charleston is known as the Holy City for its abundant churches — though residents may not be attending integrated churches. As a group, Charleston's citizens are more likely than the general population to read the Bible and listen to gospel music. Then there's the local passion for food: residents of all backgrounds are into gourmet cooking as well as chicken and seafood restaurants at rates much higher than the average American. Around here, everyone has a favorite recipe for fried chicken and she-crab soup.

| Middle-class resort and commercial seaport | Racially diverse singles and families | Less than high school educations | Professional and manufacturing jobs |
|---|---|---|---|

### Key Demographics

| | | | |
|---|---|---|---|
| Total Population: | 660,847 | Primary Ages of Adults: | 25–44 |
| Median Household Income: | $30,446 | Median Home Value: | $75,073 |

# Charleston-Huntington, West Virginia

## What's Hot | What's Not

| What's Hot | What's Not |
|---|---|
| Hunting, horse racing, car repair, the Bible | Travel, fine art, movies, health clubs |
| Fishing, camping, gardening, sewing | Tennis, boating, bicycling, golf, jogging |
| Guns, cable TV, mobile homes, pickups | PCs, CD players, home gyms, books |
| Soaps, "Unsolved Mysteries," "Inside Edition" | "Married with Children," "Joan Rivers" |
| Country, college football, religious radio | Jazz, classical, rap, rock, rhythm & blues |
| *Sports Afield, National Enquirer, Star* | *Self, Food & Wine, Wall Street Journal* |
| Pork & beans, beef stew, biscuits, snack cakes | TV dinners, rice, English muffins, Trix |
| Kool-Aid, tea, Pepsi-Cola, diet soda | Ale, imported beer, wine, herbal tea |
| Dodges, Pontiacs, Chevys, Ford Festivas | Hondas, Mazdas, Acuras, BMWs, Jaguars |
| Mail-order life and medical insurance | Visa, stocks, bonds, mutual funds |
| Conservatives, toxic waste, death penalty | Liberals, oil drilling, endangered animals |

CHARLESTON MAY BE a state capital, but it's unlike most of the other 49 capitals. Hardly a center of politics and culture, Charleston's residents have a pronounced lack of interest in current affairs, the arts, science, and finance. Among the top ten magazines for the area are the *National Enquirer,* the *Star,* and *True Story.* Among the favorite pastimes are hunting, sewing, and working on trucks (Dodge 4x4 pickups are the preferred mode of transportation). There's a parochial character to the community, as seen in the low rates of travel by plane, train, and bus. Living near the New River and extensive wilderness areas, folks around here spend an inordinate amount of time fishing and hunting — yet express little support for protecting the environment. As for saving endangered animals, forget it. In this area, living off an abundant land is not too distant a memory.

| Lower-middle-class commercial center | Predominantly white families | Less than high school educations | Farm, labor, and manufacturing jobs |
|---|---|---|---|

### Key Demographics

| | | | |
|---|---|---|---|
| Total Population: | 1,279,383 | Primary Ages of Adults: | 55+ |
| Median Household Income: | $21,371 | Median Home Value: | $48,846 |

# Charlotte, North Carolina

## What's Hot | What's Not

| What's Hot | What's Not |
|---|---|
| Home decorating, college sports, muscle cars | Movies, adult ed courses, gourmet cooking |
| Pro wrestling, gardening, crafts | Bicycling, camping, skiing, tennis, dancing |
| Lawn mowers, hot-water heaters, VCRs | Books, PCs, cameras, passports, Tupperware |
| Game shows, "Coach," "Dinosaurs," "Today" | "Letterman," "Golden Girls," "Doogie Howser" |
| Gospel, country, religious radio | Modern rock, jazz, classical, rap |
| *Colonial Homes, Prevention, Us, Redbook* | *Consumer's Digest, House Beautiful, Self* |
| Peanut butter, cold cuts, spaghetti sauce | Beef, canned tuna, yogurt, raising bread |
| Pepsi-Cola, diet soda, whole milk, orange juice | Skim milk, wine, imported beer, decaf coffee |
| Chevys, Ford Mustangs, Dodge Daytonas | Jaguars, Porsches, BMWs, Lexus ES300s |
| Home-improvement loans, mutual funds | Bonds, precious metals, stocks, Keoghs |
| Conservatives, family values, school prayer | Liberals, military cutbacks, consumerism |

CITY BOOSTERS WOULD LIKE outsiders to believe that Charlotte's skyscrapers reflect a cosmopolitan and cultured metropolis — an Atlanta wannabe. In fact, surveys of residents in North Carolina's largest city reflect a middlebrow lifestyle with a striking antipathy toward fine art, fashion, gourmet cooking, and luxury foreign cars. Although folks around here tend to be middle-class with median home values, they're more likely than average Americans to enjoy downscale good-ol'-boy activities like chewing tobacco, going fishing, working on their cars. Motorists are more likely to buy muscle machines like Chevy Camaros, Ford Mustangs, and Pontiac Firebirds than BMW 7s, Jaguar XJ6s, or anything made by Porsche. Their political views are a mix of traditional and progressive values, with support for both gay rights and pro-life advocates. If there is a sophisticated side to Charlotte, it's hidden behind closed doors: residents are into home decorating and joining country clubs at higher-than-average rates.

| Middle-class industrial city | Racially diverse families | High school educations | Manufacturing, labor, and precision jobs |
|---|---|---|---|

### Key Demographics

| | | | |
|---|---|---|---|
| Total Population: | 2,032,933 | Primary Ages of Adults: | 25–44 |
| Median Household Income: | $32,206 | Median Home Value: | $70,820 |

# Charlottesville, Virginia

## What's Hot | What's Not

| What's Hot | What's Not |
|---|---|
| College sports, movies, the arts, books | Lotteries, faxes, religious clubs, carpeting |
| Racquetball, skiing, jogging, tennis | Bowling, pro wrestling, home gyms, fishing |
| Cassette decks, PCs, power tools, used cars | Vans, sofa beds, chain saws, cable TV |
| "Seinfeld," "Sisters," "Wonder Years" | HBO, "Sally," "60 Minutes," "Loving" |
| Progressive rock, classical, jazz | News radio, middle-of-the-road, easy listening |
| *Rolling Stone, Gourmet, Self, Ski, GQ* | *Jet, Weight Watchers, New York, TV Guide* |
| Take-out, pizza, yogurt, ice cream, cheese | Cold cuts, canned tuna, biscuits, jam |
| Draft beer, wine, Diet Coke, cocktails | Tea, whole milk, orange juice, Countrytime |
| Audis, Subarus, Mazdas, Nissan 300ZXs | Chryslers, Chevys, Oldsmobiles, Ford Tempos |
| Interest checking, mutual funds, loans | Life insurance, Christmas clubs, CDs |
| Liberals, abortion rights, gay rights | Conservatives, death penalty, gun control |

AS THE HOME of the University of Virginia, Charlottesville is like many college towns: a bit more upscale, white-collar, and liberal than the average American burg. But even among college markets, this one excels, ranking first in surveys for interest in books, cultural events, and career-oriented programs. Charlottesville residents also score near the top when it comes to their passion for jogging, tennis, and exercise in general. Many of the young, educated singles are hard-core techies, involved in the latest computer gadgetry, trends in technology, even science fiction. Not surprisingly, folks around here display little interest in domestic activities like crafts, gardening, collectibles, and sewing. Perhaps their most striking expression of domesticity, according to surveys, is their support for homosexual marriages at some of the highest rates in the nation.

| Upper-middle-class college community | Predominantly white singles | College educations | Education and business jobs |
|---|---|---|---|

**Key Demographics**

| | | | |
|---|---|---|---|
| Total Population: | 111,798 | Primary Ages of Adults: | 18–34 |
| Median Household Income: | $36,030 | Median Home Value: | $110,966 |

# Chattanooga, Tennessee

## What's Hot | What's Not

| What's Hot | What's Not |
|---|---|
| Cable TV, fishing, home decorating, the Bible | Movies, plane travel, casinos, books, golf |
| Horse racing, target shooting, walking | Bicycling, jogging, swimming, skiing, sailing |
| Automotive tools, video games, garden tillers | Audio tapes, food processors, 35mm cameras |
| "American Gladiators," "Family Feud," "Cops" | "Murphy Brown," "Joan Rivers," "Honeymooners" |
| Gospel, country, heavy metal, religious radio | Rock, rap, rhythm & blues, classical music |
| *Southern Living, Field & Stream, Star* | *Time, Fortune, Travel & Leisure, Discover* |
| Sausage, canned vegetables, macaroni, doughnuts | Beef, fried chicken, yogurt, raisin bread |
| Cola, powdered drinks, cocoa, tea | Wine, imported beer, ale, skim milk |
| Chryslers, Chevys, Pontiacs, Dodge trucks | Mazdas, Acuras, VWs, Toyotas, Mercedes-Benzes |
| Money orders, life insurance, Medicare | Mutual funds, Keoghs, precious metals, AmEx |
| Conservatives, less government, endangered animals | Liberals, toxic waste, abortion rights |

FORGET GLENN MILLER'S "Chattanooga Choo-Choo." This Tennessee city isn't even served by Amtrak anymore, and few residents travel by train, plane, or even bus, for that matter. Thanks to its riverfront location surrounded by mountains, however, Chattanooga residents have plenty to do in the out-of-doors nearby. They fish and hunt at above-average rates, and their most popular magazines have titles like *Sports Afield, Field & Stream,* and *Outdoor Life.* Many residents have only modest incomes and education levels — nearly 40 percent failed to finish high school — and the result is little interest in newspapers, news magazines, and TV shows concerned with current events. Cable TV is popular, however, with locals tending to watch daytime soaps, game shows, and pro wrestling. And with the high percentage of households with children, Chattanooga also boasts high sales figures for video games, pets, crafts, and toys. Interestingly, while conservative politics are popular in the area, residents do display more liberal leanings when it comes to their children's education: in this area, parents support their kids' learning about sex, drugs, and AIDS at school.

| Lower-middle-class commercial center | Predominantly white families and couples | Less than high school educations | Manufacturing and transportation jobs |
|---|---|---|---|

**Key Demographics**

| | | | |
|---|---|---|---|
| Total Population: | 774,814 | Primary Ages of Adults: | 35–54 |
| Median Household Income: | $27,172 | Median Home Value: | $58,622 |

# Cheyenne, Wyoming—Scottsbluff, Nebraska

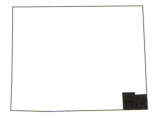

## What's Hot

Clubs, rodeos, books, car repair, photography
Bowling, skiing, hunting, camping, knitting
VCRs, audiocassettes, PCs, motorcycles
TV auto racing, "Evening Shade," "Roseanne"
Country, easy listening, religious radio
*Redbook, Reader's Digest, Popular Science*
Ham, fish, chili, canned soup, popcorn
Diet Coke, skim milk, powdered drinks
Subarus, Pontiacs, Buicks, Ford trucks
Mutual funds, annuities, CDs, auto loans
Moderates, family values, toxic waste

## What's Not

Gourmet cooking, fashion, the arts, casinos
Boating, tennis, sailing, jogging, dancing
CD players, convertibles, stereos
"Simpsons," "Hard Copy," "Donahue"
Classical music, rhythm & blues, rap
*Vogue, Food & Wine, Business Week*
TV dinners, health food, canned hash, jam
Imported beer and wine, milk, orange juice
Volvos, Acuras, Cadillacs, Toyotas
Stocks, bonds, $200,000+ home insurance
Liberals, gun control, endangered animals

A SHOTGUN MARRIAGE between a cow town and a state capital produced the Cheyenne-Scottsbluff market. Heavily influenced by the ranches on the surrounding plains, residents enjoy rodeos, horseback riding, and hunting more often than the general population. But befitting Cheyenne's role as the capital and largest city in Wyoming, the area is also a center of business and state politics, where residents form associations through business groups and fraternal orders. A higher-than-average number of residents have gone on to college, explaining the intellectual streak that colors the area's tastes. Despite few cultural opportunities — honky-tonk saloons outnumber the handful of public libraries — residents read books, see movies, and take adult-education courses at above-average rates. As for the local political perspective, this is the conservative frontier: they're down on gays, abortion rights, and big government. When the issues turn to gun control and endangered species, however, their support barely raises a blip on the screen.

| Lower-middle-class commercial center | Predominantly white families | Some college educations | Farm, craft, and construction jobs |
|---|---|---|---|

## Key Demographics

| | | | |
|---|---|---|---|
| Total Population: | 112,906 | Primary Ages of Adults: | 25–44 |
| Median Household Income: | $27,538 | Median Home Value: | $65,064 |

# Chicago, Illinois

## What's Hot

The arts, travel, pro basketball, fashion, bars
Tennis, bowling, bicycling, golf, skiing
CD players, VCRs, PCs, faxes, books
"Letterman," "In Living Color," "60 Minutes"
Jazz, classical, rhythm & blues, rock, rap
*Wall Street Journal, Essence, GQ, Vogue*
Fish, health food, take-out, Ben & Jerry's
Imported beer, wine, scotch, ale, cocktails
Acuras, Infinitis, Ferraris, Rolls-Royces
Gold cards, stocks, mutual funds, bonds
Liberals, gay rights, consumerism

## What's Not

Photography, veterans clubs, used cars, pets
Camping, gardening, woodworking, fishing
Power tools, microwaves, recliners, washers
Soaps, "Coach," "American Gladiators," Disney
Country, religious radio, college football
*McCall's, Family Handyman, True Story*
Ham, beef stew, sweet rolls, Jell-O, raisins
Pepsi-Cola, Kool-Aid, tea, lemon-lime soda
Pontiacs, Chevys, Mercurys, Dodges, Plymouths
Mail-order medical insurance, loans, Medicare
Conservatives, toxic waste, pro-lifers

IF CHICAGO IS the city of broad shoulders, those shoulders are fitted into chic designer jackets. A populace that's far more affluent, educated, and white-collar than average Americans has produced a decidedly yuppie lifestyle. Taking advantage of the area's numerous museums, jazz clubs, symphony orchestras, and dramatic groups, upscale residents go to cultural events much more often than the general population. Chicagoans have the money to buy stocks, real estate, and fine art at above-average rates. True, there's a proletarian streak in town evidenced by the popularity of bowling, horse racing, and vegging out in front of the tube while one of the local pro sports franchises does battle. As the song goes, Chicago is indeed a toddlin' town, where the popularity of alcohol is astonishing both for quantity and variety: scotch, imported beer, wine, ale — you name it, they drink it in Chicago.

| Upper-middle-class metropolis | Racially and ethnically diverse singles and families | College educations | White-collar jobs in business and finance |
|---|---|---|---|

## Key Demographics

| | | | |
|---|---|---|---|
| Total Population: | 8,588,024 | Primary Ages of Adults: | 25–44 |
| Median Household Income: | $39,753 | Median Home Value: | $109,543 |

# Chico-Redding, California

## What's Hot  What's Not

| What's Hot | What's Not |
|---|---|
| Health food, RVs, crafts, movies, pets | Health clubs, concerts, fashion, unions |
| Camping, fishing, skiing, sewing, hunting | Sailing, golf, tennis, exercise |
| Books, audiocassettes, food processors | PCs, leased cars, CD players, coupons |
| "Nightline," "Tonight Show," "Northern Exposure" | "General Hospital," "Hard Copy," Nickelodeon |
| Rock, country, golden oldies, college sports | Jazz, rhythm & blues, rap, pop music |
| *Outdoor Life, Ladies' Home Journal, Cycle* | *Time, Car & Driver, Life, New Yorker* |
| Mexican food, cheese, dried fruit, nuts | TV dinners, cold cuts, waffles, chocolates |
| Tomato juice, light beer, skim milk, cocoa | Milk, malt liquor, diet soda, imported beer |
| Mercurys, Subarus, Chryslers, Dodge trucks | Hondas, Acuras, Audis, BMWs, Mercedes-Benzes |
| Investment property, veterans life insurance | Stocks, savings bonds, precious metals |
| Moderates, pro-lifers, less government | Conservatives, gun control, toxic waste |

LOCATED IN CALIFORNIA'S remote northern interior, Chico-Redding is a magnet for the three uniquely American kinds of settlers: retirees, resort-lovers, and rural townsfolk. With more than 40 percent of adults over the age of 55, the area offers a laid-back lifestyle where residents can camp, fish, and boat in the nearby forests, lakes, and mountains. Indoors, locals tend to enjoy home-based activities, such as making crafts, knitting, sewing, and reading — everything from science fiction to the Bible. Because a significant portion of residents are recent emigrants from the state's metropolitan areas — in part, fleeing the glitz and liberal social values of the cities — they tend to be political moderates on such issues as abortion, gay rights, and pornography. And forget about the notion of government as friend of the people. In Chico-Redding, residents support cutting government, the military, and taxes; all the better to invest their money in coins, stamps, and real estate, or, better yet, save it for their grandchildren.

| Lower-middle-class agricultural area | Predominantly white couples | Some college educations | Farm, forestry, and construction jobs |
|---|---|---|---|

## Key Demographics

| | | | |
|---|---|---|---|
| Total Population: | 447,125 | Primary Ages of Adults: | 55+ |
| Median Household Income: | $26,243 | Median Home Value: | $94,497 |

# Cincinnati, Ohio

## What's Hot  What's Not

| What's Hot | What's Not |
|---|---|
| Theme parks, mall shopping, home improvement | Country clubs, gourmet cooking, casinos |
| Golf, bowling, gardening, boating, jogging | Racquetball, sailing, skiing, sewing |
| 35mm cameras, power tools, CD players | Vans, microwaves, cable TV, passports |
| TV golf, "Joan Rivers," "Wonder Years" | "Love Connection," "Fresh Prince," "Jeopardy" |
| Classic rock, golden oldies, classical, pop | Modern rock, rhythm & blues, jazz, country |
| *Discover, Popular Mechanics, 1001 Home Ideas* | *Gourmet, Ski, Ebony, American Photo, Forbes* |
| Beef, spaghetti sauce, baked beans, Pop Tarts | Health food, chili, canned chicken, jam, candy |
| Powdered drinks, domestic beer, fruit juices | Herbal tea, Diet Coke, light beer, scotch |
| Saturns, Pontiacs, Dodges, Olds Calais | Acuras, VWs, Lincolns, BMWs, Lexus SC3s |
| Christmas clubs, savings bonds, Sears cards | Medical insurance, investment property, bonds |
| Moderates, endangered animals, death penalty | Liberals, abortion rights, less government |

RICH IN ARCHITECTURE, culture, and industry, Cincinnati comes across like a blue-collar town with white-collar aspirations. Although residents are less than academically inclined — fewer than 20 percent finished college — a surprising number are science and technology buffs who read magazines like *Discover, Home Mechanix, Popular Science,* and *Popular Mechanics.* And being the home of package-goods giant Procter and Gamble has made area consumers more receptive to down-home cooking than gourmet cuisine; dry pasta, brownie mix, Stove Top stuffing, and Shake 'N Bake all sell at above-average rates here. Politically, Cincinnatians describe themselves as moderates, and they're right on target. Surveys show they're more liberal on issues concerning the environment and endangered animals, while more conservative on social concerns involving gay and abortion rights. The uproar over the homoerotic photography of Robert Mapplethorpe here could have been predicted.

| Middle-class commercial center | Predominantly white families and singles | High school educations | Manufacturing and service jobs |
|---|---|---|---|

## Key Demographics

| | | | |
|---|---|---|---|
| Total Population: | 2,077,310 | Primary Ages of Adults: | 25–44 |
| Median Household Income: | $32,994 | Median Home Value: | $74,002 |

# Clarksburg-Weston, West Virginia

## What's Hot

Mobile homes, cable TV, baking, RVs
Hunting, fishing, gardening, sewing
Trucks, 126/110 cameras, auto tools, tractors
"Current Affair," "Family Feud," "Major Dad"
Gospel, country, religious radio
*Outdoor Life, National Enquirer, TV Guide*
Frankfurters, beef stew, pudding, pie, gum
Cola, powdered drinks, Pepsi-Cola, tea
Pontiacs, Oldsmobiles, Fords, Dodge trucks
Medical insurance, investment property, CDs
Moderates, death penalty, toxic waste

## What's Not

Travel, movies, concerts, health clubs, art
Golf, bicycling, tennis, skiing, racquetball
CD players, PCs, books, stereos, condoms
"Star Trek," "National Geographic," "Sisters"
Jazz, classical, pop, rhythm & blues
*Smithsonian, Mademoiselle, Food & Wine*
TV dinners, pumpernickel, cheese, pretzels
Wine, imported beer, malt liquor, skim milk
Mazdas, Hondas, Cadillacs, Volvos, VW trucks
Stocks, mutual funds, bonds, IRAs
Liberals, gun control, gay rights

ISOLATION BREEDS SELF-SUFFICIENCY. At least, that may be the maxim here in this mountain market in central West Virginia. With half of all households earning under $20,000 a year, area residents make do with what they have — which is to say, not a lot. They're far more likely than average Americans to do their own house renovations (installing windows, roofing, lighting fixtures, and major appliances) and car repairs (sales are big for car batteries, tires, and spark plugs). Their favorite leisure pursuits are the kind that put food on the table: hunting, fishing, and gardening. By contrast, Clarksburg-Weston residents express little interest in trendy activities involving the arts, gourmet cooking, or the latest fashions. While magazine readership around here is low — except for outdoor and entertainment publications like *Outdoor Life, True Story,* and the *Star* — local folks do keep in touch with mainstream culture through television. Indeed, in the Clarksburg-Weston area, it's not uncommon to see a giant satellite dish in the backyard of a mobile home.

| *Downscale industrial town* | *Predominantly white families and couples* | *High school educations* | *Farming and mining jobs* |
|---|---|---|---|

## Key Demographics

| | | | |
|---|---|---|---|
| Total Population: | 269,149 | Primary Ages of Adults: | 55+ |
| Median Household Income: | $20,530 | Median Home Value: | $44,582 |

# Cleveland, Ohio

## What's Hot

Book clubs, pro sports, movies, lottery
Bowling, golf, home decorating, crafts
Lawn mowers, VCRs, CD players, vans
"Regis & Kathie Lee," "Empty Nest," "Roseanne"
Talk radio, classic rock, golden oldies, jazz
*Discover, Consumer's Digest, Parade, Life*
Fish, spaghetti sauce, salad dressing, doughnuts
Scotch, rum, imported wine, skim milk, Pabst
Chevys, Dodges, Pontiacs, Plymouth Sundances
Savings bonds, life insurance, JC Penney cards
Moderates, endangered animals, ocean dumping

## What's Not

Country clubs, college sports, baking, the arts
Skiing, horseback riding, tennis, hunting
Microwaves, motorcycles, passports, cameras
"Star Trek," "Meet the Press," "Full House"
Gospel, modern rock, classical, country
*Architectural Digest, True Story, Sunset*
Mexican food, rice, jam, frozen yogurt, candy
Malt liquor, cola, tea, imported beer, Bud
Porsches, Mercedes-Benzes, Isuzus, Mazda MP5s
Keoghs, mutual funds, investment property
Liberals, less government, legalizing drugs

NOTHING ABOUT CLEVELAND truly stands out. With its average incomes, home values, and education levels, Ohio's largest city stays near the mean on consuming everything from books and stocks to motorcycles and pets. Opinion polls reflect average-American views on abortion, school prayer, and gay rights. Residents tend to avoid both upscale magazines like *Architectural Digest* and downscale publications like *True Story*. With a high concentration of the workforce on the assembly line, locals shy away from yuppier sports like skiing and racquetball for more proletarian activities like bowling, playing the lottery, and watching the local pro teams on TV. Nor do residents take advantage of the abundant museums and cultural offerings that have made a resurgence in this Rust Belt community. Many keep to their own diverse ethnic groups rather than join country clubs or business groups. Cleveland residents would just as soon go their own way, which generally means a leisurely stroll down the middle of the road.

| *Middle-class industrial port* | *Predominantly white families and singles* | *High school educations* | *Manufacturing and transportation jobs* |
|---|---|---|---|

## Key Demographics

| | | | |
|---|---|---|---|
| Total Population: | 3,804,393 | Primary Ages of Adults: | 35–54 |
| Median Household Income: | $32,124 | Median Home Value: | $71,704 |

# Colorado Springs–Pueblo, Colorado

| What's Hot | What's Not |
|---|---|
| Skiing, RVs, veterans groups, theme parks | Gourmet cooking, fashion, home decorating |
| Running, camping, exercise, fishing, hunting | Tennis, pro wrestling, golf, sailing |
| Boom boxes, cameras, home gyms, bicycles | Chain saws, convertibles, pregnancy-test kits |
| "Coach," "Evening Shade," "Siskel & Ebert" | BET, HBO, "Beverly Hills, 90210," "Hard Copy" |
| Rock, middle-of-the-road, radio college sports | Gospel, rhythm & blues, jazz, news radio |
| *Flying, Skiing, New Woman, Self, Omni* | *Vogue, Star, Esquire, Fortune, Jet* |
| Health food, chili, popcorn, pizza, ice cream | Cold cuts, canned hash, French bread, cookies |
| Diet Coke, draft beer, decaf coffee, cocktails | Scotch, brandy, imported wine, milk |
| Subarus, Isuzus, Nissans, Toyota Previas | Peugeots, Infinitis, Ferraris, Volvo 940s |
| Interest checking, annuities, mutual funds | Keoghs, money orders, medical insurance |
| Conservatives, family values, toxic waste | Liberals, gun control, consumerism |

FOUNDED AS A vacation resort a century ago, this area at the foot of Pike's Peak retains its fun-loving, outdoorsy lifestyle, notwithstanding the significant presence of fundamentalist religious groups and the military. Residents, half of whom are between the ages of 25 and 44, ski, camp, jog, and exercise at rates above the national average. They also tend to read magazines related to their body-centered lifestyles, such as *Skiing, Self, Flying,* and *New Woman.* These baby boom consumers tend to buy books, listen to rock, use computers, and take adult-education courses more often than the general population. With more than half of the area economy related to the military — Colorado Springs is the home of NORAD and the U.S. Air Force Academy — veterans programs and clubs are big in the area. Despite a rise in Christian Right groups in Colorado Springs, opinion surveys find local views only moderately conservative. Indeed, with residents more concerned about privacy rights and downsizing the government than gay rights and consumerism, the area's conservatism is based less on morality than a leave-me-alone attitude.

| *Lower-middle-class residential area* | *Ethnically mixed families* | *Some college educations* | *Farm, education, and service jobs* |
|---|---|---|---|

## Key Demographics

| | | | |
|---|---|---|---|
| Total Population: | 658,789 | Primary Ages of Adults: | 25–44 |
| Median Household Income: | $28,519 | Median Home Value: | $74,595 |

# Columbia, South Carolina

| What's Hot | What's Not |
|---|---|
| Pro wrestling, college sports, the arts | Unions, movies, plane travel, gambling |
| Fishing, gardening, walking, tennis | Sailing, boating, bowling, lotteries |
| Microwaves, pickups, garden tillers, cable TV | Power tools, books, 35mm cameras, recliners |
| "I Love Lucy," game shows, "Fresh Prince" | "Face the Nation," "Joan Rivers," "Wimbledon" |
| Gospel, rhythm & blues, rap | Talk radio, jazz, rock, classical, folk |
| *Essence, Ebony, Soap Opera Digest, Health* | *Money, Smithsonian, Forbes, Stereo Review* |
| Fried chicken, BBQ sauce, rice, candy | Beef, spaghetti sauce, raisin bread, Jell-O |
| Tea, diet soda, malt liquor, cola | Imported brandy, scotch, wine, skim milk |
| Isuzus, Nissans, Pontiacs, GMC trucks | Audis, Saabs, Peugeots, Acura NSXs |
| Medical insurance, coin collecting, securities | Money-market accounts, mutual funds, Keoghs |
| Conservatives, pro-lifers, less government | Liberals, ozone depletion, nuclear waste |

A COMMERCIAL CENTER in the heart of a farming region, Columbia boasts a mix of white- and blue-collar tastes. Upscale residents enjoy fashion, the arts, and home decorating at above-average rates at the same time more downscale neighbors live for hunting and fishing. This is a low-tech area where computers, cameras, and VCRs are all bought less frequently than average Americans buy them. But it is investment conscious, with many residents collecting coins, buying securities, and looking for money-making opportunities. Given that African Americans comprise one-third of the populace, it is not surprising that the area's most popular magazines include *Essence, Ebony,* and *Jet.* Politically speaking, that racial makeup also explains why the concentration of both predominantly black liberals and typically white conservatives results in relatively few moderate views in the area. In Columbia, that extreme polarity tends to negate the two groups on social issues while uniting them in an apathetic attitude toward ecological concerns such as the ozone layer, endangered animals, and nuclear waste.

| *Middle-class commercial center* | *Racially diverse singles and families* | *High school educations* | *Manufacturing, labor, and farm jobs* |
|---|---|---|---|

## Key Demographics

| | | | |
|---|---|---|---|
| Total Population: | 847,725 | Primary Ages of Adults: | 25–44 |
| Median Household Income: | $30,417 | Median Home Value: | $70,637 |

# Columbia–Jefferson City, Missouri

| What's Hot | What's Not |
|---|---|
| College sports, crafts, fine art, baking | Movies, tennis, foreign travel, theater |
| Horseback riding, hunting, fishing, sewing | Skiing, racquetball, swimming, sailing |
| Tupperware, microwaves, 126/110 cameras | Computers, CD players, convertibles |
| "Wheel of Fortune," "Tonight Show," "Major Dad" | VH-1, "Seinfeld," "American Gladiators" |
| Country, golden oldies, adult contemporary | News radio, classical, modern, rock |
| *Reader's Digest, Ladies' Home Journal, Cycle* | *Architectural Digest, Inc., Esquire* |
| Ham, beef stew, Shake 'N Bake, candy, popcorn | TV dinners, corn on the cob, waffles, yogurt |
| Decaf coffee, tea, Pepsi-Cola, skim milk | Wine, imported beer, ale, orange juice |
| Subarus, Chryslers, Ford Crown Victorias | Acuras, Saabs, BMWs, Saturns, VW Cabriolets |
| Medical insurance, loans, mutual funds, CDs | IRAs, savings bonds, precious metals, Keoghs |
| Moderates, pro-lifers, less government | Liberals, gay rights, consumerism |

COLUMBIA MAY BE KNOWN as a classic college town and home to the University of Missouri, but its lifestyle is anything but academic. With its rural setting and a significant percentage of residents working in agriculture, this market behaves more like a redneck farm community. According to one survey, the most popular activities are chewing tobacco, attending rodeos, riding horses, and listening to country music. In another, popular collegiate pursuits such as attending concerts, watching movies, doing recreational drugs, and listening to rock, barely registered any interest. No doubt, the low income and education levels contribute to this downscale lifestyle; even with several other colleges nearby, just 20 percent of all residents hold college diplomas. Around here, the biggest connection locals have with college life is rooting for the home team on TV or radio.

| *Lower-middle-class college town* | *Predominantly white singles* | *High school educations* | *Jobs in farming and education services* |
|---|---|---|---|

**Key Demographics**

| | | | |
|---|---|---|---|
| Total Population: | 368,379 | Primary Ages of Adults: | 25–44 |
| Median Household Income: | $27,162 | Median Home Value: | $55,405 |

# Columbus, Georgia

| What's Hot | What's Not |
|---|---|
| Church events, catalog shopping, the military | Movies, country clubs, foreign travel, books |
| Fishing, hunting, sewing, exercise | Skiing, bicycling, golf, swimming, camping |
| Garden tillers, microwaves, cable TV | PCs, books, VCRs, musical instruments, cameras |
| TV sports, "Showtime at the Apollo," "Oprah" | "Cops," "20/20," "Married with Children" |
| Gospel, rap, rhythm & blues, religious radio | Classical, easy listening, modern rock |
| *Essence, Southern Living, National Enquirer* | *Popular Science, Cosmopolitan, Car & Driver* |
| Fried chicken, macaroni, snack cakes, jam | Fish, beef, pretzels, oat bran, raisins |
| Cocoa, tea, malt liquor, powdered drinks | Wine, beer, coffee, skim milk, tomato juice |
| Pontiacs, Oldsmobiles, Isuzus, Chevy pickups | Acuras, Hondas, VWs, Porsches, Audi 80/90s |
| Money orders, medical and term life insurance | Auto tellers, IRAs, bonds, annuities |
| Conservatives, pro-lifers, less government | Moderates, family values, ozone depletion |

HERE'S THE KIND OF TOWN where Norma Rae would have felt at home. With a number of textile mills in the area, union-resistant workers tend to spend their leisure time working on their cars, watching pro wrestling on the tube, attending church activities, and shopping — even if it's by catalog. Nearby Ft. Benning has attracted a lot of military families to the area, explaining the popularity of area veterans programs, video games for the kids, and weekend pursuits like fishing, hunting, and jogging. By contrast, you won't find too many cosmopolitan interests in Columbus — little in the way of gourmet cooking, fine arts, literature, or foreign travel. Few magazines are read at above-average rates, and they include titles like the *National Enquirer, Soap Opera Digest*, and three publications reflecting a high concentration of African American residents, *Essence, Ebony,* and *Jet.* As opinion pollsters discovered, Columbus is a schizo place with high concentrations of liberals and conservatives, low voter turnouts, and weak support for most issues.

| *Lower-middle-class industrial city* | *Racially diverse singles and families* | *Less than high school educations* | *Manufacturing, labor, and farm jobs* |
|---|---|---|---|

**Key Demographics**

| | | | |
|---|---|---|---|
| Total Population: | 509,234 | Primary Ages of Adults: | 18–34 |
| Median Household Income: | $24,980 | Median Home Value: | $56,744 |

# Columbus, Ohio

| What's Hot | What's Not |
|---|---|
| Books, mall shopping, rock concerts, pets | Health clubs, fraternal orders, casinos |
| Bowling, woodworking, swimming, collectibles | Tennis, fishing, racquetball, exercise |
| VCRs, faxes, bicycles, stereos, motorcycles | Cameras, smoke detectors, luxury cars |
| TV golf, "Am.'s Funniest People," "Dinosaurs" | "Nightline," "Price Is Right," "Empty Nest" |
| Rock, golden oldies, radio baseball | Jazz, rap, gospel, rhythm & blues |
| *Discover, Self, Country Living, Stereo Review* | *Time, Vogue, Forbes, American Photo* |
| Fish, biscuits, baked beans, doughnuts | Health food, canned chicken, sweet rolls |
| Diet soda, skim milk, herbal tea | Imported wine and beer, tea, spring water |
| Subarus, Fords, Pontiacs, VW Corrados | Nissans, Lincolns, Infinitis, Mazda 929s |
| Savings accounts, company stock, mutual funds | Investment property, medical insurance, bonds |
| Moderates, nuclear waste, privacy rights | Liberals, ocean dumping, oil drilling |

IN THIS STATE CAPITAL masquerading as a college town — or is it the other way around? — you've got your football-crazed Ohio State University students and your longtime residents known for their strong midwestern work ethic and traditional values. Among students and recent graduates, books, rock concerts, pets, and used cars are popular. The townies — government and factory workers — spend more of their leisure time maintaining their homes, gardening, making crafts, and hitting the golf course. With Columbus natives outnumbering the academic types, the area scores low on college educations and "good-life" activities, such as the fine arts, classical music, and travel. Surprisingly for a political town, Columbus residents are both moderate and somewhat apathetic, expressing little passion for or against such issues as abortion rights, legalizing drugs, or gay rights. (Redistricting by Republicans has helped negate the liberal student vote.) And locals are even choosy on ecological concerns: worried about nuclear waste but blasé about ocean dumping.

| *Middle-class trade center* | *Predominantly white families and singles* | *High school educations* | *Government, education, and manufacturing jobs* |
|---|---|---|---|

| **Key Demographics** | Total Population: | 1,897,818 | Primary Ages of Adults: | 25–44 |
|---|---|---|---|---|
| | Median Household Income: | $32,107 | Median Home Value: | $71,150 |

# Columbus-Tupelo, Mississippi

| What's Hot | What's Not |
|---|---|
| Church events, pro wrestling, mobile homes | News, politics, dancing, movies, junk mail |
| Hunting, fishing, sewing, gardening | Skiing, golf, exercise, boating, bowling |
| Rifles, trucks, microwaves, tractors | Food processors, PCs, VCRs, convertibles |
| Game shows, "I Love Lucy," "Sally," "Coach" | "Siskel & Ebert," "Doogie Howser," "Roseanne" |
| Gospel, country, urban contemporary radio | Jazz, news radio, classical, rock, middle-of-the-road |
| *Ebony, Essence, TV Guide, National Enquirer* | *Rolling Stone, Money, Omni, Newsweek, Self* |
| Grits, baked beans, snack cakes, macaroni | Fish, cheese, waffles, rye, TV dinners |
| Cola, diet cola, milk, powdered drinks | Wine, beer, skim milk, Diet 7-Up, Heineken |
| Pontiacs, Chevys, Isuzus, Dodge trucks | Acuras, VWs, Mazdas, Audis, Saabs, BMW 6/7s |
| Money orders, medical and life insurance | IRAs, Keoghs, gold cards, mutual funds |
| Conservatives, pro-lifers, less government | Liberals, gay rights, sex ed in schools |

HERE IN THE MISSISSIPPI DELTA, the living ain't easy. Nearly half of all households report incomes of under $20,000 a year; 40 percent of residents failed to finish high school, and many locals hold dead-end jobs. Not surprisingly, leisure activities tend to be the low-cost variety, including fishing, hunting, gardening, and sewing. For nighttime entertainment, residents meet at church, veterans clubs, or each other's homes to watch TV. Despite Tupelo's claim to fame as the birthplace of Elvis Presley, the area's most popular music isn't rock but country, gospel, and the urban contemporary sound. Compared to the rest of the nation, residents in Columbus-Tupelo rank near the bottom for interest in fine art, stock investments, and gourmet cooking. The chasm between the nation's cultural centers and this area is not limited to lifestyle. Around here, folks care little about news, politics, and the environment. While they're as conservative as other farm areas in the Deep South, their voting record is atrociously low.

| *Lower-middle-class agricultural area* | *Racially diverse families and singles* | *Less than high school educations* | *Farm and manufacturing jobs* |
|---|---|---|---|

| **Key Demographics** | Total Population: | 482,440 | Primary Ages of Adults: | 55+ |
|---|---|---|---|---|
| | Median Household Income: | $22,341 | Median Home Value: | $45,224 |

# Corpus Christi, Texas

| What's Hot | What's Not |
|---|---|
| Water sports, car repair, video games, pets | Concerts, movies, book clubs, travel |
| Fishing, sailing, jogging, sewing, hunting | Skiing, tennis, bicycling, lotteries |
| Recliners, videos, microwaves, cable TV | PCs, CD players, records, cameras |
| "Am.'s Funniest Home Videos," "Inside Edition" | "National Geographic," "Seinfeld," "Honeymooners" |
| Spanish radio, country, gospel, golden oldies | Talk radio, classical, soft rock, jazz, pop |
| *True Story, Outdoor Life, TV Guide, Cycle* | *Scientific American, Gourmet, Business Week* |
| Mexican food, fish, Fritos, doughnuts, pudding | TV dinners, canned tuna, chocolates, Wheaties |
| Cola, malt liquor, vegetable juice | Rum, wine, scotch, vodka, diet soda, tea |
| Chevys, Fords, Subaru Justys, Dodge trucks | Mazdas, Acuras, Peugeots, Audis, Saab 9000s |
| Home-improvement loans, mail-order life insurance | CDs, mutual funds, investment property |
| Conservatives, toxic waste, family values | Liberals, gay rights, buying American |

CORPUS CHRISTI is the kind of town that gives marketers gray hairs because of its multiple personalities. Settled as a trading post, it's become a center for ranching, petroleum, and military facilities. In addition, its location on the Gulf Coast has turned it into a resort town, where fishing, sailing, and water sports are popular. The local ranchers engage in hunting, horseback riding, gardening, and listening to country music more often than average Americans. The heavily Hispanic populace also explains the area's fondness for Spanish radio and Mexican food, not to mention the less-obvious pursuit of playing video games (for the typically large families). This is not a wealthy area, and surveys detect relatively little interest in gourmet cooking, foreign travel, designer fashion, and fine arts. Instead, residents try to stretch their dollars, entering sweepstakes, working on their (usually) used cars, clipping coupons, and visiting the area's windy beaches.

| *Lower-middle-class resort town* | *Ethnically diverse families* | *Less than high school educations* | *Jobs in farming, transportation, and crafts* |
|---|---|---|---|

## Key Demographics

| | | | |
|---|---|---|---|
| Total Population: | 516,720 | Primary Ages of Adults: | 25–44 |
| Median Household Income: | $24,788 | Median Home Value: | $51,616 |

# Dallas–Ft. Worth, Texas

| What's Hot | What's Not |
|---|---|
| Exercise, videos, computers, self-improvement | Investment property, bicycling, veterans clubs |
| Jogging, boating, racquetball, weight training | Bowling, skiing, gardening, woodworking |
| PCs, 35mm cameras, faxes, VCRs, home gyms | Recliners, 126/110 cameras, lawn mowers |
| "Simpsons," "Wonder Years," "Letterman" | Game shows, "Nightline," "Fresh Prince" |
| Talk radio, classical, rock, pro football | Country, religious radio, adult contemporary |
| *Inc., New Woman, Omni, GQ, Travel & Leisure* | *Star, Popular Mechanics, Woman's Day, Jet* |
| Fish, beef, rice cakes, chili, sour cream | Cold cuts, pasta, baked beans, snack cakes |
| Imported beer, wine, cocktails, herbal tea | Tea, powdered drinks, tomato juice, Diet Pepsi |
| Infinitis, Jaguars, Acuras, Toyota trucks | Buicks, Oldsmobiles, Dodges, Pontiac 6000s |
| Stocks, annuities, gold cards, bonds | Life insurance, Medicare, Christmas clubs |
| Liberals, gay rights, oil drilling | Moderates, ocean dumping, abortion rights |

YOU WON'T FIND a lot of similarities between the real Dallas and the oily lifestyle popularized by the Ewings of South Fork. But with nearly one-third of all households earning over $50,000 a year, the Metroplex, as the Dallas–Ft. Worth market is known, registers some decidedly upscale activities. Folks around here enjoy fashion, fine art, and foreign travel at above-average rates. And they're big on self-improvement, creating one of the nation's top markets for health clubs, adult-education courses, self-help books, and magazines like *Shape, Self,* and *Inc.* Area residents can be classified as techies, considering their passion for computers, CD players, VCRs, and anything remotely scientific. An aspect many share with the status-conscious Ewings is a high-style taste for designer labels, status imports like Jaguars, and new vacation spots — all pursued at rates above the national average. In the Metroplex, the color of money colors the predominant lifestyle.

| *Middle-class metropolitan sprawl* | *Racially and ethnically diverse families* | *College educations* | *White-collar executives and professionals* |
|---|---|---|---|

## Key Demographics

| | | | |
|---|---|---|---|
| Total Population: | 4,864,023 | Primary Ages of Adults: | 25–44 |
| Median Household Income: | $34,938 | Median Home Value: | $79,975 |

# Davenport, Iowa–Rock Island–Moline–East Moline, Illinois

| What's Hot | What's Not |
|---|---|
| Home improvement, collectibles, grandchildren | Current affairs, casinos, rock concerts |
| Golf, bowling, fishing, sewing, crafts | Skiing, tennis, jogging, sailing, camping |
| Garden tillers, tools, VCRs, motorcycles | CD players, microwaves, sofas, toaster ovens |
| TV sports, "Young & Restless," "Evening Shade" | "Wonder Years," "American Gladiators," "Oprah" |
| Country, golden oldies, radio baseball | News radio, classical, soft rock, jazz, rap |
| *Field & Stream, Home Mechanix, Woman's World* | *Mademoiselle, New Yorker, Barron's, Sunset* |
| Ham, beef, Stove Top stuffing, canned soup | Health food, fried chicken, rice, Häagen-Dazs |
| Coffee, powdered drinks, Diet 7-Up, cocoa | Imported beer and wine, herbal tea, Diet Coke |
| Pontiacs, Oldsmobiles, Dodges, Ford trucks | Hondas, Saabs, Acuras, Mercedes-Benzes |
| Loans, life insurance, CDs, JC Penney cards | Stocks, bonds, precious metals, Visa cards |
| Conservatives, toxic waste, pro-lifers | Liberals, gun control, gay rights |

TIME PASSES SLOWLY in this heartland market known as Quad Cities. The elderly population is considerable—more than one in four household heads is over 65—and traditional. They tell opinion pollsters that "history is more important than current events." Indeed, relatively few read newspapers, watch public affairs programs, and listen to radio news. But they're a sociable lot. When locals hop into their mid- to large-size American cars, it's often to meet other residents of nearby small towns or to visit with grown children and grandchildren. In the Quad Cities market, residents are more likely than average Americans to belong to veterans clubs, business clubs, religious clubs, and unions. Liberals, however, need not apply.

| Middle-class commercial center | Predominantly white families | High school educations | Farm, labor, and manufacturing jobs |
|---|---|---|---|

**Key Demographics**

| | | | |
|---|---|---|---|
| Total Population: | 793,660 | Primary Ages of Adults: | 55+ |
| Median Household Income: | $28,578 | Median Home Value: | $47,388 |

# Dayton, Ohio

| What's Hot | What's Not |
|---|---|
| Book clubs, unions, bowling, coupons | Fine arts, foreign travel, wine, RVs |
| Crafts, boating, woodworking, sewing | Skiing, hunting, tennis, jogging, sailing |
| Recliners, lawn mowers, microwaves, VCRs | CD players, weights, station wagons |
| "Northern Exposure," "Regis & Kathie Lee" | "Face the Nation," "Honeymooners," "Donahue" |
| Heavy metal, country, classic rock | News radio, jazz, modern rock, classical |
| *Family Handyman, 1001 Home Ideas, Parents* | *Architectural Digest, Forbes, Vogue* |
| Nuts, frozen potatoes, biscuits, Pop Tarts | Chili, canned chicken, sweet rolls, rice |
| Skim milk, diet soda, vegetable juice | Imported beer, orange juice, tea, ale |
| Pontiacs, Chevys, Dodges, Plymouth Sundances | Saabs, Volvos, Lexuses, Infinitis, BMW 5s |
| Christmas clubs, savings bonds, auto loans | Keoghs, medical insurance, bonds, gold cards |
| Moderates, sex ed in schools, nuclear waste | Liberals, gay rights, legalizing drugs |

LIKE MANY MIDWESTERN middle-class cities, Dayton is filled with stable blue-collar workers pursuing conforming, middle-brow lifestyles. Residents are more likely than average Americans to watch television, go bowling, and belong to business and hobby clubs. Indeed, the group mentality is so strong here that locals belong to book clubs at above-average rates while being less likely than the general population to buy individual books. Still there is a streak of ambition among Dayton's populace. Residents tend to decorate their homes and take adult-education courses, and they tell pollsters that they like to try new foods and find new ways to invest their money. The goal, however, seems less to rise in class than to maintain a mid-level lifestyle. In Dayton, people are more likely to spend their leisure time putting their feet up in a recliner than shopping-till-they-drop.

| Middle-class industrial city | Predominantly white families | High school educations | Labor, craft, and service jobs |
|---|---|---|---|

**Key Demographics**

| | | | |
|---|---|---|---|
| Total Population: | 1,348,501 | Primary Ages of Adults: | 35–54 |
| Median Household Income: | $32,581 | Median Home Value: | $66,488 |

# Denver, Colorado

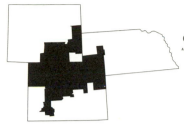

| What's Hot | What's Not |
|---|---|
| Travel, PCs, skiing, pets, self-improvement | Catalog shopping, home improvement, soaps |
| Exercise, bicycling, jogging, camping, tennis | Boating, walking, bowling, coin-collecting |
| Cassette decks, cameras, books, radar detectors | Garden tillers, pickups, crossword puzzles |
| "Murphy Brown," "Simpsons," "Tonight Show" | "Sally," "Family Matters," "Bold & Beautiful" |
| Modern rock, classical, easy listening, country | Gospel, urban contemporary, religious radio |
| *Ski, Scientific American, Gourmet, Self* | *Weight Watchers, Jet, Field & Steam, Star* |
| Mexican food, fish, frozen yogurt, rye, cheese | Sausage, cold cuts, peanut butter, biscuits |
| Diet Coke, wine, imported beer, spring water | Tea, milk, orange juice, powdered drinks |
| Audis, Infinitis, Acuras, Lexus SC3s, VW vans | Oldsmobiles, Buicks, Pontiacs, Chevy Caprices |
| Homeowner's insurance, mutual funds, AmEx | Medical insurance, securities, money orders |
| Liberals, gay rights, ozone depletion | Moderates, school prayer, endangered animals |

WHATEVER HAPPENED TO the Cuisinart-loving y-people of the '80s, those young urban professionals? Well, enough of them have been drawn to cosmopolitan Denver to create a decidedly yuppie lifestyle. Surveys show locals belong to health clubs, travel abroad, and attend movies, plays, and concerts at rates far above the national average. The city ranks among the nation's top ten markets in the ownership of computers, cameras, and stereos. Many residents are serious about skiing, exercise, and bicycling — thanks to the nearby Rockies, which contain some of the nation's most challenging ski and cycling terrain. But unlike other metropolitan areas where upscale residents are preoccupied with status activities like wearing designer clothes, decorating their homes, and investing in real estate, Denver's residents are generally casual, educated, and socially conscious. According to opinion polls, the majority are liberal, concerned about toxic waste and air pollution, and supportive of abortion and gay rights — despite the continuing controversy over the state's gay anti-discrimination legislation.

| *Middle-class metropolis* | *Ethnically diverse families and singles* | *College educations* | *White-collar professionals and administrators* |
|---|---|---|---|

### Key Demographics

| | | | |
|---|---|---|---|
| Total Population: | 2,741,687 | Primary Ages of Adults: | 25–44 |
| Median Household Income: | $34,779 | Median Home Value: | $91,543 |

# Des Moines, Iowa

| What's Hot | What's Not |
|---|---|
| Civic activities, baking, dancing, TV sports | Health food, concerts, casinos, theme parks |
| Fishing, golf, hunting, sewing, walking | Boating, jogging, tennis, skiing |
| Motorcycles, VCRs, tractors, food processors | Pregnancy-test kits, PCs, toaster ovens |
| "NBC Nightly News," "Coach," "Full House" | HBO, "Fresh Prince," "Loving," "Hard Copy" |
| Country, middle-of-the-road, radio baseball | News radio, soft rock, classical, talk radio |
| *Outdoor Life, Ladies' Home Journal, Parents* | *Glamour, Fortune, GQ, Travel & Leisure* |
| Ham, cheese, canned soup, oatmeal | Mexican foods, TV dinners, canned hash, rice |
| Draft beer, powdered drinks, skim milk | Imported wine and beer, milk, orange juice |
| Buicks, Mercurys, Olds 88s, Dodge trucks | Volvos, Porsches, Infinitis, Peugeot 405s |
| Medical insurance, CDs, life insurance | Bonds, stocks, gold cards, ATM cards |
| Moderates, death penalty, family values | Liberals, ocean dumping, gun control |

LIKE MANY CAPITALS of farming states, Des Moines is somewhat a contradiction. On the one hand, government and insurance professionals pursue a fast-track lifestyle, engaging in political activities, taking business trips, and joining country clubs at above-average rates. On the other, tradition-steeped farmers move at a slower pace, going hunting, riding horses, doing their own car repair, and renovating their homes more often than the general population. Although Des Moines is a national center for publishing, locals read relatively few magazines, and most of those are concerned with outdoor sports and home services. More residents are interested in television, especially prime-time programming and sports coverage of golf, horse racing, and auto racing. With one-third of Des Moines citizens retirees or homemakers, made-from-scratch meals are de rigueur. Yet, few residents claim any interest in gourmet cooking, relying on stuffings, breadings, and puddings for their culinary flourishes. Des Moines is the nation's number one market for Jell-O.

| *Middle-class commercial center* | *Predominantly white families and singles* | *Some college educations* | *Jobs in farming, education, and insurance* |
|---|---|---|---|

### Key Demographics

| | | | |
|---|---|---|---|
| Total Population: | 973,276 | Primary Ages of Adults: | 55+ |
| Median Household Income: | $29,620 | Median Home Value: | $51,017 |

# Detroit, Michigan

## What's Hot | What's Not

| What's Hot | What's Not |
|---|---|
| Cars, investments, movies, concerts, unions | Civic activities, home improvement, coupons |
| Bowling, golf, fishing, boating, lotteries | Gardening, woodworking, hunting, camping |
| Radar detectors, faxes, condoms, 35mm cameras | Power tools, microwaves, recliners, pickups |
| "Seinfeld," "Cops," "Oprah," NBA Basketball | "Cheers," "Evening Shade," "Guiding Light" |
| Rhythm & blues, rap, jazz, classical | Country, heavy metal, college football |
| *Jet, Barron's, Inc., Esquire, Mademoiselle* | *Country Living, TV Guide, Prevention* |
| Take-out, fish, waffles, bagels, yogurt | Bacon, sausage, chili, canned vegetables, gum |
| Imported wine, beer, malt liquor, diet soda | Tea, cola, lemon-lime soda, Kool-Aid |
| Cadillacs, Saturns, Mercedes-Benzes, Volvos | Subarus, Dodge trucks, Daihatsu Charades |
| Stocks, savings bonds, mutual funds, IRAs | Medicare, medical insurance, loans |
| Liberals, oil drilling, abortion rights | Conservatives, less government, death penalty |

EVEN WHEN THE auto industry is struggling, Detroit remains a car-crazy town. Out of 243 car models sold in the U.S., area residents buy 220 at above-average rates — including a surprising number of Japanese and European models. And unlike in other major metros, the residents in this, the nation's sixth-largest city, work on their cars more often than the general population. Still, Detroit's lifestyle is like that of many older American cities with a taste for movies, concerts, and cultural events. There's also a preoccupation with money, as residents invest in stocks, buy real estate, and read a number of financial magazines at highest rates. This upscale behavior is in contrast to middlebrow leisure pursuits that are popular among Detroit's numerous blue-collar workers: bowling, powerboating, and lottery playing. But whatever socioeconomic profile, area citizens remember their roots, and not just in automotive matters. Surveys show that in Motown, the most popular music is rhythm & blues.

| *Upper-middle-class urban metropolis* | *Racially diverse families and singles* | *High school educations* | *Business and transportation jobs* |
|---|---|---|---|

### Key Demographics

| | | | |
|---|---|---|---|
| Total Population: | 4,735,784 | Primary Ages of Adults: | 35–54 |
| Median Household Income: | $38,109 | Median Home Value: | $74,324 |

# Dothan, Alabama

## What's Hot | What's Not

| What's Hot | What's Not |
|---|---|
| Veterans programs, trucks, cable TV, the Bible | Dancing, health clubs, theater, travel |
| Fishing, hunting, horseback riding | Skiing, tennis, golf, sailing, exercise |
| Gardening tools, mobile homes, recliners | PCs, bicycles, weights, books, cameras |
| BET, "Fresh Prince," "Rescue 911," "Sally" | VH-1, "Siskel & Ebert," "Wonder Years" |
| Gospel, country, urban contemporary | Talk radio, jazz, classical, modern rock |
| *True Story, Southern Living, Ebony, TV Guide* | *Architectural Digest, Food & Wine, Discover* |
| Hot dogs, bacon, BBQ sauce, rice, Fritos, jam | Canned tuna, spaghetti sauce, Ben & Jerry's |
| Tea, cola, diet soda, orange juice | Wine, imported and draft beer, skim milk |
| Pontiacs, Chryslers, Isuzus, GMC trucks | Saturns, Audis, Volvos, Saabs, Ferraris |
| Money orders, medical and term life insurance | Mutual funds, annuities, bonds, IRAs |
| Conservatives, school prayer, pro-lifers | Liberals, gun control, gay rights |

ANYONE WITH PROGRESSIVE notions of life in Dixie should visit this city of 90,000 in southeast Alabama. Surrounded by peanut farms, lumber mills, textile factories, and nearby Fort Rucker, Dothan is a study in downscale lifestyles typical of the Deep South. With nearly 40 percent of residents over the age of 55, activities like gardening, crafts, and sewing are popular — not to mention spoiling grandchildren with video games. With African Americans comprising 40 percent of the populace, media tastes lean toward rap and blues as well as publications like *Ebony* and *Essence*. And with the area's military presence, residents take advantage of veterans programs, hunting, and jogging at rates above the national average. Granted, there are at least two passions that unite these diverse groups: pickup trucks and old-time religion. Besides buying 189 truck models at rates above the national average, locals also spend their time listening to religious radio, reading the Bible, and supporting issues like school prayer. Dothan is God-and-gun country.

| *Lower-middle-class farm and timber area* | *Racially diverse families and couples* | *Less than high school educations* | *Farm, timber, and manufacturing jobs* |
|---|---|---|---|

### Key Demographics

| | | | |
|---|---|---|---|
| Total Population: | 243,576 | Primary Ages of Adults: | 55+ |
| Median Household Income: | $25,473 | Median Home Value: | $51,476 |

# Duluth, Minnesota–Superior, Wisconsin

| What's Hot | What's Not |
|---|---|
| Home improvement, fishing, crossword puzzles | Casinos, movies, theater, country clubs |
| Crafts, hunting, golf, boating, camping | Tennis, jogging, exercise, racquetball |
| Auto tools, Tupperware, VCRs, RVs | CD players, PCs, books, antiques |
| "Young & Restless," "Major Dad," "Cheers" | "David Brinkley," "Married with Children" |
| Golden oldies, country, adult contemporary | Jazz, rap, classical, modern rock |
| *Sports Afield, Woman's Day, Home Mechanix* | *Travel & Leisure, Vogue, Financial World* |
| Fish, ham, baked beans, pudding, pie, popcorn | Health food, canned chicken, raisin bread |
| Countrytime, ground coffee, diet soda | Imported wine and beer, orange juice, tea |
| Pontiacs, Buicks, Chevys, Mercury Topazes | Saabs, Sterlings, Acuras, Nissan 300ZXs |
| Life insurance, home-improvement loans, CDs | Bonds, gold cards, homeowner's insurance |
| Moderates, toxic waste, sex ed in schools | Liberals, ozone depletion, gun control |

THE RESIDENTS OF THESE twin ports, not far from rugged wilderness, make the most of the area's pristine lakes and timberland. They fish, camp, hunt, and go boating at some of the highest rates in the nation. A large percentage of retirees also make indoor activities like needlework, crafts, and crossword puzzles popular in this market. With modest incomes and education levels, residents express little interest in good-life activities, such as fashion, fine art, and foreign travel. On the other hand, they do engage in civic activities much more often than average Americans, and they really get riled up over threats to wildlife and the environment. Given the abundance of fish and game, however, locals care little about endangered animals.

| Lower-middle-class ports | Predominantly white families | High school educations | Jobs in timber, mining, and transportation |
|---|---|---|---|

## Key Demographics

| | | | |
|---|---|---|---|
| Total Population: | 438,183 | Primary Ages of Adults: | 55+ |
| Median Household Income: | $24,170 | Median Home Value: | $43,654 |

# El Centro, California–Yuma, Arizona

| What's Hot | What's Not |
|---|---|
| Gambling, car repair, vitamins, veterans clubs | Health clubs, movies, books, pregnancy-test kits |
| Horseback riding, woodworking, sewing, camping | Tennis, racquetball, skiing, weight training |
| Microwaves, cable TV, 126/110 cameras, tools | PCs, VCRs, chain saws, stereos, toaster ovens |
| TV news, "Coach," World Series, "Empty Nest" | Showtime, "Hard Copy," "Doogie Howser" |
| Country, religious radio, adult contemporary | Modern rock, rhythm & blues, news radio |
| *Outdoor Life, Ladies' Home Journal, Flying* | *People, Playboy, Fortune, Car & Driver* |
| Mexican foods, beef stew, dried fruit, nuts | Fish, cold cuts, rice cakes, pretzels, rye |
| Powdered drinks, decaf coffee, light beer | Imported beer, Coca-Cola, orange juice |
| Lincolns, Mercurys, Subaru, Nissan trucks | Peugeots, Acuras, Volvos, Hyundai Sonatas |
| Medical insurance, mutual funds, auto loans | Savings accounts, bonds, stocks, IRAs |
| Moderates, nuclear waste, death penalty | Liberals, endangered animals, abortion rights |

YUMA HAS BEEN DESCRIBED as an oversized pit stop for cross-country truckers, a confluence of diners and motels in the middle of the desert. Nearby El Centro, however, is more the farm town, thanks to irrigation water from the Colorado River. Together they offer a laid-back rural lifestyle that's attracted a sizable number of retirees, farmers, and military families affiliated with the nearby testing grounds. In this market, residents engage in woodworking, sewing, and walking for their health at higher-than-average rates. They rank first in the nation in the ownership of recreational and four-wheel-drive vehicles, the better to explore the nearby desert. With the strong elderly presence, denture cleansers and hair color products are big sellers at local drug stores. And befitting this area's crossroads locale, residents are motor-heads: they work on their cars and watch TV auto races at above-average rates. When they go out to eat, it's very often to drive to one of the local truck stop diners.

| Downscale desert communities | Ethnically diverse families and couples | Less than high school educations | Farm, transportation, and construction jobs |
|---|---|---|---|

## Key Demographics

| | | | |
|---|---|---|---|
| Total Population: | 240,348 | Primary Ages of Adults: | 25–44 |
| Median Household Income: | $25,330 | Median Home Value: | $72,768 |

# El Paso, Texas

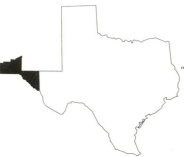

## What's Hot

Veterans programs, foreign travel, fast food
Camping, exercise, coin collecting
Boom boxes, microwaves, home workshops
"NBC Boxing," "Simpsons," "Star Trek," "Cops"
Spanish radio, rap, rhythm & blues, jazz
*Playboy, TV Guide, Soap Opera Digest, Glamour*
Mexican food, yogurt, candy bars, doughnuts
Imported beer, Coca-Cola, spring water, tea
Nissan Sentras, Toyota Tercels, Isuzu trucks
Money orders, savings accounts, Ward cards
Liberals, toxic waste, abortion rights

## What's Not

Country clubs, movies, unions, low-cal food
Fishing, boating, golf, skiing, tennis
VCRs, power tools, 35mm cameras, new cars
"Letterman," U.S. Open, "Donahue," "Sisters"
Country, classical, religious radio
*Consumer's Digest, Inc., House Beautiful*
Cheese, popcorn, Jell-O, pasta, canned tuna
Skim milk, diet sodas, light beer, cocoa
Chevys, Eagles, Dodges, Porsches, Ford Tempos
Life insurance, CDs, mutual funds, Keoghs
Conservatives, death penalty, privacy rights

IMAGINE A UTOPIAN multicultural city where Americans of varied ancestry live side by side, speaking different languages and sharing in the celebration of their different ethnic cultures. Now consider El Paso. The country's largest bilingual metropolis — with 64 percent of its 600,000 residents Latino — is a somewhat shabby city on the Mexican border colored by nationalist tensions, smelly copper mills, and the massive Fort Bliss military base. The high concentration of singles explains the area's passion for aerobic exercise, four-wheel-drive vehicles, *Playboy*, and fast-food joints. Residents frequent Taco Bell, Denny's, Popeye's, and Church's Fried Chicken at above-average rates. Not surprisingly, they also seem to have an aversion to dietetic food, consuming relatively little yogurt, skim milk, diet soda, light beer, and Weight Watchers sherbet. With low incomes, there's not a lot of money for big-ticket items like cars; only a handful of imported subcompacts are purchased at above-average rates. Then again, who needs them? To visit another country, it's not a big hassle to walk across the Cordova Bridge into Mexico.

| *Lower-middle-class commercial center* | *Ethnically diverse families and singles* | *Less than high school educations* | *Labor, service, and manufacturing jobs* |
|---|---|---|---|

**Key Demographics**

| | | | |
|---|---|---|---|
| Total Population: | 791,054 | Primary Ages of Adults: | 25–44 |
| Median Household Income: | $24,807 | Median Home Value: | $62,858 |

# Elmira, New York

## What's Hot

Mall shopping, cable TV, baking, RVs
Hunting, needlework, gardening, crafts
Power tools, lawn furniture, ceiling fans
"Am.'s Funniest People," "Cheers," "Sally"
Adult contemporary, heavy metal, radio baseball
*Redbook, Country Living, Reader's Digest*
Hot dogs, canned vegetables, pasta, pretzels
Pepsi-Cola, diet sodas, decaf coffee
Oldsmobiles, Chevys, Pontiacs, Subaru Justys
Coin collecting, CDs, auto loans, Sears cards
Moderates, less government, pro-lifers

## What's Not

Foreign travel, fashion, current affairs
Jogging, skiing, tennis, bicycling, boating
CD players, PCs, 35mm cameras, sofa beds
VH-1, "National Geographic," "Murphy Brown"
News radio, classical, jazz, rhythm & blues
*Working Woman, Vanity Fair, Time, Sunset*
Health food, TV dinners, rice, French bread
Wine, imported beer, malt liquor, cocktails
Volvos, Acuras, Ferraris, Mercedes-Benz 500s
Stocks, precious metals, Keoghs, AmEx cards
Liberals, gun control, air pollution

THERE'S NO SMALL IRONY that Elmira, the punchline of jokes about godforsaken places, is the burial site of Mark Twain. Like many aging industrial cities, Elmira has a sedate lifestyle far removed from Twain's hard-drinking, cigar-smoking, pool-playing ways. The area's many retirees — half the residents are over 50 years old — prefer activities like coin collecting, making crafts, doing crossword puzzles, and gardening. Comparatively few are into current affairs, the latest movies, and news magazines covering popular culture. In blue-collar Elmira, residents are into anaerobic athletics, more interested in bowling and listening to baseball on the radio than jogging or playing tennis. And yet for all their staid pursuits, Elmira residents believe strongly in the right of individuals to be as iconoclastic as Samuel Clemens. In opinion polls, they support more privacy protections, less government regulations, and no particular preferences for the elderly because of their age or experience.

| *Lower-middle-class manufacturing center* | *Predominantly white couples and singles* | *High school educations* | *Manufacturing and transportation jobs* |
|---|---|---|---|

**Key Demographics**

| | | | |
|---|---|---|---|
| Total Population: | 238,379 | Primary Ages of Adults: | 55+ |
| Median Household Income: | $27,832 | Median Home Value: | $52,587 |

# Erie, Pennsylvania

## What's Hot | What's Not

| What's Hot | What's Not |
|---|---|
| Baking, lotteries, videos, book clubs | Health clubs, gambling casinos, travel, wine |
| Woodworking, golf, boating, bowling, walking | Tennis, exercise, bicycling, racquetball |
| VCRs, microwaves, grills, recliners | CD players, stereos, PCs, sofa beds |
| "Current Affair," "Major Dad," "Sisters" | "In Living Color," "Geraldo," "Nightline" |
| Golden oldies, classic rock, country | News radio, jazz, urban contemporary |
| *Popular Mechanics, Woman's World, Star* | *Architectural Digest, Fortune, Essence* |
| Fish, pudding, spaghetti sauce, pasta, nuts | Take-out, chili, canned chicken, yogurt, jam |
| Powdered drinks, skim milk, ground coffee | Diet Coke, orange juice, herbal tea |
| Chevys, Pontiacs, Eagles, Dodge trucks | BMWs, Volvos, Ferraris, Saabs, Audis |
| Christmas clubs, savings bonds, auto loans | Homeowner's insurance, stocks, gold cards |
| Moderates, buying American, privacy rights | Liberals, family values, gun control |

THOSE IN SEARCH OF the perfect bowling alley — you know who you are — should not pass up a visit to Erie. Here in this Rust Belt shipping center, there are 37 bowling alleys — about one lane for every 350 homes. But the popularity of bowling is just one sign of Erie's blue-collar predilections. Residents also have a fondness for unions, powerboating, woodworking, and playing the lottery. And with a significant number of area women working at home, cooking and eating are popular sports. Indeed, Erie residents consume relatively large amounts of Shake 'N Bake and Stove Top stuffing along with beef, chicken, and fish — all the ingredients for middlebrow home-cooked meals. And this image of the old-fashioned household is completed in the driveway, where locals still tend to drive midsize cars made in nearby Detroit. Erie is buy-American country.

| Lower-middle-class port city | Predominantly white families and singles | High school educations | Transportation, craft, and manufacturing jobs |
|---|---|---|---|

**Key Demographics**

| | | | |
|---|---|---|---|
| Total Population: | 414,885 | Primary Ages of Adults: | 55+ |
| Median Household Income: | $28,192 | Median Home Value: | $53,515 |

# Eugene, Oregon

## What's Hot | What's Not

| What's Hot | What's Not |
|---|---|
| The arts, travel, jogging, books, health food | Theater, fashion, home furnishing, lotteries |
| Bicycling, boating, skiing, camping, fishing | Tennis, walking, stamp collecting |
| PCs, cameras, VCRs, microwaves, 4WD vehicles | Convertibles, Tupperware, kitchen improvements |
| "Saturday Night Live," "Northern Exposure" | "Family Feud," "Geraldo," "Murder, She Wrote" |
| Modern rock, golden oldies, baseball | News radio, jazz, classical, rhythm & blues |
| *Self, Field & Stream, Omni, Rolling Stone* | *Life, Ebony, Star, Business Week, Vogue* |
| Fish, apples, cheese, popcorn, pizza | TV dinners, cold cuts, canned hash, pie |
| Light beer, skim milk, cocktails, cocoa | Whole milk, orange juice, tea, Diet Coke |
| Subarus, Chryslers, Chevys, GMC trucks | BMWs, Volvos, Peugeots, Lexus LS400s |
| Mutual funds, loans, savings accounts | Keoghs, bonds, life insurance |
| Moderates, death penalty, toxic waste disposal | Liberals, gun control, gay rights |

THERE'S A '60s feel to this rustic college town, with its mix of students and professionals, hippies and loggers. Running and biking are big in Eugene thanks to the numerous trails and paths crisscrossing the town; in fact, locals claim to have launched the '70s jogging revolution. The presence of the University of Oregon has also spawned a lively cultural scene, and residents express an interest in literature, photography, live music (mostly rock), and fine art. But Eugene's rural setting has also attracted its share of loggers and retirees who've made fishing, hunting, and gardening among the most popular activities in town. This unlikely demographic mix has created an odd political perspective, a kind of frontier liberalism where locals support the death penalty and less government regulation while opposing gay rights and gun control.

| Lower-middle-class college town | Predominantly white couples and singles | Some college educations | Education and forestry jobs |
|---|---|---|---|

**Key Demographics**

| | | | |
|---|---|---|---|
| Total Population: | 456,329 | Primary Ages of Adults: | 35–54 |
| Median Household Income: | $26,533 | Median Home Value: | $65,546 |

# Eureka, California

| What's Hot | What's Not |
|---|---|
| Gourmet cooking, photography, wine, pets | Gambling, theater, health clubs, fashion |
| Camping, skiing, fishing, collectibles | Tennis, golf, sailing, exercise |
| Cable TV, VCRs, tape players, camcorders | PCs, CD players, car batteries, stereos |
| "Evening Shade," "Northern Exposure," "Cops" | "All My Children," "Donahue," "Wonder Years" |
| Country, rock, golden oldies, religious radio | Urban contemporary, easy listening, classical |
| *Outdoor Life, Colonial Homes, Redbook, Cycle* | *Parade, Consumer's Digest, Forbes, Newsweek* |
| Health food, beef, cheese, raisins, Wheaties | Spaghetti sauce, cold cuts, canned hash, rye |
| Light beer, skim milk, lemon-lime soda, cocoa | Imported beer and wine, orange juice, Tab |
| Dodges, Pontiacs, Buicks, Subaru Loyales | Mercedes-Benzes, Jaguars, Audis, Saturns |
| Medical insurance, investment property, CDs | Homeowner's insurance, mutual funds, bonds |
| Moderates, ozone depletion, toxic waste | Liberals, endangered animals, consumerism |

EUREKA IS SOMETHING of a paradox: an industrial city at the gateway of some of the nation's oldest redwood and sequoia forests. Accordingly, the lifestyle of residents — a mix of working-class loggers, yuppies escaping the smog of the state's big cities, and corporate execs living in Victorian mansions — is a stew of high- and lowbrow activities. Compared to the national average, residents are more likely to read books, collect fine art, and buy investment property as well as hunt, work on their cars, and enter sweepstakes. The rugged wilderness nearby helps explain the local passion for camping, hiking, and fishing. And Eureka's location near California's prime wine-producing valleys also explains the popularity of wine and gourmet cooking. For politicians, however, satisfying Eureka's disparate voters is a nightmare: on environmental issues, surveys find that residents worry about toxic waste, air pollution, and the depletion of the ozone layer while expressing little concern for endangered animals, oil drilling, and ocean dumping. Tree huggers would do better elsewhere.

| *Lower-middle-class industrial town* | *Predominantly white singles and couples* | *Some college educations* | *Fishing and forestry jobs* |
|---|---|---|---|

| **Key Demographics** | | | | |
|---|---|---|---|---|
| Total Population: | 150,434 | Primary Ages of Adults: | 25–44 |
| Median Household Income: | $26,216 | Median Home Value: | $94,078 |

# Evansville, Indiana

| What's Hot | What's Not |
|---|---|
| Veterans clubs, home furnishing, collectibles | Movies, fashion, the arts, gourmet cooking |
| Bowling, fishing, hunting, knitting, crafts | Camping, jogging, skiing, tennis, bicycling |
| Powerboats, cable TV, video games, Tupperware | PCs, 35mm cameras, VCRs, stereos |
| "Indianapolis 500," "Price Is Right," "Coach" | "Meet the Press," "Married with Children" |
| Golden oldies, religious radio, country | Urban contemporary, news radio, soft rock |
| *Reader's Digest, Family Handyman, Parents* | *Cosmopolitan, Time, Food & Wine, Ebony* |
| Ham, sausage, canned soup, pasta, snack cakes | TV dinners, take-out, yogurt, English muffins |
| Decaf coffee, Pepsi-Cola, diet sodas | Wine, imported beer, herbal tea, cocktails |
| Chevys, Pontiacs, Oldsmobiles, Dodge Rams | Toyotas, Mitsubishis, Mazdas, Cadillacs |
| Life insurance, auto loans, money orders | Stocks, bonds, gold cards, Keoghs |
| Moderates, pro-lifers, less government | Liberals, legalizing drugs, gay rights |

AS A COMMERCIAL CENTER for an agricultural and manufacturing area, Evansville boasts an old-fashioned lifestyle for its working-class households. Men hunt, women bake from scratch, and the cut of your lawn means more than the cut of your designer suit. In this market, there's little interest in foreign travel, gourmet cooking, or the arts. Residents take advantage of the number of bowling alleys, as well as area lakes and fields for fishing and hunting. Although local voters describe themselves as moderates, their values are heartland conservative, and they worry about what they perceive as urban ills (read: drugs and the gay culture) coming to their community. In Evansville, residents live by their hands, in the fields and factories as well as away from work with activities like gardening, sewing, and car repair.

| *Lower-middle-class commercial center* | *Predominantly white families* | *High school educations* | *Farm, mining, and manufacturing jobs* |
|---|---|---|---|

| **Key Demographics** | | | | |
|---|---|---|---|---|
| Total Population: | 693,903 | Primary Ages of Adults: | 55+ |
| Median Household Income: | $27,254 | Median Home Value: | $50,410 |

# Fargo, North Dakota

## What's Hot

| What's Hot | What's Not |
|---|---|
| Clubs, mall shopping, college sports, baking | Movies, pro sports, travel, fashion, the arts |
| Hunting, fishing, bowling, sewing, camping | Racquetball, sailing, exercise, tennis, golf |
| Power tools, radios, recliners, RVs | CD players, hatchbacks, VCRs, PCs |
| TV news, "Major Dad," "Full House," "Cheers" | VH-1, "Joan Rivers," "In Living Color" |
| Middle-of-the-road, country, religious radio | Rap, modern rock, classical, rhythm & blues |
| *Ladies' Home Journal, Popular Mechanics* | *People, Gourmet, Barron's, Cosmopolitan* |
| Beef, baked beans, tortilla chips, pudding | Health food, spaghetti sauce, French bread |
| Light beer, ground coffee, skim milk | Imported beer, ale, wine, orange juice |
| Buicks, Pontiacs, Dodges, Geos, Olds 98s | Mazdas, Cadillacs, Hondas, Toyota trucks |
| Medical insurance, CDs, first mortgages | Savings bonds, gas credit cards, mutual funds |
| Conservatives, pro-lifers, less government | Liberals, military cutbacks, ozone depletion |

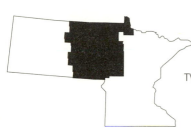

THE RESIDENTS OF North Dakota's largest city are, for the most part, conservative, civic-minded, and collegiate. With three colleges in the area, surveys reflect the popularity of college sports, adult-education courses, bicycling, and motorcycles. The high percentage of farm families around Fargo also makes for a classic rural American lifestyle, with residents enjoying fishing, hunting, gardening, and home-based activities like sewing, making crafts, and reading the Bible. Fargo's role as a commercial center in this big and sparsely populated prairie state draws people together in groups, and membership rates are high for business clubs, country clubs, fraternal orders, and veterans groups. Local voters long ago developed a prairie populism on the otherwise conservative landscape. Even during bitter winters, locals attend political forums of local legislators — if only to vote for less government intrusion in their lives.

| *Lower-middle-class farming center* | *Predominantly white families and singles* | *Some college educations* | *Farming and education jobs* |
|---|---|---|---|

## Key Demographics

| | | | |
|---|---|---|---|
| Total Population: | 574,013 | Primary Ages of Adults: | 25–44 |
| Median Household Income: | $25,521 | Median Home Value: | $53,257 |

# Flagstaff, Arizona

## What's Hot

| What's Hot | What's Not |
|---|---|
| The arts, rodeos, videos, self-improvement | Home furnishing, fashion, concerts, lotteries |
| Skiing, exercise, jogging, bicycling, camping | Bowling, golf, tennis, sailing, fishing |
| Cameras, microwaves, tillers, minivans | CD players, cable TV, Tupperware, video games |
| "Inside Edition," "Blossom," Wimbledon | "Siskel & Ebert," "Wonder Years," "60 Minutes" |
| Spanish radio, country, adult contemporary | Rhythm & blues, rap, pop, classical music |
| *McCall's, Soap Opera Digest, Outdoor Life* | *House & Garden, Forbes, Weight Watchers* |
| Health food, chili, dried fruit, pasta | Cold cuts, canned tuna, English muffins, jam |
| Cola, powdered drinks, draft beer | Vodka, scotch, wine, milk, imported beer |
| Subarus, Chryslers, Isuzus, Mazda 323s | Infinitis, Volvos, Saturns, BMWs, VW Jettas |
| Education loans, Keoghs, investment property | Savings bonds, mutual funds, precious metals |
| Conservatives, toxic waste, school prayer | Moderates, gay rights, ocean drilling |

FLAGSTAFF IS A PRETTY pure version of how a Wild West town evolved to a modern, culturally diverse community. Hispanics and Native Americans make up more than one-third of the population, and students (at Arizona State University) and tourists are an important part of the local economy. As a result, the area's popular activities range from exercise, jogging, and skiing to horseback riding, woodworking, and sewing. Thanks to its location as a transportation center — the heart of the town was bisected by Route 66 and the Santa Fe Railroad — Flagstaff has also been a cosmopolitan center for decades. In contrast to inhabitants of other small towns in the Southwest, residents are interested in art, antiques, film, literature, and cultural events. But there's still something of the frontier quirkiness in the political views of Flagstaff folks: residents describe themselves as conservatives supporting less government, more military spending, banning abortions, and instituting school prayer. Hardly the usual collegiate agenda.

| *Middle-class trade center* | *Ethnically diverse singles and families* | *College educations* | *Farming, education, and transportation jobs* |
|---|---|---|---|

## Key Demographics

| | | | |
|---|---|---|---|
| Total Population: | 103,692 | Primary Ages of Adults: | 25–44 |
| Median Household Income: | $29,690 | Median Home Value: | $89,440 |

# Flint-Saginaw—Bay City, Michigan

| What's Hot | What's Not |
|---|---|
| New cars, bowling, mall shopping, civic affairs | Health clubs, travel, concerts, casinos |
| Boating, golf, camping, gardening, skiing | Tennis, sailing, racquetball, jogging |
| Charcoal grills, power tools, radar detectors | Toaster ovens, CD players, stereos, sofa beds |
| "Young & Restless," "Coach," TV bowling | "Entertainment Tonight," "Geraldo," "Simpsons" |
| Heavy metal, country, golden oldies, rap | Jazz, rhythm & blues, classical, modern rock |
| *Family Handyman, Home Mechanix, Family Circle* | *Scientific American, House & Garden, Fortune* |
| Cold cuts, fish, peanut butter, corn chips | Health food, canned hash, frozen yogurt, jam |
| Powdered drinks, skim milk, ground coffee | Herbal tea, wine, imported beer, orange juice |
| Pontiacs, Chevys, Dodges, Mercury Topazes | Audis, Porsches, Saabs, Alfa Romeos, BMW 6/7s |
| Home-improvement loans, savings bonds, CDs | Keoghs, investment property, stocks, Medicare |
| Moderates, toxic waste, death penalty | Liberals, gay rights, less government |

CARS SEEM TO DRIVE the lifestyle in this market on Michigan's Lower Peninsula. A significant number of residents are blue-collar workers whose factories produce vehicles and auto parts. Even more tend to work on their cars, drive RVs and motorcycles, and buy new cars every few years — made in the U.S., natch. Like their assembly-line jobs that rely on teamwork to succeed, popular pastimes are often group related: residents belong to unions, business clubs, and veterans clubs at above-average rates. And this is the number one market for bowling in the nation. On their own, residents spend a lot of time maintaining their homes — installing their own lights, windows, and carpeting — and getting tips on home improvement from magazines like *Family Handyman* and *Popular Mechanics*. Unlike many union-yes communities with a liberal political tradition, however, the economic hard times engulfing the auto industry have tempered local voters, who now describe themselves as moderates. Here, government regulation means protecting U.S. jobs from the Japanese car invasion.

| Middle-class industrial towns | Predominantly white families | High school educations | Transportation, farm, and forestry jobs |
|---|---|---|---|

| **Key Demographics** | Total Population: | 1,250,201 | Primary Ages of Adults: | 35–54 |
|---|---|---|---|---|
| | Median Household Income: | $29,540 | Median Home Value: | $50,680 |

# Florence—Myrtle Beach, South Carolina

| What's Hot | What's Not |
|---|---|
| Junk mail, fashion, stock cars, cable TV | Gourmet cooking, movies, art, foreign travel |
| Fishing, hunting, gardening, bicycling | Skiing, tennis, exercise, sailing, lotteries |
| Tillers, microwaves, washers, mobile homes | PCs, VCRs, CD players, 35mm cameras |
| "Blossom," BET, "Another World," "Rescue 911" | "David Brinkley," "Roseanne," "Joan Rivers" |
| Gospel, country, rap, religious radio | Jazz, middle-of-the-road, classical, radio baseball |
| *Southern Living, True Story, Ebony, Essence* | *Gourmet, House Beautiful, Self, Inc., Vogue* |
| Seafood, pizza, doughnuts, corn on the cob, candy | Beef, TV dinners, yogurt, raisin bread, Trix |
| Tea, cola, diet sodas, Kool-Aid, cocoa | Imported beer, ground coffee, spring water |
| Pontiacs, Isuzus, Nissan Stanzas | Volvos, BMWs, VWs, Audis, Saabs, Peugeot 505s |
| Medical insurance, money orders, loans | Bonds, IRAs, annuities, stocks, gold cards |
| Conservatives, school prayer, ocean dumping | Liberals, gun control, ozone depletion |

IT'S PERHAPS FITTING that this market in South Carolina's low country has a corresponding lowbrow lifestyle. In a region of textile mills, tobacco farms, and ocean beaches, popular activities range from salt-water fishing, swimming, and sewing to pro wrestling, miniature golf, and stock-car racing. With nearly half of all adults having failed to complete high school, there's little interest in reading books, traveling abroad, or attending the theater. Residents have a wide variety of tacky discos and fast-food joints to visit along the beachfront. Or they can stay home and wallow in junk mail: Florence–Myrtle Beach is one of the nation's best areas for responding to catalogs, sweepstakes, and coupons. When it comes to political appeals, those that are "right from the start" get the highest response rates, thanks to the conservative white majority. Voters oppose abortion rights, gay rights, and most environmental concerns except ocean dumping. No surprise there, considering that beach tourists are a major source of revenue.

| Lower-middle-class mill town | Racially diverse families and singles | Less than high school educations | Farm and textile manufacturing jobs |
|---|---|---|---|

| **Key Demographics** | Total Population: | 430,043 | Primary Ages of Adults: | 35–44 |
|---|---|---|---|---|
| | Median Household Income: | $25,829 | Median Home Value: | $61,576 |

# Fresno–Visalia, California

| What's Hot | What's Not |
|---|---|
| Gardening, horses, fraternal orders | Books, movies, health clubs, unions, casinos |
| Fishing, bicycling, camping, sewing | Jogging, skiing, swimming, sailing, golf |
| Power tools, microwaves, tillers, RVs | PCs, VCRs, CD players, convertibles, cable TV |
| "Am.'s Funniest Home Videos," "Major Dad" | "Hard Copy," "Fresh Prince," "Honeymooners" |
| Country, golden oldies, Spanish radio | Rhythm & blues, classical, pop, news radio |
| *Sports Afield, 1001 Home Ideas, Home Mechanix* | *Working Woman, Life, Esquire, Forbes* |
| Mexican food, cheese, raisins, Shake 'N Bake | TV dinners, pasta, English muffins, yogurt |
| Powdered drinks, lemon-lime soda, draft beer | Imported beer, wine, milk, Diet Coke |
| Subarus, Chryslers, Ford Crown Victorias | Audis, Acuras, Infinitis, BMWs, Toyota vans |
| Life insurance, loans, investment property | IRAs, mutual funds, stocks, precious metals |
| Conservatives, family values, toxic waste | Liberals, gun control, abortion rights |

IT'S NO SURPRISE that some of the richest agricultural land in the U.S. has taken on a Norman Rockwell kind of lifestyle. Here in California's Central Valley residents are into the same activities that have been enjoyed for generations: fishing, hunting, horseback riding, and crafts. Locals are more likely to belong to fraternal orders and veterans clubs than book clubs and health clubs. Indeed, there's little sign of yuppie consumers in this area, given the lack of interest in jogging, movies, sailing, health food, and y-brand elixirs, like Heineken and Diet Coke. These old-fashioned folks tend to keep their shotguns in their pickups and their kitchens well stocked with the local harvest — grapes, plums, tomatoes, and cantaloupes. Their idea of modern life is zapping frozen stewed tomatoes in microwavable Tupperware.

| *Lower-middle-class agricultural area* | *Ethnically diverse families* | *Less than high school educations* | *Farm, transportation, and craft jobs* |
|---|---|---|---|

| **Key Demographics** | Total Population: | 1,465,645 | Primary Ages of Adults: | 25–44 |
|---|---|---|---|---|
| | Median Household Income: | $28,172 | Median Home Value: | $87,400 |

# Ft. Myers–Naples, Florida

| What's Hot | What's Not |
|---|---|
| Travel, investments, recliners, grandchildren | Fashion, movies, car repair, catalog shopping |
| Bowling, boating, golf, fishing, walking | Skiing, racquetball, sailing, jogging |
| Microwaves, VCRs, workbenches, hair color | CD players, PCs, pregnancy-test kits |
| "Meet the Press," "Murder, She Wrote," TV golf | Disney, "Roseanne," "Arsenio," soaps |
| Pop, country, radio football | Rhythm & blues, modern rock, heavy metal |
| *Colonial Homes, Architectural Digest, Sunset* | *Discover, Soap Opera Digest, Us, Glamour* |
| Health food, chicken, oat bran, dried fruit | TV dinners, beef stew, pizza, rice, Twinkies |
| Skim milk, wine, decaf coffee, tomato juice | Herbal tea, powdered drinks, lemon-lime soda |
| Rolls-Royces, Cadillacs, Lincolns, Jaguars | Subarus, Eagles, Plymouths, Hyundai Sonatas |
| Medical insurance, mutual funds, bonds, CDs | Home insurance, IRAs, term insurance |
| Moderates, less government, family values | Liberals, gay rights, nuclear waste |

THE TWENTYSOMETHING sun-worshipers have yet to discover the beaches on Florida's Gulf coast, but the retirees have. In the Ft. Myers–Naples market, where 40 percent of all residents are over 65 years old, the lifestyle is elderly-driven. Many of the most popular activities — knitting, reading books, doing crossword puzzles — are geared to sedentary individuals. The more energetic locals engage in sports like golf, tennis, and bicycling. Residents have money enough to be investment-crazy, purchasing property, mutual funds, and precious metals at rates far above the national average. And they have the time to travel — to Europe and the Caribbean at above-average rates — taking along reading material such as *Travel & Leisure, National Geographic,* and *Field & Stream.* Like many golden-age communities, voters here are right-of-center, especially on social issues. At this stage in their lives, many would just as soon not be bothered by controversies surrounding gays, abortion rights, and nuclear waste. A big event here is watching the sun sink into the gulf at dusk.

| *Middle-class retirement communities* | *Predominantly white couples* | *High school educations* | *Farm, construction, and financial jobs* |
|---|---|---|---|

| **Key Demographics** | Total Population: | 699,684 | Primary Ages of Adults: | 65+ |
|---|---|---|---|---|
| | Median Household Income: | $32,681 | Median Home Value: | $94,996 |

# Ft. Smith, Arkansas

## What's Hot

Rodeos, baking, fraternal orders, the Bible
Hunting, horseback riding, fishing, sewing
Chain saws, microwaves, 126/110 cameras
"Beverly Hills, 90210," "Inside Edition"
Country, gospel, radio college football
*Outdoor Life, National Enquirer, McCall's*
Ham, sausage, peanut butter, Jell-O, doughnuts
Cola, tea, diet sodas, powdered drinks
Chevys, Pontiacs, Subarus, Dodge trucks
Medical insurance, investment property
Moderates, school prayer, death penalty

## What's Not

Dancing, movies, the arts, foreign travel
Bicycling, jogging, skiing, bowling, boating
PCs, home gyms, CD players, 35mm cameras
"Letterman," "Wonder Years," "Joan Rivers"
Rock, rap, modern rock, classical, jazz
*Time, Scientific American, Fortune, Shape*
Mexican food, Italian bread, fish, yogurt
Fruit juice, light beer, malt liquor, wine
Audis, Volvos, Acuras, Jaguars, Saab 9000s
Stocks, mutual funds, bonds, gold cards
Liberals, ozone depletion, gun control

THIS INDUSTRIAL CITY still retains an Old West flavor from its early days as a rowdy frontier town. Residents enjoy country music, hunting, and chewing tobacco at above-average rates. They like to bet on the ponies at Blue Ribbon Downs or attend the town's annual rodeo. With only 13 percent of adults having college degrees, there's not a lot of interest in reading books, attending cultural events, or subscribing to news magazines; the area's most popular titles include supermarket tabloids like the *National Enquirer* and the *Star*. While locals take their religion seriously — reading the Bible and listening to gospel music are popular pursuits — there's still some of the outlaw spirit in area political views. The majority want no part of gun control or government regulation.

| *Working-class industrial city* | *Predominantly white couples and families* | *High school educations* | *Farm, transportation, and manufacturing jobs* |
| --- | --- | --- | --- |

### Key Demographics

| | | | | |
| --- | --- | --- | --- | --- |
| Total Population: | 514,787 | | Primary Ages of Adults: | 25–44 |
| Median Household Income: | $25,378 | | Median Home Value: | $52,442 |

# Ft. Wayne, Indiana

## What's Hot

Home furnishing, golf, bowling, collectibles
Fishing, bicycling, gardening, knitting
Power tools, cameras, VCRs, motorcycles, PCs
TV auto racing, "Designing Women," "Coach"
Golden oldies, middle-of-the-road, country
*Family Circle, Popular Mechanics, TV Guide*
Fish, beef, baked beans, shredded wheat
Powdered drinks, skim milk, diet sodas
Dodges, Oldsmobiles, Pontiacs, GMC trucks
Christmas clubs, home-improvement loans, CDs
Moderates, pro-lifers, nuclear waste

## What's Not

Foreign travel, gourmet cooking, the arts
Jogging, skiing, exercise, tennis, boating
CD players, microwaves, stereos, woks
"Simpsons," "Honeymooners," "Nightline"
Urban contemporary, soft rock, talk radio
*Financial World, Esquire, Harper's Bazaar*
Health food, grits, sweet rolls, yogurt
Orange juice, tea, wine, imported beer
Alfa Romeos, Porsches, Sterlings, Mazda 929s
Mutual funds, stocks, investment property
Liberals, oil drilling, death penalty

AT ONE TIME, marketers bet the ranch on rolling out a new product in Peoria, Ill., a city filled with average citizens who typified the American mainstream. Today, everyone knows the mass market is dead, but demographically "average" cities remain, and Ft. Wayne seems to be so blessed. In most key measures, this midsize politically moderate city sticks close to the median (in income, age, and education). In lifestyle terms, this market could pass for the capital of middlebrowism, with residents engaging in sports like golf, bowling, and fishing and nonideological home pursuits such as sewing, knitting, and crafts as well as coin- and stamp collecting. This is the kind of community where residents have a passion for collecting souvenirs from what few journeys they take: ashtrays, Elvis plates, or snow-globes of smooching flamingos from Florida. When locals do work up a sweat, it's generally to keep their used cars and relatively cheap homes up with the Joneses: home improvement and car repair are popular activities in Ft. Wayne. Status is a basement workshop with socket wrenches in inches *and* millimeters.

| *Middle-class factory town* | *Predominantly white families* | *High school educations* | *Manufacturing, farm, and craft jobs* |
| --- | --- | --- | --- |

### Key Demographics

| | | | | |
| --- | --- | --- | --- | --- |
| Total Population: | 643,961 | | Primary Ages of Adults: | 25–44 |
| Median Household Income: | $33,221 | | Median Home Value: | $57,869 |

# Gainesville, Florida

## What's Hot

Books, exercise, dancing, the arts, PCs
Jogging, boating, tennis, fishing, camping
CD players, 126/110 cameras, microwaves
"Northern Exposure," NCAA Basketball, "Star Trek"
Folk, classical, country, rock, rap
*Rolling Stone, Mademoiselle, Field & Stream*
Fast food, chili, biscuits, pizza, Pop Tarts
Cola, light beer, lemon-lime soda, Diet Coke
Subarus, Mazdas, Isuzus, Mitsubishi trucks
Education loans, savings accounts
Liberals, pro-lifers, ozone depletion

## What's Not

Home furnishing, fashion, car repair, casinos
Bowling, golf, hunting, sewing, crafts
VCRs, garden tools, home gyms, carpeting
"Arsenio," "Primetime Live," "Empty Nest"
Jazz, easy listening, middle-of-the-road, news radio
*Parade, Food & Wine, Omni, Star, Forbes*
Beef, cold cuts, canned tuna, waffles, Trix
Domestic wine, orange juice, ground coffee
Saturns, Cadillacs, Mercedes-Benzes, Porsches
IRAs, life insurance, mutual funds, bonds
Moderates, gun control, school prayer

LIKE MANY COLLEGE TOWNS — this one's the backdrop for the University of Florida — Gainesville is a buzzing progressive island set in a traditional agricultural landscape. The town's main residents do what students everywhere do: a lot of reading, running around, tapping on their computers, and pondering the Timeless Questions of Existence and more timely concerns about getting a job. Although the area's median income is relatively low — few locals have been in the workforce that long — residents manage to spend a lot of money on CDs and tapes, athletic apparel, movies, college sporting events, and rock concerts. Away from campus, longtime residents enjoy a more rural lifestyle, engaging in fishing and horseback riding, listening to country music, and chewing tobacco at above-average rates. The diverse populace results in schizophrenic literary tastes: *GQ* and *Rolling Stone* for the students, and *Field & Stream* and *Outdoor Life* for the farm families. And the Deep Dixie location of this market also affects political attitudes. While residents call themselves liberal, they're at best neo-liberals who support the prolife movement but oppose gun control.

| *Working-class college town* | *Racially diverse singles* | *College educations* | *Jobs in education and farming* |
|---|---|---|---|

**Key Demographics**

| | | | |
|---|---|---|---|
| Total Population: | 239,422 | Primary Ages of Adults: | 18–34 |
| Median Household Income: | $24,386 | Median Home Value: | $67,957 |

# Grand Junction–Durango, Colorado

## What's Hot

Photography, camping, car repair, pets
Skiing, bicycling, fishing, hunting
VCRs, cameras, chain saws, motorcycles, RVs
TV baseball, "Coach," "Evening Shade," "Cops"
Country, '40s–'60s pop, heavy metal
*Reader's Digest, Ladies' Home Journal, Cycle*
Canned chicken, American cheese, popcorn
Light beer, fruit juice, decaf coffee
Chryslers, Subarus, Lincolns, Dodge Colts
Medical insurance, loans, investment property
Conservatives, family values, toxic waste

## What's Not

Movies, foreign travel, cable TV, health clubs
Boating, bowling, golf, jogging, tennis
PCs, CD players, toaster ovens, convertibles
"Family Feud," Nickelodeon, "Siskel & Ebert"
Classical, rhythm & blues, rap, talk radio
*Fortune, House Beautiful, Life, Esquire, Jet*
Corn on the cob, canned hash, chocolates, rye
Diet sodas, party wines, malt liquor
Volvos, Ferraris, Acuras, Lexus SC3/SC4s
Stocks, savings bonds, gold cards, IRAs
Liberals, gun control, legalizing drugs

MINERS AND COWBOYS have given way to backpackers and cyclists in the mountains and desert near these central Colorado communities. The tourists are drawn to an outdoorsy lifestyle heavy on activities like camping, hunting, fishing, and skiing — not to mention attendant products like cameras, RVs, and powerboats for finding and capturing the stunning vistas. In recent years, the Grand Junction–Durango area has also attracted its share of retirees, who spend time indoors sewing, making crafts, and reading a wide range in literature. While residents tend to be educated and politically active — two criteria often associated with liberal thinking — this is a conservative area where the hot-button issues are family values, the pro-life movement, and privacy rights.

| *Lower-middle-class agricultural and tourist area* | *Predominantly white families and couples* | *Some college educations* | *Farm, mining, and construction jobs* |
|---|---|---|---|

**Key Demographics**

| | | | |
|---|---|---|---|
| Total Population: | 169,796 | Primary Ages of Adults: | 35–54 |
| Median Household Income: | $26,237 | Median Home Value: | $70,007 |

# Grand Rapids—Kalamazoo—Battle Creek, Michigan

## What's Hot

Home improvement, golf, book clubs, lotteries
Bowling, boating, gardening, fishing, crafts
PCs, VCRs, power tools, motorcycles
"Cheers," "Northern Exposure," TV auto racing
Heavy metal, golden oldies, '40s–'60s pop
*Family Handyman, Redbook, Colonial Homes*
Beef, fish, macaroni, canned soup, pretzels
Cola, fruit juice, skim milk, domestic beer
Pontiacs, Oldsmobiles, Dodges, Chevy S10s
Company stocks, savings bonds, auto loans
Moderates, consumerism, toxic waste

## What's Not

Gourmet cooking, country clubs, casinos, books
Racquetball, jogging, tennis, sailing
CD players, toaster ovens, diesel cars
"Family Feud," "National Geographic"
Modern rock, rap, gospel, classical
*Working Woman, Business Week, Jet, Sunset*
Health food, rice, frozen yogurt, canned hash
Rum, vodka, imported beer, herbal tea, milk
Audis, Saabs, Jaguars, BMWs, Lexus ES250s
Medical insurance, Keoghs, gold cards
Liberals, gun control, family values

THIS TRIO OF industrial cities on Michigan's agricultural plain proves that good factory jobs can still create comfortable middle-class lifestyles. Many of the baby boom residents — half the household heads are under 44 — hold decent jobs, thanks to several dominant industries: breakfast cereals (Battle Creek), pharmaceuticals (Kalamazoo), and furniture (Grand Rapids). As consumers, residents buy their American cars new and spend an inordinate amount of time maintaining their homes, gardening in the yard, and hanging out at the bowling alley, golf course, or American Legion Hall. They'd rather watch TV than read a book, but they belong to book clubs more for middlebrow status than any literary bent. With their stable jobs and comfortable homes, these folks are easy marks for bank lenders, and borrow they do: home-improvement loans, car loans, and education loans are all popular in this market. The thinking is that if I have to borrow my way to the American Dream, just show me where to sign.

| Middle-class industrial cities | Predominantly white families | High school educations | Farm, manufacturing, and crafts jobs |
|---|---|---|---|

### Key Demographics

| | | | |
|---|---|---|---|
| Total Population: | 1,750,626 | Primary Ages of Adults: | 25–44 |
| Median Household Income: | $33,162 | Median Home Value: | $63,953 |

# Great Falls, Montana

## What's Hot

Car repair, rodeos, crafts, PCs, mobile homes
Hunting, horseback riding, fishing, camping
Microwaves, 126/110 cameras, food processors
"CBS This Morning," "Major Dad," "Full House"
Country, ethnic radio, college sports
*Outdoor Life, Reader's Digest, Popular Science*
Ham, beef, baked beans, BBQ sauce, oatmeal
Draft and light beer, ground coffee, Kool-Aid
Subarus, Buicks, Chryslers, Chevy trucks
Medical insurance, mutual funds, CDs
Moderates, less government, death penalty

## What's Not

Health clubs, foreign travel, movies, unions
Golf, boating, hiking, swimming, sailing
VCRs, 35mm cameras, PCs, CD players
HBO, "Beverly Hills, 90210," "Seinfeld"
Gospel, rock, pop, rhythm & blues, jazz
*Smithsonian, Self, Omni, Money, Gourmet*
Take-out, canned tuna, Italian bread, rice
Wine, diet sodas, Coca-Cola, imported beer
Volvos, Audis, Saturns, Ferraris, Peugeots
IRAs, stocks, bonds, precious metals
Liberals, endangered animals, oil drilling

THIS IS HIGH PLAINS COUNTRY, where getting around the wide open spaces is serious business. Accordingly, car repair is more popular in Great Falls than in any other market in the country, and horseback- and motorcycle riding aren't far behind. With four in ten adults home during the day — as homemakers and retirees — daytime television is also big, especially soaps and game shows. Indeed, nightlife in the form of movies, theater, or discos are distinctly unpopular. In this early-to-bed, early-to-rise country, locals are more interested in camping and gardening than in reading books and doing crossword puzzles. A citizenry that's 10 percent Native American is also more likely than the general population to enjoy crafts, ethnic radio, and outdoor activities like fishing and hunting. The rugged landscape has helped forge a right-of-center political ideology. Faced with classic liberal concerns, like endangered animals and environmental hazards from oil drilling, these residents gun their engines and drive off into the sunset.

| Working-class industrial city | Predominantly white families | High school educations | Jobs in farming, mining, and transportation |
|---|---|---|---|

### Key Demographics

| | | | |
|---|---|---|---|
| Total Population: | 172,905 | Primary Ages of Adults: | 25–44 |
| Median Household Income: | $25,049 | Median Home Value: | $55,741 |

# Green Bay–Appleton, Wisconsin

## What's Hot / What's Not

| What's Hot | What's Not |
|---|---|
| Home workshops, pro football, bowling, unions | Photography, fashion, catalog shopping, books |
| Golf, skiing, walking, hunting, fishing | Jogging, racquetball, exercise, tennis |
| VCRs, Tupperware, tillers, power tools | PCs, CD players, stereos, cameras, cable TV |
| TV baseball, "Another World," "Evening Shade" | "I Love Lucy," "Hard Copy," "Letterman" |
| Country, heavy metal, golden oldies | Pop music, rock, classical, rhythm & blues |
| *Home Mechanix, TV Guide, Good Housekeeping* | *Scientific American, Business Week, GQ, Jet* |
| Beef, frozen potatoes, canned fruit, pie, candy | TV dinners, rice cakes, canned chicken, yogurt |
| Cocoa, ground coffee, light beer, fruit juice | Pop wines, imported beer, orange juice, wine |
| Dodges, Pontiacs, Ford Crown Victorias | Nissans, Hondas, Porsches, VWs, Volvo 940s |
| CDs, home-improvement loans, life insurance | Keoghs, stocks, gold cards, annuities |
| Moderates, pro-lifers, nuclear waste | Liberals, gay rights, oil drilling |

GREEN BAY AND APPLETON are the kinds of classic blue-collar towns one might think disappeared with the Corvair. Thanks to the midscale incomes paid by area paper mills and high-skill manufacturers, residents have stable jobs, decent homes, and comfortable lifestyles. They spend their free time on weekends engaged in home improvement, gardening, and woodworking. And they take their sports seriously, especially outdoor pursuits like fishing, hunting, skiing, and golf. Given the cold weather that engulfs this area so much of the year, it's no wonder that watching TV sports is one of the most popular indoor activities. On the other hand, that doesn't stop hearty residents from donning parkas and ski masks to root for the area's pride and joy, the Green Bay Packers, the nation's only municipally owned National Football League franchise.

| Middle-class commercial center | Predominantly white families | High school educations | Jobs in farming, forestry, and manufacturing |
|---|---|---|---|

### Key Demographics

| | | | |
|---|---|---|---|
| Total Population: | 1,048,480 | Primary Ages of Adults: | 25–44 |
| Median Household Income: | $31,316 | Median Home Value: | $59,917 |

# Greensboro-Winston-Salem–High Point, North Carolina

## What's Hot / What's Not

| What's Hot | What's Not |
|---|---|
| Home decorating, the Bible, mall shopping | Theme parks, book clubs, travel, unions |
| Walking, golf, tennis, pro wrestling | Woodworking, skiing, swimming, jogging |
| Tillers, power tools, sweepstakes, pickups | VCRs, microwaves, powerboats, minivans |
| Game shows, "Fresh Prince," "Sally," "Loving" | Showtime, "60 Minutes," "Empty Nest" |
| Gospel, country, urban contemporary | Rhythm & blues, rap, classical, news radio |
| *Southern Living, Star, Jet, Us* | *National Geographic, House Beautiful, Time* |
| Peanut butter, sausage, pasta, brownies | Mexican food, canned tuna, sour cream, Trix |
| Cola, milk, tea, orange juice | Wine, draft and imported beer, skim milk |
| Chevy Camaros, Ford Mustangs, Dodge trucks | Saab 9000s, Volvo 740s, BMW 5s, Peugeot 405s |
| Medicare, money orders, life insurance | Mutual funds, bonds, investment property |
| Conservatives, family values, death penalty | Liberals, military cutbacks, consumerism |

O YE OF FAITH, this market will surely provide some comfort. Residents in these industrial cities enjoy reading the Bible, buying gospel records, and tuning in to religious radio at some of the highest rates in the nation. With many jobs based in factories — producing furniture, textiles, and cigarettes — residents share a lot of lifestyle activities found in other Southern mill towns: a fondness for pro wrestling, hunting, and fishing. But there's also an upscale streak to this market, influenced in part by the presence of a handful of colleges, including Wake Forest, UNC-Greensboro, and North Carolina A&T. As a result, locals are more likely than average Americans to enjoy college sports and civic activities. Although Greensboro helped launch the civil rights movement with the 1960s lunch counter sit-ins, today the area is staunchly conservative, with voters opposed to issues like gun control, gay rights, and drug legalization (and neutral on issues concerning social pluralism).

| Middle-class industrial cities | Racially diverse couples and singles | Less than high school educations | Manufacturing, transportation, and craft jobs |
|---|---|---|---|

### Key Demographics

| | | | |
|---|---|---|---|
| Total Population: | 1,373,419 | Primary Ages of Adults: | 35–54 |
| Median Household Income: | $31,213 | Median Home Value: | $72,142 |

# Greenville–New Bern–Washington, North Carolina

| What's Hot | What's Not |
|---|---|
| Fashion, home decorating, crafts, dieting | Country clubs, movies, the arts, wine, books |
| Fishing, hunting, sewing, exercise, bicycling | Golf, bowling, skiing, camping, racquetball |
| Tillers, trucks, tobacco products, microwaves | VCRs, PCs, CD players, 35mm cameras, RVs |
| "Today," "NBC Boxing," "Rescue 911" | "Tonight Show," "Married with Children," "Sisters" |
| Gospel, country, rap, urban contemporary | Classical, rock, pop, easy listening |
| *Ebony, Essence, Sports Afield, TV Guide* | *Newsweek, Self, Money, Sunset, Omni* |
| Fried chicken, beef stew, grits, snack cakes | Chicken, TV dinners, waffles, cheese, oatmeal |
| Cola, fruit juice, malt liquor, milk | Wine, imported beer, skim milk, Diet 7-Up |
| Isuzus, Pontiacs, Oldsmobiles, Ford Broncos | Saabs, Audis, Acuras, Mercedes-Benzes, BMW 5s |
| Mail-order medical insurance, money orders | IRAs, Keoghs, savings bonds, VISA cards |
| Conservatives, pro-lifers, less government | Liberals, gun control, endangered animals |

AT FIRST GLANCE, this market looks firmly embedded on Tobacco Road, a place where men work at blue-collar jobs — in textile mills, food processing plants, or tobacco fields — and nearly one in five women is a homemaker, explaining the popularity of home decorating, sewing, crafts, and catalog shopping. But the local military and college presence (from East Carolina University) also affect local lifestyles. Dieting and aerobic athletic activities are big among these twentysomething adults. And they're also into self-improvement, taking adult-education courses, becoming involved in local church and school groups — one-third of all adults have children at home — and signing up for veterans programs. This is an old area — New Bern was the 18th-century home of the state capital at Tryon Palace — and values are traditional. Residents describe themselves as conservatives and supporters of the death penalty, a strong military, and family values.

| Lower-middle-class trade center | Racially diverse singles and families | High school educations | Farm, forestry, and manufacturing jobs |
|---|---|---|---|

## Key Demographics

| | | | |
|---|---|---|---|
| Total Population: | 647,899 | Primary Ages of Adults: | 25–44 |
| Median Household Income: | $26,044 | Median Home Value: | $63,626 |

# Greenville-Spartanburg, South Carolina–Asheville, North Carolina

| What's Hot | What's Not |
|---|---|
| Walking, photography, bluegrass, vitamins | Foreign travel, the arts, news, casinos |
| Fishing, camping, gardening, crafts, sewing | Bicycling, bowling, golf, running, skiing |
| Microwaves, 126/110 cameras, mobile homes | Cassette decks, PCs, VCRs, RVs, 35mm cameras |
| "American Gladiators," "Blossom," "Rescue 911" | "Face the Nation," "Simpsons," TV tennis |
| Country, urban contemporary, gospel | Golden oldies, jazz, soft rock, news radio |
| *Outdoor Life, Star, Redbook, TV Guide* | *Business Week, Shape, Discover, Newsweek* |
| Sausage, beef stew, corn on the cob, popcorn | Mexican food, fish, yogurt, pumpernickel |
| Tea, cola, orange juice, powdered drinks | Light beer, wine, decaf coffee, skim milk |
| Ford Mustangs, Chevy Camaros, Dodge Daytonas | Saabs, Porsches, Acuras, Infinitis, Jaguars |
| Life insurance, loans, first mortgages | Homeowner's insurance, mutual funds, stocks |
| Conservatives, school prayer, death penalty | Liberals, abortion rights, military cutbacks |

ASHEVILLE NATIVE SON Thomas Wolfe wrote that you can't go home again, but perhaps he just didn't *want* to go home. His quiet mountain resort community today is surrounded by two grim textile mill towns, and the combined Greenville-Spartanburg-Asheville market is a downscale place with high concentrations of poorly educated factory workers and outdoors-loving retirees. With the majestic Great Smoky Mountains to the west, locals are big on fishing and hiking as well as photography and reading magazines like *Sports Afield* and *Outdoor Life*. Because only 15 percent of the residents completed college, this is a relatively unsophisticated place with low rates for foreign travel, gourmet cooking, and reading news magazines. As for the high number of elderly residents, they're drawn to the mountain air as well as the many hospitals and clinics in Asheville; not surprisingly, health foods and vitamins are big sellers in area stores. For many locals, Wolfe's adage about not being able to go home has more to do with never having left in the first place.

| Lower-middle-class commercial centers | Predominantly white couples | Less than high school educations | Manufacturing, transportation, and craft jobs |
|---|---|---|---|

## Key Demographics

| | | | |
|---|---|---|---|
| Total Population: | 1,757,744 | Primary Ages of Adults: | 55+ |
| Median Household Income: | $28,638 | Median Home Value: | $62,349 |

# Greenwood-Greenville, Mississippi

| What's Hot | What's Not |
|---|---|
| The Bible, the blues, bus travel, cable TV | Movies, health clubs, the arts, clubs, books |
| Hunting, fishing, sewing, gardening, walking | Boating, bowling, golf, tennis, skiing |
| RVs, tobacco products, rifles, records | VCRs, microwaves, CD players, motorcycles |
| BET, Cinemax, "Family Feud," "Coach," "Sally" | "Cops," "David Brinkley," "Sisters" |
| Gospel, rap, religious radio | Classical, modern rock, jazz, '40s–'60s pop |
| *Ebony, Essence, Southern Living, True Story* | *Forbes, Bon Appetit, Cosmopolitan, Discover* |
| Bacon, peanut butter, aerosol cheese, jam | TV dinners, beef, canned tuna, yogurt, nuts |
| Tea, powdered drinks, milk, cola, Tab | Cocktails, imported beer, wine, skim milk |
| Isuzus, Nissan Stanzas, Olds 98s, Ford F350s | Audis, Alfa Romeos, VWs, Toyota Previas |
| Money orders, medical and term life insurance | Mutual funds, stocks, savings bonds, Keoghs |
| Conservatives, pro-lifers, oil drilling | Moderates, gay rights, ozone depletion |

THE BLUES WERE HATCHED in these sleepy Mississippi Delta towns — and for good reason. There's plenty of misery to share among residents who are predominantly poor, poorly educated (45 percent fail to finish high school), and have Third World health care. Amid the cotton and catfish farms, living is often at basic survival levels: locals are into fishing, hunting, and gardening to help put food on the table. For relaxation, there are church socials, local music clubs, and whatever's on cable. Given the bleak reality of this area, it's no wonder that they rely on their faith to better their lives: they read the Bible, listen to gospel music, and enter sweepstakes at some of the highest rates in the nation. For more practical escapism, they simply get out of town — to Jackson, Memphis, or Chicago; residents here may not buy a lot of new cars, but they hop the bus and train at higher-than-average rates. It's that or breaking into a soulful riff by native sons Muddy Waters or W. C. Handy, who knew whereof they sang.

| *Poor Delta farm towns* | *Racially diverse families and singles* | *Less than high school educations* | *Farm, labor, and manufacturing jobs* |
|---|---|---|---|

| **Key Demographics** | Total Population: | 217,662 | Primary Ages of Adults: | 55+ |
|---|---|---|---|---|
| | Median Household Income: | $17,232 | Median Home Value: | $42,592 |

# Hagerstown, Maryland

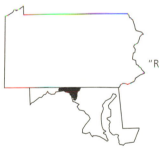

| What's Hot | What's Not |
|---|---|
| Home workshops, collectibles, pets, unions | Clubs, college sports, adult-ed courses |
| Bowling, gardening, woodworking, camping | Golf, hiking, racquetball, jogging, exercise |
| Video games, lawn furniture, power tools | PCs, CD players, books, toaster ovens |
| "Regis & Kathie Lee," "Another World," "Coach" | "Murphy Brown," "Arsenio," "Face the Nation" |
| Country, golden oldies, easy listening | Jazz, rhythm & blues, modern rock, classical |
| *Mother Earth News, Home Mechanix, Parents* | *GQ, Gourmet, Financial World, House Beautiful* |
| Cold cuts, spaghetti sauce, pasta, doughnuts | Mexican food, canned chicken, raisin bread |
| Powdered drinks, ground coffee, skim milk | Imported wine, herbal tea, orange juice |
| Chevys, Mercurys, Buicks, Dodge trucks | BMWs, Volvos, Sterlings, Lexus LS400s |
| Home-improvement loans, savings bonds, CDs | Gold cards, bonds, precious metals, stocks |
| Moderates, nuclear waste, death penalty | Liberals, ocean dumping, drug legalization |

THERE AREN'T MANY SMALL middle-American towns close to metropolitan behemoths the size of Washington and Baltimore, but Hagerstown is different. In this picket-fence community, residents spend a lot of time caring for their homes, from the furniture on the porch to the decorative plates and dolls over the mantel. The town's location amid western Maryland's rolling farms and green mountains encourages outdoor activities like hunting, hiking, and gardening. A high percentage of families also results in big market sales for kid-oriented products, such as video games, video rentals, powdered drinks, and household pets. The stable economy geared toward light industrial jobs also makes for enough financial security to borrow liberally: residents have a high rate for taking out home-improvement, education, and car loans. But that's about as liberal as these folks get: they're down on gays, illegal drugs, and abortion rights. This part of Maryland has been Republican since the Civil War.

| *Middle-class commercial town* | *Predominantly white couples and families* | *High school educations* | *Transportation, craft, and manufacturing jobs* |
|---|---|---|---|

| **Key Demographics** | Total Population: | 124,780 | Primary Ages of Adults: | 35–54 |
|---|---|---|---|---|
| | Median Household Income: | $32,693 | Median Home Value: | $89,300 |

# Harrisburg-York-Lancaster-Lebanon, Pennsylvania

## What's Hot

Civic activities, TV sports, videos, lotteries
Woodworking, knitting, walking, hunting
VCRs, recliners, cable TV, power tools
USA network, "Roseanne," "Evening Shade"
Rock, rap, country, middle-of-the-road
*Family Handyman, Sports Afield, Woman's Day*
Fish, beef, pasta, baked beans, sweet rolls
Skim milk, cocoa, tomato juice, ground coffee
Eagles, Dodges, Chevys, Ford Aerostars
Savings bonds, auto loans, mutual funds
Moderates, nuclear waste, death penalty

## What's Not

Health clubs, rodeos, gourmet cooking
Tennis, sailing, jogging, racquetball
CD players, microwaves, sofa beds
A&E, "60 Minutes," "Honeymooners"
Classical, gospel, rhythm & blues
*Playboy, Life, Smithsonian, Forbes, Sunset*
Mexican food, canned chicken, frozen yogurt
Wine, herbal tea, imported beer, spring water
Acuras, Toyotas, BMWs, Volvos, Jeep Cherokees
Medical insurance, stocks, investment property
Liberals, legalizing drugs, gay rights

YOU CAN LEAVE the mainstream behind in this central Pennsylvania region, traveling from the busy state capital, Harrisburg, to the languid Pennsylvania Dutch farms surrounding Lancaster. But the market as a whole is a comfortable middle-class area with a diverse economic base: residents work at farming, government services, or factories run by giants like Hershey's and Armstrong. As a result, local lifestyles are varied, with above-average interest in videos and book clubs as well as hunting and woodworking. Perhaps surprisingly, residents show relatively low rates of involvement in "good-life" activities, such as the arts, fashion, gourmet cooking, and foreign travel. Then again, with many area farms, it's no wonder that families are more into domestic activities like knitting, making crafts, and collecting antiques. Politically, this is a centrist area except on environmental issues. With the memory of Three Mile Island still fresh for many, residents express high rates of concern about nuclear waste disposal, ozone depletion, and toxic waste.

| *Middle-class commercial centers* | *Predominantly white families and couples* | *High school educations* | *Jobs in manufacturing, transportation, and crafts* |
|---|---|---|---|

## Key Demographics

| | | | |
|---|---|---|---|
| Total Population: | 1,554,044 | Primary Ages of Adults: | 35–54 |
| Median Household Income: | $35,857 | Median Home Value: | $86,280 |

# Harrisonburg, Virginia

## What's Hot

Home improvement, hunting, collectibles, pets
Gardening, knitting, woodworking, sewing
Chain saws, microwaves, 126/110 cameras
Game shows, "Today," "Am.'s Funniest People"
Country, gospel, heavy metal, religious radio
*Working Mother, Prevention, Home Mechanix*
American cheese, beef stew, sausage, pudding
Cola, diet sodas, powdered drinks
Chevys, Pontiacs, Subarus, Dodge trucks
Loans, medical insurance, savings accounts
Moderates, school prayer, less government

## What's Not

Clubs, current affairs, books, casinos, travel
Jogging, swimming, sailing, skiing, tennis
PCs, CD players, 35mm cameras, stereos
"Joan Rivers," "Wonder Years," "Letterman"
Rhythm & blues, rap, soft rock, classical
*Consumer's Digest, Fortune, Jet, Vogue*
Canned tuna, sour cream, take-out, TV dinners
Wine, imported beer, ale, skim milk
Nissans, Acuras, Audis, Ferraris, Volvo 940s
Investment property, precious metals, Visa
Liberals, gay rights, ocean dumping

IN THIS PART of the Shenandoah Valley, you won't find people enjoying tennis, racquetball, or bowling at above-average rates. Harrisonburg was settled in 1739, and area lifestyles appear steeped in the past. The biggest athletic pursuits are hunting, fishing, and horseback riding. Many of the adults work in factories preparing meat, poultry, and dairy products for market, and residents like to spend their off-hours working around their house, decorating the living room with collectibles, digging a well-stocked garden, displaying their handmade crafts. With several colleges nearby — among them, James Madison University — residents enjoy watching college sports. But these people on the edge of the Blue Ridge Mountains have an insular quality: they're not into foreign travel, adult-education courses, movies, or even catalog shopping. Among older residents — one in four is over 65 years old — the Bible may be one of the few books they own.

| *Lower-middle-class industrial city* | *Predominantly white families and couples* | *High school educations* | *Farming, transportation, and manufacturing jobs* |
|---|---|---|---|

## Key Demographics

| | | | |
|---|---|---|---|
| Total Population: | 234,669 | Primary Ages of Adults: | 55+ |
| Median Household Income: | $30,471 | Median Home Value: | $73,786 |

# Hartford–New Haven, Connecticut

## What's Hot | What's Not

| What's Hot | What's Not |
|---|---|
| Foreign travel, theater, movies, country clubs | Gambling, car repair, veterans clubs, crafts |
| Tennis, jogging, swimming, skiing, golf | Hunting, fishing, camping, horseback riding |
| Woks, PCs, VCRs, microwaves, cable TV | Mobile homes, garden tillers, pregnancy-test kits |
| VH-1, HBO, "Seinfeld," "Face the Nation" | Soaps, "Beverly Hills, 90210," "Family Feud" |
| Classical, jazz, Broadway musicals, rock | Heavy metal, rap, country, rhythm & blues |
| *Smithsonian, Food & Wine, Self, New Yorker* | *Star, Jet, Playboy, True Story* |
| Fish, salad, cheese, oat bran, bagels | Ham, sausage, chili, sweet rolls, snack cakes |
| Diet Coke, wine, imported beer, decaf coffee | Tea, milk, Kool-Aid, Coca-Cola |
| Audis, Porsches, Saabs, Toyota Previas | Chevys, Pontiacs, Cadillacs, Oldsmobile 98s |
| IRAs, stocks, mutual funds, gold cards | Personal loans, medical insurance, securities |
| Liberals, abortion rights, ozone depletion | Moderates, school prayer, legalizing drugs |

THE RICH MAY NOT live differently than the rest of us; they just have the money to do more of what most Americans do. A case in point is the Hartford–New Haven market. In one readership survey of 106 magazines, locals read 84 of them at above-average rates. In an ownership poll involving 228 car models, they drive all but 12 more often than the general population — and the highest percentage are luxury imports. Since well before the turn of the century, Hartford has had one of the nation's highest median incomes, and it still ranks near the top, thanks to well-paying jobs in insurance and defense. Area residents enjoy traveling abroad, going to the theater, and belonging to country clubs all at rates above the U.S. average. And the progressive ideas bubbling at area colleges like Yale have also had an impact, resulting in leftist views on such issues as abortion and gay rights. Despite the flinty Connecticut Yankees who settled the area, today's residents are liberal with their money, attitudes, and consuming tastes.

| *Affluent urban area* | *Predominantly white couples and singles* | *College educations* | *White-collar jobs in insurance and defense* |
|---|---|---|---|

### Key Demographics

| | | | |
|---|---|---|---|
| Total Population: | 2,465,457 | Primary Ages of Adults: | 25–44 |
| Median Household Income: | $46,640 | Median Home Value: | $182,619 |

# Helena, Montana

## What's Hot | What's Not

| What's Hot | What's Not |
|---|---|
| Art, car repair, dancing, photography, rifles | Fashion, health clubs, concerts, theme parks |
| Skiing, hunting, horseback riding, camping | Golf, sailing, tennis, crossword puzzles |
| PCs, woks, camcorders, calculators, books | CD players, convertibles, coupons |
| "Tonight Show," "Saturday Night Live," "Cheers" | "Geraldo," "Beverly Hills, 90210," "Loving" |
| Country, classic rock, '40s–'60s pop | Rap, rhythm & blues, urban contemporary |
| *Mother Earth News, National Geographic, Self* | *Vogue, Fortune, Esquire, Life, New Yorker* |
| Mexican food, ham, beef, popcorn, dried fruit | Fried chicken, cold cuts, Pop Tarts |
| Draft beer, coffee, skim milk, diet soda | Herbal tea, orange juice, imported wine |
| Subarus, Isuzus, Chryslers, Dodge trucks | Ferraris, Sterlings, Infinitis, Lexus ES250s |
| Mutual funds, first mortgages, personal loans | Bonds, IRAs, stocks, money orders |
| Conservatives, privacy rights, less government | Liberals, endangered animals, oil drilling |

GUNS AND ARTWORK? At first glance, the interests of Helena residents may seem as wide as the Montana sky. In this market, with its concentration of jobs in government, tourism, and farming, tastes range from literature and film to bowling and car repair. The area's stunning snowcapped mountains and wooded valleys no doubt encourage the popularity of fishing, hunting, and camping; Helena is one of the nation's top markets for skiing as well as one of the areas where residents are most concerned about threats to the environment as long as it doesn't interfere with their oil-based economy. As a state capital, Helena also attracts people who are involved in politics, community affairs, and business clubs. Indeed, the lure of the land for recreation and investment opportunities has also drawn a number of Japanese citizens to this western outpost. One result: this is Subaru country, with the top three models coming from that Japanese car–maker.

| *Middle-class state capital* | *Predominantly white families and singles* | *College educations* | *Jobs in farming and public administration* |
|---|---|---|---|

### Key Demographics

| | | | |
|---|---|---|---|
| Total Population: | 49,906 | Primary Ages of Adults: | 25–44 |
| Median Household Income: | $28,685 | Median Home Value: | $65,759 |

# Houston, Texas

| What's Hot | What's Not |
|---|---|
| Fashion, electronics, health clubs, dancing | Cable TV, gourmet cooking, motorcycles |
| Racquetball, tennis, skiing, weight training | Horse racing, bowling, woodworking, knitting |
| CD players, tape decks, 35mm cameras, handguns | Gardening tools, 126/110 cameras, recliners |
| "Simpsons," NBA Basketball, "Wonder Years" | "Wheel of Fortune," "Major Dad," "Blossom" |
| Modern rock, jazz, rhythm & blues, talk radio | Adult contemporary, country, religious radio |
| *Ebony, Vanity Fair, Money, Architectural Digest* | *American Photo, Star, Woman's World* |
| Take-out, Mexican food, TV dinners, yogurt | Sausage, crackers, baked beans, pudding, gum |
| Cocktails, imported beer, skim milk, Diet Coke | Tea, powdered drinks, milk, orange juice |
| Infinitis, Ferraris, Porsches, Toyota trucks | Dodges, Pontiacs, Buicks, Ford Tempos |
| Homeowner's insurance, stocks, gold cards | Life insurance, CDs, medical insurance |
| Liberals, ozone depletion, gay rights | Moderates, pro-lifers, buy American |

THIS FREEWHEELING SPRAWL of a city — with rich and poor, singles and families, whites, African Americans, and Latinos — produces a lifestyle hodgepodge. In Houston, residents are into high-tech electronics, theater, and ethnic festivals as well as boating, fishing, and working on their cars. In their garages sit plenty of Porsches and Ferraris, not to mention beat-up trucks and discarded computers. The high percentage of young singles and divorcés results in a higher-than-average interest in fashion, jogging, and aerobic exercise. But it's difficult to gauge the pulse of Houston because of the disparity of worlds coexisting among the downtown skyscrapers and the crumbling shacks nearby. Here's a city where residents listen to classical, modern rock, rap, and jazz all at rates above the national average. And this is also a city where there are twice as many gunshops as in any other metro area in the U.S. Only on political issues do you find some convergence of ideas. Houston is a liberal haven where residents share a concern for gays, abortion rights, and environmental threats caused by oil refineries.

| Middle-class metropolitan sprawl | Racially and ethnically diverse families | College educations | Jobs in finance, trade, and recreation |
|---|---|---|---|

**Key Demographics**

| | | | |
|---|---|---|---|
| Total Population: | 4,266,902 | Primary Ages of Adults: | 25–44 |
| Median Household Income: | $33,220 | Median Home Value: | $66,802 |

# Huntsville-Decatur-Florence, Alabama

| What's Hot | What's Not |
|---|---|
| Muscle cars, home decorating, electronics | Travel, the arts, movies, clubs, photography |
| Fishing, hunting, sewing, gardening | Bicycling, skiing, tennis, sailing |
| Cable TV, video games, mobile homes | PCs, CD players, Tupperware, 35mm cameras |
| "I Love Lucy," soaps, "Full House," "Cheers" | "Letterman," "Empty Nest," "Roseanne" |
| Gospel, country, religious radio | Jazz, soft rock, middle-of-the-road, rap |
| *True Story, Star, Playboy, Working Mother* | *Omni, Ebony, GQ, Shape, Fortune, Sunset* |
| Canned hash, corn on the cob, macaroni | Chicken, take-out, waffles, frozen yogurt |
| Diet Coke, tea, Kool-Aid, orange juice | Wine, light beer, skim milk, decaf coffee |
| Subarus, Pontiacs, Chryslers, Dodge trucks | Peugeots, BMWs, Acuras, Jaguar XJ6s |
| First mortgages, life insurance, money orders | IRAs, savings bonds, mutual funds, stocks |
| Conservatives, school prayer, death penalty | Moderates, military cutbacks, toxic waste |

OLD AND NEW LIFESTYLES clash in this market along Alabama's northern border. Many residents are back-country farmers and small-town people with a fondness for traditional rural passions such as hunting, pickups, and country music. But in the 30 years since NASA opened the Marshall Space Flight Center, Huntsville has been transformed into a high-tech boomtown whose 200,000 residents also exhibit a taste for electronics, video games, muscle cars, and publications like *Playboy* and *Working Mother*. The result in Huntsville is a neotraditional culture where all residents support old-fashioned values, such as home, family, religion, and sports (especially the Alabama college football teams). And, on the tube, residents are less likely to watch hip shows like "The Simpsons" and "David Letterman" than messageless sitcoms like "I Love Lucy" and "Full House." The biggest political concerns involve military cutbacks, with everyone fearing the potential loss of jobs and a weakened military presence abroad.

| Lower-middle-class mixed farm and research area | Predominantly white families and couples | Less than high school educations | Jobs in farming, transportation, and crafts |
|---|---|---|---|

**Key Demographics**

| | | | |
|---|---|---|---|
| Total Population: | 820,383 | Primary Ages of Adults: | 25–44 |
| Median Household Income: | $29,230 | Median Home Value: | $63,112 |

# Idaho Falls–Pocatello, Idaho

## What's Hot

Wilderness sports, photography, rodeos, RVs
Skiing, camping, fishing, hunting, sewing
PCs, video games, boats, books, motorcycles
"Northern Exposure," "Roseanne," "Nightline"
Country, heavy metal, golden oldies
*Outdoor Life, McCall's, Popular Science*
Beef, canned vegetables, potatoes, nuts
Powdered drinks, draft beer, skim milk
Subaru, Oldsmobiles, Chevys, GMC Sierras
Medical insurance, life insurance, loans, CDs
Moderates, family values, nuclear waste

## What's Not

Fashion, art, frequent flying, dieting
Tennis, jogging, exercise, crossword puzzles
CD players, convertibles, weights, cable TV
"Geraldo," "Inside Edition," "Am. Detective"
Jazz, rhythm & blues, rap, classical
*Vogue, Esquire, Inc., Travel & Leisure, Jet*
Take-out, pumpernickel, rice, chocolates
Orange juice, imported wine and beer
Volvos, Acuras, Porsches, Sterlings, BMW 6/7s
Mutual funds, stocks, homeowner's insurance
Liberals, gay rights, endangered animals

MANY PEOPLE IN THIS PART of Idaho still live down on the farm. But they manage to make the most of the nearby wilderness areas, turning this into one of the top ten markets for camping, skiing, fishing, and hunting. The natural attractions in the northwest part of the state also encourage the local interest in photography, off-road vehicles, and environmental concerns. Inside their homes, residents live like many farm families: baking from scratch, listening to country music, making crafts, and sewing. But nearly half of all locals have gone to college, and they're also big on adult-education courses and magazines like *Popular Science, National Geographic,* and *Home Mechanix.* These educated, recent migrants came for the cleaner living and slower pace of small-town America. In this market, residents worry about family values and government intrusions in their lives; having escaped the urban ills, they just want to be left alone.

| Lower-middle-class agricultural area | Predominantly white families | Some college educations | Jobs in farming, construction, and crafts |
| --- | --- | --- | --- |

## Key Demographics

| | | | |
| --- | --- | --- | --- |
| Total Population: | 339,837 | Primary Ages of Adults: | 25–44 |
| Median Household Income: | $29,024 | Median Home Value: | $59,736 |

# Indianapolis, Indiana

## What's Hot

Bowling, book clubs, TV sports, unions
Golf, swimming, gardening, knitting, crafts
VCRs, lawn furniture, cameras, home gyms
TV auto racing, "Coach," "Regis & Kathie Lee"
Middle-of-the-road, modern rock, radio baseball
*Outdoor Life, 1001 Home Ideas, Home Mechanix*
Ham, spaghetti, pizza, American cheese, pudding
Light beer, ground coffee, diet sodas, cocoa
Dodge Daytonas, Pontiac Sunbirds, Ford Tempos
Home improvement loans, savings bonds, CDs
Moderates, military cutbacks, ozone depletion

## What's Not

Travel, the arts, fashion, country clubs
Skiing, jogging, racquetball, tennis
CD players, convertibles, sailboats
"Jeopardy," "Siskel & Ebert," "Fresh Prince"
Classical, gospel, rhythm & blues, news radio
*Food & Wine, Time, Essence, Sunset, Vogue*
Chili, canned chicken, rice cakes, brownies
Malt liquor, tea, milk, wine, imported beer
Peugeots, Mercedes-Benzes, Lexus LS400s
Investment property, medical insurance, bonds
Liberals, legalizing drugs, oil drilling

BEYOND THE OFFICE COMPLEXES and oversized parks, Indianapolis resembles a blue-collar factory town with somewhat staid, middlebrow lifestyles. Residents are into bowling, crafts, lotteries, and boating at rates above the national average. Their political views are near the norm on issues ranging from abortion and gay rights to concern about government regulation and the environment. Locals shy away from upscale interests like gourmet cooking, foreign travel, and the arts as well as downscale pursuits like casino gambling, hunting, and bus travel. With the recent opening of several new sports arenas, in addition to the Indianapolis Motor Speedway and the National Track and Field Hall of Fame, the city is trying to become the sports capital of the nation — to middling success. Other than a fondness for the area's pro teams — the Indiana Pacers and the Indianapolis Colts — the most athletic activity residents do is channel-surf to find the best TV sports program.

| Middle-class state capital and commercial center | Predominantly white singles and couples | High school educations | Jobs in manufacturing, crafts, and transportation |
| --- | --- | --- | --- |

## Key Demographics

| | | | |
| --- | --- | --- | --- |
| Total Population: | 2,377,619 | Primary Ages of Adults: | 25–44 |
| Median Household Income: | $32,255 | Median Home Value: | $60,797 |

# Jackson, Mississippi

| What's Hot | What's Not |
|---|---|
| Fashion, cable TV, the Bible, crafts, dogs | Theater, gourmet cooking, car repair, casinos |
| Fishing, hunting, walking, sewing | Boating, bowling, golf, skiing, crafts |
| Cable TV, garden tillers, mobile homes | PCs, CD players, VCRs, microwaves, books |
| BET, Disney, "Family Matters," "Guiding Light" | "Letterman," "Married with Children," US Open |
| Gospel, rhythm & blues, rap | Jazz, modern rock, easy listening, folk |
| *Ebony, Essence, National Enquirer, TV Guide* | *Smithsonian, Cosmopolitan, Newsweek, Inc.* |
| Fried chicken, grits, aerosol cheese, pie | Canned tuna, pasta, sour cream, pancakes, Trix |
| Cola, orange juice, tea, lemon-lime sodas | Wine, beer, decaf coffee, scotch |
| Nissans, Isuzus, Ford Festivas, Mazda 929s | Porsches, Alfa Romeos, Saabs, Infiniti M30s |
| Money orders, medical insurance | Gold cards, Keoghs, mutual funds, IRAs |
| Conservatives, pro-lifers, oil drilling | Liberals, death penalty, ozone depletion |

MISSISSIPPI'S LARGEST URBAN AREA — albeit with under a million people — has little to boast of compared to other grand Southern cities, such as Atlanta, Nashville, and New Orleans. In Jackson, with its mix of upper-middle-class white and down-scale African American communities, the overall lifestyle is without much personality. Locals are less likely than average Americans to read magazines, drive new cars, and own high-tech electronic equipment like computers and CD players. Indeed, Jackson citizens would rather engage in outdoor sports like fishing and hunting as well as domestic pursuits like gardening, needlework, and reading the Bible. It's difficult to find political issues they strongly favor: they're down on gun control, the death penalty, gay rights, school prayer, and many environmental issues. With the surprising exception of an interest in fashion — this is, after all, a state capital — Jackson rates barely a blip on one of the most important barometers of civilized cities: only one out of one hundred residents reads the Sunday *New York Times*.

| Lower-middle-class state capital | Racially mixed singles and families | Less than high school educations | Farm and manufacturing jobs |
|---|---|---|---|

| Key Demographics | | | |
|---|---|---|---|
| | Total Population: | 822,406 | Primary Ages of Adults: 25–44 |
| | Median Household Income: $23,196 | | Median Home Value: $52,918 |

# Jackson, Tennessee

| What's Hot | What's Not |
|---|---|
| Home furnishing, sweepstakes, the Bible | Health clubs, movies, casinos, current events |
| Rodeos, target shooting, sewing, crafts | Skiing, bicycling, bowling, golf, jogging |
| RVs, 126/110 cameras, tobacco products | PCs, convertibles, CD players, books, VCRs |
| "Family Feud," "Today," "I Love Lucy" | "In Living Color," "Joan Rivers," "Sisters" |
| Religious radio, country, gospel | Classical, jazz, middle-of-the-road, modern rock |
| *True Story, Soap Opera Digest, Ebony* | *Changing Times, House & Garden, Omni* |
| Sausage, peanut butter, white bread, candy | Beef, yogurt, salads, cheese, raisin bread |
| Tea, diet sodas, cola, Kool-Aid, milk | Wine, imported beer, skim milk |
| Ford Mustangs, Chevy Camaros, Olds 98s | Jaguars, Peugeots, Audis, Toyota MR2s |
| Money orders, medical insurance, loans | Stocks, mutual funds, savings bonds |
| Conservatives, school prayer, death penalty | Liberals, gay rights, military cutbacks |

SETTLED NEARLY two centuries ago, Jackson remains a modest industrial city on the flat farmland of western Tennessee. Local tastes resemble those of many rural Southern communities: listening to country music, drinking cola, chewing tobacco, and watching cable TV are all enjoyed at above-average rates. And residents are people of faith, who tune in to religious radio, read the Bible, and enter sweepstakes at some of the highest rates in the nation. Politically, Jackson is a Democratic area, although many residents have conservative good-ol'-boy values that date to the plantation owners prior to the Confederacy. In this part of the South, people support such issues as family values, school prayer, less government, and more military spending. They're perfect examples of Southern Democrats who vote Republican at the drop of the Kennedy name.

| Lower-middle-class farming area | Predominantly white families and couples | Less than high school educations | Farm, manufacturing, and transportation jobs |
|---|---|---|---|

| Key Demographics | | | |
|---|---|---|---|
| | Total Population: | 164,775 | Primary Ages of Adults: 55+ |
| | Median Household Income: $24,182 | | Median Home Value: $48,939 |

# Jacksonville, Florida

| What's Hot | What's Not |
|---|---|
| Gourmet cooking, dieting, electronics, veterans | Travel, art, movies, adult-ed courses, books |
| Bicycling, camping, fishing, exercise | Skiing, bowling, walking, racquetball, knitting |
| Mobile homes, cable TV, motorcycles | PCs, stereos, weights, Tupperware, tools |
| "Am.'s Funniest Home Videos," "Sally" | "Empty Nest," "Showtime at the Apollo" |
| Urban contemporary, country, gospel | Soft rock, jazz, golden oldies, news radio |
| *Southern Living, Jet, Sports Afield, Redbook* | *Cosmopolitan, Discover, Rolling Stone, Money* |
| Canned hash, macaroni, pizza, candy, Wendy's | TV dinners, French bread, pretzels, yogurt |
| Cola, malt liquor, diet sodas, tea | Imported wine and beer, ale, skim milk |
| Isuzus, Subarus, Chevys, Chryslers, Buicks | Mazdas, VWs, Acuras, BMWs, Volvos, Audis |
| Investment property, medical insurance, loans | IRAs, savings bonds, mutual funds, Keoghs |
| Conservatives, school prayer, toxic waste | Liberals, death penalty, legalizing drugs |

THINK OF JACKSONVILLE as the Rodney Dangerfield of Florida's cities—a metropolis that no matter how hard it tries just can't get any respect. It's usually ignored by out-of-towners more interested in Florida's beaches, the laid-back Keys, or the fantasy rides of Disney World. Yet this racially mixed, growing community boasts a diversified economic base in insurance, transportation, and the military, and its citizens have an enviable lifestyle. Jacksonville is a strong market for home decorating, gourmet cooking, physical fitness, and electronics. With a higher-than-average concentration of families, unlike the park-benched retirees of southern Florida, area residents engage in active sports like riding bicycles or taking aerobics classes. And there are enough conservative veterans and protective parents to worry about family values, military cutbacks, and toxic waste fouling the local beaches. Interestingly, when it comes to day trips, Jacksonville residents would rather visit a state fair than a theme park.

| *Middle-class state capital* | *Racially diverse singles and couples* | *College educations* | *Finance, transportation, and service jobs* |
|---|---|---|---|

**Key Demographics**

| | | | |
|---|---|---|---|
| Total Population: | 1,291,951 | Primary Ages of Adults: | 25–44 |
| Median Household Income: | $31,563 | Median Home Value: | $71,396 |

# Johnstown-Altoona, Pennsylvania

| What's Hot | What's Not |
|---|---|
| Cable TV, car repair, crafts, gardening, dogs | The arts, travel, movies, books, clubs, cats |
| Hunting, fishing, hiking, woodworking, sewing | Tennis, skiing, jogging, bicycling, golf |
| Power tools, VCRs, microwaves, motorcycles | 35mm cameras, CD players, stereos, PCs |
| USA network, "Current Affair," "Evening Shade" | "Wonder Years," "Meet the Press," "Donahue" |
| Country, adult contemporary, radio baseball | Gospel, folk, modern rock, rhythm & blues |
| *Family Handyman, Woman's World, Star* | *Psychology Today, Omni, Bon Appetit, Ebony* |
| Hot dogs, spaghetti sauce, Wheaties, Jell-O | Health food, take-out, chili, corn on the cob |
| Diet sodas, fruit juices, powdered drinks | Wine, ale, spring water, herbal tea |
| Pontiacs, Chevys, Buicks, Dodges, Chryslers | Mazdas, Hondas, Nissans, Saabs, Audis |
| Car loans, personal loans, CDs, savings bonds | Gold cards, stocks, mutual funds, annuities |
| Moderates, buying American, death penalty | Liberals, gay rights, gun control |

THESE ONCE-THRIVING steel and railroad towns have seen better days; for a half-century, their population has been steadily declining. Today, residents still work in aging factories, on small farms, and in a few new biotech industries, but the overall lifestyle is relatively downscale. There are no "good-life" activities pursued at above-average rates — not travel, fashion, the arts, or gourmet cooking. And forget about any market-wide interest in high-tech electronics, science, or technology. Thanks to the surrounding Allegheny Mountains, most locals enjoy outdoor pursuits like hunting, fishing, camping, and hiking. And there's a strong streak of self-reliance in the area: many of the residents work on their cars and motorcycles, do their own home improvements, and like to sew, knit, and make crafts. While few activities here rank among the nation's top markets, in one area Johnstown-Altoona does excel: this is unions-forever, buy-American country. No one would be caught dead driving a foreign car, drinking an imported beer, or supporting more military bases abroad.

| *Lower-middle-class industrial towns* | *Predominantly white* | *High school educations* | *Jobs in manufacturing, transportation, and farming* |
|---|---|---|---|

**Key Demographics**

| | | | |
|---|---|---|---|
| Total Population: | 770,129 | Primary Ages of Adults: | 55+ |
| Median Household Income: | $24,992 | Median Home Value: | $47,610 |

# Jonesboro, Arkansas

| What's Hot | What's Not |
|---|---|
| Rodeos, baking, crossword puzzles, pets, RVs | Art, golf, lotteries, adult-ed courses |
| Hunting, fishing, sewing, gardening | Bowling, exercise, skiing, tennis, hiking |
| Recliners, garden tillers, chain saws, trucks | PCs, CD players, VCRs, food processors |
| Soaps, "Current Affair," "Unsolved Mysteries" | "Doogie Howser," "ABC Wide World of Sports" |
| Country, religious radio, heavy metal | Jazz, '40s–'60s pop, rock, rap music |
| *Country Living, Reader's Digest, McCall's* | *Glamour, Consumer's Digest, Discover, Money* |
| Ham, biscuits, canned vegetables, Twinkies | Take-out, beef, fish, sweet rolls, cheese |
| Tea, decaf coffee, diet sodas, cola | Wine, herbal tea, skim milk, Cold Duck |
| Ford Festivas, Dodge Dynastys, Olds 98s | Cadillacs, Saturns, Saabs, Mercedes-Benzes |
| Medical insurance, investment property, loans | Gas cards, annuities, savings bonds, stocks |
| Conservatives, pro-lifers, privacy rights | Liberals, ozone depletion, consumerism |

JONESBORO IS A retirement community, pure and simple, where 30 percent of the residents are over 65, and pollsters find that one of the most popular pursuits is, in a word, "grandchildren." Jonesboro is a prime market for crafts, sewing, and knitting — with residents whipping together, no doubt, goofy mittens and hats for the grandkids. The aging citizenry is also big on gardening, crossword puzzles, walking for health, and pets (more dogs than cats). Most of the working people of Jonesboro are into farming and light industry, and they spend their off-hours hunting, horseback riding, and listening to country music. In terms of their political views, however, Jonesboro's residents would just as soon shut the door on the rest of the world: in attitudinal polls, they support less government, more military cutbacks, and increased privacy rights.

| *Poor farming and retirement area* | *Predominantly white couples* | *Less than high school educations* | *Jobs in agriculture and light industry* |
|---|---|---|---|

| **Key Demographics** | Total Population: | 214,668 | Primary Ages of Adults: | 55+ |
|---|---|---|---|---|
| | Median Household Income: | $20,832 | Median Home Value: | $41,107 |

# Joplin, Missouri–Pittsburg, Kansas

| What's Hot | What's Not |
|---|---|
| Gardening, sewing, junk mail, crafts, RVs | Foreign travel, the arts, fashion, casinos |
| Walking, fishing, camping, collectibles | Skiing, jogging, tennis, bicycling, golf |
| Video games, power tools, lawn mowers | Microwaves, 35mm cameras, radar detectors |
| "NBC Nightly News," "I Love Lucy," "Full House" | "Simpsons," "David Brinkley," "Fresh Prince" |
| Adult contemporary, middle-of-the-road, gospel | Classical, jazz, modern rock, news radio |
| *Redbook, Colonial Homes, Sports Afield* | *Vogue, GQ, New Yorker, Self, Financial World* |
| Shake 'N Bake, canned soup, shredded wheat | TV dinners, canned tuna, yogurt, rice cakes |
| Milk, ground coffee, tea, diet sodas | Fruit juice, imported wine and beer, skim milk |
| Pontiacs, Chevys, Chryslers, Lincoln Town Cars | VWs, Ferraris, Saabs, BMWs, Acura Legends |
| Medical insurance, life insurance, CDs | IRAs, bonds, precious metals, mutual funds |
| Moderates, death penalty, school prayer | Liberals, endangered animals, oil drilling |

THIS IS OZARK COUNTRY, a place of retirement condominiums and hardscrabble farms, where the incomes are below average but so are the living costs. More than half the residents are over 50, and it shows in the popularity of crafts, collectibles, woodworking, and sewing. And like other retirement markets, folks here are big on Medicare and other forms of medical insurance. Politically, Joplin-Pittsburg is far from cosmopolitan America — in distance as well as ideology — and many folks are right-leaning moderates who support family values, the pro-life movement, and school prayer. But the rolling mountains are also prime terrain for outdoor activities, and residents take advantage of their free time to go fishing and camping. Around here, the main form of aerobic exercise is walking to the crafts shop.

| *Poor farming and retirement area* | *Predominantly white singles and couples* | *High school educations* | *Jobs in agriculture and light industry* |
|---|---|---|---|

| **Key Demographics** | Total Population: | 357,251 | Primary Ages of Adults: | 55+ |
|---|---|---|---|---|
| | Median Household Income: | $22,364 | Median Home Value: | $35,695 |

# Kansas City, Missouri—Kansas City, Kansas

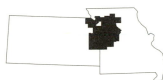

| What's Hot | What's Not |
|---|---|
| Business clubs, pro sports, fine art, movies | Gourmet cooking, fashion, casinos, RVs |
| Golf, bicycling, exercise, swimming, knitting | Tennis, skiing, coin collecting |
| Home gyms, CD players, VCRs, 35mm cameras | Microwaves, convertibles, mobile homes |
| "Northern Exposure," TV sports, "Letterman" | "Beverly Hills, 90210," "Hard Copy," "Blossom" |
| Jazz, classical, rock, middle-of-the-road | Rap, rhythm & blues, gospel, country |
| *USA Today, Money, New Woman, Popular Science* | *TV Guide, Playboy, Star, Car & Driver* |
| Beef, fish, BBQ sauce, canned soup, nuts | Health food, beef stew, snack cakes, rice, jam |
| Domestic wine, skim milk, light beer | Tea, orange juice, milk, Pepsi-Cola |
| Saturns, Audis, Acuras, Chevy Astros | Rolls-Royces, Daihatsus, Nissan Stanzas |
| Mutual funds, stocks, annuities, IRAs | Medical insurance, investment property |
| Moderates, abortion rights, family values | Liberals, gun control, oil drilling |

RISING OUT OF THE CENTER of the Great Plains, Kansas City comes on like a marketing colossus. Despite having only moderate incomes, attitudes, and educational levels, area residents are extraordinary consumers with eclectic tastes. They buy nearly every car sold in America at above-average rates — Fords and Ferraris, Mazdas and Mercedes-Benzes. From soup to nuts, they buy everything in the supermarket at levels greater than the general population. They like to watch TV *and* read a lot of magazines. Plus, it's hard to find a sport or activity they don't enjoy, including fishing, hunting, golf, sailing, gardening, and knitting. Unlike in the big cities on the coast, residents here are slightly more conservative in their views, supporting issues involving family values while opposing the death penalty, gay rights, and gun control. If there's one area where these residents don't excel, it's in traveling far from home. Then again, given their consumption patterns, they've already got everything they need in Kansas City.

| *Middle-class metropolitan sprawl* | *Predominantly white singles and couples* | *High school educations* | *Jobs in education, services, and farming* |
|---|---|---|---|

**Key Demographics**

| | | | |
|---|---|---|---|
| Total Population: | 2,025,887 | Primary Ages of Adults: | 25–44 |
| Median Household Income: | $32,564 | Median Home Value: | $67,671 |

# Knoxville, Tennessee

| What's Hot | What's Not |
|---|---|
| Home decorating, TV sports, car repair, dogs | Dancing, the arts, gourmet cooking, casinos |
| Sewing, gardening, hunting, walking | Bicycling, bowling, golf, tennis, exercise |
| Cable TV, video games, charcoal grills | CD players, 35mm cameras, radar detectors |
| Soaps, "Cops," "Family Feud," "Sally" | "Nightline," "Honeymooners," "Wonder Years" |
| Country, religious radio, college sports | Rhythm & blues, classic rock, jazz, news radio |
| *Southern Living, TV Guide, Field & Stream* | *Esquire, Business Week, Shape, Bon Appetit* |
| Sausage, baked beans, peanut butter, pies | Health food, raisin bread, cheese, rice, Trix |
| Cola, milk, tea, vegetable juices, coffee | Fruit juice, rum, vodka, light beer, Heineken |
| Pontiacs, Chevys, Subaru Justys, Dodge pickups | BMWs, Acuras, Volvos, VW Golfs, Mazda RX-7s |
| Loans, money orders, mail-order life insurance | IRAs, annuities, bonds, stocks |
| Conservatives, less government, pro-lifers | Liberals, consumerism, gay rights |

SOMETIMES, you can take the city out of the wilderness but not the wilderness out of the city. A case in point is Knoxville, carved out of mountains by the first pioneers who crossed the Appalachians two centuries ago. Today the city is a melange of modern skyscrapers, older brick buildings, and renovated shops, galleries, and restaurants. Yet the lifestyle is still steeped in the hillbilly traditions of the surrounding mountains. Compared to average Americans, residents are more likely to engage in outdoor activities like fishing, hunting, and gardening as well as such domestic pursuits as sewing, woodworking, and reading the Bible. Thanks to the local University of Tennessee, residents are fans of college sports. But many lack college degrees and display relatively little interest in science, technology, or current affairs. Even with the government's Tennessee Valley Authority providing cheap power to spur local growth, Knoxville voters are stubbornly conservative, opposing government regulation, military spending, and social welfare programs.

| *Lower-middle-class industrial city* | *Predominantly white couples and singles* | *Less than high school educations* | *Jobs in farming, transportation, and manufacturing* |
|---|---|---|---|

**Key Demographics**

| | | | |
|---|---|---|---|
| Total Population: | 1,104,575 | Primary Ages of Adults: | 35–54 |
| Median Household Income: | $24,744 | Median Home Value: | $56,744 |

# La Crosse—Eau Claire, Wisconsin

## What's Hot

Home workshops, baking, cable TV, rodeos
Bicycling, hunting, fishing, camping, knitting
Microwaves, powerboats, pickups, recliners
CNN, Learning Channel, Daytona 500, "Cheers"
Country, middle-of-the-road, radio baseball
*Outdoor Life, Reader's Digest, Redbook*
Ham, sweet rolls, dried fruit, oatmeal, Jell-O
Draft and light beer, skim milk, Kool-Aid
Oldsmobiles, Buicks, Pontiacs, Ford Festivas
Medical insurance, life insurance, auto loans
Moderates, death penalty, pro-lifers

## What's Not

Theme parks, frequent flying, movies, book clubs
Swimming, jogging, exercise, tennis, golf
PCs, convertibles, stereos, toaster ovens
"Married with Children," "Geraldo," "Hard Copy"
Gospel, modern rock, rap, classical
*Forbes, Food & Wine, Working Woman, Ebony*
Take-out, spaghetti sauce, canned tuna, rice
Wine, vodka, malt liquor, orange juice, tea
Infinitis, Porsches, Nissans, Volvo 780s
Gold cards, stocks, bonds, precious metals
Liberals, endangered animals, legalizing drugs

HERE IN THE HEART of the nation's dairyland, there's not much cream to skim off the top. Residents are less likely than average Americans to engage in typical upscale interests like traveling abroad, collecting art, or attending plays. Horseback riding, hunting, and camping are all popular, as is sewing, gardening, and making crafts. Baking from scratch is also common—nearly one-quarter of the area's residents are homemakers or retirees—although gourmet cooking is not big among these households. Interestingly, residents are above-average purchasers at supermarkets of fresh foods already found on the farm, such as beef, pork, and ice cream. Living so close to Milwaukee, it's no wonder that locals are drawn to sports that can be enjoyed while downing copious quantities of beer—activities like bowling, fishing, and boating. But folks around here are loyal to their state, which is said to have as many cows as people. When they go out to a drive-in, their first choice is Dairy Queen.

| *Lower-middle-class agricultural area* | *Predominantly white couples and singles* | *High school educations* | *Jobs in farming and transportation* |
| --- | --- | --- | --- |

**Key Demographics**

| | | | |
| --- | --- | --- | --- |
| Total Population: | 459,925 | Primary Ages of Adults: | 25–44 |
| Median Household Income: | $27,322 | Median Home Value: | $54,149 |

# Lafayette, Indiana

## What's Hot

Self-improvement, movies, PCs, travel, science
Exercise, jogging, bicycling, golf, racquetball
Home gyms, cameras, VCRs, stereos, microwaves
"Roseanne," "Saturday Night Live," college sports
Modern rock, golden oldies, classical, folk
*Smithsonian, GQ, Ladies' Home Journal, Cycle*
Fast food, fish, pizza, yogurt, pretzels, candy
Herbal tea, light beer, diet sodas, cocktails
Subarus, Dodges, Eagles, Mazdas, GMC Safaris
Mutual funds, interest checking, loans
Moderates, abortion rights, ozone depletion

## What's Not

Fashion, gourmet cooking, casinos, wine, RVs
Skiing, fishing, hunting, walking
Bedroom furnishings, chain saws, power boats
HBO, BET, "American Detective," "Geraldo"
Jazz, rhythm & blues, urban contemporary
*Forbes, Vogue, Weight Watchers, TV Guide*
Beef stew, corn on the cob, waffles, rice
Cola, malt liquor, whole milk, orange juice
Chryslers, Cadillacs, Sterlings, Alfa Romeos
Medical insurance, stocks, bonds, Keoghs
Conservatives, family values, school prayer

YOU'VE GOT TO HAND IT to those college kids. Although students make up only about one-tenth of Lafayette's population—the vast majority attending Purdue University—their sneakers leave a deep imprint on the community's lifestyle. Compared to average Americans, residents are more likely to be involved in aerobic sports like jogging, exercise, and bicycling, as well as cultural activities like photography, art, and the theater. The college-educated labor pool is big on high-tech interests like electronics, computers, and science; among the popular magazines are *Smithsonian, Discover,* and *Popular Science.* But the market also includes the neat farms and picket-fence small towns of western Indiana, and the rural influence can be seen in the popularity of fishing, gardening, and veterans clubs as well as publications like *Ladies' Home Journal* and *Family Handyman.* Although local members of Congress have generally been conservative Republicans, Lafayette voters typically claim liberal views, favoring sex- and AIDS education over prayer in the schools, and gay rights over the gun lobby.

| *Middle-class college town* | *Predominantly white singles* | *College educations* | *Jobs in education, farming, and manufacturing* |
| --- | --- | --- | --- |

**Key Demographics**

| | | | |
| --- | --- | --- | --- |
| Total Population: | 135,008 | Primary Ages of Adults: | 18–34 |
| Median Household Income: | $30,447 | Median Home Value: | $71,069 |

# Lafayette, Louisiana

| What's Hot | What's Not |
|---|---|
| Fishing, Cajun cooking, cable TV, sweepstakes | Travel, the arts, books, coupons, health clubs |
| Hunting, walking, sewing, gardening | Skiing, tennis, golf, bowling, racquetball |
| Charcoal grills, 126/110 cameras, video games | PCs, 35mm cameras, VCRs, stereos, home gyms |
| "American Gladiators," "Guiding Light," soaps | A&E, VH-1, "Siskel & Ebert," "Sisters" |
| Country, gospel music, urban contemporary | Classical, jazz, soft rock, talk radio |
| *True Story, Ebony, Outdoor Life, TV Guide* | *Inc., Sunset, Omni, House Beautiful, Shape* |
| Seafood, sausage, rice, BBQ sauce, biscuits | Mexican food, chicken, salad, French bread |
| Malt liquor, diet sodas, powdered drinks, tea | Spring water, beer, wine, decaf coffee |
| Pontiacs, Fords, Chryslers, Dodge trucks | VWs, Volvos, Audis, Peugeots, Saabs |
| Money orders, loans, medical insurance | Mutual funds, credit cards, savings bonds |
| Conservatives, toxic waste, school prayer | Moderates, gay rights, military cutbacks |

LAFAYETTE, LOUISIANA, is known mostly for two things: oil and Cajuns. As the geographical heart of Cajun country, the town is home to a significant number of people who speak not English but Cajun French, and who have their own traditions in culture and cuisine. Though marketing surveys typically don't pick up ethnic quirks, food surveys show some of the Cajun influence in the popularity of ham, sausage, seafood, and rice — all the ingredients of jambalaya. And residents are more likely to spend their off-time hunting, gardening, and fishing; it's said that one's first fishing trip is as important a rite of passage here as a bar mitzvah is in New York. Because many locals are poor and poorly educated — 40 percent failed to finish high school — there's relatively little interest in books, newspapers, or magazines. And few locals have the disposable income to travel or invest in real estate. The vagaries of the oil industry have shifted the area's employment base toward tourism, and local family-run restaurants are among the big attractions. Reportedly, Lafayette is the nation's top market for per capita restaurant sales.

| *Poor commercial center* | *Racially diverse families and singles* | *Less than high school educations* | *Jobs in farming, mining, and manufacturing* |
|---|---|---|---|

## Key Demographics

| | | | |
|---|---|---|---|
| Total Population: | 539,684 | Primary Ages of Adults: | 25–44 |
| Median Household Income: | $20,776 | Median Home Value: | $49,665 |

# Lake Charles, Louisiana

| What's Hot | What's Not |
|---|---|
| Wildlife, car repair, the Bible, dieting, dogs | Civic activities, theme parks, clubs, cats |
| Fishing, hunting, sewing, crafts, gardening | Golf, jogging, exercise, tennis, bowling |
| Cable TV, video games, pickups, RVs | VCRs, PCs, Tupperware, 35mm cameras, books |
| BET, TV wrestling, "Current Affair," "Full House" | "Letterman," "Face the Nation," "Loving" |
| Country, gospel, rap, college sports | Classical, modern rock, jazz, '40s-'60s pop |
| *Outdoor Life, Family Handyman, Woman's World* | *People, Newsweek, Mademoiselle, Barron's* |
| Ham, hash, peanut butter, snack cakes, grits | TV dinners, beef, pumpernickel, rice cakes |
| Cola, powdered drinks, milk, vegetable juices | Wine, imported and draft beer, skim milk |
| Chevys, Oldsmobiles, Pontiac Sunbirds | Ferraris, Saabs, Audis, Nissan 300ZXs |
| Whole-term insurance, Medicare, loans | Stocks, bonds, annuities, mutual funds, IRAs |
| Conservatives, pro-lifers, less government | Liberals, oil-drilling, ozone depletion |

IT'S BARELY A STONE'S THROW across the bayou from Lake Charles to Lafayette, the previous market described. And, not surprisingly, the lifestyles are much alike: this is still Cajun country, where local cooks are said to use every part of a pig but its squeal. With a tough blue-collar workforce — oil refining is the biggest source of work here — Lake Charles ranks high among residents who do their own home improvements, work on their cars, and go fishing and hunting to put food on the table (hunting dogs are a prized commodity). Locals are so self-sufficient that they rarely belong to clubs — not veterans groups, religious groups, or bowling leagues. And compared to average Americans, they're less likely to engage in high-tech activities, owning relatively few computers, VCRs, cameras, and other electronic gear. Although their employers are big polluters of the air and water, locals apparently have a high tolerance for ecological threats; they express little concern for water pollution caused by refineries.

| *Lower-middle-class commercial port* | *Racially diverse families* | *High school educations* | *Jobs in manufacturing, mining, and transportation* |
|---|---|---|---|

## Key Demographics

| | | | |
|---|---|---|---|
| Total Population: | 234,220 | Primary Ages of Adults: | 25–44 |
| Median Household Income: | $24,752 | Median Home Value: | $53,852 |

# Lansing, Michigan

| What's Hot | What's Not |
|---|---|
| Career activities, art, movies, books, unions | Fashion, gourmet cooking, rodeos, casinos |
| Bicycling, boating, bowling, skiing, hiking | Tennis, walking, coin collecting |
| Food processors, power tools, PCs, VCRs | Microwaves, cameras, diesel autos, passports |
| "Northern Exposure," "Simpsons," "Cheers" | Game shows, "People's Court," "I Love Lucy" |
| Classical, heavy metal, rap, rock | Gospel, rhythm & blues, jazz, folk |
| *Home Mechanix, Omni, 1001 Home Ideas, Parents* | *Harper's Bazaar, Time, Esquire, Star* |
| Fish, canned soup, popcorn, oat bran, macaroni | Health food, rice, jam, brownies, cookies |
| Powdered drinks, light beer, herbal tea | Tea, milk, orange juice, imported beer, ale |
| Subaru, Dodges, Oldsmobiles, Chevy Luminas | Peugeots, Nissans, Lincolns, BMW 6/7s |
| Christmas clubs, savings accounts, auto loans | Investment property, stocks, gold cards |
| Moderates, toxic waste, death penalty | Liberals, family values, gay rights |

TIME WAS WHEN America was known as the land of the Great Middle Class, a nation where mainstream communities like Lansing were commonplace. Today, Lansing is still middlebrow, but it comes across as a rare and somewhat contradictory community. With incomes, home values, and political attitudes near the national average, residents tend to avoid upscale pursuits like foreign travel, wearing designer clothes, and gourmet cooking. Moreover, they shy away from activities typical of more downscale communities, such as watching daytime soaps, entering sweepstakes, and reading the Bible. Lansing's well-paying factory jobs provide residents with the time and money to golf, bowl, collect local art, and travel — though domestically rather than abroad. And their literary tastes, likely influenced by local Michigan State University, make them fans of sports, science, and fiction. Voters here claim to be moderates, yet they keep political analysts guessing with their opposition to both gay rights and family values.

| *Middle-class industrial city* | *Predominantly white singles* | *Some college educations* | *Manufacturing and crafts jobs* |
|---|---|---|---|

| **Key Demographics** | Total Population: | 639,721 | Primary Ages of Adults: | 25–44 |
|---|---|---|---|---|
| | Median Household Income: | $33,908 | Median Home Value: | $62,983 |

# Laredo, Texas

| What's Hot | What's Not |
|---|---|
| Foreign travel, car repair, cable TV, vitamins | The arts, theme parks, gardening, movies |
| Walking, fishing, sewing | Golf, bowling, boating, skiing, bicycling |
| Microwaves, washers, pregnancy-test kits | CD players, PCs, home gyms, toaster ovens |
| "Inside Edition," "Rescue 911," boxing | "Designing Women," "Seinfeld," Wimbledon |
| Spanish radio, urban contemporary, gospel | Classical, modern rock, easy listening |
| *Playboy, Essence, Jet, Star, TV Guide* | *U.S. News, Redbook, Food & Wine, Prevention* |
| Mexican food, canned chicken, potato chips, gum | Fish, pasta, yogurt, oat bran, nuts |
| Cola, milk, tea, domestic beer, diet sodas | Cocktails, draft and light beer, cocoa |
| Hyundais, Daihatsu Charades, Nissan trucks | Volvos, Acuras, Jaguars, Porsches, Saab 900s |
| Money orders, mail-order life insurance | Stocks, annuities, mutual funds, Keoghs |
| Liberals, family values, privacy rights | Moderates, school sex ed, gay rights |

THIS DUSTY BORDER TOWN still retains many frontier traditions from its 19th-century days as the capital of Zapata's Republic of the Rio Grande. Residents today enjoy rodeos, target shooting, and fishing as much as their forebears. And there are plenty of cheap restaurants where locals can enjoy enchiladas washed down with beer — domestic brands like Lone Star are preferred. The short walk over a bridge into Mexico helps explain the high rate of foreign travel as well as the popularity of electronics and vitamins (cheaper over the border). In this downscale area, lacking both money and educational achievement, residents make do by keeping up their homes and used cars; of 228 car models, only 2 models are bought new at above-average rates compared to nearly 75 truck nameplates. Although the voting district generally supports Democrats, the voting rate is low and many citizens are social conservatives. Indeed, a significant percentage of residents still feel a greater allegiance to Mexico than to the United States.

| *Poor border trade area* | *Predominantly Hispanic families* | *Less than high school educations* | *Jobs in transportation and manufacturing* |
|---|---|---|---|

| **Key Demographics** | Total Population: | 157,297 | Primary Ages of Adults: | 25–44 |
|---|---|---|---|---|
| | Median Household Income: | $20,008 | Median Home Value: | $52,480 |

# Las Vegas, Nevada

## What's Hot

Casino gambling, fashion, dancing, travel
Skiing, golf, jogging, camping, collectibles
Home gyms, CD players, PCs, woks, condoms
"Siskel & Ebert," "Simpsons," "Doogie Howser"
Modern rock, pop, classical, rhythm & blues
*Sunset, New Woman, Shape, Bon Appetit, Inc.*
Mexican food, fish, cheese, croissants, yogurt
Spring water, cocktails, wine, ground coffee
Saturns, Isuzus, Mitsubishis, Mazdas, Toyotas
Credit cards, IRAs, mutual funds, bonds, stocks
Liberals, gay rights, ozone depletion

## What's Not

The arts, photography, clubs, the Bible
Bicycling, fishing, hunting, sewing
Microwaves, power tools, lawn furniture
"Cosby Show," "Price Is Right," "Major Dad,"
Gospel, country, jazz, late-night radio
*Outdoor Life, Soap Opera Digest, Prevention*
Pizza, baked beans, cold cuts, pasta, pies
Tea, powdered drinks, orange juice, cocoa
Ferraris, Buicks, Oldsmobiles, Lincolns
Keoghs, CDs, loans, medical insurance
Moderates, family values, buying American

RAISE A SHOT GLASS to gambling and greed, the twin sins that built Las Vegas. Most residents here earn their middle-class incomes in entertainment and recreation services, and the lack of income- and corporate taxes fosters an enviable lifestyle. Locals have the money to enjoy fashion, gourmet cooking, pop concerts, high-tech toys — this is one of the top markets for VCRs and video games — and traveling within the U.S. and abroad. There's a preoccupation with making more money, and not just at the casinos. Compared to average Americans, residents are more likely to buy stocks, precious metals, and investment property, as well as coins, stamps, and decorative plates. There's not much in the way of wilderness sports, unless you count visiting the Mirage Hotel's man-made rain forest and volcano (which erupts every 15 minutes at night). But the locals know that the Lord had nothing to do with Las Vegas: this is a terrible market for the spiritual who care about gospel music, religious radio, or the Bible. In Vegas, the pursuit of money is the dominant religion.

| *Middle-class gambling resort* | *Ethnically diverse singles and couples* | *Some college educations* | *Jobs in finance and recreation services* |
| --- | --- | --- | --- |

### Key Demographics

| | | | |
| --- | --- | --- | --- |
| Total Population: | 889,114 | Primary Ages of Adults: | 25–44 |
| Median Household Income: | $33,836 | Median Home Value: | $100,244 |

# Laurel-Hattiesburg, Mississippi

## What's Hot

Mobile homes, gardening, car repair, the Bible
Fishing, hunting, walking, sewing, knitting
Chain saws, microwaves, VCRs
Morning news, "I Love Lucy," "Fresh Prince"
Country, urban contemporary, religious radio
*True Story, Southern Living, Ebony, TV Guide*
Bacon, beef stew, biscuits, macaroni, snack cakes
Cola, tea, orange juice, Kool-Aid, cocoa
Olds 98s, Cadillac Broughams, Ford trucks
Medical insurance, loans, money orders
Conservatives, school prayer, oil drilling

## What's Not

Movies, books, theme parks, travel, newspapers
Golf, tennis, bowling, boating, collectibles
Cameras, food processors, PCs, books, radios
"Nightline," "Joan Rivers," "In Living Color"
Soft rock, jazz, classical, radio baseball
*Glamour, Rolling Stone, Newsweek, Discover*
TV dinners, French bread, canned tuna, pretzels
Tomato juices, imported beer, wine, skim milk
Saabs, Acuras, Peugeots, Volvos, VW vans
Savings bonds, stocks, mutual funds, Keoghs
Liberals, gun control, ozone depletion

HERE IN THE PINEY WOODS of southern Mississippi, the residents of Laurel and Hattiesburg seem caught in a no-man's land between the rich farmland to the north and lucrative tourist trade along the Gulf Coast. There's not much money or education among locals, who tend to work in paper mills or on hardscrabble farms, and their lifestyle is somewhat dreary. Residents are more likely to go fishing and hunting than bowling or to the movies. With many young people leaving for better jobs elsewhere, this is an older area — one-quarter of the population is over 65 — where denture cleansers and hair color are big sellers at the drug stores. Although few cars are bought at above-average rates, the ones that do sell well tend to be sturdy pickups or large American cruisers, such as the Ford Crown Victoria and the Oldsmobile 98, that can handle the area's rugged back roads. This part of Mississippi is conservative, religious, and known as the Bible Belt for good reason: people read the Bible here at the highest rate in the nation.

| *Poor farming area* | *Racially diverse singles and couples* | *Less than high school educations* | *Farm, manufacturing, and transportation jobs* |
| --- | --- | --- | --- |

### Key Demographics

| | | | |
| --- | --- | --- | --- |
| Total Population: | 253,553 | Primary Ages of Adults: | 55+ |
| Median Household Income: | $20,490 | Median Home Value: | $45,538 |

# Lexington, Kentucky

| What's Hot | What's Not |
|---|---|
| Home furnishing, horseback riding, baking | Travel, the arts, current affairs, health food |
| Gardening, fishing, hunting, walking | Bicycling, skiing, tennis, bowling, golf |
| Garden tillers, charcoal grills, cable TV | Microwaves, VCRs, PCs, cameras, power tools |
| "Murder, She Wrote," "Primetime Live," "Cops" | "Married with Children," "Masters Golf," "Sisters" |
| Country, gospel, radio college sports | Rap, classic rock, classical, radio pro sports |
| *Country Living, National Enquirer, McCall's* | *Business Week, Ebony, Food & Wine, Shape* |
| Fried chicken, hot dogs, biscuits, brownies | Take-out, beef, canned tuna, frozen yogurt |
| Bourbon, orange juice, cola, milk, tea | Rum, imported brandy, scotch, wine, skim milk |
| Ford Festivas, Subaru Loyales, Dodge trucks | Mercedes-Benzes, Saabs, Acuras, Peugeot 505s |
| Life insurance, Keoghs, mortgage loans | Gold cards, savings bonds, mutual funds |
| Conservatives, pro-lifers, less government | Liberals, school sex ed, endangered animals |

DESPITE THE RECENT ARRIVAL of industrial giants like IBM and Toyota, Lexington remains steeped in the traditions of bluegrass country: growing tobacco, breeding horses, and producing whiskey. Residents tend to enjoy outdoor activities like horseback riding, gardening, and fishing more than tennis, golf, and jogging. With the large number of antebellum houses, home decorating is popular in the area, along with crafts, needlework, and magazines like *Country Living* and *1001 Home Ideas*. Locals also are into college sports, thanks to the area's perennial powerhouse, the University of Kentucky. And though the image of the horsey set is generally one of upscale gentry pursuing travel, fashion, and gourmet cooking, in fact there's little of that in the Lexington market. Most residents lead more prosaic lives; the closest many come to the Kentucky Derby is watching it on their living room TV sets.

| *Lower-middle-class commercial center* | *Predominantly white couples and singles* | *Less than high school educations* | *Jobs in farming, transportation, and manufacturing* |
|---|---|---|---|

### Key Demographics

| | | | |
|---|---|---|---|
| Total Population: | 993,429 | Primary Ages of Adults: | 25–44 |
| Median Household Income: | $23,947 | Median Home Value: | $58,184 |

# Lima, Ohio

| What's Hot | What's Not |
|---|---|
| Home furnishing, TV sports, collectibles, RVs | Health clubs, theme parks, fashion, travel |
| Bowling, golf, fishing, bicycling, crafts | Sailing, exercise, jogging, skiing, tennis |
| Video games, cable TV, VCRs, cameras, grills | Stereos, CD players, sofa beds, convertibles |
| Nickelodeon, Daytona 500, "Evening Shade" | HBO, "Night Court," "Star Trek," "Loving" |
| Golden oldies, country, adult contemporary | Jazz, rhythm & blues, modern rock, talk radio |
| *Outdoor Life, Popular Mechanics, Redbook* | *Travel & Leisure, Gourmet, Ebony, Forbes* |
| Fish, spaghetti sauce, pudding, shredded wheat | Mexican food, corn on the cob, hash, pancakes |
| Vegetable juices, powdered drinks, skim milk | Imported wine, malt liquor, tea, imported beer |
| Pontiacs, Oldsmobiles, Chevys, Dodge Daytonas | Hondas, VWs, Acuras, Volvos, Jaguars, BMW 6/7s |
| Home-improvement loans, stocks, CDs | Bonds, precious metals, medical insurance |
| Moderates, school sex ed, privacy rights | Liberals, gay rights, legalizing drugs |

THIS IS AMERICA'S industrial heartland and, like the factories around Lima, the locals are getting a bit long in the tooth. Nearly 40 percent of all adults are over 55 years old, and the most popular activities include woodworking, knitting, and collecting stamps and coins. Many locals avoid aerobic sports like jogging and exercise in favor of golf and fishing. And when it comes to magazines, locals prefer home decorating and fix-it publications; indeed, these are the folks for whom bankers invented home-improvement loans. Living on the edge of the Rust Belt — Lima's biggest employer is General Dynamics, maker of the M-1 Abrams tank — residents describe themselves as patriotic moderates. They buy American cars and spend their vacations in this country rather than abroad, but they're somewhat ambivalent on the issue of military spending. In the 1980 primary election, for instance, they voted for George Bush over Ronald Reagan.

| *Lower-middle-class industrial city* | *Predominantly white families and singles* | *High school educations* | *Manufacturing, labor, and crafts jobs* |
|---|---|---|---|

### Key Demographics

| | | | |
|---|---|---|---|
| Total Population: | 109,894 | Primary Ages of Adults: | 55+ |
| Median Household Income: | $29,394 | Median Home Value: | $55,027 |

# Lincoln-Hastings-Kearney, Nebraska

| What's Hot | What's Not |
|---|---|
| Clubs, mall shopping, adult-ed courses, baking | Frequent flying, movies, lotteries, unions |
| Walking, hunting, fishing, sewing, knitting | Racquetball, jogging, tennis, skiing |
| Home gyms, power tools, microwaves, Tupperware | VCRs, PCs, CD players, station wagons |
| Game shows, "Tonight Show," "Roseanne" | "Geraldo," "Hard Copy," "Beverly Hills, 90210" |
| Golden oldies, heavy metal, middle-of-the-road | Pop, rap, jazz, soft rock, news radio |
| *Field & Stream, National Geographic, McCall's* | *Fortune, Cosmopolitan, Architectural Digest* |
| Pizza, ham, canned fruit, crackers, popcorn | Take-out, canned hash, tuna, chocolates, rice |
| Light and draft beer, skim milk, ground coffee | Wine, imported beer, orange juice, herbal tea |
| Buicks, Dodges, Oldsmobiles, Ford Festivas | Saabs, Audis, Alfa Romeos, Volvo 940s |
| Medical insurance, mutual funds, CDs | IRAs, savings bonds, Keoghs, stocks |
| Moderates, less government, pro-lifers | Liberals, endangered animals, legalizing drugs |

LOCAL COLLEGES LIKE the University of Nebraska save these three cities from forming just another farmer's market. Residents tend to read books, take adult-education classes, and light up the bars and restaurants in downtown Lincoln. Otherwise, this is a fairly sober area as state capitals go, with residents big on public activities and belonging to business and veterans groups. Outside the three cities are neat farms and orderly towns that color the market's overall lifestyle. Compared to the general population, locals are more likely to enjoy rodeos, horseback riding, and gardening, as well as read magazines like *Mother Earth News, Field & Stream,* and *Ladies' Home Journal.* Politically, this is a land of moderates who vote Republican on the national level and Democrat on the state level. Even the students are right-of-center, opposing gay rights, abortion rights, and legalizing drugs.

| *Lower-middle-class trade area* | *Predominantly white couples and singles* | *High school educations* | *Jobs in farming, transportation, and education* |
|---|---|---|---|

### Key Demographics

| | | | |
|---|---|---|---|
| Total Population: | 632,274 | Primary Ages of Adults: | 55+ |
| Median Household Income: | $26,812 | Median Home Value: | $48,909 |

# Little Rock, Arkansas

| What's Hot | What's Not |
|---|---|
| Rodeos, pro wrestling, baking, the Bible | Travel, the arts, books, casinos, coupons |
| Fishing, hunting, sewing, crafts | Jogging, tennis, golf, bicycling, skiing |
| Chain saws, microwaves, 126/110 cameras, RVs | Food processors, 35mm cameras, CD players, PCs |
| Daytime news, "Family Feud," "Days of Our Lives" | MTV, "Wonder Years," "Face the Nation" |
| Country, rhythm & blues, gospel, religious radio | Soft rock, classical, golden oldies, middle-of-the-road |
| *National Enquirer, Southern Living, Ebony* | *Newsweek, People, Discover, GQ, Bon Appetit* |
| Ham, peanut butter, BBQ sauce, chili, grits | TV dinners, cheese, canned tuna, raisin bread |
| Cola, powdered drinks, malt liquor, tea | Fruit juices, imported wine, draft beer |
| Chryslers, Dodges, Chevys, Dodge trucks | Toyotas, Saturns, VWs, Audis, Range Rovers |
| Medical insurance, loans, first mortgages | Mutual funds, bonds, stocks, gold cards |
| Conservatives, school sex ed, less government | Liberals, consumerism, gay rights |

IT'S HARD TO BELIEVE that Bill Clinton spent most of his adult life in this sleepy state capital. Little Rock residents are less likely than average Americans to jog, read books, travel abroad, or express an interest in technology — no wonder Bill wanted to move to Washington. According to surveys, these Arkansans would rather fish, hunt, garden, and watch cable TV. Their favorite magazines include supermarket tabloids like the *National Enquirer* and the *Star* as well as those chroniclers of television programming, *TV Guide* and *Soap Opera Digest.* With one-quarter of the residents retired, this is an area marketers of senior products cherish, from crossword puzzles to RVs. But Little Rock still resembles a backwater Southern burg with conservative leanings, which helps explain the forcible resistance to integrated schools in 1957. Today residents still oppose government regulation, gay rights, and the efforts of consumer advocates, though race relations have improved. If there is one thing that Clinton shares with Little Rock locals, it's a strong faith in politics and religion; around here folks read the Bible, listen to religious radio, and become involved in public activities far more often than average Americans.

| *Lower-middle-class commercial center* | *Racially diverse couples and singles* | *High school educations* | *Jobs in farming, labor, and manufacturing* |
|---|---|---|---|

### Key Demographics

| | | | |
|---|---|---|---|
| Total Population: | 1,210,516 | Primary Ages of Adults: | 55+ |
| Median Household Income: | $24,941 | Median Home Value: | $53,218 |

# Los Angeles, California

| What's Hot | What's Not |
|---|---|
| Movies, fashion, travel, art, books, casinos | Home furnishing, gardening, crafts, pets |
| Exercise, jogging, tennis, bicycling, skiing | Fishing, hunting, bowling, golf, walking |
| Home gyms, PCs, cassette decks, faxes, cameras | Power tools, video games, microwaves, pickups |
| HBO, C-SPAN, "Letterman," "In Living Color" | Game shows, "Major Dad," "Days of Our Lives" |
| Modern rock, jazz, classical, rap, talk radio | Country, gospel, religious radio, heavy metal |
| *Forbes, Vanity Fair, Cosmopolitan, GQ, Sunset* | *True Story, Star, Popular Mechanics* |
| Health food, Mexican food, yogurt, rye bread | Beef stew, pudding, pasta, canned soup, doughnuts |
| Domestic wine, spring water, vodka, rum | Tomato juice, lemon-lime sodas, milk, cocoa |
| Ferraris, Porsches, Rolls-Royces, Jaguars | Oldsmobiles, Chevys, Pontiacs, Dodges, Buicks |
| Investment property, stocks, bonds, IRAs | CDs, life insurance, auto and personal loans |
| Liberals, legalizing drugs, oil drilling | Moderates, pro-lifers, endangered animals |

IF HOLLYWOOD NEEDED a backdrop of trendy glitz and glamour, it could hardly have done much better than Los Angeles. This sprawling city by the sea ranks among the nation's top ten markets for interest in movies, music, fashion, foreign travel, and the arts. Compared to average Americans, Los Angelenos own more computers, CD players, and VCRs per capita than residents of nearly any other city in the U.S. As home of California's body-conscious set, the city is also one of America's best markets for health clubs, health food, and aerobic exercise. To be sure, not everyone shops on Rodeo Drive: L.A. has an underclass of poorly educated Hispanics and under-employed African Americans (whose anger fueled the deadly riots of 1992). But at its core, the City of Angels deals in Rolls-Royce–sized dreams, with residents who gamble at high rates on everything from casino games to real estate to lotteries. If the films and TV shows originating in Los Angeles seem to bear so little resemblance to heartland America, it's for good reason. L.A. is a mecca of liberalism, where residents back abortion rights, gay pride, environmental awareness, and nude beaches. The heartland is far away — geographically and psychologically.

| *Affluent metropolitan sprawl* | *Ethnically diverse singles* | *Some college educations* | *Jobs in business, finance, and entertainment* |
|---|---|---|---|

| **Key Demographics** | Total Population: | 15,129,009 | Primary Ages of Adults: | 25–44 |
|---|---|---|---|---|
| | Median Household Income: | $41,482 | Median Home Value: | $227,929 |

# Louisville, Kentucky

| What's Hot | What's Not |
|---|---|
| Home decorating, horse racing, city parks, pets | Current affairs, theme parks, dancing, cats |
| Fishing, hunting, gardening, camping, crafts | Golf, tennis, skiing, bicycling, jogging |
| Video games, cable TV, power tools, Tupperware | Toaster ovens, 35mm cameras, microwaves |
| Morning news, "Sally," "Current Affair" | VH-1, "Murphy Brown," "Nightline," "Simpsons" |
| Country, heavy metal, gospel, golden oldies | Rhythm & blues, rap, modern rock, '40s–'60s pop |
| *Field & Stream, Southern Living, Parents* | *New Woman, Rolling Stone, Smithsonian, Omni* |
| Ham, baked beans, snack cakes, Lucky Charms | Chicken, canned tuna, French bread, sour cream |
| Powdered drinks, tea, bourbon, milk | Herbal tea, wine, beer, skim milk, diet sodas |
| Chevys, Pontiacs, Oldsmobiles, Ford Tempos | Volvos, Jaguars, Alfa Romeos, Lexus SC3/SC4s |
| Term life insurance, Christmas clubs | IRAs, savings bonds, mutual funds, Keoghs |
| Moderates, school prayer, death penalty | Liberals, ozone depletion, consumerism |

AS THE HOME of the Kentucky Derby, Louisville conjures up genteel images of mint juleps on the veranda. In fact, this city is an industrial giant that produces bourbon, cigarettes, meat, and refined oil, although the area is reminiscent of a small Southern mill town. Residents are into home decorating, college sports, and muscle cars at above-average rates. Their favorite reading matter, next to the Bible, includes magazines like *Southern Living* and *Colonial Homes*. Compared to the general population, Louisville has a high concentration of homemakers and retirees, resulting in the popularity of crafts, crossword puzzles, home cooking, and video games (for the kiddies and grandkids). The numerous city parks that once lured native son Muhammad Ali for his early morning workouts now draw senior citizens for a quiet stroll.

| *Lower-middle-class manufacturing city* | *Predominantly white couples and singles* | *High school educations* | *Jobs in manufacturing, transportation, and services* |
|---|---|---|---|

| **Key Demographics** | Total Population: | 1,469,902 | Primary Ages of Adults: | 25–44 |
|---|---|---|---|---|
| | Median Household Income: | $28,694 | Median Home Value: | $56,771 |

# Lubbock, Texas

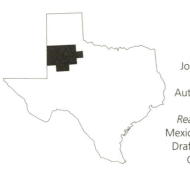

| What's Hot | What's Not |
|---|---|
| Electronics, baking, art, rodeos, the Bible | The arts, gourmet cooking, books, bicycles |
| Jogging, skiing, hunting, sewing, collectibles | Boating, bowling, tennis, walking, gambling |
| PCs, recliners, cable TV, grills, trucks | Radar detectors, CD players, lawn furniture |
| Auto races, "American Gladiators," "Cheers" | Soaps, "Oprah," "Hard Copy," "Seinfeld" |
| Country, modern rock, folk, golden oldies | Rap, middle-of-the-road, rhythm & blues, classical |
| *Reader's Digest, Cycle, Outdoor Life, McCall's* | *Life, House Beautiful, Financial World, Ebony* |
| Mexican food, beef stew, dried fruit, BBQ sauce | Chicken, take-out, rice cakes, frozen yogurt |
| Draft beer, tea, tomato juice, powdered drinks | Cocktails, wine, imported beer, orange juice |
| Chevy Geos, Subaru Loyales, Dodge Omnis | Peugeot 505s, Volvo 240s, Audi 80/90s |
| Medical insurance, education loans, CDs | Savings bonds, stocks, IRAs, gold cards |
| Conservatives, pro-lifers, less government | Liberals, gay rights, military cutbacks |

THIS ONE-TIME COW TOWN in the Texas panhandle has long since diversified into oil, cotton farming, and catering to the students of Texas Tech as well as the soldiers at Reese Air Force Base. But the diverse economic base has also bred an idiosyncratic lifestyle. Residents are into fashion, fine art, and electronics, as well as hunting, motorcycles, and the Bible. The large percentage of young singles has made popular jogging, skiing, and camping. But the rural flavor of area farms has also resulted in above-average interest in crafts, collectibles, sewing, and needlework. Perhaps in no other area are these eclectic tastes more pronounced than in the native music: Buddy Holly, Roy Orbison, and Waylon Jennings called Lubbock home, and their individual styles have influenced country, folk, and rock 'n' roll well beyond the Texas border for decades.

| *Lower-middle-class commercial center* | *Ethnically diverse couples and singles* | *Less than high school educations* | *Farm, education, and transportation jobs* |
|---|---|---|---|

**Key Demographics**

| | | | |
|---|---|---|---|
| Total Population: | 517,412 | Primary Ages of Adults: | 25–44 |
| Median Household Income: | $28,559 | Median Home Value: | $58,205 |

# Macon, Georgia

| What's Hot | What's Not |
|---|---|
| Veterans groups, home restoration, music | Frequent flying, movies, skiing, theme parks |
| Walking, fishing, hunting, sewing | Golf, bowling, tennis, bicycling, knitting |
| Garden tillers, chain saws, microwaves | Cameras, VCRs, PCs, recliners, motorcycles |
| "Fresh Prince," "I Love Lucy," "Family Matters" | A&E, "Joan Rivers," "Married with Children" |
| Gospel, rap, rhythm & blues | Modern rock, classical, jazz, golden oldies |
| *Ebony, Jet, Sports Afield, Seventeen, Health* | *Working Mother, U.S. News, Self, Gourmet, Omni* |
| Beef stew, peanut butter, corn, fast food | TV dinners, canned tuna, chocolates, soup, nuts |
| Cola, diet sodas, milk, tea, orange juice | Draft beer, skim milk, scotch, imported brandy |
| Isuzus, Nissans, Mazda 626s, Chevy Camaros | VWs, Audis, Jaguars, Porsches, Saab 9000s |
| Medical insurance, term life insurance | Annuities, bonds, mutual funds, IRAs |
| Conservatives, school prayer, toxic waste | Moderates, privacy rights, gun control |

THE HOME OF legendary musicians Otis Redding, Little Richard, and the Allman Brothers, Macon is a big music town. One lifestyle survey found that purchasing records and tapes — gospel, rap, country, and rhythm & blues — accounted for half of the ten most popular activities in the market. Residents are also into the video media: they're much more likely to watch soaps, game shows, and pro wrestling than to read newspapers, magazines, and books. The downscale economy, based on low-wage jobs in farm, textile, and paper products, makes this a weak market for computers, financial products, and such sports as golf and sailing. Although Macon residents have voted Democratic since Sherman marched through Georgia, they are conservative Democrats who oppose gay and abortion rights as well as government regulation. Still, the invasion of larger city problems, such as drugs and AIDS, has tempered their rightist views; today a significant percentage support AIDS- and sex education in the classroom — along with school prayer.

| *Lower-middle-class industrial center* | *Racially diverse families and singles* | *High school educations* | *Manufacturing, transportation, and farm jobs* |
|---|---|---|---|

**Key Demographics**

| | | | |
|---|---|---|---|
| Total Population: | 517,412 | Primary Ages of Adults: | 25–44 |
| Median Household Income: | $28,559 | Median Home Value: | $58,205 |

# Madison, Wisconsin

## What's Hot

Politics, photography, books, movies, dancing
Bowling, golf, skiing, bicycling, camping
Cassette decks, musical instruments, motorcycles
"Siskel & Ebert," "Northern Exposure," "Coach"
Rock, country, pop, heavy metal
*Mother Earth News, Self, Redbook, Omni, Health*
Fish, pizza, baked beans, canned soup, pretzels
Draft beer, skim milk, coffee, cocoa
Buick, Dodges, Subarus, Pontiacs, Chevy pickups
Medical insurance, mutual funds, auto loans
Moderates, toxic waste, pro-lifers

## What's Not

Gourmet cooking, fashion, theater, dieting
Tennis, jogging, coin collecting, the Bible
CD players, newspapers, cable TV, convertibles
Soaps, "Geraldo," "People's Court," "60 Minutes"
Rhythm & blues, rap, gospel, news radio
*People, Forbes, Car & Driver, Ebony, Esquire*
TV dinners, health food, chili, cold cuts, pie
Wine, tea, imported beer, cola, malt liquor
Nissans, Porsches, Acuras, Hyundais, BMW 6/7s
Bonds, money orders, investment property
Liberals, gun control, legalizing drugs

THIS LONGTIME LIBERAL BASTION, capital of a progressive state, and home to the University of Wisconsin, is perhaps best summed up by a popular local T-shirt that reads: "THE ALTERNATIVE TO REALITY." Thanks to the high concentration of young, intellectually inclined singles, locals are more likely than average Americans to read books, attend art gallery openings, and take adult-education courses. The city thrives with New Age stores and cafés, and the shady trees surrounding the state capitol make bicycling and walking popular local pursuits. Like other college towns, Madison's liberal mores are tempered somewhat by the surrounding rural residents who display a passion for activities like fishing, woodworking, and gardening, as well as a conservative streak on issues like drugs, abortion, and gay rights. And you really see the intersection of state government and the academic community in Madison's preoccupation with ideas. While residents once were caught up in the drug and protest scene, today's citizens are more interested in politics, science, and technology.

| *Middle-class state capital* | *Predominantly white singles* | *College educations* | *Education, farming, and craft jobs* |
|---|---|---|---|

## Key Demographics

| | | | | |
|---|---|---|---|---|
| Total Population: | 748,033 | Primary Ages of Adults: | 25–44 |
| Median Household Income: | $33,236 | Median Home Value: | $69,553 |

# Mankato, Minnesota

## What's Hot

Crafts, casinos, dancing, RVs, grandchildren
Fishing, camping, hunting, bowling, golf
Cable TV, microwaves, grills, recliners
Game shows, "Major Dad," Indianapolis 500
Country, golden oldies, adult contemporary
*Field & Stream, Ladies' Home Journal, TV Guide*
Sausage, hot dogs, corn chips, pizza, candy
Powdered drinks, light beer, skim milk, Miller
Dodges, Ford Crown Victorias, Buick Park Avenues
Medical insurance, CDs, savings accounts
Moderates, death penalty, less government

## What's Not

Theme parks, the arts, books, health food
Jogging, skiing, sailing, tennis
VCRs, CD players, 35mm cameras, toaster ovens
"Star Trek," "Wonder Years," "Oprah," "Loving"
Pop, jazz, rhythm & blues, religious radio
*Barron's, Food & Wine, Working Woman, Time*
Chicken, take-out, canned tuna, rice, brownies
Orange juice, tea, spring water, wine, rum
Nissans, Alfa Romeos, VW Corrados, BMW 325s
Gold cards, bonds, precious metals, IRAs
Liberals, gay rights, gun control

IN THE MID-1980S, local promoters billed Mankato as the nation's "wellness capital" because of a community-wide health program that had residents reducing their intake of fatty foods, smoking, and drinking. No longer. According to surveys, today they're more likely to consume pizza, candy bars, corn chips, and sausage — not to mention over-the-counter diet and indigestion pills. As for exercise, residents are less likely than average Americans to belong to health clubs, partake of aerobic exercise, or buy health foods and vitamins. Mankato's location in a dairy farming area along the Blue Earth River makes outdoor activities like fishing, hunting, and camping popular. And an older-than-average population also pursues activities like walking, watching TV sports, and spending time with their grandchildren. These folks are belongers — to fraternal orders, veterans groups, and political clubs — but their views are strictly right of center: supportive of pro-lifers and family values, opposed to gay rights and big government.

| *Lower-middle-class farming town* | *Predominantly white singles* | *High school educations* | *Jobs in farming, education, and transportation* |
|---|---|---|---|

## Key Demographics

| | | | |
|---|---|---|---|
| Total Population: | 83,008 | Primary Ages of Adults: | 55+ |
| Median Household Income: | $26,036 | Median Home Value: | $50,245 |

# Marquette, Michigan

| What's Hot | What's Not |
|---|---|
| Veterans clubs, college sports, skiing, bowling | Fashion, frequent flying, movies, dieting |
| Woodworking, knitting, boating, walking, hunting | Exercise, golf, jogging, tennis, sailing |
| Microwaves, cable TV, power tools, motorcycles | Home gyms, CD players, faxes, 35mm cameras |
| "Unsolved Mysteries," "Current Affair," "Coach" | "Nightline," "Dinosaurs," "Joan Rivers" |
| Country, heavy metal, adult contemporary, gospel | News radio, pop, classical, easy listening |
| *Mother Earth News, Cycle World, TV Guide* | *New Woman, Bon Appetit, Omni, Essence* |
| Bacon, beef stew, pasta, snack cakes, gum | TV dinners, croissants, rice, yogurt, doughnuts |
| Powdered drinks, tea, lemon-lime soda, coffee | Imported beer, wine, orange juice, cola |
| Oldsmobiles, Pontiacs, Chevys, Dodge pickups | Volvos, Peugeots, BMW 3/5s, Acuras, Mazda RX-7s |
| Investment property, life insurance, auto loans | Keoghs, stocks, mutual funds, bonds, IRAs |
| Conservatives, less government, pro-lifers | Liberals, endangered animals, oil drilling |

HERE IN MICHIGAN'S UPPER PENINSULA, it's best to keep your long underwear handy. It snows more than half the year, and residents cope with the long winters by cocooning with a vengeance. They're more likely than average Americans to read, sew, collect coins, make crafts, and do crossword puzzles. On the other hand, the heartier souls of this iron-mining range enjoy fishing, skiing, and camping. With a high percentage of senior citizens — one-quarter of all locals are retirees — Marquette is one of the nation's best markets for knitting, woodworking, and walking. By contrast, residents seem to accept their distance — geographically and psychologically — from the nation's cosmopolitan centers. There's no one "good-life" activity they enjoy at above-average rates: not theater, art, fashion, travel, or gourmet cooking. While voters no doubt enjoy the environment, they're not liberal enough to care about oil pollution or other ecological threats from the mining or forestry industries. And wild animals had best lay low around Marquette; this is a top market for hunting.

| *Lower-middle-class industrial area* | *Predominantly white singles and couples* | *High school educations* | *Jobs in mining, logging, and education* |
|---|---|---|---|

## Key Demographics

| | | | |
|---|---|---|---|
| Total Population: | 153,461 | Primary Ages of Adults: | 55+ |
| Median Household Income: | $23,294 | Median Home Value: | $39,607 |

# McAllen-Brownsville, Texas

| What's Hot | What's Not |
|---|---|
| Rodeos, fishing, car repair, baking, dogs | Business trips, pop music, casinos, unions |
| Hunting, horseback riding, walking, sewing | Boating, bowling, golf, skiing, tennis |
| Microwaves, tillers, trucks, guns, cigarettes | Radar detectors, weights, PCs, cameras |
| "Beverly Hills, 90210," "Family Matters," "Oprah" | Wimbledon, "Honeymooners," "Doogie Howser" |
| Spanish radio, country, religious radio | Rap, rhythm & blues, classic rock, '40s–'60s pop |
| *National Enquirer, Soap Opera Digest, McCall's* | *Newsweek, USA Today, Discover, Self, Money* |
| Mexican food, canned chicken, pudding, biscuits | Canned hash, TV dinners, yogurt, rice cakes |
| Cola, powdered drinks, decaf coffee | Brandy, scotch, mixed drinks, ale, skim milk |
| Subaru Justys, Ford Festivas, Dodge trucks | Audis, Volvos, Porsches, Toyota Previas |
| Mail-order life insurance, Keoghs, home loans | Mutual funds, stocks, savings bonds, Visa |
| Conservatives, school prayer, privacy rights | Liberals, gun control, buying American |

TO GET TO MCALLEN-BROWNSVILLE, you leave much of contemporary America behind. The extreme southern tip of Texas is one of the nation's poorest areas, a border frontier, home largely to downscale Hispanic Americans. With less than half the population having completed high school, there's relatively little interest in science or the arts. Except for Detroit-made pickup trucks, motorists buy few vehicles at above-average rates. In this rugged agricultural area, locals are likely to engage in outdoor activities typical of the area for the last century: fishing, hunting, and horseback riding. Today, a big date is heading for a rodeo or watching a pro wrestling match. There's plenty of Mexican influence in the local preferences for food, radio programming, and *novellas* (Spanish soaps) beamed from local stations. But the lack of money and education causes many residents to consider themselves removed from the nation's majority culture: they tend to be politically apathetic except on issues affecting their personal freedom, such as legalizing drugs (for) and gun control (against).

| *Poor commercial center* | *Predominantly Hispanic families and singles* | *Less than high school educations* | *Farm, mining, and manufacturing jobs* |
|---|---|---|---|

## Key Demographics

| | | | |
|---|---|---|---|
| Total Population: | 760,941 | Primary Ages of Adults: | 35–54 |
| Median Household Income: | $18,265 | Median Home Value: | $38,423 |

# Medford, Oregon

| What's Hot | What's Not |
|---|---|
| Gardening, cable TV, casinos, photography, cats | Foreign travel, tennis, movies, dancing |
| Camping, skiing, sewing, woodworking, hunting | Jogging, exercise, weight training |
| Food processors, woks, Tupperware, microwaves | Convertibles, CD players, PCs, stereos |
| CNN, "Evening Shade," "Jeopardy," "Empty Nest" | "Donahue," "Married with Children," "Seinfeld" |
| Country, gospel, '40s–'60s pop, golden oldies | Rock, rhythm & blues, rap, classical, jazz |
| *Field & Stream, Good Housekeeping, TV Guide* | *U.S. News, Star, Vogue, Gourmet* |
| Health food, canned vegetables, shredded wheat | Take-out, cold cuts, waffles, corn on the cob |
| Powdered drinks, skim milk, ground coffee | Orange juice, wine, diet soda, whole milk |
| Chryslers, Buicks, Cadillac Broughams, Olds 98s | Saabs, Audis, Acuras, Mercedes-Benz 300s |
| Medical insurance, investment property, loans | IRAs, savings bonds, stocks, gold cards |
| Moderates, family values, less government | Liberals, ocean dumping, gay rights |

MIX A RICH FARMING REGION with timber wilderness and you get a lifestyle much like Medford's. Residents, many of whom work at logging and farming, are outdoorsy people who love to fish, camp, and make crafts. The nearby national parks have attracted retirees — the median age is 50 — who also like to fish and camp as well as go hiking and boating. But with the recent immigration of city-dwellers from the West Coast, some urban tastes have come to the country. Medford residents are more likely than average Americans to enjoy wok-cooking, photography, casino gambling, and investing in property. And local demographics has caused the cat population — and popularity — to soar for two reasons: the farmfolk keep barn cats outside to catch field mice; the elderly retirees keep lap cats inside for companionship.

| *Lower-middle-class farm and resort area* | *Predominantly white couples* | *High school educations* | *Jobs in farming, logging, and crafts* |
|---|---|---|---|

| **Key Demographics** | Total Population: | 364,065 | Primary Ages of Adults: | 55+ |
|---|---|---|---|---|
| | Median Household Income: | $25,632 | Median Home Value: | $74,504 |

# Memphis, Tennessee

| What's Hot | What's Not |
|---|---|
| Music, home furnishing, fashion, sweepstakes | Art, movies, casinos, health food, lotteries |
| Walking, sewing, fishing, hunting | Boating, bicycling, golf, skiing, tennis |
| Cable TV, mobile homes, microwaves, trucks | Home gyms, VCRs, gardening tools, 35mm cameras |
| BET, "You Bet Your Life," "Fresh Prince" | World Series, "20/20," "Married with Children" |
| Rhythm & blues, soul, gospel, rap | Classical, jazz, middle-of-the-road, modern rock |
| *Ebony, Jet, National Enquirer, Esquire* | *Family Circle, Inc., Smithsonian, Discover* |
| Fried chicken, ham, peanut butter, BBQ sauce | Health food, French bread, beef, popcorn, yogurt |
| Cola, pop wine, tea, milk, orange juice | Beer, skim milk, decaf coffee, ale |
| Isuzus, Ford Crown Victorias, Dodge pickups | Infinitis, Audi 100/200s, BMW 6/7s, Toyota MR2s |
| Medical insurance, securities, money orders | CDs, education loans, mutual funds, Keoghs |
| Conservatives, pro-lifers, endangered animals | Liberals, military cutbacks, gay rights |

MEMPHIS IS SYNONYMOUS with music for its role in the development of blues, soul, and rock 'n' roll — not to mention the Elvis Presley legend. But today Memphis is also known as an agribusiness center and the largest city in Tennessee. The town enjoys a contemporary Southern lifestyle, which is to say that residents enjoy home furnishing, car repair, and reading the Bible at higher-than-average rates. But Memphis is not a particularly well-off or well-educated city, and it's one of the more racially polarized metro areas in the country, with the family income of African Americans only 47 percent of the median white income in 1990. The result is a market with lower-than-average interest in movies, travel, books, and magazines, except for a handful of publications like *Essence, Jet,* and *Ebony.* And the flight of conservative white voters to the suburbs overwhelms the liberal views of the 55 percent of African Americans still living in the city. According to opinion surveys, Memphis is not an accommodating community for gay and abortion rights, environmental concerns, or consumer issues. And despite Graceland's notoriety, legalizing drugs has few fans in Memphis.

| *Lower-middle-class commercial center* | *Racially diverse singles* | *Less than high school educations* | *Service, transportation, and manufacturing jobs* |
|---|---|---|---|

| **Key Demographics** | Total Population: | 1,661,797 | Primary Ages of Adults: | 25–44 |
|---|---|---|---|---|
| | Median Household Income: | $25,978 | Median Home Value: | $59,312 |

# Meridian, Mississippi

| What's Hot | What's Not |
|---|---|
| Gardening, dieting, fishing, the Bible | Travel, mall shopping, books, casinos, science |
| Walking, hunting, gardening, sewing, knitting | Bowling, golf, skiing, boating, crafts |
| Cable TV, video games, mobile homes, trucks | Cameras, lawn furniture, PCs, radios |
| Game shows, "Oprah," "Showtime at the Apollo" | TV tennis, "Letterman," "Murphy Brown" |
| Urban contemporary, rap, gospel | Golden oldies, easy listening, jazz, classical |
| *Ebony, True Story, Weight Watchers, Star* | *Working Mother, Business Week, Time, Self* |
| Grits, pork & beans, aerosol cheese, rice, jam | Take-out, salad, cheese, waffles, fresh fruit |
| Powdered drinks, tea, diet sodas, orange juice | Wine, imported beer, skim milk, tomato juice |
| Isuzus, Buick Roadmasters, Olds 88s, GMC pickups | Saturns, Porsches, Honda Civics, Mazda Miatas |
| Medical and term life insurance, money orders | Savings accounts, bonds, annuities, mutual funds |
| Conservatives, oil drilling, school prayer | Liberals, endangered animals, military cutbacks |

ONCE THE FLASHPOINT for the civil rights movement, Meridian today is a sleepy trade and industrial center in a farming and timber region. With more than one-quarter of the residents over 65, a number of popular activities are sedentary: watching videos, sewing, knitting, and fishing. There's little disposable income to spend on travel, gourmet dining, or financial investments; indeed, Meridian is one of the nation's worst markets for stocks, mutual funds, and insurance annuities. As in many small Southern communities, religion plays an important role in the lives of locals, and residents are more likely than average Americans to read the Bible, listen to gospel music, and watch religious programming on cable. Local consumers do enjoy Southern cooking — rich with bacon, peanut butter, and fried chicken — but they well know the results. They're into dieting and reading *Weight Watchers* magazine much more than the general population.

| *Poor agricultural and industrial trade area* | *Racially diverse singles* | *Less than high school educations* | *Jobs in farming, manufacturing, and labor* |
|---|---|---|---|

### Key Demographics

| | | | |
|---|---|---|---|
| Total Population: | 182,279 | Primary Ages of Adults: | 55+ |
| Median Household Income: | $21,123 | Median Home Value: | $44,548 |

# Miami–Ft. Lauderdale, Florida

| What's Hot | What's Not |
|---|---|
| Foreign travel, fashion, casinos, health food | Home decorating, videos, crafts, pets |
| Sailing, exercise, jogging, dancing, tennis | Bowling, golf, skiing, camping, knitting |
| Toaster ovens, convertibles, CD players, books | Microwaves, Tupperware, VCRs, trucks |
| HBO, VH-1, "Meet the Press," "In Living Color" | Disney, "Wheel of Fortune," "Designing Women" |
| Spanish radio, rap, jazz, classical, modern rock | Country, heavy metal, classic rock, golden oldies |
| *New York, Travel & Leisure, Forbes, Sunset* | *Southern Living, Parents, Popular Science* |
| Seafood, chicken, frozen yogurt, rye bread | Beef, ham, pasta, white bread, pie, Jell-O |
| Wine, imported beer, scotch, vodka, rum | Diet soda, regular milk, light beer, cocoa |
| Rolls-Royces, Ferraris, Alfa Romeos, BMWs | Subarus, Pontiacs, Oldsmobiles, Chevrolets |
| Investment property, bonds, stocks, gold cards | Loans, life insurance, Christmas clubs |
| Liberals, gun control, legalizing drugs | Moderates, death penalty, pro-lifers |

THE SUN, SURF, and pastel buildings have had their impact on the lifestyle of the Miami–Ft. Lauderdale market. Like a "Miami Vice" episode, the local scene is filled with trendy fashions, sports cars, gourmet restaurants, and lively nightlife for reggae and *merengue* dancing. There's money enough among those who dwell in the high-rise condos and Art Deco apartments for above-average investing in stocks, bonds, and real estate. In this ethnic polyglot, with one-third of the population Hispanic (mostly from Cuba), the Latin American influence is easy to see in the popularity of Spanish radio, electronics, and gambling — on lotteries, sweepstakes, and casino games. The high concentration of retirees — 40 percent of all residents are over 55 — also makes this a good market for vitamins and magazines like *Sunset* and *Health*. But not all is sunny in this seaside area: there are plenty of pockets of poverty — one-third of residents earn under $20,000 — as well as high crime areas that prompt residents to back gun control. And threats to the ocean can really get their backs up — and not just to even out their tans. Ft. Lauderdale, as always, remains home to "where the boys are" during spring break.

| *Middle-class metropolitan sprawl* | *Racially and ethnically diverse couples and singles* | *Less than high school educations* | *Financial, entertainment, and business jobs* |
|---|---|---|---|

### Key Demographics

| | | | |
|---|---|---|---|
| Total Population: | 3,420,767 | Primary Ages of Adults: | 55+ |
| Median Household Income: | $31,706 | Median Home Value: | $95,774 |

# Milwaukee, Wisconsin

| What's Hot | What's Not |
|---|---|
| Unions, stocks, health clubs, bowling, movies | Veterans clubs, gourmet cooking, politics, pets |
| Golf, boating, skiing, bicycling, gardening | Jogging, tennis, sewing, target shooting |
| VCRs, CD players, PCs, power tools, Tupperware | RVs, trucks, chain saws, garden tillers |
| "Roseanne," "Regis & Kathie Lee," Daytona 500 | "Full House," "Bold & Beautiful," "I Love Lucy" |
| Golden oldies, rock, classical, talk radio | Country, rhythm & blues, urban contemporary |
| *Shape, Discover, Home Mechanix, Inc., Life* | *Playboy, National Enquirer, Outdoor Life* |
| Beef, fish, canned macaroni, sour cream, nuts | Ham, chili, beef stew, rice, sweet rolls |
| Domestic and draft beer, powdered drinks, milk | Tea, cola, imported beer, orange juice |
| Saturns, Dodge Daytonas, Mercury Cougars | Subarus, Isuzus, Audis, Volvos, Porsche 911s |
| Savings bonds, term life insurance, IRAs, CDs | Stocks, medical insurance, bonds, money orders |
| Moderates, military cutbacks, school sex ed | Conservatives, school prayer, family values |

THE SMOKESTACK INDUSTRIES are declining, but Milwaukee is still a factory town with comfortable blue-collar lifestyles. Consumers here drink domestic beer, drive American-made cars, and belong to bowling leagues at some of the steepest rates in the nation: Many baby boom adults tend to join health clubs, see a lot of movies, and watch TV sports. Stable union wages have made retirees comfortable and able to enjoy pursuits like casino gambling, crafts, and traveling throughout the U.S. Milwaukee residents are more likely than average Americans to work on their lawns and cars rather than attend cultural events. The high concentrations of ethnic German and Polish neighborhoods also create tight-knit social enclaves where residents enjoy entertaining at home, meeting at local bars, or dining at ethnic restaurants. When the Milwaukee-based public radio show "Whaddaya Know?" recently conducted a search to find the quintessential city resident, the winner (who used to drive a Rambler and live in a duplex with his in-laws) received an award his neighbors surely envied: a four-foot-long, 25-pound kielbasa.

| *Middle-class industrial center* | *Predominantly white singles and families* | *High school educations* | *Jobs in manufacturing, transportation, and services* |
|---|---|---|---|

## Key Demographics

| | | | |
|---|---|---|---|
| Total Population: | 2,119,542 | Primary Ages of Adults: | 25–44 |
| Median Household Income: | $35,061 | Median Home Value: | $76,985 |

# Minneapolis–St. Paul, Minnesota

| What's Hot | What's Not |
|---|---|
| Domestic travel, the arts, PCs, golf, casinos | Fashion, mobile homes, pro wrestling, comedy |
| Bicycling, boating, skiing, fishing, hunting | Coin collecting, gourmet cooking |
| Power tools, cameras, food processors, recliners | Microwaves, faxes, cable TV, convertibles |
| "20/20," "Northern Exposure," "Siskel & Ebert" | MTV, "Hard Copy," "Fresh Prince," "Geraldo" |
| Classical, rock, pop, country, middle-of-the-road | Rhythm & blues, gospel, rap, jazz |
| *Popular Science, National Geographic, Self* | *Ebony, Vogue, Esquire, TV Guide, Food & Wine* |
| Fish, dried fruit, corn chips, pudding, oat bran | Beef stew, corn on the cob, chili, grits, pie |
| Skim milk, domestic wine, vegetable juice | Ale, malt liquor, milk, tea, orange juice |
| Saturns, Sterlings, Audis, Plymouths, Dodges | Peugeots, Nissan Stanzas, Hyundai Sonatas |
| Mutual funds, stocks, annuities, IRAs, CDs | Securities, mail-order medical insurance |
| Moderates, toxic waste, abortion rights | Liberals, gun control, endangered animals |

THOSE IN SEARCH of the all-American lifestyle need look no further than the Twin Cities. By some happy coincidence of baby boom demographics — half of all household heads are under 44 years old and earn over $35,000 annually — residents are voracious consumers of seemingly everything offered in the American marketplace. They buy 223 of 226 automobile models sold in the U.S. at above-average rates. They enjoy virtually every leisure sport and athletic activity — from skiing and golf to hunting and fishing — more often than the general population, and they take advantage of the many trails and paths around the area's parks for walking and cycling. Granted, the Twin Cities have a relatively white-bread culture, with few minorities and little interest in, say, jazz, rap, or the progressive sound produced by hometown favorite Prince. But thanks to local corporate support of the arts, residents are big on attending theaters, concerts, and galleries. Indeed, it seems impolite among locals to dislike anything: they register almost no below-average concern for any political issue. What they don't enjoy is complacency, like vegging out in front of a TV set. The area motto ought to be: So much to do, so little time.

| *Upper-middle-class metropolitan sprawl* | *Predominantly white families and singles* | *College educations* | *Jobs in farming, trade, and white-collar services* |
|---|---|---|---|

## Key Demographics

| | | | |
|---|---|---|---|
| Total Population: | 3,768,256 | Primary Ages of Adults: | 25–44 |
| Median Household Income: | $36,251 | Median Home Value: | $86,356 |

# Minot-Bismarck-Dickinson, North Dakota—Glendive, Montana

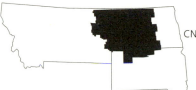

| What's Hot | What's Not |
|---|---|
| Gardening, knitting, crafts, car repair, cats | Gourmet cooking, theme parks, the arts, dogs |
| Hunting, fishing, bowling, walking, camping | Golf, exercise, jogging, bicycling |
| Power tools, calculators, 126/110 cameras | Books, VCRs, PCs, 35mm cameras, convertibles |
| CNN, ESPN, "Major Dad," "Letterman," Daytona 500 | TV news, "Star Trek," "Geraldo," "Simpsons" |
| Golden oldies, country, religious radio | Gospel, modern rock, '40s–'60s pop, rap, folk |
| *Mother Earth News, Redbook, Popular Mechanics* | *Parade, Glamour, Discover, Architectural Digest* |
| Ham, beef, BBQ sauce, canned soup, nuts, Trix | Take-out, spaghetti sauce, canned tuna, pancakes |
| Powdered drinks, light beer, skim milk | Imported wine and beer, orange juice, vodka |
| Oldsmobiles, Pontiacs, Chryslers, Chevy pickups | Mazdas, Toyotas, Volvos, Acuras, BMW 5s |
| Medical insurance, mortgages, mutual funds | Precious metals, investment property, bonds |
| Conservatives, pro-lifers, school prayer | Liberals, consumerism, ozone depletion |

IN MANY RESPECTS, this region is still the American frontier. Bismarck is a state capital with a small-town lifestyle; the other cities are agricultural trading centers that reflect the traditional tastes of farm families throughout the nation's heartland. Residents are into fishing and hunting, sewing and woodworking. And this is one of the best markets in the nation for gardening, knitting, and crafts. Locals tend to be self-sufficient, doing their own home improvements and fixing their own cars (and tractors). And they're too far from big-city trend-centers to care much about fashion, art, or theater. These folks are more likely than average Americans to enjoy rodeos, outdoors magazines, and religious radio. Like many rural communities, the residents are graying — one-quarter of all adults are over 65 — and they take special pleasure in their grandchildren, their cats, and their collectibles. The aging populace also makes for old-time values, and these voters care little for untraditional sexual attitudes and social concerns.

| *Lower-middle-class agricultural area* | *Predominantly white families and couples* | *High school educations* | *Jobs in farming, transportation, and crafts* |
|---|---|---|---|

**Key Demographics**

| | | | |
|---|---|---|---|
| Total Population: | 363,207 | Primary Ages of Adults: | 55+ |
| Median Household Income: | $24,336 | Median Home Value: | $49,280 |

# Missoula, Montana

| What's Hot | What's Not |
|---|---|
| Skiing, photography, rodeos, clubs, guns | Fashion, theater, theme parks, frequent flying |
| Camping, hunting, fishing, boating, bicycling | Jogging, swimming, sailing, tennis, golf |
| Gardening tools, recliners, microwaves, VCRs | CD players, PCs, cable TV, station wagons |
| Evening news, "Kentucky Derby," "Roseanne" | "Inside Edition," "Seinfeld," "Dinosaurs" |
| Country, heavy metal, rock, middle-of-the-road | Jazz, classical, modern rock, rhythm & blues, rap |
| *Outdoor Life, Self, Cycle World, Reader's Digest* | *Life, Working Woman, Bon Appetit, Fortune* |
| Health food, hot dogs, chili, biscuits, popcorn | TV dinners, rice, cold cuts, chocolates |
| Light and draft beer, skim milk, ground coffee | Orange juice, wine, imported beer, diet sodas |
| Chryslers, Subarus, Chevrolets, Dodge trucks | Porsches, Infinitis, Acuras, Suzuki Sidekicks |
| Medical insurance, home-improvement loans, CDs | Gold cards, savings bonds, IRAs, mutual funds |
| Conservatives, privacy rights, school sex ed | Liberals, endangered animals, oil drilling |

MISSOULA IS LOCATED at the crossroads of a college campus (the University of Montana) and a blue-collar sawmill town. Bookstores and vegetarian cafés sit alongside truck lots and gun stores. And consuming patterns are similarly polarized. Many of the 10,000 students are into art, photography, and rock 'n' roll. But a large number of residents are also into activities reminiscent of other mill towns, such as boating, hunting, heavy metal music, and fraternal orders. Bicycling has been popular since 1896, when the 25th Infantry Bicycle Corps took over the local army fort. And all Missoula residents seem to share a local passion for outdoor activities like camping, skiing, and riding motorcycles. Politically, though, this is a tough town to pin down; like other isolated communities on the western frontier, most residents care a lot about privacy rights and prefer to keep to themselves.

| *Lower-middle-class college town* | *Predominantly white singles and couples* | *Some college educations* | *Education, farm, and construction jobs* |
|---|---|---|---|

**Key Demographics**

| | | | |
|---|---|---|---|
| Total Population: | 203,311 | Primary Ages of Adults: | 35–54 |
| Median Household Income: | $24,723 | Median Home Value: | $67,479 |

# Mobile, Alabama–Pensacola, Florida

| What's Hot | What's Not |
|---|---|
| Home decorating, veterans, baking, cable TV | Dancing, politics, casinos, health clubs |
| Fishing, camping, hunting, sewing, woodworking | Tennis, bowling, golf, camping, racquetball |
| Tupperware, guns, power tools, garden tillers | Microwaves, VCRs, PCs, CD players, motorcycles |
| Soaps, "Coach," "Oprah," "Beverly Hills, 90210" | "Tonight Show," "60 Minutes," "Honeymooners" |
| Gospel, rap, country, religious radio | Classical, modern rock, jazz, news radio |
| *Southern Living, Ebony, National Enquirer, Jet* | *Sports Illustrated, Popular Science, Money, GQ* |
| Seafood, fried chicken, potato chips, snack cakes | Beef, canned tuna, pretzels, sour cream, Wheaties |
| Tea, powdered drinks, diet sodas, cola | Wine, herbal tea, beer, skim milk, scotch, vodka |
| Chevy Camaros, Nissan Stanzas, Isuzu Styluses | Lexus LS400s, BMW 5s, Volvo 780s, Porsche 911s |
| First mortgages, loans, medical insurance | Stocks, CDs, mutual funds, savings bonds |
| Conservatives, pro-lifers, school prayer | Liberals, military cutbacks, legalizing drugs |

THEY CALL THESE TWO CITIES along the Gulf Coast the "Redneck Riviera" after their rarely used beaches, which are more than a cut below Florida's glitzier Gold Coast. But nearby military bases have made hunting, veterans clubs, and patriotic politics popular in this corner of the U.S. And retirees from the South, drawn to the white-sand beaches, also exhibit above-average interest in crafts, coin collecting, and crossword puzzles. Mobile was ignored by Union soldiers during the Civil War, and the many antebellum buildings today make home decorating a fashionable activity among residents. The military- and seniors-filled population have turned this market into a hotbed of conservative politics. In 1988, area residents gave George Bush his highest margin of victory outside Texas, and local voters continuously back issues like increased military spending, less government regulation, and the return of prayer to the classroom.

| *Lower-middle-class industrial ports* | *Racially mixed singles and couples* | *High school educations* | *Transportation and manufacturing jobs* |
|---|---|---|---|

**Key Demographics**

| | | | |
|---|---|---|---|
| Total Population: | 1,144,609 | Primary Ages of Adults: | 25–44 |
| Median Household Income: | $27,294 | Median Home Value: | $61,965 |

# Monroe, Louisiana–El Dorado, Arkansas

| What's Hot | What's Not |
|---|---|
| Pro wrestling, rodeos, tobacco, the Bible, dogs | Frequent flying, movies, casinos, concerts, cats |
| Hunting, fishing, gardening, sewing, crafts | Skiing, exercise, jogging, bicycling, walking |
| Cable TV, mobile homes, trucks, used cars | PCs, CD players, microwaves, woks, camcorders |
| Game shows, "You Bet Your Life," "Rescue 911" | "Letterman," "Saturday Night Live," "Sisters" |
| Urban contemporary, country, rap, gospel | Modern rock, jazz, classical, news-talk radio |
| *True Story, Outdoor Life, Soap Opera Digest* | *People, Popular Science, Photography, Vogue* |
| Seafood, sausage, grits, beef stew, rice, jam | Cheese, pasta, canned soup, rice cakes, yogurt |
| Powdered drinks, tea, cola, orange juice | Skim milk, beer, wine, ground coffee |
| Isuzus, Chevy Camaros, GMC Sierras, Ford trucks | Saturns, Toyotas, Sterlings, Audis, VW trucks |
| Medical and term-life insurance, money orders | Savings accounts, CDs, mutual funds, Keoghs |
| Conservatives, toxic waste, pro-lifers | Moderates, gun control, gay rights |

HUNTING, HOME-BASED CRAFTS, and the Bible: these are the interests of this Deep South market, where folks live in small towns surrounded by cotton fields and piney woods, and where the values and lifestyles are time-honored. Far from the cosmopolitan cities, the residents of Monroe and El Dorado (pronounced dor-AY-doh) care little for foreign travel, fashion, the arts, or gourmet cooking. With locals twice as likely as average Americans to live in mobile homes, there's not a lot of money for cameras or computers, CD players, or VCRs. Around here, people are more interested in fishing, gardening, knitting, and sewing. They take pride in their gardens, their grandchildren, and the fate of the teams at Northeast Louisiana University. And there's a special sense of vanity that goes with having a good hunting dog perched squarely on the passenger seat of a beat-up pickup. Cats, however, have no practical purpose.

| *Poor industrial cities* | *Racially diverse singles* | *Less than high school educations* | *Jobs in mining, forestry, and transportation* |
|---|---|---|---|

**Key Demographics**

| | | | |
|---|---|---|---|
| Total Population: | 479,366 | Primary Ages of Adults: | 55+ |
| Median Household Income: | $20,563 | Median Home Value: | $45,215 |

# Montgomery-Selma, Alabama

| What's Hot | What's Not |
|---|---|
| Veterans, sweepstakes, TV sports, the Bible | Movies, casinos, health clubs, theme parks |
| Walking, fishing, hunting, gardening | Skiing, bowling, golf, bicycling, exercise |
| Cable TV, muscle cars, chain saws | VCRs, radar detectors, Tupperware, CD players |
| BET, "Fresh Prince," "People's Court," "Donahue" | "60 Minutes," "Simpsons," "Joan Rivers" |
| Gospel, rhythm & blues, urban contemporary | Easy listening, modern rock, jazz |
| *Ebony, Jet, TV Guide, Field & Stream* | *Changing Times, Newsweek, Smithsonian, Self* |
| Fried chicken, sausage, rice, brownies | Fish, yogurt, salad, pasta, canned soup, nuts |
| Tea, milk, diet soda, orange juice | Fruit juices, beer, ground coffee, scotch |
| Mazda 929s, Buick Roadmasters, Isuzu pickups | BMW 325s, Infiniti Q45s, Alfa Romeo 164s |
| Money orders, medical and term life insurance | Bonds, CDs, IRAs, mutual funds, stocks |
| Conservatives, school prayer, oil drilling | Liberals, military cutbacks, school sex ed |

MONTGOMERY AND SELMA will forever be etched in the nation's consciousness for their role in the civil rights movement. Today, these cities in the heart of the Black Belt — originally named for the loamy soil but later used to refer to the high concentration of African Americans — are still sleepy, God-fearing communities that remain racially polarized. Thanks to Montgomery's Maxwell Air Force Base, residents are into veterans groups, outdoor activities like jogging and hunting, and conservative political views. A higher-than-average concentration of retirees has also made popular quiet domestic pursuits like watching TV sports, gardening, and walking. Surveys don't usually pick up many consuming patterns targeted by race, but this market, which is 42 percent African American, is big on rhythm & blues recordings, Black Entertainment Television, and gospel radio. All locals seem to take their religion seriously — they read the Bible at twice the national average — but most churches remain divided along racial lines.

| *Lower-middle-class commercial center* | *Racially diverse singles and couples* | *Less than high school educations* | *Jobs in farming, manufacturing, and services* |
|---|---|---|---|

## Key Demographics

| | | | |
|---|---|---|---|
| Total Population: | 589,121 | Primary Ages of Adults: | 55+ |
| Median Household Income: | $24,342 | Median Home Value: | $55,457 |

# Nashville, Tennessee

| What's Hot | What's Not |
|---|---|
| Country music, home furnishing, the Bible, pets | Theater, foreign travel, casinos, skiing, wine |
| Gardening, hunting, fishing, walking, sewing | Sailing, bicycling, golf, tennis, exercise |
| Tupperware, 126/110 cameras, video games | PCs, CD players, radar detectors, microwaves |
| College sports, "Today," "Full House" | VH-1, "Joan Rivers," "Empty Nest," "Sisters" |
| Gospel, urban contemporary, religious radio | Classical, jazz, middle-of-the-road, radio baseball |
| *Southern Living, Redbook, TV Guide, Star* | *Forbes, Food & Wine, Smithsonian, Discover* |
| Ham, beef stew, grits, cheese, sweet rolls | Fish, Mexican food, Wheaties, rice cakes, Trix |
| Tea, powdered drinks, milk, colas, orange juice | Imported and draft beer, skim milk, scotch |
| Pontiacs, Chevys, Ford Festivas, Nissan Stanzas | BMWs, Audis, Acuras, Infiniti G20s, Saab 9000s |
| Life insurance, personal loans, money orders | Mutual funds, stocks, precious metals, IRAs |
| Conservatives, pro-lifers, less government | Liberals, legalizing drugs, military cutbacks |

IT'S KNOWN BY various nicknames: the Athens of the South for its sixteen area colleges, including Vanderbilt and Fisk; the Gold Buckle of the Bible Belt for its whopping 700 churches; and, of course, the home of country music, a $6 billion industry that attracts six million fans each year to Opryland, the Grand Ole Opry, and the Country Music Hall of Fame. But nicknames aside, surveys reveal Nashville to be a pedestrian city with a middlebrow lifestyle. Unlike in college towns, there's relatively little interest in science, current affairs, or the arts. The favored outdoor activities are not what you'd expect from a major metropolis but more akin to the surrounding farmlands: hunting, fishing, and gardening. Indoors, residents are less likely to own computers and CD players than sewing machines and power tools. True, country music is king in Nashville, but locals also listen to heavy metal music as in other factory towns. With its cheesy neon and numerous gift emporia offering tacky C&W collectibles, a more appropriate monicker might be "Nash-Vegas."

| *Lower-middle-class metropolitan area* | *Predominantly white couples and singles* | *Less than high school educations* | *Jobs in farming, transportation, and manufacturing* |
|---|---|---|---|

## Key Demographics

| | | | |
|---|---|---|---|
| Total Population: | 1,953,481 | Primary Ages of Adults: | 25–44 |
| Median Household Income: | $28,919 | Median Home Value: | $68,044 |

# New Orleans, Louisiana

| What's Hot | What's Not |
|---|---|
| Gourmet cooking, fashion, live music, TV sports | Frequent flying, camping, theme parks, clubs |
| Fishing, gardening, bicycling, sewing | Golf, tennis, skiing, knitting, bowling, crafts |
| VCRs, cable TV, stereos, microwaves | Cameras, CD players, power tools, toaster ovens |
| BET, Cinemax, "Fresh Prince," "Family Feud" | "Primetime Live," World Series, "Roseanne" |
| Jazz, rhythm & blues, rap, religious radio | Heavy metal, modern rock, easy listening |
| *Ebony, Vogue, Esquire, Food & Wine, New Woman* | *Scientific American, US News, Family Circle* |
| Fried chicken, seafood, BBQ sauce, po'boys, pie | Beef, pasta, canned soup, oat bran, dried fruit |
| Ground coffee, milk, ale, malt liquor, pop wine | Domestic wine, skim milk, imported beer, cocoa |
| Isuzus, Hyundais, Chevy Camaros, Ford Mustangs | Mercedes-Benzes, Alfa Romeos, Ford Tauruses |
| Securities, medical and homeowners insurance | Mutual funds, Keoghs, savings bonds, IRAs |
| Liberals, gay rights, oil-drilling | Moderates, death penalty, buying American |

HERE IN THE "BIG EASY," life is a cabaret — especially at its heart in the French Quarter. With numerous nightclubs and restaurants spread throughout the city, New Orleans is a perpetual party town. Residents tend to enjoy gourmet cooking, live music, and nightlife. While lacking gambling casinos (when this was written), they nonetheless bet at high rates on sweepstakes and lottery tickets. But beyond the conspicuous consumption, this city also has a downbeat side, an underclass where 40 percent of all households earn less than $20,000 a year, and many are headed by African Americans working menial jobs. Media tastes reflect this racial gap, split between those reading *Jet, Ebony,* and *Essence* and others subscribing to *Food & Wine, Southern Living,* and *Country Living.* Still, all residents share a passion for religion (from voodoo to Catholicism), food (Creole gumbo and Cajun jambalaya), and politics. Although this market includes the district that elected ex-Klansman David Duke to the state house, the high rate of African American voters gives New Orleans a liberal cast.

| *Lower-middle-class metropolis* | *Racially diverse families and singles* | *Less than high school educations* | *Service, transportation, and entertainment jobs* |
|---|---|---|---|

**Key Demographics**

| | | | |
|---|---|---|---|
| Total Population: | 1,692,504 | Primary Ages of Adults: | 25–44 |
| Median Household Income: | $25,344 | Median Home Value: | $69,490 |

# New York, New York

| What's Hot | What's Not |
|---|---|
| The arts, fashion, books, dancing, travel, casinos | Gardening, crafts, the Bible, car repair, pets |
| Tennis, jogging, exercise, skiing, photography | Golf, boating, hunting, fishing, camping |
| PCs, CD players, stereos, floor lamps, condoms | VCRs, charcoal grills, microwaves, Tupperware |
| "Honeymooners," "In Living Color," "60 Minutes" | "Cops," "Price Is Right," "Evening Shade" |
| Jazz, classical, folk, rap, talk radio | Country, gospel, heavy metal, religious radio |
| *New York, Essence, GQ, Forbes, Vanity Fair* | *Parents, Good Housekeeping, Family Handyman* |
| Health food, tuna, bagels, pasta, Ben & Jerry's | Ham, beef stew, canned soup, hot dogs, doughnuts |
| Wine, scotch, orange juice, decaf coffee | Cocoa, light beer, tomato juice, powdered drinks |
| Ferraris, Rolls-Royces, Infinitis, Jaguars | Pontiacs, Chevrolets, Chryslers, Oldsmobiles |
| Mutual funds, stocks, bonds, gold cards, IRAs | Loans, CDs, savings accounts, medical insurance |
| Liberals, abortion rights, ocean dumping | Moderates, school prayer, toxic waste |

AS THE SONG unabashedly declares, New York, New York, is indeed "at the top of the heap," according to many measures of cosmopolitan living. New Yorkers rank in the top five markets when it comes to interest in fashion, foreign travel, wine, and gourmet cooking. Their passion for the arts — theater, literature, and music — is unparalleled. And befitting its reputation as the financial capital of the world, New York boasts one of the nation's highest median incomes as well as a healthy desire to accumulate more money, by investing in stocks and bonds or gambling at casinos and the track. Indeed, this is an unconventional city, overpopulated at 6.8 million households, hostile to middle-class families, a haven for gays, and a magnet for all races and ethnic groups. Forty-five percent of all residents are single, yet New York is one of the belongingest areas in the nation, with high rates of memberships in business, health, and country clubs. Given the city's celebrated ethnic stew, voters tend to be tolerant on civil liberty issues, liberal on economic issues, and conservative on social ones. The result is a political cauldron that outrages someone at almost any time.

| *Affluent metropolitan sprawl* | *Racially and ethnically diverse singles* | *College educations* | *Service, finance, and health jobs* |
|---|---|---|---|

**Key Demographics**

| | | | |
|---|---|---|---|
| Total Population: | 18,682,687 | Primary Ages of Adults: | 35–54 |
| Median Household Income: | $44,974 | Median Home Value: | $209,265 |

# Norfolk-Portsmouth–Newport News–Hampton, Virginia

| What's Hot | What's Not |
|---|---|
| Veterans groups, theme parks, antiques | Movies, health food, politics, casinos |
| Jogging, tennis, exercise, bicycling | Skiing, golf, hunting, camping, gardening |
| PCs, home workshops, stereos, CD players | Food processors, microwaves, recliners, cameras |
| Disney Channel, "American Gladiators," | "Face the Nation," "Santa Barbara," "Evening Shade" |
| Gospel, rhythm & blues, rap, jazz | Country, golden oldies, middle-of-the-road, classical |
| *New Woman, Ebony, Cycle World, Parade* | *Travel & Leisure, New Yorker, Prevention, Omni* |
| Fried chicken, fast food, rice, sweet rolls | Beef, spaghetti sauce, pasta, pudding, Wheaties |
| Cola, malt liquor, pop wine, tea, milk | Ground coffee, skim milk, light beer |
| Isuzus, Nissans, Mitsubishis, Mazdas, Saturns | Peugeots, Saabs, Audis, Porches, Ferraris |
| Securities, life insurance, precious metals | IRAs, savings bonds, CDs, Keoghs, annuities |
| Conservatives, pro-lifers, less government | Moderates, military cutbacks, legalizing drugs |

STRADDLING THE JAMES RIVER and Chesapeake Bay, these four cities together form the nation's largest naval base, with a populace dominated by the families of young servicemen and -women. Residents have high rates of involvement in outdoor activities like jogging and bicycling, and they have plenty of options for entertaining youngsters: Busch Gardens Theme Park, the Virginia Zoological Park, and Jamestown are all close by. Area stores cater to families, recording big sales for video games, throwaway cameras, cookies, and home pregnancy-test kits. And as one of the busiest seaports along the Atlantic, this market is a major entry point for Japanese cars; hence their local popularity. Norfolk has been a thriving port for two centuries, a vestige of Old Virginia that still supports a thriving cultural scene: locals are into art, antiques, and the decorative arts at above-average rates. But the palpable presence of Uncle Sam also makes for conservative politics, and local voters can always be counted on to support family values and higher military spending.

| *Middle-class port cities* | *Racially diverse families and singles* | *College educations* | *Jobs in the military and public administration* |
|---|---|---|---|

## Key Demographics

| | | | |
|---|---|---|---|
| Total Population: | 1,703,522 | Primary Ages of Adults: | 25–44 |
| Median Household Income: | $33,503 | Median Home Value: | $92,162 |

# North Platte, Nebraska

| What's Hot | What's Not |
|---|---|
| Crafts, clubs, baking from scratch, rodeos | The arts, fashion, dancing, exercise, books |
| Hunting, fishing, sewing, gardening | Jogging, tennis, skiing, hiking, bicycling |
| Microwaves, food processors, power tools, RVs | CD players, PCs, 35mm cameras, sofa beds |
| TV sports, "As the World Turns," "Cheers" | C-SPAN, "Loving," "Hard Copy," "Seinfeld" |
| Country, adult contemporary, '40s–'60s pop | Modern rock, rap, rhythm & blues, classical |
| *Outdoor Life, Reader's Digest, Woman's Day* | *Rolling Stone, Working Woman, Business Week* |
| Ham, beef, baked beans, pudding, cheese, pies | Cold cuts, raisin bread, rice, frozen yogurt |
| Skim milk, decaf coffee, tea, light beer | Wine, spring water, imported beer, milk, vodka |
| Buicks, Mercurys, Subarus, Chryslers, Olds 88s | VWs, Saabs, Saturns, Volvos, BMW 6/7s |
| Medical insurance, investment property, CDs | Mutual funds, IRAs, savings bonds, stocks |
| Moderates, less government, privacy rights | Liberals, gay rights, gun control |

ONE OF THE NATION'S smallest markets, North Platte is the place where area farmers go when they "head into town." As with other agrarian communities, residents tend to enjoy traditional heartland lifestyles and are more likely than average Americans to fish and hunt than play tennis or exercise. While many Americans don't give much thought to their houses beyond making sure the roof doesn't leak, North Platte residents — half of whom are over 50 years old — take great pride in maintaining neat, comfortable residences, decorating their living areas with flowers and crafts, and filling their pantries with fresh-baked cakes and pies. Though they have below-average incomes, they achieve some sense of financial well-being by collecting stamps, coins, decorative plates, and figurines. Folks here find satisfaction in groups and are more likely than the general population to belong to business clubs and fraternal orders. But on political issues, they tend to value independence and old-fashioned capitalism; these folks don't place too much stock in consumerism or the environmental movement.

| *Lower-middle-class agricultural trade center* | *Predominantly white couples and singles* | *High school educations* | *Jobs in farming, crafts, and construction* |
|---|---|---|---|

## Key Demographics

| | | | |
|---|---|---|---|
| Total Population: | 45,249 | Primary Ages of Adults: | 55+ |
| Median Household Income: | $25,740 | Median Home Value: | $43,069 |

# Odessa-Midland, Texas

| What's Hot | What's Not |
|---|---|
| Home furnishing, car repair, the Bible, dogs | Travel, gourmet cooking, casinos, politics |
| Hunting, fishing, camping, woodworking | Tennis, bicycling, skiing, jogging, golf |
| Power tools, cable TV, recliners, trucks | Tupperware, PCs, weights, CD players |
| Morning news, "Coach," "Young & Restless" | "Wonder Years," "People's Court," "Siskel & Ebert" |
| Spanish, adult contemporary, religious radio | Gospel, pop, jazz, rap, urban contemporary |
| *Field & Stream, Ladies' Home Journal, Cycle* | *Consumer's Digest, People, Bon Appetit* |
| TV dinners, Mexican food, biscuits, hot dogs | Take-out, canned tuna, pumpernickel, yogurt |
| Tea, powdered drinks, ground coffee, cola | Milk, cocktails, imported beer, brandy |
| Chryslers, Chevrolets, Pontiacs, Subarus | Acuras, Porsches, Saabs, Volvos |
| Life insurance, auto loans, money orders | Mutual funds, interest checking, bonds |
| Conservatives, pro-lifers, military cutbacks | Liberals, endangered animals, gun control |

THIS IS TEXAS CRUDE COUNTRY, home of the oil and gas fields where George Bush first struck paydirt in the '50s. But the '80s oil bust left many area families with below-average incomes and less-than-luxurious lifestyles. Today, after working gritty jobs around oil rigs, men come home to tinker with their cars and do their own home improvements; their idea of relaxing is hunting, fishing, or taking off into the desert on a motorcycle or in a utility vehicle. Nearly one in five women is a homemaker, resulting in this market's above-average rates for sewing, knitting, and baking from scratch. As in other rural communities, there's not much cultural life in Odessa or Midland, and locals are less likely than average Americans to go to plays, movies, live concerts, or art exhibits. What they don't lack is the gambler's streak of the wildcatter: they enter sweepstakes at one of the highest rates in the nation.

| *Lower-middle-class industrial cities* | *Ethnically diverse families and couples* | *Less than high school educations* | *Jobs in mining, transportation, and manufacturing* |
|---|---|---|---|

**Key Demographics**

| Total Population: | 385,971 | Primary Ages of Adults: | 25–44 |
|---|---|---|---|
| Median Household Income: | $26,294 | Median Home Value: | $46,013 |

# Oklahoma City, Oklahoma

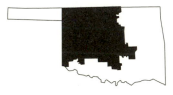

| What's Hot | What's Not |
|---|---|
| Baking, mall shopping, rodeos, college sports | Casinos, theater, health clubs, unions, movies |
| Hunting, horseback riding, fishing, crafts | Tennis, golf, sailing, skiing, walking |
| Grills, antiques, campers, power tools | Toaster ovens, PCs, CD players, sofa beds |
| "Major Dad," "Evening Shade," "Full House" | "Meet the Press," "General Hospital" |
| Adult contemporary, country, religious radio | Folk, rhythm & blues, jazz, news radio |
| *Outdoor Life, Reader's Digest, Omni* | *Financial World, American Photo, Vogue* |
| Beef, baked beans, chili, Twinkies, oat bran | Italian bread, tuna, salad, aerosol cheese |
| Vegetable juice, cocoa, skim milk, Diet Coke | Spring water, wine, imported beer, scotch |
| Subarus, Chryslers, Ford Crown Victorias | Acuras, Volvos, Mercedes-Benz 500s |
| Medical insurance, mutual funds, auto loans | Precious metals, gold cards, Keoghs, IRAs |
| Conservatives, less government, death penalty | Liberals, ocean dumping, consumerism |

OIL WELLS DOT THIS state capital almost to the governor's mansion, and that's instructive. Oklahoma City is an industrial center in the midst of farm and grazing land, and its prosperity is tied to oil's boom-and-bust cycles. The '80s oil slump has left the city a bit punch-drunk, and it's a long way from the cutting edge when it comes to the arts, designer fashion, or gourmet cooking. Residents do enjoy domestic pursuits, such as baking, collecting antiques, and making crafts, at above-average rates. And with Oklahoma City being a large cattle market — besides the home of the National Cowboy Hall of Fame — this is one of the nation's top markets for horseback riding and rodeos. Several local colleges and the University of Oklahoma, a half hour drive to the south, make rooting for college sports a popular pastime. As for politics, this is an area of prairie populism with residents strongly opposed to government regulation. At the city's Enterprise Square USA attraction, the glories of free enterprise are sung by bobbing George Washington heads on massive dollar bills.

| *Lower-middle-class oil city* | *Predominantly white singles and couples* | *Some college educations* | *Jobs in mining, ranching, and education* |
|---|---|---|---|

**Key Demographics**

| Total Population: | 1,500,378 | Primary Ages of Adults: | 25–44 |
|---|---|---|---|
| Median Household Income: | $27,021 | Median Home Value: | $52,205 |

# Omaha, Nebraska

| What's Hot | What's Not |
|---|---|
| Stocks, collectibles, crafts, baking, casinos | Health clubs, foreign travel, theater, books |
| Bowling, golf, walking, hunting, gardening | Tennis, skiing, boating, bicycling, camping |
| Food processors, video games, cameras, tillers | Microwaves, CD players, stereos, PCs |
| CNN, "Siskel & Ebert," "Evening Shade" | HBO, "Geraldo," "Seinfeld," "In Living Color" |
| Golden oldies, adult contemporary, country | Soft rock, urban contemporary, classical |
| *Reader's Digest, McCall's, Popular Mechanics* | *Working Woman, Fortune, New Yorker, Jet* |
| Beef, ham, sour cream, Wheaties, canned fruit | Health food, rice, canned hash, French bread |
| Light beer, coffee, diet sodas, powdered drinks | Cola, ale, party wine, milk, orange juice, tea |
| Oldsmobiles, Buicks, Dodges, Chevy Luminas | Volvos, Alfa Romeos, Saabs, Nissan Stanzas |
| Medical and life insurance, mutual funds, bonds | Keoghs, securities, gold cards, money orders |
| Moderates, pro-lifers, family values | Liberals, gun control, legalizing drugs |

THE LOCAL STOCKYARDS helped make Omaha the third-largest livestock marketplace in the country, but this is no cow town. Omaha today is a quiet metropolis linked less to agricultural products than to telecommunications services, with 10,000 people working at 1-800 and 1-900 telemarketing centers. Despite the suburban sprawl that characterizes much of the city, residents in this market still have the heartland values and homespun tastes of the Farm Belt. Residents here believe in self-sufficiency, enjoying outdoor activities like fishing and hunting, canning their own fruits and vegetables, and performing their own home improvements. In addition, locals enjoy getting together with friends and workmates at one of the myriad bowling lanes or golf courses. For those interested in the big-city pleasures of the arts, health food, and professional sports, this is not the place to settle. In Omaha, folks are conservative in their outlook, favoring a return to traditional religious and family values while opposing pornography, homosexuality, and feminism; they'd rather have prayer than sex education in the schools.

| *Middle-class commercial center* | *Predominantly white families* | *High school educations* | *Farm and service jobs* |
|---|---|---|---|

**Key Demographics**

| | | | |
|---|---|---|---|
| Total Population: | 963,929 | Primary Ages of Adults: | 25–44 |
| Median Household Income: | $30,483 | Median Home Value: | $56,752 |

# Orlando—Daytona Beach—Melbourne, Florida

| What's Hot | What's Not |
|---|---|
| Clubs, the arts, travel, pop music, barbecuing | Fashion, lotteries, health clubs, movies |
| Tennis, bicycling, boating, swimming | Sailing, skiing, racquetball, gardening |
| VCRs, cable TV, boom boxes, toaster ovens | CD players, faxes, convertibles, tillers |
| "Nightline," "I Love Lucy," "Jeopardy," "Cops" | A&E, "General Hospital," "Roseanne," "Blossom" |
| Gospel, easy listening, country, heavy metal | Classical, rap, rhythm & blues, news radio |
| *Colonial Homes, New Woman, Omni, Shape* | *Home Mechanix, Life, Glamour, Business Week* |
| Health food, soup, canned fruit, pudding | TV dinners, cold cuts, canned macaroni, doughnuts |
| Skim milk, decaf coffee, domestic wine, cocoa | Milk, imported wine, tea, domestic beer, rum |
| Chryslers, Mitsubishis, Mercurys, Chevy Geos | BMWs, Alfa Romeos, Infinitis, Chevy Berettas |
| Stocks, bonds, investment property, CDs | Savings bonds, term insurance, IRAs |
| Moderates, family values, legalizing drugs | Liberals, death penalty, abortion rights |

B.D. — BEFORE DISNEY — arrived in 1971, this central Florida market used to be sleepy farm country. Today it's home to one of the world's most popular tourist attractions — Orlando's Walt Disney World — and America's largest collegiate blow-out — Daytona Beach during spring break. The eclectic year-round populace consists of retirees and baby boom families drawn to the sand, the high-growth service economy, and the resort living. As a result, tastes drift all over the map. When it comes to magazines, this market is hot for *Colonial Homes* as well as *Shape*. Residents are fans of both C-SPAN and "A Current Affair." And the high concentration of newcomers to the area makes club memberships a sign of status: Orlando boasts more than 800 tennis courts. Though they're not much on reading financial magazines, residents do enjoy investing their money in everything from stocks and bonds to CDs and real estate. As for political views, these Floridians shred traditional labels: they support family values as well as legalizing drugs.

| *Middle-class resort area* | *Predominantly white couples and singles* | *Some college educations* | *Entertainment, construction, and service jobs* |
|---|---|---|---|

**Key Demographics**

| | | | |
|---|---|---|---|
| Total Population: | 2,451,889 | Primary Ages of Adults: | 55+ |
| Median Household Income: | $32,038 | Median Home Value: | $84,880 |

# Ottumwa, Iowa–Kirksville, Missouri

## What's Hot

Grandchildren, antiques, baking, gardening, cats
Hunting, fishing, camping, sewing, knitting
Cable TV, power tools, recliners, trucks, RVs
TV news, "Bold & Beautiful," "Full House"
Country, religious radio, adult contemporary
*Sports Afield, Mother Earth News, Woman's World*
Ham, bacon, beef stew, canned vegetables, Jell-O
Powdered drinks, tea, milk, tomato juice
Pontiacs, Buicks, Oldsmobiles, Chevy pickups
Medical insurance, personal loans, CDs
Conservatives, less government, pro-lifers

## What's Not

Movies, PCs, theme parks, technology, unions
Skiing, tennis, bicycling, bowling, hiking
VCRs, video games, CD players, radar detectors
TV sports, "Beverly Hills, 90210," "Geraldo"
Heavy metal, classic rock, jazz, classical, rap
*Harper's Bazaar, Discover, GQ, Financial World*
Health food, take-out, fish, waffles, grits
Imported beer, party wine, spring water
Nissans, Hondas, VWs, Volvo 740/760s
Savings accounts, precious metals, stocks
Liberals, ozone depletion, gay rights

IT'S TEMPTING TO SAY that since crude comic Tom Arnold left Ottumwa-based Iowa Beef Processing for Hollywood, the quality of life has improved in this farmer's market, but that wouldn't be true. In recent years, farms have been disappearing, the population has been declining, and the median age has been increasing: today, half of all area residents are over 50 years old and Ottumwa-Kirksville leads the nation in the popularity of grandchildren. In addition, residents are big on low-stress domestic activities like sewing, making crafts, and collecting antiques. Outside, locals enjoy pursuits that help put food on the table, such as fishing, gardening, and hunting. Indeed, there's not much money to fritter away on fashion, art, stocks, or gambling casinos. And though residents describe themselves as moderate, they really mean middle-of-the-road Republicans whose idea of high technology is a La-Z-Boy recliner.

| *Lower-class agricultural area* | *Predominantly white couples and singles* | *High school educations* | *Jobs in farming, mining, and transportation* |
|---|---|---|---|

**Key Demographics**

| | | | |
|---|---|---|---|
| Total Population: | 87,058 | Primary Ages of Adults: | 55+ |
| Median Household Income: | $20,951 | Median Home Value: | $35,510 |

# Paducah, Kentucky–Cape Girardeau, Missouri–Harrisburg-Marion, Illinois

## What's Hot

Baking, gardening, pro wrestling, the Bible
Hunting, fishing, sewing, woodworking
Video games, cable TV, motorcycles, tillers
Network news, "Price Is Right," "Blossom"
Gospel, country, religious radio
*Southern Living, Woman's World, Reader's Digest*
Biscuits, beef stew, crackers, pudding, fruit
Cola, cocoa, tomato juice, ground coffee
Pontiacs, Chevrolets, Ford Festivas, Dodge Rams
Medical insurance, term insurance, loans
Conservatives, family values, death penalty

## What's Not

Dancing, theme parks, the arts, foreign travel
Bowling, jogging, exercise, tennis, bicycling
Camcorders, faxes, food processors, CD players
"Nightline," "Simpsons," "Joan Rivers"
Jazz, modern rock, pop, news radio
*Changing Times, Food & Wine, Self, Omni*
Pumpernickel, Trix, sour cream, Ben & Jerry's
Spring water, mixed drinks, skim milk, wine, beer
Saabs, Nissans, BMWs, Acuras, Toyota MR2s
Keoghs, mutual funds, stocks, savings bonds
Liberals, legalizing drugs, abortion rights

TO STAND-UP COMICS, Paducah has always been the end of the line, the least prestigious place for an entertainer to play. And in many respects, the Paducah-et-al. market is the opposite of a glittery cosmopolis, an area of strip mines and small farms that time forgot. Residents are into activities that their ancestors engaged in when they settled the land two centuries ago: fishing, hunting, sewing, and gardening. The populace is relatively old — the median age is 50 — and comparatively poor. There's not much money for nightlife, and locals tend to entertain themselves around the dinner table or television set (soap stars are preferred over TV comics). This part of the nation is also filled with people of faith who keep their Bible nearby, listen to religious radio, and look forward to the annual Big Singing in the Benton, Ky., courthouse every May, featuring old-time hymn performers. The political views of voters are similarly conservative, despising what they perceive as threats to the traditional family.

| *Lower-class agricultural and mining area* | *Predominantly white singles and couples* | *Less than high school educations* | *Jobs in farming, mining, and transportation* |
|---|---|---|---|

**Key Demographics**

| | | | |
|---|---|---|---|
| Total Population: | 862,016 | Primary Ages of Adults: | 55+ |
| Median Household Income: | $21,748 | Median Home Value: | $41,844 |

# Palm Springs, California

| What's Hot | What's Not |
|---|---|
| Investment property, gourmet cooking, fashion | Home workshops, photography, fishing, unions |
| Golf, tennis, walking, bicycling, gambling | Jogging, boating, skiing, hunting, camping |
| Toaster ovens, RVs, convertibles, PCs, VCRs | Tupperware, CD players, tillers, subcompacts |
| "Meet the Press," PGA Tournaments, "Cops" | "Another World," "Family Matters," "NBC Boxing" |
| Classical, '40s–'60s pop, easy listening | Modern rock, country, rhythm & blues |
| *Sunset, Gourmet, Smithsonian, Forbes, Omni* | *Us, Car & Driver, Working Mother, Playboy* |
| Health food, sweet rolls, canned fruit, cheese | TV dinners, pizza, white bread, Twinkies |
| Domestic wine, cocktails, skim milk, scotch | Powdered drinks, tea, lemon-lime soda, ale |
| Rolls-Royces, Jaguars, Porsches, Cadillacs | Eagles, Hyundais, Chevrolets, Pontiacs |
| Stocks, mutual funds, CDs, bonds, gold cards | Securities, money orders, home-improvement loans |
| Conservatives, less government, school prayer | Liberals, consumerism, school sex ed |

SURROUNDED BY CALIFORNIA DESERT, Palm Springs is a man-made oasis of sprawling golf courses, sparkling swimming pools, and ritzy condos. Although more than 40 percent of its residents are Hispanics earning under $20,000 annually, the community is better known as a year-round playground for showbiz millionaires — Sonny Bono is the town mayor — with lifestyles to match. This is one of the nation's top markets for art, fashion, travel, casino gambling, and investing in stocks and real estate. There are few places in the country with more golf aficionados and only a handful more devoted to tennis. Less than 10 percent of the local populace earns more than $100,000 a year, but that group is large enough to account for some of the nation's highest ownership rates of Rolls Royces, Jaguars, and BMWs. Perhaps surprisingly, locals have not completely succumbed to living in paradise: they still get up in the morning to exercise, eat health food, watch the morning news shows, and argue politics. It's no coincidence that former Republican presidents Gerald Ford and Dwight Eisenhower — not to mention Frank Sinatra and Spiro Agnew — all once called Palm Springs home.

| *Middle-class retirement resort* | *Ethnically diverse singles and couples* | *College educations* | *Jobs in finance, entertainment, and business* |
|---|---|---|---|

**Key Demographics**

| Total Population: | 248,065 | Primary Ages of Adults: | 55+ |
|---|---|---|---|
| Median Household Income: | $33,165 | Median Home Value: | $135,515 |

# Panama City, Florida

| What's Hot | What's Not |
|---|---|
| Mobile homes, baking, veterans groups, cable TV | Skiing, frequent flying, book clubs, movies |
| Fishing, hunting, gardening, woodworking | Exercise, bowling, golf, racquetball, bicycling |
| Microwaves, 126/110 cameras, trucks, RVs | VCRs, PCs, toaster ovens, 35mm cameras |
| "I Love Lucy," "Rescue 911," "Inside Edition" | "In Living Color," "Wonder Years," "L.A. Law" |
| Country, gospel, urban contemporary | Modern rock, classical, easy listening |
| *TV Guide, Southern Living, National Enquirer* | *Food & Wine, Inc., Travel & Leisure, Tennis* |
| Baked beans, ham, grits, snack cakes, Jell-O | Beef, canned tuna, bagels, rice cakes |
| Orange juice, tea, powdered drinks, Pepsi-Cola | Rum, imported beer, lemon-lime soda, cognac |
| Chryslers, Buick Roadmasters, Lincoln Town Cars | Hondas, Saturns, Volvo 940s, Peugeot 405s |
| Medical insurance, investment property, loans | Bonds, savings accounts, mutual funds, annuities |
| Conservatives, family values, death penalty | Liberals, oil-drilling, endangered animals |

MANY BLUE-COLLAR SOUTHERNERS know this Gulf Coast resort as one of the destination points along Florida's "Redneck Riviera." Nearly one-third of the residents are retired, making this a popular place for fishing, woodworking, and gardening. The white-sand beaches and nearby military installations also attract servicemen who tend to enjoy professional wrestling, hunting, and veterans groups. But while Panama City is a port of entry, it's hardly a worldly place. Locals are less likely than average Americans to care about news, politics, and the arts, and few magazines are read at above-average rates. TV is the medium of choice, though viewers avoid news telecasts in favor of soaps, game shows, and cop-shock re-creations like "American Detective," "Cops," and "Rescue 911." The preference for video vérité cop shows is understandable: in this military-dense area, locals are tough on crime, support the death penalty, and oppose gun control (except for the bad guys).

| *Lower-middle-class resort* | *Predominantly white singles and couples* | *Less than high school educations* | *Jobs in farming, transportation, and crafts* |
|---|---|---|---|

**Key Demographics**

| Total Population: | 261,631 | Primary Ages of Adults: | 35–54 |
|---|---|---|---|
| Median Household Income: | $25,370 | Median Home Value: | $58,574 |

# Parkersburg, West Virginia

| What's Hot | What's Not |
|---|---|
| Home improvements, mall shopping, the Bible | Health clubs, rock concerts, travel, books |
| Gardening, fishing, bowling, sewing, camping | Jogging, tennis, sailing, bicycling, exercise |
| Radar detectors, lawn furniture, power tools | Stereos, 35mm cameras, CD players, sofa beds |
| "Coach," "Evening Shade," Daytona 500 | "Face the Nation," "Family Feud," U.S. Open |
| Adult contemporary, country, religious radio | Urban contemporary, jazz, classical, talk radio |
| *Outdoor Life, Redbook, Prevention, Parents* | *Newsweek, Cosmopolitan, Fortune, Esquire, Ski* |
| Cold cuts, Lucky Charms, canned soup, popcorn | TV dinners, yogurt, canned chicken, rye bread |
| Powdered drinks, tea, ground coffee, skim milk | Imported wine, ale, malt liquor, Diet 7-Up |
| Pontiacs, Eagles, Dodge Daytonas, Chevy Luminas | Acuras, Nissans, Cadillacs, Mercedes-Benz 420s |
| Christmas clubs, auto loans, savings bonds | IRAs, stocks, Keoghs, mutual funds, bonds |
| Moderates, privacy rights, military cutbacks | Liberals, consumerism, gay and abortion rights |

A THRIVING RAILROAD TOWN at the turn of the century, Parkersburg grew as the industrial heart of a coal, steel, and timber region. But in recent years a number of factories have closed, the population has dwindled, and many residents have abandoned the downtown for suburban subdivisions and malls. What's left is a lower-middle-class market with little interest in such big-city concerns as the arts, fashion, and gourmet cooking, but a hearty appetite for rustic small-town pursuits like hunting, fishing, camping, and gardening. Parkersburg residents enjoy such domestic activities, such as sewing, knitting, and woodworking, and status is having a well-organized home workshop. Having witnessed so much uncertainty as their city has declined, locals cling to their faith: listening to religious radio is big in Parkersburg. Liberal politics is not: this is a place where local politicians earn points bashing Ralph Nader, gay congressman Barney Frank, and women's advocate Eleanor Smeal.

| *Lower-middle-class industrial center* | *Predominantly white couples and singles* | *High school educations* | *Jobs in transportation, crafts, and manufacturing* |
|---|---|---|---|

| **Key Demographics** | Total Population: | 149,854 | Primary Ages of Adults: | 55+ |
|---|---|---|---|---|
| | Median Household Income: | $27,030 | Median Home Value: | $53,649 |

# Peoria-Bloomington, Illinois

| What's Hot | What's Not |
|---|---|
| Collectibles, shopping malls, barbecuing, unions | Movies, plays, concerts, country clubs, travel |
| Bowling, woodworking, fishing, swimming, golf | Racquetball, skiing, tennis, sailing, exercise |
| VCRs, Tupperware, recliners, cameras | Faxes, RVs, CD players, toaster ovens |
| TV sports, "Days of Our Lives," "Major Dad" | "Geraldo," "Beverly Hills 90210," "60 Minutes" |
| Heavy metal, country, classic rock, golden oldies | Rhythm & blues, rap, gospel, classical |
| *Family Handyman, 1001 Home Ideas, Parade, Cycle* | *Barron's, Cosmopolitan, Bon Appetit, Life* |
| Fish, Wheaties, Pop Tarts, potatoes, cheese | Chili, corn on the cob, canned chicken, grits |
| Fruit juice, skim milk, light beer, diet soda | Cola, scotch, imported beer and wine, tea |
| Dodges, Oldsmobiles, Chevrolets, Pontiac 6000s | Sterlings, Nissans, Volvos, Range Rovers |
| Loans, savings bonds, mutual funds, annuities | Stocks, gold cards, money orders, bonds |
| Moderates, school sex ed, death penalty | Liberals, legalizing drugs, buying American |

WILL IT PLAY IN PEORIA? That used to be the cry of businessmen (and Nixon aide John Ehrlichman) when they sought an archetypical Middle American city to test their products and ideas. Today, the Peoria-Bloomington market is still close to the midpoint on many demographic measures, but it behaves like a typical American community of a generation past: a blue-collar factory town — Caterpillar is a big employer — where residents like to bowl, share a beer at the local lodge, and join friends for backyard barbecues. And yet locals haven't completely tuned out the high-tech revolution: they enjoy their VCRs, channel-surf through their cable stations, and buy foreign-made goods. But many of these folks have borrowed their way to the American Dream: loans are popular in this area for everything from home improvements to new cars and boats. And the early '90s recession has moderated this once-staunch Republican area. Voters no longer automatically think big government is bad or buying American products is good; what plays in Peoria is value for your money.

| *Middle-class industrial market* | *Predominantly white couples and singles* | *High school educations* | *Jobs in manufacturing, crafts, and transportation* |
|---|---|---|---|

| **Key Demographics** | Total Population: | 600,648 | Primary Ages of Adults: | 25–44 |
|---|---|---|---|---|
| | Median Household Income: | $31,248 | Median Home Value: | $53,161 |

# Philadelphia, Pennsylvania

## What's Hot | What's Not

| What's Hot | What's Not |
|---|---|
| Theme parks, fashion, casinos, travel, the arts | Baking, clubs, sweepstakes, crafts, pets |
| Tennis, exercise, walking, golf, swimming | Gardening, hunting, fishing, bicycling, camping |
| Woks, radar detectors, CD players, faxes | Power tools, video games, motorcycles |
| "Joan Rivers," "Doogie Howser," "In Living Color" | "Price Is Right," "Cheers," "Full House" |
| Jazz, rap, classical, rock, rhythm & blues | Country, adult contemporary, religious radio |
| *Ebony, Inc., Discover, Mademoiselle, Life, GQ* | *Reader's Digest, Parents, Outdoor Life, Playboy* |
| Bagels, tuna, pretzels, chocolate, fruit | Fast food, ham, Pop Tarts, dried fruit, pudding |
| Wine, cocktails, orange juice, domestic beer | Vegetable juice, diet sodas, powdered drinks |
| Peugeots, Infinitis, Jaguars, Porsches, Audis | Chryslers, Chevrolets, Subarus, Pontiacs |
| Homeowners insurance, stocks, IRAs, mutual funds | Medical insurance, savings accounts, auto loans |
| Liberals, gay and abortion rights, consumerism | Moderates, less government, privacy rights |

FORGET ITS FOUNDING as William Penn's City of Brotherly Love. Surveys today show that Philadelphia residents actively dislike the brotherhood of unions, business clubs, fraternal orders, and veterans groups. They're even less likely than average Americans to hold backyard barbecues. But even if they do go their own way, it's difficult to put down their lifestyle. Philadelphia is one of the nation's prime markets when it comes to the arts, film, literature, fashion, and gourmet cooking. Locals are passionate about their music — whatever the genre — and like to crank up their sophisticated CD players. Demographically speaking, the town is a bit schizophrenic, racially and ethnically divided, with pockets of poverty not far from yuppie enclaves. But there *is* money in Philadelphia, thanks to jobs in health and financial services. There's also a hard edge to the city, reflected in the popularity of craps tables in nearby Atlantic City as well as a jaundiced eye on current affairs. When locals watch TV, they're less likely to tune in TV news than shock-and-schlock gabmeisters like Joan, Oprah, and Phil.

| *Upper-middle-class metropolitan sprawl* | *Racially mixed singles* | *High school educations* | *Health, finance, and service jobs* |
|---|---|---|---|

**Key Demographics**

| | | | |
|---|---|---|---|
| Total Population: | 7,262,042 | Primary Ages of Adults: | 25–44 |
| Median Household Income: | $40,229 | Median Home Value: | $112,456 |

# Phoenix, Arizona

## What's Hot | What's Not

| What's Hot | What's Not |
|---|---|
| Domestic travel, dancing, crafts, casinos, dogs | Religious clubs, home furnishing, tobacco, cats |
| Bicycling, skiing, golf, exercise, camping | Boating, jogging, fishing, gardening, knitting |
| Toaster ovens, books, CD players, weights, PCs | Microwaves, chain saws, pickups, clothes dryers |
| "Star Trek," "Tonight Show," U.S. Open | "People's Court," "General Hospital," "Arsenio" |
| Modern rock, classical, '40s–'60s pop, jazz | Gospel, country, soft rock, urban contemporary |
| *Sunset, Scientific American, Shape, Forbes* | *Woman's World, Home Mechanix, Soap Opera Digest* |
| Health food, oat bran, chili, cheese, popcorn | Cold cuts, pasta, canned stew, snack cakes |
| Spring water, ground coffee, domestic wine | Lemon-lime soda, tea, powdered drinks, Pabst |
| Porsche 928s, Cadillac Allantes, Jaguar XJSs | Dodge Shadows, Ford Tempos, Chevrolet Luminas |
| Mutual funds, precious metals, annuities, bonds | Home-improvement loans, medical insurance |
| Moderates, school prayer, death penalty | Apolitical voters, endangered animals, gay rights |

SUNSHINE AND DRY AIR helped transform Phoenix from a farming community into a tourist haven and health resort. Today, Arizona's state capital and largest city caters to a population of retirees and baby boomers drawn to the jobs at high-tech firms, such as IBM and Motorola. This is one of the nation's top markets for outdoor sports like golf, bicycling, skiing, and camping. The area's highly educated residents are also more likely than average Americans to enjoy books, movies, current affairs, and science; among the favorite magazines are *Scientific American, Omni, National Geographic*, and *Smithsonian*. The snowbirds who moved to Phoenix have helped make it a politically active area — with above-average rates of liberals, conservatives, and moderates — concerned about family values and school prayer, apathetic about environmental threats and endangered animals. But it's difficult to get a rise out of them even on the issue of ozone depletion; apparently they're too busy worrying about their golf games to notice.

| *Middle-class commercial center* | *Ethnically diverse couples and singles* | *College educations* | *Jobs in finance and recreation services* |
|---|---|---|---|

**Key Demographics**

| | | | |
|---|---|---|---|
| Total Population: | 2,818,227 | Primary Ages of Adults: | 25–44 |
| Median Household Income: | $32,045 | Median Home Value: | $89,557 |

# Pittsburgh, Pennsylvania

| What's Hot | What's Not |
|---|---|
| Mall shopping, TV sports, car repair | Art, boating, politics, theater, casinos, pets |
| Bowling, golf, walking, woodworking, gardening | Exercise, weight training, bicycling, sailing |
| VCRs, microwaves, power tools, lawn furniture | PCs, 35mm cameras, video games, sofa beds |
| "Roseanne," "Another World," "Regis & Kathie Lee" | Sunday talk shows, "Simpsons," "Wonder Years" |
| Heavy metal, classic rock, golden oldies | Pop, jazz, modern rock, rhythm & blues, gospel |
| *Family Handyman, Weight Watchers, Redbook, Us* | *Changing Times, Tennis, House Beautiful, Time* |
| Beef, pasta, spaghetti sauce, pretzels, waffles | Canned hash, Mexican food, rice, grits, jam |
| Cocoa, orange juice, powdered drinks, Pepsi-Cola | Imported beer, herbal tea, wine, spring water |
| Chevrolets, Oldsmobiles, Dodges, Buick Regals | Volvos, Audis, Jaguars, Hondas, Mazda Miatas |
| Savings bonds, life insurance, auto loans, CDs | Gold cards, medical insurance, mutual funds |
| Moderates, buying American, nuclear waste | Liberals, gay rights, oil drilling |

FOR A CENTURY, Pittsburgh has thrived as the heart of the nation's steel industry, weathering recent industrial declines by encouraging high-tech job growth. But despite attempts to earn a yuppie reputation — after all, the city is home to several universities and museums as well as "Mister Rogers' Neighborhood" — Pittsburgh still behaves like a blue-collar factory town. Residents would rather go bowling or hunting than play tennis or racquetball. They're less likely than average Americans to enjoy art, theater, fashion, or travel. With 30 percent of adults home during the day as homemakers or retirees, watching TV is a popular pastime, and Pittsburgh is one of the nation's top markets when it comes to watching televised sports — especially football, hockey, and auto races. Indeed, locals seem to nurture a sit-down culture: they buy recliners and porch furniture at above-average rates and have made crossword puzzles a popular pursuit. Pittsburgh's passion for cars has remained strong over the years, with motorists buying more than 50 models at above-average rates, mostly subcompacts and muscle cars, and all made in America. In Steeltown, foreign car–makers are the enemy.

| *Middle-class industrial and residential market* | *Predominantly white couples and singles* | *High school educations* | *Jobs in manufacturing, transportation, and crafts* |
|---|---|---|---|

**Key Demographics**

| | | | |
|---|---|---|---|
| Total Population: | 2,968,003 | Primary Ages of Adults: | 55+ |
| Median Household Income: | $27,945 | Median Home Value: | $57,152 |

# Portland, Oregon

| What's Hot | What's Not |
|---|---|
| Photography, art, rock concerts, books, cats | Fashion, rap, country clubs, sweepstakes |
| Camping, bicycling, boating, skiing, golf | Bowling, tennis, jogging, coin collecting |
| Food processors, PCs, CD players, VCRs, RVs | Cable TV, microwaves, tillers, convertibles |
| "Northern Exposure," "Murphy Brown" | "Guiding Light," "Inside Edition," "Geraldo" |
| Modern rock, folk, easy listening, talk radio | Urban contemporary, jazz, classical, country |
| *Photography, Shape, Rolling Stone, Discover* | *Star, Food & Wine, Vogue, Ebony, New Yorker* |
| Fish, cheese, shredded wheat, canned soup, nuts | Beef stew, raisin bread, rice, brownies, gum |
| Local microbrewed beer, domestic wine, coffee | Malt liquor, cola, tea, milk, orange juice |
| Toyotas, Saturns, Subarus, Isuzus, Chevy Geos | Lincolns, Oldsmobiles, Peugeots, Dodge pickups |
| Precious metals, stocks, dental insurance, IRAs | Medical insurance, securities, money orders |
| Moderates, school sex ed, ozone depletion | Apolitical voters, gun control, endangered animals |

IT MAY HAVE BEEN BORN a blue-collar port, but today, Portland's collars are shiny New-Age white. A mostly young populace — half the residents are under 44 years old — pursues a go-go lifestyle, popularizing everything from skiing and rock concerts to camping and beer drinking (thanks to a slew of local microbreweries). This is one of the nation's best markets for cultural sophisticates who enjoy photography, books, art, and theater, in part because of a dozen area colleges. Dotted with parks, Portland also draws fans for bicycling, hiking, walking, and white-water rafting. True, middle-class incomes tend to diminish interests at the upper and lower end of the socioeconomic ladder: relatively few locals are into country clubs or gospel music, European fashion or rap. And while dockworkers temper the liberal attitudes of area baby boomers, everyone seems concerned about environmental threats, such as nuclear waste and ozone depletion; the misty weather makes this one of the nation's best cities for healthy skin. Recycling is so popular that there aren't enough outlets to handle all the recycled materials.

| *Middle-class river port city* | *Predominantly white singles and families* | *Some college educations* | *Jobs in crafts, construction, and recreation* |
|---|---|---|---|

**Key Demographics**

| | | | |
|---|---|---|---|
| Total Population: | 2,442,610 | Primary Ages of Adults: | 25–44 |
| Median Household Income: | $32,090 | Median Home Value: | $73,544 |

# Portland–Poland Spring, Maine

## What's Hot    What's Not

| What's Hot | What's Not |
|---|---|
| State fairs, boating, gourmet cooking, cats | Theme parks, business clubs, movies, lotteries |
| Skiing, walking, camping, woodworking, knitting | Jogging, tennis, exercise, weight training |
| Microwaves, rifles, Tupperware, VCRs, RVs | PCs, 35mm cameras, CD players, station wagons |
| Morning news, "Cheers," "Cops," "Major Dad" | Talk shows, "Letterman," "Fresh Prince" |
| Country, adult contemporary, religious radio | Modern rock, rhythm & blues, classical |
| *Sports Afield, Ladies' Home Journal, Prevention* | *Architectural Digest, Forbes, Bon Appetit* |
| Ham, baked beans, biscuits, snack cakes, Jell-O | Fast food, French bread, canned chicken, rice |
| Powdered drinks, vegetable juices, ground coffee | Wine, imported beer, spring water, cocktails |
| Pontiacs, Chryslers, Chevrolets, Dodge Omnis | Hondas, Ferraris, Sterlings, Lexus ES250s |
| First mortgages, loans, life insurance, CDs | Mutual funds, Keoghs, stocks, gold cards, IRAs |
| Moderates, family values, death penalty | Liberals, consumerism, oil-drilling |

THIS "DOWN EAST" MARKET is seemingly lost in time, drifting between its past as a blue-collar home of loggers and long-shoremen and its current incarnation as a booming center of high-tech and service jobs. The quiet, craggy coast surrounding Portland and Poland Spring has lured young, educated city-dwellers seeking relaxed lifestyles. And they've found it, enjoying activities like boating, golf, and woodworking at higher-than-average rates. But they've also brought some of their urban values with them, including a taste for gourmet cooking, politics, and current affairs; residents here are big on morning network news shows. The area was made for outdoor activities like camping, skiing, and hiking, and residents are suitably attired thanks to L. L. Bean's headquarters located in nearby Freeport. Although this is a center for producing spring water, natural toothpaste, and organic foods, many residents will have none of them, preferring a hearty, cholesterol-filled diet of pork products, processed foods, and snack cakes.

| Middle-class commercial center | Predominantly white singles and couples | High school educations | Jobs in farming, transportation, and crafts |
|---|---|---|---|

## Key Demographics

| | | | |
|---|---|---|---|
| Total Population: | 892,216 | Primary Ages of Adults: | 25–44 |
| Median Household Income: | $34,571 | Median Home Value: | $111,784 |

# Presque Isle, Maine

## What's Hot    What's Not

| What's Hot | What's Not |
|---|---|
| Hunting, crafts, coin collecting, dieting, RVs | The arts, fashion, frequent flying, politics |
| Walking, fishing, knitting, skiing, gardening | Golf, bowling, jogging, tennis, dancing |
| Cable TV, hot-water heaters, 126/110 cameras | Toaster ovens, PCs, 35mm cameras, condoms |
| Game shows, "Guiding Light," "Full House" | Talk shows, "Honeymooners," "Doogie Howser" |
| Country, gospel, religious, all-night radio | Jazz, soft rock, classical, Spanish, news radio |
| *Field & Stream, McCall's, National Enquirer* | *Newsweek, Discover, Business Week, Sunset* |
| Beef stew, baked beans, canned fruit, doughnuts | Health food, fish, rice, cheese, raisin bread |
| Cocoa, tomato juice, colas, tea, Pepsi-Cola | Wine, fruit juices, spring water, light beer |
| Buicks, Pontiacs, Ford Festivas, Oldsmobile 98s | Mazdas, Volkswagens, Hondas, BMWs, Acura Vigors |
| Medical insurance, home-improvement loans | Savings bonds, annuities, Keoghs, stocks |
| Conservatives, privacy rights, buying American | Liberals, ozone depletion, endangered animals |

MANY PEOPLE THINK of Maine as a coastal string of fishing ports, but Presque Isle sits in the middle of a wild, isolated area where residents work on hardscrabble potato farms or log the evergreen forests. Like other rural areas, this market is big on activities where the land plays a crucial role: hunting, fishing, and gardening. With an older-than-average populace, Presque Isle also ranks as one of the nation's top markets for sewing, knitting, and coin collecting. Living hundreds of miles from the closest metropolis, folks around here are not up on current affairs, the arts, or the latest fashion. Since they're surrounded by miles of wilderness, residents are skeptical of environmental threats. And though Presque Isle residents claim to be more concerned about dieting than any other market in the nation, you wouldn't know it by looking into their pantries. Food surveys reveal a local passion for high-calorie processed foods and a striking distaste for health foods. Perhaps dieting in Presque Isle means never having to say you're hungry.

| Lower-middle-class rural shipping center | Predominantly white families and couples | High school educations | Jobs in farming, forestry, and manufacturing |
|---|---|---|---|

## Key Demographics

| | | | |
|---|---|---|---|
| Total Population: | 86,206 | Primary Ages of Adults: | 25–44 |
| Median Household Income: | $25,656 | Median Home Value: | $50,097 |

# Providence, Rhode Island–New Bedford, Massachusetts

| What's Hot | What's Not |
|---|---|
| Lotteries, videos, gourmet cooking, fashion | Baking, crafts, adult-ed courses, the Bible |
| Bowling, skiing, tennis, walking, exercise | Fishing, hunting, racquetball, jogging, sewing |
| Charcoal grills, cable TV, porch furniture | VCRs, PCs, cameras, light fixtures, mini-vans |
| MTV, C-SPAN, "Letterman," "People's Court" | BET, CNN, "Beverly Hills, 90210," "Rescue 911" |
| Rock, easy listening, talk radio | Rhythm & blues, country, gospel, folk, classical |
| *Discover, Consumer's Digest, Cosmopolitan, Time* | *Sports Afield, Country Living, Parents, Esquire* |
| Fish, TV dinners, rye bread, Wheaties, pretzels | Ham, chili, dried fruit, Pop Tarts, potato chips |
| Diet Coke, domestic beer, milk, cocktails | Powdered drinks, decaf coffee, light beer, tea |
| Hyundais, Saturns, Plymouths, Peugeot 405s | Lincolns, BMWs, Alfa Romeos, Mercedes-Benz 500s |
| Savings bonds, life insurance, CDs, Sears cards | Investment property, credit lines, mutual funds |
| Moderates, gay rights, ocean dumping | Conservatives, legalizing drugs, oil-drilling |

THIS IS AN ODD DUCK of a market, a state capital crossed with a college town crossed with a commercial port. The result is a socioeconomic stew: pockets of well-heeled residents in Newport; downscale Portuguese in New Bedford; and Ivy League students at Brown University in Providence. And yet the combined lifestyle of Providence–New Bedford is comfortably middle-class. Residents are more likely than average Americans to enjoy mall shopping, fashion, and gourmet cooking. And though there's usually a correlation between education and income, in this market residents have the brains but not yet the bucks. They're big on reading smart magazines like *Discover, Consumer's Digest, Newsweek,* and *Scientific American,* yet they're more likely to invest in lottery tickets than stocks and bonds. Where the true eclectic character of this market presents itself is in political issues: as moderates, they favor issues on the left — supporting gay rights and sex education in the schools — as well as the right — opposing gun control and legalizing drugs.

| Upper-middle-class commercial center | Predominantly white couples and singles | High school educations | Service, manufacturing, and transportation jobs |
|---|---|---|---|

**Key Demographics**

| | | | |
|---|---|---|---|
| Total Population: | 1,533,636 | Primary Ages of Adults: | 25–44 |
| Median Household Income: | $36,824 | Median Home Value: | $150,303 |

# Quincy, Illinois–Hannibal, Missouri

| What's Hot | What's Not |
|---|---|
| Collectibles, gardening, hunting, grandchildren | Foreign travel, fashion, gourmet cooking, books |
| Bowling, fishing, walking, woodworking, sewing | Sailing, golf, skiing, jogging, backpacking |
| Tillers, power tools, microwaves, recliners | Faxes, CD players, radar detectors, PCs |
| Soaps, "Current Affair," "Northern Exposure" | "American Gladiators," "Meet the Press," "Cops" |
| Country, middle-of-the-road, golden oldies | Soft rock, jazz, classical, Spanish, news radio |
| *Ladies' Home Journal, Sports Afield, TV Guide* | *Photography, Working Woman, Rolling Stone, Inc.* |
| Sausages, baked beans, canned soup, sweet rolls | Take-out, spaghetti sauce, canned chicken, grits |
| Powdered drinks, lemon-lime soda, skim milk | Cocktails, domestic beer, orange juice, scotch |
| Buicks, Olds 88s, Dodge Omnis, Chevy Berettas | VWs, Saabs, Acura Legends, Mazda RX-7s |
| Medical and life insurance, CDs, auto loans | Mutual funds, savings bonds, stocks, IRAs |
| Moderates, death penalty, pro-lifers | Liberals, gun control, nuclear waste |

HANNIBAL, MISSOURI, was a rowdy frontier riverport when writer Mark Twain lived there as a youth. Today, Hannibal and sister city Quincy, Illinois, have aged, slowed a bit, weathered the Flood of '93, and grown more conservative. Nearly one-quarter of the residents are retired — this is one of the top ten markets for interest in grandchildren — and homemakers constitute one-fifth of the population. Still, the predominant lifestyle would probably be appreciated by Twain characters Tom Sawyer and Huck Finn: fishing, hunting, and gardening are all enjoyed at above-average rates. Residents also are less likely than average Americans to be interested in citified pursuits, such as foreign travel, theater, and classical music. Political analysts have nicknamed this area Little Dixie because its original settlers were pro-slavery southerners, and it's still a haven for right-of-center thinking. A sad irony is that the birthplace of one of America's greatest writers has below-average interest in reading books.

| Lower-middle-class river ports | Predominantly white couples and singles | High school educations | Jobs in farming, crafts, and transportation |
|---|---|---|---|

**Key Demographics**

| | | | |
|---|---|---|---|
| Total Population: | 276,405 | Primary Ages of Adults: | 55+ |
| Median Household Income: | $23,962 | Median Home Value: | $38,285 |

# Raleigh–Durham, North Carolina

| What's Hot | What's Not |
| --- | --- |
| Science, the arts, college sports, baking, dogs | Gambling, movies, gourmet cooking, theme parks |
| Exercise, tennis, hunting, walking | Bowling, skiing, bicycling, swimming, crafts |
| Cable TV, mobile homes, microwaves, mattresses | CD players, VCRs, recliners, 35mm cameras |
| BET, "Blossom," "Guiding Light," "Donahue" | "David Brinkley," "Roseanne," "Love Connection" |
| Gospel, rhythm & blues, country, religious radio | Classical, modern rock, jazz, radio baseball |
| *Southern Living, Essence, Seventeen, Flying* | *People, Smithsonian, Architectural Digest, Inc.* |
| Fried chicken, BBQ, grits, pies | Fish, cheese, rye bread, canned fruit, popcorn |
| Tea, colas, powdered drinks, malt liquor | Imported wine, fruit juices, ale, spring water |
| Mazdas, Isuzus, Chevrolets, Nissans, GMC trucks | Peugeots, Acuras, Porsches, Ford Econolines |
| Medical insurance, education loans, bank cards | Savings bonds, mutual funds, IRAs |
| Conservatives, school prayer, toxic waste | Moderates, military cutbacks, gay rights |

ALONG WITH CHAPEL HILL, these two cities form the boundaries of North Carolina's Research Triangle, an area with more Ph.D.s than anywhere else in the nation. But not everyone around here has a diploma; in fact, the local populace is a mix of high-tech workers, downscale tobacco growers, and students attending Duke, the University of North Carolina, and N.C. State. The resultant lifestyle is stretched among residents who are more likely than average Americans to attend the theater as well as work on their cars, to chew tobacco as well as play tennis. The student influence is especially apparent in the popularity of aerobic exercise and area college basketball teams. Local farmers keep subscription rates high for magazines like *Mother Earth News* and *Field & Stream*. Although political views are divided between the liberal college community and more conservative rural residents, traditional religious values are shared by most voters. Local congressman David Price — a Democrat, former political science professor, and lay Baptist preacher — epitomizes the area's crazy salad profile.

| Middle-class commercial centers | Racially diverse singles and and couples | Some college educations | Jobs in manufacturing, transportation, and services |
| --- | --- | --- | --- |

## Key Demographics

| | | | |
| --- | --- | --- | --- |
| Total Population: | 2,037,818 | Primary Ages of Adults: | 25–44 |
| Median Household Income: | $31,221 | Median Home Value: | $78,043 |

# Rapid City, South Dakota

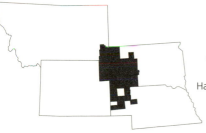

| What's Hot | What's Not |
| --- | --- |
| Veterans clubs, motorcycles, car repair, baking | Travel, movies, electronics, health food, dancing |
| Hunting, fishing, horseback riding, bowling | Tennis, boating, exercise, weight training |
| Charcoal grills, garden tools, 126/110 cameras | VCRs, radar detectors, CD players, convertibles |
| Morning news, "Price Is Right," "Full House" | Soaps, "Wonder Years," "Hard Copy," "Seinfeld" |
| Country, golden oldies, Native American ethnic | Rhythm & blues, classical, modern rock |
| *Outdoor Life, Parents, Home Mechanix* | *Business Week, Bon Appetit, Life, New Yorker* |
| Ham, baked beans, biscuits, Lucky Charms, Jell-O | Canned hash, waffles, raisin bread, chocolates |
| Light beer, skim milk, tomato juice, Kool-Aid | Orange juice, imported beer and wine, milk |
| Subaru, Oldsmobiles, Mercurys, Dodge Omnis | Sterlings, Acuras, Ferraris, Nissan Maximas |
| Mutual funds, CDs, first mortgages, auto loans | Gold cards, savings bonds, precious metals |
| Moderates, family values, privacy rights | Liberals, endangered animals, oil drilling |

SETTLED MORE THAN A CENTURY ago by gold miners, Rapid City is still a center for mining and ranching as well as a draw for tourists exploring the nearby Black Hills. The prevailing lifestyle is prairie populist: hunting, fishing, and horseback riding are all enjoyed at above-average rates. The opening of casinos in nearby Deadwood has made gambling popular among Rapid City residents, but typical expressions of the "good life" are otherwise lacking, such as the arts, fashion, gourmet cooking, and dancing — at least dancing in nightclubs. Kevin Costner's film *Dances with Wolves* was shot in part on the area's local landscape, which features rolling plains and grain farms. Native Americans represent 9 percent of this market's population, helping boost the popularity of crafts, ethnic radio, and, that modern equine equivalent, motorcycles. On political issues, this is a moderate area — conservative on economic issues, more liberal on foreign ones — but most of all residents cherish their privacy.

| Lower-middle-class ranching area | Predominantly white families and couples | Some college educations | Jobs in farming, transportation, and crafts |
| --- | --- | --- | --- |

## Key Demographics

| | | | |
| --- | --- | --- | --- |
| Total Population: | 243,023 | Primary Ages of Adults: | 25–44 |
| Median Household Income: | $25,932 | Median Home Value: | $53,875 |

# Reno, Nevada

| What's Hot | What's Not |
|---|---|
| Casinos, skiing, books, rodeos, gourmet cooking | Home furnishing, the arts, dieting, the Bible |
| Bicycling, boating, jogging, camping, hunting | Tennis, walking, gardening, knitting, sewing |
| Woks, CD players, RVs, PCs, cameras, recliners | Lawn mowers, microwaves, washing machines |
| "Cops," "Letterman," "Murphy Brown" | "All My Children," "Geraldo," "People's Court" |
| Classical, rock, jazz, heavy metal | Rap, gospel, rhythm & blues, news radio |
| *Sunset, Omni, Travel & Leisure, New Woman* | *Star, Inc., Soap Opera Digest, Vogue* |
| Beef, chili, yogurt, oat bran, sweet rolls | Spaghetti, cold cuts, aerosol cheese, Pop Tarts |
| Spring water, domestic wine, light beer | Orange juice, milk, imported wine, cocoa, tea |
| Subarus, Mazdas, Isuzus, Mitsubishis, Hondas | Oldsmobiles, Infinitis, Rolls-Royces, Buicks |
| Investment property, mutual funds, annuities | Medical insurance, Christmas clubs, money orders |
| Liberals, abortion rights, toxic waste | Moderates, endangered animals, ocean dumping |

IT BILLS ITSELF AS "the biggest little city in the world," but Reno is better known as a haven for tacky weddings, quickie divorces, and legalized gambling. Surveys show it's the nation's second-best market for casinos (after Las Vegas), and it sits near the top of all markets when it comes to skiing, camping, bicycling, and watching videos. The ethnically diverse populace — with above-average concentrations of Hispanics, Asians, and Native Americans — has the money to travel, join health clubs, and enjoy the local nightlife. They also have the youth, education, and sophistication to be interested in reading, health food, and athletics; locals pursue nearly every kind of outdoor sport known in America, from bicycling and jogging to fishing and hiking in the nearby Sierra Nevada. Cross all this energy with a high number of chapels and you'll see another characteristic of the area: residents are more likely than the general population to be married.

| *Middle-class resort community* | *Ethnically diverse singles and couples* | *Some college educations* | *Jobs in public administration and entertainment* |
|---|---|---|---|

| **Key Demographics** | | | |
|---|---|---|---|
| Total Population: | 512,748 | Primary Ages of Adults: | 25–44 |
| Median Household Income: | $34,500 | Median Home Value: | $113,066 |

# Richmond, Virginia

| What's Hot | What's Not |
|---|---|
| Home furnishing, the arts, college sports, pets | Health food, movies, adult-ed courses, golf |
| Tennis, jogging, hunting, knitting, gardening | Racquetball, bowling, fishing, woodworking |
| Microwaves, cable TV, garden tillers | VCRs, cameras, radar detectors, recliners |
| "Nightline," "Wonder Years," "Fresh Prince" | "Tonight Show," "Face the Nation," "Honeymooners" |
| Urban contemporary, gospel, rhythm & blues | Heavy metal, country, modern rock, folk |
| *Esquire, Parade, Ebony, Health, Food & Wine* | *Glamour, Scientific American, Popular Mechanics* |
| Fried chicken, biscuits, rice, beef stew, grits | Fish, English muffins, canned fruit, pretzels |
| Diet soda, colas, powdered drinks, malt liquor | Draft beer, imported wine, ground coffee, vodka |
| Nissans, Mazdas, Volvos, Cadillacs, Lincolns | Dodges, Plymouths, Oldsmobiles, Alfa Romeos |
| Savings accounts, whole life insurance, money orders | Savings bonds, Keoghs, mutual funds, IRAs |
| Conservatives, less government, school prayer | Moderates, military cutbacks, legalizing drugs |

VIRGINIA'S STATE CAPITAL — and once the seat of the Confederacy — remains a modest-size city with deep Southern roots. Antebellum homes are carefully maintained along shady avenues punctuated with monuments to Confederate war heroes. With above-average rates of college educations, residents have a strong interest in the arts, antiques, and classical music. The half-dozen local colleges — including Virginia Commonwealth University — attract students who've popularized fitness, art, and cheering on their campus teams. But this is a racially mixed market — nearly one-third of all residents are African American — and you can see the split media tastes in the consumption of black-oriented *Jet* and "The Fresh Prince of Bel Air" coupled with the larger white audiences drawn to *Southern Living* and "The Wonder Years." Ideologically, the heavily white suburbs tilt this area into the conservative column. But Richmond stands as one of those rare communities with eclectic tastes for everything from contemporary film to state fairs.

| *Middle-class commercial center* | *Racially mixed singles and couples* | *College educations* | *Jobs in services, manufacturing, and transportation* |
|---|---|---|---|

| **Key Demographics** | | | |
|---|---|---|---|
| Total Population: | 1,190,192 | Primary Ages of Adults: | 25–44 |
| Median Household Income: | $35,852 | Median Home Value: | $84,136 |

# Roanoke—Lynchburg, Virginia

## What's Hot

Gardening, car repair, pro wrestling, the Bible
Fishing, hunting, target-shooting, sewing
Tillers, microwaves, 126/110 cameras, pickups
Soaps, "I Love Lucy," "Blossom," "Rescue 911"
Country, gospel, rap, urban contemporary
*True Story, Field & Stream, Soap Opera Digest*
Sausage, peanut butter, canned macaroni, pudding
Colas, tea, powdered drinks, orange juice, milk
Pontiac Grand Ams, Ford Mustangs, Chevy Luminas
Personal loans, medical insurance, securities
Conservatives, pro-lifers, death penalty

## What's Not

Theater, dancing, health clubs, lotteries, unions
Jogging, racquetball, golf, bicycling, skiing
PCs, toaster ovens, stereos, woks
"60 Minutes," "Empty Nest," "20/20"
Rhythm & blues, classical music, '40s–'60s pop
*Self, Fortune, Discover, Sunset, Bon Appetit*
Beef, canned tuna, cheese, waffles, rice cakes
Skim milk, wine, light and draft beer, diet sodas
Porsche 928s, Volvo 940s, Acura Integras
Stocks, mutual funds, annuities, Keoghs, IRAs
Liberals, gay rights, military cutbacks

SURROUNDED BY THE Blue Ridge Mountains, this market is a religious fundamentalist's dream: conservative, hawkish, and the home of Jerry Falwell's Moral Majority. Area lifestyles are not too distant from the earliest settlers' world of 200 years ago: residents are into fishing, gardening, and sewing at above-average rates. They appear far removed — figuratively and literally — from cosmopolitan tastes in current affairs, news, and media; forget about the investigative journalism of TV shows like "60 Minutes" and "20/20." Gay pride is an oxymoron. Although there are a number of small colleges nearby, most residents fail to complete high school. Yet they do compensate for nominal incomes with a high degree of self-sufficiency, working on their cars and doing their own home improvements. What they lack is leisure: you just won't find too many area folks into golf, bowling, tennis, or skiing.

| Lower-middle-class commercial center | Predominantly white couples and singles | Less than high school educations | Farm, manufacturing, and transportation jobs |
|---|---|---|---|

## Key Demographics

| | | | |
|---|---|---|---|
| Total Population: | 1,020,651 | Primary Ages of Adults: | 55+ |
| Median Household Income: | $27,687 | Median Home Value: | $61,745 |

# Rochester, New York

## What's Hot

Photography, the arts, frequent flying, dancing
Golf, bowling, boating, skiing, bicycling
CD players, power tools, PCs, 35mm cameras
"ABC Wide World of Sports," "Seinfeld," "Sisters"
Modern rock, classical, jazz, easy listening
*Discover, Inc., Shape, Rolling Stone, Newsweek*
Fish, French bread, spaghetti, cheese, waffles
Cold Duck, wine, imported beer, skim milk
Peugeots, Saturns, Saabs, Mazdas, Acuras
Mutual funds, savings bonds, gold cards, IRAs
Liberals, ozone depletion, endangered animals

## What's Not

Baking, fashion, rodeos, investment property
Walking, fishing, hunting, sewing
Microwaves, 126/110 cameras, chain saws, trucks
"Family Feud," "Inside Edition," "Simpsons"
Country, urban contemporary, religious radio
*Mother Earth News, Weight Watchers, Sports Afield*
Ham, canned chicken, pizza, dried fruit, jam
Lemon-lime soda, tea, milk, powdered drinks
Rolls-Royces, Chevy Geos, Ford Crown Victorias
Medical insurance, money orders, personal loans
Conservatives, school prayer, legalizing drugs

"WELCOME, TECHIES" ought to be the sign that greets visitors to Rochester. With a slew of local high-tech firms — including Eastman Kodak, Bausch and Lomb, and Xerox — this market is a magnet for upscale, educated professionals. Residents are more likely than average Americans to own products like computers, CD players, and cameras — and not the cheapie 126/110 models, thank-you, but the high-end 35mm gear. They have the brains and bucks to enjoy Rochester's cultural offerings at museums, theaters, and art galleries. And with few couch potatoes here — TV fans tend to watch nightly news shows and urban-based sitcoms — Rochester is a strong market for active consumers with eclectic tastes. They enjoy sports ranging from bowling to golf to skiing, and it's difficult to find a car model they won't buy at above-average rates. Interestingly, given their passion for cutting-edge art and science, Rochester residents shy away from the trendiest consumption patterns: they dislike fashion, gourmet cooking, and seminars on self-improvement. Perhaps the techies are too caught up in their software to notice style.

| Upper-middle-class industrial city | Predominantly white singles | College educations | Jobs in finance, business, and health services |
|---|---|---|---|

## Key Demographics

| | | | |
|---|---|---|---|
| Total Population: | 1,024,447 | Primary Ages of Adults: | 25–44 |
| Median Household Income: | $38,108 | Median Home Value: | $93,178 |

# Rochester, Minnesota—Mason City, Iowa—Austin, Minnesota

## What's Hot

Barbecuing, collectibles, knitting, grandchildren
Bicycling, skiing, walking, fishing, hunting
Cable TV, RVs, recliners, lawn mowers
TV news, "Evening Shade," "Wheel of Fortune"
Country, middle-of-the-road, adult contemporary
*Field & Stream, Redbook, Popular Science*
Ham, baked beans, dried fruit, crackers, Jell-O
Vegetable juice, powdered drinks, ground coffee
Oldsmobiles, Subarus, Buicks, Dodge 4x4 trucks
Medical insurance, mutual funds, CDs, auto loans
Moderates, family values, pro-lifers

## What's Not

Foreign travel, art, movies, theme parks, pets
Boating, jogging, exercise, tennis, sailing
Microwaves, PCs, CD players, sofa beds
"I Love Lucy," "Star Trek," "America's Most Wanted"
Soft rock, jazz, classical, urban contemporary
*Forbes, Vogue, GQ, Mademoiselle, Food & Wine*
Health food, canned hash, rye, oat bran
Cocktails, tea, imported beer, wine, ale
Acuras, BMWs, Volvos, Jaguars, Suzuki Sidekicks
Stocks, gold cards, Keoghs, precious metals
Liberals, environmental concerns, gun control

THIS TRIO OF HEARTLAND communities serves as a trading center for a rich agricultural region. But there are some wrinkles in that pastoral portrait. Rochester is the home of the Mayo Clinic, which has lured thousands of white-collar professionals to the area. And Austin is the headquarters of the Hormel meat-packing firm, which has had to contend with bitter strikes by its blue-collar workers (as well as the hundredth anniversary celebration of Spam). The result is an uncommon rural market where residents are big on network and cable news as well as magazines like *Popular Science, National Geographic,* and *Popular Mechanics.* With nearly 40 percent of all adults retired or working as homemakers, domestic activities like knitting and wood-working are popular. In part that's to cope with the relatively bleak cultural life; locals have to drive 90 minutes to the Twin Cities for professional theater, sports, or entertainment. It's easier to enjoy the outdoor scene: the dozens of cross-country ski trails in the winter or the trout streams in Whitewater State Park in the summer.

| Lower-middle-class agricultural area | Predominantly white families and couples | High school educations | Farm and crafts jobs |
|---|---|---|---|

### Key Demographics

| | | | |
|---|---|---|---|
| Total Population: | 354,240 | Primary Ages of Adults: | 55+ |
| Median Household Income: | $29,646 | Median Home Value: | $53,578 |

# Rockford, Illinois

## What's Hot

Home furnishing, car repair, videos, unions
Bowling, fishing, gardening, woodworking
VCRs, radar detectors, PCs, motorcycles
"Santa Barbara," "Dinosaurs," "Coach"
Heavy metal, classic rock, '40s–'60s pop music
*Family Handyman, Family Circle, Parade*
Cold cuts, canned vegetables, Lucky Charms
Powdered drinks, cocoa, diet sodas, draft beer
Dodge Daytonas, Chevy Corsicas, Olds Cieras
First mortgages, auto loans, term life insurance
Moderates, school sex ed, toxic waste

## What's Not

Theater, rock concerts, country clubs, casinos
Tennis, jogging, skiing, sailing, reading
CD players, stereos, home gyms, convertibles
"Entertainment Tonight," "I Love Lucy," "Geraldo"
Jazz, rhythm & blues, classical, gospel, rap
*Money, New Woman, New Yorker, Bon Appetit*
Seafood, chili, corn on the cob, rice cakes, jam
Imported beer and wine, herbal tea, spring water
Nissan 300ZXs, Porsche 911s, BMW 6/7s, Acura NSXs
Investment property, precious metals, bonds
Liberals, legalizing drugs, gay rights

THIS CITY WAS BUILT on smokestack industries producing machinery, hardware, and tools. And even the 1980s recession that gave Rockford one of the nation's highest unemployment rates failed to shake the area's middle-class lifestyles. As in many factory towns, residents here are big on group activities: they belong to unions, play in bowling leagues, and attend Tupperware parties at higher-than-average rates. Local tastes prove a correlation between loud assembly-line work and things that make a lot of noise, such as motorcycles, muscle cars, and heavy metal music. Rockford is not a big market for more reflective pursuits like reading, attending plays, or listening to classical music, but residents do read magazines if the subject is home improvements, sewing ideas, and car repair. And while this congressional district gave birth to both liberal presidential candidate John Anderson and conservative President Ronald Reagan, Rockford mostly breeds moderates, in favor of protecting both the environment and the family.

| Middle-class industrial city | Predominantly white couples and families | High school educations | Manufacturing, transportation, and craft jobs |
|---|---|---|---|

### Key Demographics

| | | | |
|---|---|---|---|
| Total Population: | 425,676 | Primary Ages of Adults: | 25–44 |
| Median Household Income: | $33,604 | Median Home Value: | $63,233 |

# Sacramento-Stockton, California

## What's Hot

Theme parks, casinos, foreign travel, movies
Skiing, hiking, racquetball, bicycling, jogging
Radar detectors, charcoal grills, CD players
"Letterman," "Wonder Years," NBA Basketball
Modern and classic rock, easy listening
*Sunset, Golf Digest, New Woman, Shape*
Fish, yogurt, canned fruit, rice cakes, nuts
Domestic wine, spring water, vegetable juice
Subarus, Mazdas, Isuzus, Hondas, Saturn SCs
Investment property, mutual funds, gold cards
Conservatives, less government, school prayer

## What's Not

Fashion, home furnishing, sweepstakes, dieting
Hunting, knitting, tennis, walking, bowling
Microwaves, chain saws, pickups, cable TV
"Sally," "Family Matters," "Seinfeld"
Rhythm & blues, gospel, country, religious radio
*Soap Opera Digest, Prevention, Home Mechanix*
Cold cuts, beef stew, macaroni, biscuits, doughnuts
Cocoa, herbal tea, powdered drinks, milk
Ferraris, Buicks, Plymouths, Chryslers, Olds 98s
Medical insurance, Keoghs, home-improvement loans
Apolitical voters, legalizing drugs, gun control

THE FIRST SETTLERS to the area were miners joining the Gold Rush of 1849. Today's immigrants are more likely lawyers, lobbyists, or consultants, drawn to Sacramento's massive state government employment base and upscale lifestyle. Like other California boomtowns, this is an area where residents enjoy aerobic sports, such as jogging, skiing, and exercise, and high-tech electronics, including computers, camcorders, and CD players. Although the community lacks cultural outlets, residents do make up for it in their high rates of attending movies and gambling casinos across the Nevada border. At home, these Californians are into collecting antiques, restoring the area's many Victorian homes, and pursuing a local culinary passion. They're more likely than average Americans to be into gourmet cooking, baking from scratch, and buying health food. Despite California's reputation for inhabiting a political Left Coast, this market is filled with voters representing all ideological stripes and concerns.

| *Upper-middle-class commercial and government center* | *Ethnically diverse families and singles* | *Some college educations* | *Jobs in recreation, finance, and public administration* |
|---|---|---|---|

**Key Demographics**

| Total Population: | 3,094,929 | Primary Ages of Adults: | 25–44 |
|---|---|---|---|
| Median Household Income: | $35,827 | Median Home Value: | $142,301 |

# Salinas-Monterey, California

## What's Hot

Fine art, foreign travel, exercise, books
Jogging, camping, skiing, bicycling, tennis
CD players, PCs, 35mm cameras, radar detectors
"Letterman," "Simpsons," "Doogie Howser"
Easy listening, modern rock, classical, Spanish
*Architectural Digest, Forbes, Omni, Self*
Health food, sweet rolls, cheese, dried fruit
Domestic wine, imported beer, spring water
Rolls-Royces, Ferraris, Jaguars, Porsche 928s
Mutual funds, stocks, bonds, savings accounts
Liberals, abortion rights, toxic waste

## What's Not

Home furnishing, car repair, crafts, the Bible
Fishing, hunting, bowling, crossword puzzles
Tillers, Tupperware, lawn mowers, trucks, rifles
"Sally," "Guiding Light," "Family Matters"
Urban contemporary, rap, gospel, religious radio
*Woman's World, Sports Afield, Inc., True Story*
Macaroni, canned hash, beef stew, gum
Cocoa, milk, powdered drinks, tea
Oldsmobiles, Chevrolets, Pontiacs, Ford Tempos
Life insurance, home-improvement loans, Medicare
Moderates, death penalty, gun control

THIS MARKET ALONG California's central coast is a place of geographic extremes: from the fertile valley farms of Salinas to the rocky cliffs of the Monterey Peninsula. But most of the lifestyles in this area lean toward the upscale and are more reflective of the local village of Carmel, where ex-mayor Clint Eastwood presided over this retreat for millionaires. Residents comprise one of the nation's top markets for interest in fine art, photography, and theater. They have the money and taste to travel abroad, invest in real estate, and collect wine. Yet the local citizens also care about their health, buying health food at high rates as well as engaging in jogging, exercise, and bicycling. Given the area's dramatic scenery, it's no wonder residents are into camping, hiking, and boating more than average Americans. What is surprising, given the long distance to the nation's political centers, is the preoccupation with politics, influenced by the immigration of liberal boomers to the area. Political analysts call them "the Sierra Club calendar generation."

| *Upper-middle-class agricultural and resort area* | *Ethnically diverse singles and couples* | *College educations* | *Jobs in recreation, farming, and finance* |
|---|---|---|---|

**Key Demographics**

| Total Population: | 643,835 | Primary Ages of Adults: | 25–44 |
|---|---|---|---|
| Median Household Income: | $40,058 | Median Home Value: | $247,111 |

# Salisbury, Maryland

| What's Hot | What's Not |
|---|---|
| Fraternal orders, baking, collectibles, junk mail, pets | Theme parks, dancing, the arts, travel, PCs |
| Bicycling, fishing, knitting, crossword puzzles | Tennis, skiing, jogging, golf, exercise |
| Lawn mowers, recliners, 126/110 cameras, tillers | Food processors, radar detectors, motorcycles |
| BET, "Blossom," "Evening Shade," "Fresh Prince" | "Joan Rivers," "Married with Children," "Sisters" |
| Urban contemporary, country, religious radio | Golden oldies, jazz, classical, modern rock |
| *Outdoor Life, Seventeen, Family Handyman, Health* | *House & Garden, Money, Scientific American, GQ* |
| Seafood, chicken, corn on the cob, brownies, candy | Beef, cheese, Italian bread, pretzels, Wheaties |
| Malt liquor, powdered drinks, diet sodas, milk | Light beer, skim milk, wine, lemon-lime sodas |
| Chryslers, Lincolns, Pontiac Firebirds, Mazda 929s | Saturns, VWs, Jaguars, Audi 80/90s |
| Investment property, medical insurance, securities | Precious metals, IRAs, stocks, annuities, Keoghs |
| Conservatives, family values, school prayer | Liberals, consumerism, oil drilling |

CROSS THE CHESAPEAKE BAY to Maryland's Eastern Shore and time seems to slow down. Residents of Salisbury tend to farm, fish for crabs, and raise chickens much like their ancestors did — though tender entrepreneur Frank Perdue has industrialized the poultry business here. This is still a rural area, where self-sufficient locals like to boat, fish, garden, and do their own needlework. With nearly 40 percent of the populace either retirees or homemakers, daytime TV is popular, especially soaps and talk shows. And though booming Baltimore and Washington are only a few hours away, Salisbury residents display a striking lack of interest in art, theater, film, and music, and rarely head west for the cultural offerings. In this area, folks who want a night out may take in a country singer at a bar or head for the honky-tonk nightlife of nearby Ocean City. Otherwise, they gather for a church social or around the cable TV. Despite having once elected a gay Republican congressman, Robert Bauman, Salisbury voters tend to be conservative and down on gays, gun control, and consumerism.

| Middle-class trade center | Racially mixed singles and couples | High school educations | Manufacturing, farm, and transportation jobs |
|---|---|---|---|

### Key Demographics

| | | | |
|---|---|---|---|
| Total Population: | 259,127 | Primary Ages of Adults: | 55+ |
| Median Household Income: | $30,852 | Median Home Value: | $82,099 |

# Salt Lake City, Utah

| What's Hot | What's Not |
|---|---|
| Theme parks, baking, car repair, the Bible, RVs | Fashion, gourmet cooking, politics, dieting |
| Camping, skiing, hunting, golf, boating, crafts | Walking, coin collecting, collectibles, dancing |
| PCs, charcoal grills, camcorders, power tools | Microwaves, bedroom furniture, crossword puzzles |
| "Coach," "Roseanne," "Siskel & Ebert" | "American Detective," "In Living Color" |
| Golden oldies, soft rock, radio pro sports | Urban contemporary, Spanish, rhythm & blues, rap |
| *Country Living, Woman's World, Family Handyman* | *Esquire, Food & Wine, Barron's, New Yorker* |
| Mexican food, pizza, ice cream, pudding, Pop Tarts | Fried chicken, beef stew, rice, snack cakes |
| Skim milk, powdered drinks, Diet 7-Up | Orange juice, coffee, tea, wine, beer, brandy |
| GMC Safaris, Mitsubishi Mini-Vans, Chevy Geos | BMW 6/7s, Jaguar XJ6s, Mercedes-Benz 560s |
| Mutual funds, interest checking, auto loans | Medical insurance, Keoghs, bonds, stocks |
| Conservatives, pro-lifers, less government | Liberals, gay rights, legalizing drugs |

HEADQUARTERS OF THE Mormon Church, the Salt Lake City market encompasses most of Utah and is no place for those who enjoy a stiff drink while arguing the merits of liberal concerns. A confluence of young families and the dramatic Wasatch Front make this a sporting paradise: Nearly every known sport in the nation is pursued here at above-average rates, from boating and skiing to jogging and aerobics. The concentration of white-collar professionals and students makes Salt Lake City a prime market for computers, high-tech electronics, adult-education courses, and books (everything from science fiction to the Bible). With 40 percent of all households filled with children — far above the national average — locals are also into theme parks, video games, sneakers, and bulk food purchases; among the big sellers are puddings, American cheese, and pretzels. But Salt Lake City still lacks the cultural attractions of comparably sized cities, and residents display relatively little interest in fine art, antiques, and fashion. While there's money in town, little of it ends up in stocks, bonds, and real estate.

| Middle-class commercial center | Predominantly white families | Some college educations | Jobs in farming, mining, and education |
|---|---|---|---|

### Key Demographics

| | | | |
|---|---|---|---|
| Total Population: | 1,976,647 | Primary Ages of Adults: | 25–44 |
| Median Household Income: | $32,153 | Median Home Value: | $73,089 |

# San Angelo, Texas

## What's Hot

Veterans, cable TV, coin collecting, sewing, pets
Camping, fishing, hunting, knitting, gardening
Recliners, video games, lawn mowers, trucks, RVs
"American Gladiators," "Designing Women"
Country, adult contemporary, Spanish radio
*Sports Afield, Good Housekeeping, Sunset, Flying*
Beef, bacon, biscuits, canned vegetables, nuts
Vegetable juices, powdered drinks, light beer
Fords, Buicks, Mercurys, Subarus, Chevy Geos
Medical and life insurance, personal loans, CDs
Conservatives, family values, death penalty

## What's Not

Collectibles, plays, movies, travel, casinos
Skiing, golf, bicycling, exercise, tennis
Faxes, VCRs, CD players, radar detectors, PCs
"Hard Copy," "Geraldo," "Fresh Prince"
Jazz, classical, modern rock, folk, rap
*Changing Times, Playboy, Self, Parents*
Canned chicken, bagels, rice cakes, brownies
Rum, scotch, diet sodas, imported beer
Acuras, Volvos, Porsches, Sterlings, BMW 5s
Stocks, bonds, investment property, IRAs
Liberals, gun control, oil-drilling pollution

THIS CENTER FOR OIL and ranching still recalls its days as a rowdy frontier town in the late 19th century. Residents are more likely than average Americans to enjoy horseback riding, hunting, target-shooting, and rodeos. The pleasures of cosmopolitan America are hard to find; locals rarely attend movies, plays, or contemporary music concerts. With a lower-middle-class workforce, costly leisure activities like boating, skiing, and tennis fare poorly in San Angelo. And relatively few area consumers purchase high-tech electronics like computers, VCRs, and CD players. On the other hand, the older-than-average populace pursues traditional domestic activities with a vengeance. This is one of the nation's best markets for needlework, sewing, and knitting, and no wonder: San Angelo happens to be one of the nation's biggest producers of mohair.

| *Lower-middle-class* | *Ethnically mixed singles and couples* | *Less than high school educations* | *Jobs in farming, mining, and manufacturing* |
| --- | --- | --- | --- |

### Key Demographics

| | | | |
| --- | --- | --- | --- |
| Total Population: | 134,837 | Primary Ages of Adults: | 25–44 |
| Median Household Income: | $24,783 | Median Home Value: | $48,980 |

# San Antonio–Victoria, Texas

## What's Hot

Dancing, car repair, crafts, dogs, dieting
Camping, exercise, hunting, sewing, walking
Microwaves, cable TV, boom boxes, sofa beds
BET, "Simpsons," "Inside Edition," "Rescue 911"
Spanish, heavy metal, golden oldies, modern rock
*TV Guide, Vogue, Forbes, Harper's Bazaar*
Mexican food, canned vegetables, Lucky Charms
Spring water, colas, ales, milk, herbal teas
Hondas, Chryslers, Cadillacs, Nissan trucks
Savings accounts, mail-order life insurance
Liberals, toxic waste, big government

## What's Not

Gourmet cooking, skiing, books, theater, casinos
Gardening, tennis, boating, bicycling, knitting
Food processors, recliners, 35mm cameras, RVs
"Seinfeld," "Letterman," "Wide World of Sports"
Classical, soft rock, urban contemporary, country
*Popular Science, USA Today, Seventeen, Gourmet*
Sausage, tuna, pasta, pizzas, sweet rolls, nuts
Wine, skim milk, fruit drinks, light beer
Audis, Saabs, Subarus, Buicks, Plymouth trucks
Mutual funds, CDs, Keoghs, term insurance
Conservatives, school sex ed, gay rights

WITH A POPULATION that's 48 percent Hispanic, the San Antonio–Victoria market likely wouldn't top many lists as a middle-American community. Yet surveys reveal that the age breakdowns and lifestyle activities of many residents are close to the national average. Residents follow the U.S. norm when it comes to their interest in art, fashion, politics, and photography. They have average tastes in TV shows, tuning in to such shows as "60 Minutes," "Good Morning, America," and "In Living Color." To be sure, area families do have particular passions for Spanish media, Mexican food, crafts, and pets. And while relatively downscale socioeconomic levels put a crimp in new-car purchases, this is a strong market for improvement, whether that means repairing the car, renovating the house, or taking adult-education courses. Some market analysts consider this market the '90s version of Peoria.

| *Lower-middle-class* | *Ethnically diverse families and couples* | *Some college educations* | *Farm, transportation, and service jobs* |
| --- | --- | --- | --- |

### Key Demographics

| | | | |
| --- | --- | --- | --- |
| Total Population: | 1,822,062 | Primary Ages of Adults: | 25–44 |
| Median Household Income: | $27,271 | Median Home Value: | $59,016 |

# San Diego, California

## What's Hot

The arts, fashion, dancing, travel, health food
Jogging, exercise, camping, bicycling, tennis
Cassette decks, CD players, PCs, 35mm cameras
"Letterman," "Meet the Press," "Wonder Years"
Rock, classical, Spanish, folk, jazz
*Forbes, Scientific American, New Yorker, Vogue*
Cheese, canned chicken, waffles, croissants
Domestic wine, imported beer, spring water, rum
Porsches, Ferraris, Infinitis, BMW 3/5s
Investment property, precious metals, bonds
Liberals, legalizing drugs, gun control

## What's Not

Baking, TV sports, rodeos, crafts, car repair
Bowling, sewing, knitting, woodworking
Video games, power tools, lawn mowers, tillers
"Current Affair," "Family Feud," "Major Dad"
Adult contemporary, country, gospel, religious
*Colonial Homes, Woman's Day, Soap Opera Digest*
Ham, hot dogs, pasta, peanut butter, snack cakes
Powdered drinks, colas, milk, malt liquor, ale
Buicks, Dodges, Plymouths, Pontiac Bonnevilles
Home-improvement loans, life insurance, Medicare
Moderates, pro-lifers, death penalty

IT USUALLY PLAYS second fiddle to Los Angeles, but San Diego — smog-free, beach-filled, and leisurely paced — has a more-than-enviable lifestyle. With its high concentration of young singles, San Diego is a prime market for travel and fitness: residents are more likely than average Americans to belong to health clubs, eat health food, and enjoy outdoor sports like jogging, skiing, and tennis. A handful of local colleges attract an academic crowd who express a strong interest in science, politics, and high-tech electronics; they also buy the latest computers, cameras, and CD players at above-average rates. And with their upscale incomes and tastes, residents are big on attending rock concerts and casinos, plays and movies. The pleasant weather, with sunny skies 70 percent of the time, keeps most locals out of the house: San Diego is one of the nation's worst markets for domestic activities like sewing, knitting, and woodworking.

| *Upper-middle-class commercial center* | *Ethnically mixed singles* | *College educations* | *Jobs in finance and recreation* |
| --- | --- | --- | --- |

**Key Demographics**

| | | | |
| --- | --- | --- | --- |
| Total Population: | 2,653,089 | Primary Ages of Adults: | 25–44 |
| Median Household Income: | $39,872 | Median Home Value: | $205,937 |

# San Francisco–Oakland–San Jose, California

## What's Hot

Travel, the arts, exercise, gourmet cooking
Tennis, jogging, skiing, camping, sailing
Woks, PCs, CD players, food processors, faxes
"Siskel & Ebert," "Simpsons," "In Living Color"
Jazz, classical, modern rock, Broadway musicals
*Architectural Digest, Vanity Fair, Gourmet, GQ*
Chicken, rice cakes, fruit, Ben & Jerry's
Tomato juice, spring water, wine, imported beer
Acuras, Hondas, Mazdas, Infinitis, Jaguars
Stocks, AmEx cards, mutual funds, Keoghs
Liberals, gay and abortion rights, legalizing drugs

## What's Not

Wrestling, home workshops, rodeos, sewing, dogs
Bowling, fishing, horseback riding, hunting
Gardening tools, charcoal grills, Tupperware
Soaps, "Coach," "Current Affair," "Sally"
Religious radio, country, gospel, golden oldies
*Field & Stream, National Enquirer, McCall's*
Bacon, pizza, white bread, sausage, pudding
Cocoa, powdered drinks, cola, tea, milk
Chevrolets, Dodges, Mercurys, Oldsmobile 88s
Personal loans, mail-order life insurance
Moderates, death penalty, oil drilling

LIKE MANY OF AMERICA'S great port cities, San Francisco is a sprawling metropolis whose polyglot society is filled with recent immigrants from Asia and Central America. The concentration of college-educated and affluent residents contributes to a sophisticated consumer society that seeks out the latest trends in film, theater, and contemporary jazz. Compared to the general population, Bay Area residents tend to travel abroad — Europe is their most popular destination — drive foreign cars — Japanese over German — and purchase the latest-generation PCs and CD players. In contrast, they disdain such popular Middle American activities as going bowling, throwing Tupperware parties, listening to religious radio, and watching daytime soap operas. Known as a haven for hippies, lesbians, and gays, San Francisco is a center for liberalism and New Age spiritualism. One telling survey found that, although residents live in one of the wealthiest cities in America, they still reject the notion that money is the best measure of success; they find more satisfaction in personal fulfillment.

| *Upscale metropolis* | *Ethnically diverse singles and couples* | *College educations* | *White-collar executives and professionals* |
| --- | --- | --- | --- |

**Key Demographics**

| | | | |
| --- | --- | --- | --- |
| Total Population: | 6,132,898 | Primary Ages of Adults: | 25–44 |
| Median Household Income: | $47,836 | Median Home Value: | $283,374 |

# Santa Barbara—Santa Maria—San Luis Obispo, California

## What's Hot

Fine art, books, health food, bicycling, cats
Exercise, skiing, camping, sailing, racquetball
PCs, 35mm cameras, toaster ovens, weights, RVs
"Nightline," British Open, "Simpsons," "Cheers"
Classical, '40s–'60s pop, soft rock, folk
*Sunset, Smithsonian, Cycle World, Shape, Omni*
Fish, cheese, frozen yogurt, rice cakes, oat bran
Wine, light beer, vegetable juice, skim milk
Mercedes-Benzes, Ferraris, VW vans, Lexus SC3s
Mutual funds, stocks, interest checking, Keoghs
Liberals, ozone depletion, military cutbacks

## What's Not

Fashion, crafts, coin collecting, lotteries
Bowling, golf, fishing, hunting, sewing
Video games, power tools, tillers, trucks
"Geraldo," "Another World," "Fresh Prince"
Gospel, rhythm & blues, country, news radio
*TV Guide, Prevention, Inc., Jet, Seventeen*
Sausage, canned chicken, baked beans, doughnuts
Milk, tea, orange juice, Pabst, Coca-Cola
Chevrolets, Hyundais, Ford Tempos, Dodge Monacos
Term insurance, securities, life insurance
Conservatives, pro-lifers, gun control

FORGET THE AREA'S Spanish Revival buildings echoing the early 19th century, when California was ruled by Spain and Mexico. This resort market is thoroughly contemporary, with trendy, upscale lifestyles to match. Residents read books, see movies, and own computers all at high rates. With a number of local museums — and the Hearst Castle — residents can indulge their affection for fine art, antiques, photography, and cultural events. The high concentration of under-25-year-olds helps explain the local passion for outdoor fitness activities like jogging, skiing, bicycling, and tennis. And this sun-drenched coastal area is America's top market for purchasing health foods and vitamins. What locals lack is an appreciation of blue-collar pursuits, such as sewing, woodworking, and playing the lottery. And despite Santa Barbara's being Ronald Reagan's home district, area voters are liberal on many issues, strong supporters of consumerism, and big opponents of military involvement abroad.

| Upper-middle-class resort area | Ethnically mixed singles and couples | College educations | Jobs in education, business and recreation |
|---|---|---|---|

### Key Demographics

| | | | |
|---|---|---|---|
| Total Population: | 609,755 | Primary Ages of Adults: | 25–44 |
| Median Household Income: | $39,064 | Median Home Value: | $252,705 |

# Sarasota, Florida

## What's Hot

Domestic travel, stocks, golf, crossword puzzles
Bicycling, boating, walking, tennis, knitting
Microwaves, recliners, VCRs, convertibles
"Today," "Honeymooners," "Joan Rivers"
Folk, '40s–'60s pop, news-talk radio
*American Photo, Travel & Leisure, Barron's*
Chicken, pumpernickel, dried fruit, sour cream
Cold Duck, ground coffee, diet sodas, vodka
Rolls-Royces, Cadillacs, Jaguars, Lincolns
CDs, precious metals, bonds, Keoghs, Medicare
Conservatives, privacy rights, less government

## What's Not

Theme parks, casinos, movies, car repair, unions
Hiking, jogging, skiing, gardening, racquetball
Boom boxes, condoms, calculators, cigarettes
"Letterman," "Roseanne," "Night Court"
Rap, rock, rhythm & blues, gospel, country
*Ebony, Outdoor Life, Popular Mechanics, Glamour*
Pork, chili, American cheese, pizza, breath mints
Powdered drinks, milk, lemon-lime soda
Eagles, Plymouths, Subarus, Hyundais, Chevrolets
Loans, money orders, term insurance, savings bonds
Liberals, gay rights, oil-drilling pollution

IF YOU HAVE ANY DOUBT that America's current crop of retirees is the wealthiest and most active in history, check out Sarasota. Boasting a median age of 61, this Gulf Coast market is geared toward elderly consumers who enjoy the finer things in life. Culturally speaking, residents are into books and plays but not movies and classical concerts. In terms of sports, they like boating and bicycling but not hunting and skiing. They have the money to travel, enjoy gourmet restaurants, and look for money-making opportunities; indeed, this is the nation's best market for investing in stocks and bonds. But while these Americans are supposedly slowing down, they show a surprising lack of interest in domestic pursuits like collecting stamps, making crafts, and gardening. Indeed, their only nod to sedentary activities seems to be a fondness for crossword puzzles. Sarasota is number one among all markets when it comes to working the small squares.

| Middle-class retirement area | Predominantly white couples and singles | Some college educations | Jobs in finance, entertainment, and business |
|---|---|---|---|

### Key Demographics

| | | | |
|---|---|---|---|
| Total Population: | 293,341 | Primary Ages of Adults: | 65+ |
| Median Household Income: | $34,522 | Median Home Value: | $96,533 |

# Savannah, Georgia

## What's Hot | What's Not

| What's Hot | What's Not |
|---|---|
| Baking, fashion, veterans, wrestling, the Bible | Travel, art, casinos, movies, health clubs |
| Hunting, bicycling, tennis | Skiing, bowling, golf, camping, woodworking |
| Cable TV, mobile homes, tillers, trucks | PCs, CD players, microwaves, Tupperware, books |
| "Oprah," "American Gladiators," "Rescue 911" | "Simpsons," "Tonight Show," "Empty Nest" |
| Country, gospel, rhythm & blues, urban contemporary | Jazz, classical, rock, heavy metal |
| *Jet, Essence, Southern Living, Field & Stream* | *Newsweek, House Beautiful, Money, Mademoiselle* |
| Seafood, beef stew, corn on the cob, grits, pies | TV dinners, beef, yogurt, chocolate, raisin bread |
| Tea, powdered drinks, milk, diet soda, Tab | Spring water, cocktails, wine, beer, skim milk |
| Nissan Stanzas, Ford Festivas, Dodge pickups | Infiniti Q45s, Alfa Romeo 164s, Lexus ES250s |
| Money orders, medical insurance, securities | Savings bonds, mutual funds, IRAs, annuities |
| Conservatives, pro-lifers, death penalty | Liberals, military cutbacks, endangered animals |

SETTLED MORE THAN 250 years ago, Savannah today is an industrial city with a backward glance. Although paper mills and chemical plants have replaced tobacco- and cotton-farming as important industries, area residents still behave like farm families, enjoying fishing, hunting, and baking at above-average rates. Local military installations have attracted young servicemen who've popularized owning muscle cars and watching TV sports. A populace that's nearly one-third African American also results in high rates for subscribing to *Jet, Ebony,* and *Essence,* along with listening to rap, rhythm & blues, and jazz; Savannah has a number of clubs that feature big band, bebop, and contemporary jazz. Unlike downscale markets where residents save money by baking from scratch, consumers here like to bake as well as enjoy gourmet cuisine, especially at the local seafood restaurants. In this part of the South, residents take their cooking and religion seriously; more than one-quarter of the residents regularly read the Bible.

| Lower-middle-class industrial port | Racially mixed singles and families | High school educations | Manufacturing, farm, and transportation jobs |
|---|---|---|---|

### Key Demographics

| | | | |
|---|---|---|---|
| Total Population: | 675,235 | Primary Ages of Adults: | 25–44 |
| Median Household Income: | $27,499 | Median Home Value: | $65,144 |

# Seattle–Tacoma, Washington

## What's Hot | What's Not

| What's Hot | What's Not |
|---|---|
| Health clubs, the arts, travel, photography | Fashion, home furnishing, dieting, wrestling |
| Racquetball, camping, skiing, bicycling | Bowling, tennis, walking, fishing, hunting |
| PCs, CD players, VCRs, radar detectors, books | Tupperware, cable TV, tillers, crafts, trucks |
| TV golf, "Simpsons," "Wonder Years," "Coach" | "Hard Copy," "Family Feud," "Sally" |
| Modern rock, classical, jazz, folk | Gospel, urban contemporary, Spanish radio |
| *Omni, Architectural Digest, Self, Forbes* | *National Enquirer, Seventeen, TV Guide, Jet* |
| Imported cheese, canned chicken, popcorn | Baked beans, American cheese, snack cakes |
| Rum, vodka, spring water, wine, ground coffee | Cola, milk, powdered drink, orange juice |
| Audis, Lexuses, Infinitis, Toyota Landcruisers | Plymouth Horizons, Dodge Monacos, Suzuki Samarais |
| Annuities, mutual funds, precious metals, IRAs | Home-improvement loans, Medicare, money orders |
| Liberals, gay rights, consumerism, toxic waste | Moderates, family values, buying American |

ONCE AN INDUSTRIAL CITY swarming with loggers and shipbuilders, Seattle today is a thoroughly white-collar metropolis, a sleepless, high-rise boomtown fueled by employers like Microsoft, Boeing, and Nordstroms. Locals have the money to enjoy the "good life": traveling abroad, enjoying gourmet cuisine — especially espresso from numerous coffee bars — and investing in stock, bonds, and real estate at some of the highest rates in the nation. This is a great market in which to be a spectator, with three major-league teams and more than a dozen professional theaters and orchestras. The high concentration of young singles has even created a thriving grunge music scene (celebrated in the movie *Singles*), as well as busy jogging trails, fitness clubs, and nearby ski slopes. Opinion polls show residents to be of the brie-and-chablis set, supporters of gay rights, legalizing drugs, and consumer activism. Still, life is tempered somewhat by the rainy, drizzly weather that socks in Seattle for nearly eight months of the year. In this market, residents are 50 percent more likely to own cats than dogs, the more accommodating of housebound pets.

| Upper-middle-class metropolis | Predominantly white singles and couples | College educations | White-collar jobs in finance and public administration |
|---|---|---|---|

### Key Demographics

| | | | |
|---|---|---|---|
| Total Population: | 3,800,790 | Primary Ages of Adults: | 25–44 |
| Median Household Income: | $36,663 | Median Home Value: | $118,644 |

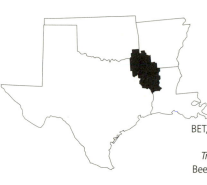

# Shreveport, Louisiana–Texarkana, Arkansas–Texarkana, Texas

## What's Hot

Rodeos, junk mail, crafts, the Bible, dogs
Fishing, hunting, gardening, sewing, knitting
Cable TV, rifles, chain saws, RVs
BET, soaps, "Geraldo," "Family Matters," "Cosby"
Country, gospel, rap, religious radio
*True Story, Ebony, Sports Afield, Woman's World*
Beef, canned hash, stew, chili, sweet rolls, crackers
Tea, powdered drinks, milk, malt liquor
Chevy Camaros, Pontiac Firebirds, Ford Mustangs
Money orders, medical insurance, personal loans
Conservatives, school prayer, oil drilling

## What's Not

The arts, movies, casinos, lotteries, unions
Skiing, bowling, tennis, golf, collectibles
VCRs, microwaves, food processors, PCs
"Doogie Howser," "Joan Rivers," "In Living Color"
Modern rock, jazz, classical, folk
*Business Week, Food & Wine, Discover, Self*
TV dinners, canned tuna, pumpernickel, oatmeal
Wine, draft beer, skim milk, ground coffee
Peugeot 505s, Acura Legends, Saab 900s, BMW 5s
Stocks, mutual funds, money-market accounts
Liberals, ocean dumping, gay rights

THE LIFESTYLE OF Shreveport-Texarkana is like a Southern gumbo — filled with disparate ingredients not always blending together. The local populace includes rowdy oil workers as well as fundamentalist Baptists, and their combined passions range from raucous rodeos and heavy metal music to religious radio and Bible reading. Living on the border of Ark-La-Tex, many householders behave like Old West ranch families, tending to pursue activities like fishing, hunting, gardening, and sewing. With below-average incomes, there's not a lot of money to pursue upscale activities like buying designer clothes, seeing plays, or collecting fine art — nor do residents have the cultural inclination to travel to big cities to enjoy these cosmopolitan offerings. While they buy few new cars at above-average rates, the ones they do purchase are testosterone laden. In this area, status is having a fast horse or a souped-up muscle car.

| *Lower-middle-class industrial area* | *Racially diverse singles and couples* | *Less than high school educations* | *Transportation, farm, and manufacturing jobs* |
|---|---|---|---|

**Key Demographics**

| | | | |
|---|---|---|---|
| Total Population: | 998,126 | Primary Ages of Adults: | 55+ |
| Median Household Income: | $22,584 | Median Home Value: | $48,590 |

# Sioux City, Iowa

## What's Hot

Baking, golf, veterans, sewing, grandchildren
Walking, bowling, fishing, hunting, woodworking
Power tools, recliners, cable TV, motorcycles
Morning news, "Northern Exposure," World Series
Country, '40s–'60s pop, adult contemporary
*Mother Earth News, Reader's Digest, McCall's*
Ham, canned soup, baked beans, Jell-O, Trix
Light beer, lemon-lime soda, tomato juice
Oldsmobiles, Buicks, Ford Festivas, Chevy K2500s
Medical insurance, CDs, home-improvement loans
Moderates, family values, death penalty

## What's Not

Movies, casinos, travel, book clubs, theater
Racquetball, tennis, sailing, weight training
VCRs, CD players, cameras, PCs, cassette players
"American Gladiators," "Hard Copy," "Star Trek"
Rock, rhythm & blues, classical, rap, jazz
*Life, Bon Appetit, Cosmopolitan, Forbes*
Fish, rice, French bread, waffles, yogurt
Wine, imported beer, milk, tea, orange juice
Porsches, Acuras, Volvo 960s, Toyota Previas
IRAs, Keoghs, stocks, bonds, precious metals
Liberals, endangered animals, nuclear waste

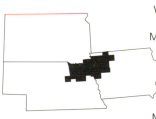

ONCE A THRIVING market town on the Great Plains, Sioux City has been in slow decline for most of this century. Downtown stores have fled to suburban shopping malls, and the waterfront no longer hums with the activity of boatmen and stockyard workers. Sioux City is still home to farmers and those who ship agricultural products, but the population is aging; half the adults are over 50 years old, and residents are more likely than average Americans to collect stamps and work crossword puzzles. They tend to avoid strenuous aerobic activities in favor of sports like bowling, golf, and fishing. With only working-class incomes, there's not the money for a vibrant nightlife, and locals have a comparatively low rate of seeing movies, going to casinos, and traveling outside the area. Indeed, they're more likely to bake at home than blow the bucks on a gourmet meal. They even fail to get too excited over politics: local congressman Fred Grandy, who once played Gopher on "The Love Boat," has described himself as a "knee-jerk moderate."

| *Lower-middle-class agricultural trade center* | *Predominantly white families and couples* | *High school educations* | *Farm and transportation jobs* |
|---|---|---|---|

**Key Demographics**

| | | | |
|---|---|---|---|
| Total Population: | 417,359 | Primary Ages of Adults: | 55+ |
| Median Household Income: | $25,733 | Median Home Value: | $41,987 |

# Sioux Falls–Mitchell, South Dakota

| What's Hot | What's Not |
|---|---|
| Rodeos, fishing, fraternal orders, crafts | Fashion, books, health clubs, lotteries, rap |
| Hunting, knitting, bicycling, bowling | Skiing, tennis, exercise, jogging, swimming |
| Cable TV, calculators, charcoal grills | VCRs, 35mm cameras, CD players, faxes |
| Game shows, "Major Dad," "Full House," "Coach" | "Hard Copy," "Seinfeld," "Married with Children" |
| Country, adult contemporary, ethnic radio | Jazz, classical, rhythm & blues, modern rock |
| *Outdoor Life, Family Handyman, Woman's Day* | *People, New Yorker, Barron's, Rolling Stone* |
| Ham, sausage, biscuits, canned fruit, pies | Spaghetti, aerosol cheese, TV dinners, yogurt |
| Light beer, ground coffee, tea, skim milk | Imported beer, orange juice, cocktails, scotch |
| Oldsmobiles, Buicks, Pontiacs, Subaru Justys | Volvos, Infinitis, Saabs, Ferraris, Acura Vigors |
| Liability insurance, CDs, home-improvement loans | Precious metals, stocks, gold cards, mutual funds |
| Moderates, pro-lifers, toxic waste | Liberals, consumerism, gun control, gay rights |

YOU'D THINK THAT the largest market in a state would be a magnet for culture and commerce, a place where one could go out on a shopping spree, have a fancy meal, or take in a show. Not so, Sioux Falls–Mitchell. This agricultural shipping center has low rates for interest in the arts, literature, live music, and dance. In contrast, residents are big on outdoor activities like hunting, fishing, gardening, and camping; there are 170 parks and recreation areas across the state. And folks can indulge their passion for sewing, knitting, and woodworking — all done at above-average rates — while occasionally taking time off to visit the Enchanted World Doll Museum in Mitchell (filled with dolls ranging from Shirley Temple to Princess Di). Although residents don't have the money to travel, buy high-tech electronics, or invest in the stock market, they do share one trait with other big cities: clubs. In this area, almost everyone seems to belong to a fraternal order, veterans club, or business group. And that's where locals go for nightlife.

| *Lower-middle-class farm center* | *Predominantly white couples and singles* | *High school educations* | *Jobs in farming and transportation* |
|---|---|---|---|

| **Key Demographics** | | | |
|---|---|---|---|
| Total Population: | 583,583 | Primary Ages of Adults: | 55+ |
| Median Household Income: | $25,238 | Median Home Value: | $45,066 |

# South Bend–Elkhart, Indiana

| What's Hot | What's Not |
|---|---|
| Home decorating, art, unions, Tupperware, VCRs | Foreign travel, health clubs, rock concerts |
| Fishing, golf, bicycling, bowling, gardening | Sailing, skiing, walking, jogging, reading |
| Lawn mowers, video games, motorcycles | CD players, PCs, dining room furniture |
| Soaps, "Regis & Kathie Lee," "Northern Exposure" | "Donahue," "America's Most Wanted" |
| Country, adult contemporary, golden oldies | Jazz, modern rock, classical, rap, gospel |
| *McCall's, TV Guide, Outdoor Life, Home Mechanix* | *Cosmopolitan, Smithsonian, Time, Barron's* |
| Cold cuts, peanut butter, pizza, pudding, Trix | TV dinners, chili, canned chicken, raisin bread |
| Fruit juice, colas, diet sodas, ground coffee | Ale, scotch, orange juice, spring water, wine |
| Pontiacs, Chevrolets, Dodges, Eagle Summits | Mazdas, VWs, Saabs, Porsche 928s |
| Christmas clubs, life insurance, auto loans | Mutual funds, Keoghs, money-market accounts |
| Moderates, privacy rights, death penalty | Liberals, gun control, legalizing drugs |

DECADES OF PLANT CLOSINGS have taken the bloom off industrial cities like South Bend and Elkhart. But the sprouting of new companies on the countryside — including the nation's largest maker of mobile homes — has allowed the area to retain its middle-class status. Locals here are big on bowling and golf, power tools and collectibles. This is one of the few markets where folks still speak of unions with pride, and American nameplates dominate the car-buying market. Although Notre Dame is located here, South Bend–Elkhart is not a center for intellectual pursuits like science, electronics, politics, and the arts normally found in college communities. Indeed, residents have only average rates for reading books and are comparatively weak subscribers of magazines like *Smithsonian, Time,* and *Scientific American.* The biggest connection many locals have to the nation's most famous Roman Catholic college is rooting for the Fighting Irish sports teams.

| *Middle-class industrial market* | *Predominantly white families and couples* | *High school educations* | *Crafts, manufacturing, and farm jobs* |
|---|---|---|---|

| **Key Demographics** | | | |
|---|---|---|---|
| Total Population: | 820,955 | Primary Ages of Adults: | 25–44 |
| Median Household Income: | $31,525 | Median Home Value: | $57,617 |

# Spokane, Washington

## What's Hot          What's Not

| What's Hot | What's Not |
|---|---|
| Mall shopping, rodeos, photography, motorcycles | Movies, tennis, travel, theater, dieting |
| Skiing, fishing, horseback riding, camping, sewing | Bowling, exercise, walking, racquetball |
| Microwaves, chain saws, recliners, power boats | CD players, PCs, VCRs, cable TV, sofa beds |
| "Tonight Show," "Roseanne," "Jeopardy" | "Primetime Live," "Family Feud," "Joan Rivers" |
| Golden oldies, country, middle-of-the-road | Urban contemporary, classical, soft rock |
| *Field & Stream, Reader's Digest, Redbook* | *Vogue, Financial World, Food & Wine, Jet* |
| Mexican food, pizza, sausage, pudding, Wheaties | Canned hash, English muffins, frozen yogurt |
| Draft beer, powdered drinks, skim milk, tea | Imported wine and beer, milk, malt liquor |
| Subarus, Chryslers, Chevy Celebritys, Dodge Colts | Alfa Romeos, Sterlings, BMWs, Volvo 740/760s |
| CDs, loans, investment property, mutual funds | Bonds, gold cards, stocks, precious metals |
| Moderates, nuclear waste, family values | Liberals, ocean dumping, consumerism |

POLITICAL ANALYSTS HAVE DESCRIBED Spokane as an island of Middle America in a barren desert, yet its consumer tastes have a decidedly Western flavor. Residents are more likely than average Americans to enjoy woodworking, gardening, sewing, and knitting. Surrounded by wild rivers and northern prairies, locals are also big on outdoor sports, such as camping, fishing, hunting, and skiing — along with related products, such as cameras, RVs, and sport/utility vehicles. You won't find the yuppified tastes of cities like Seattle here in eastern Washington: Spokane residents have relatively little interest in the arts, travel, health food, and high-tech electronics. And though this is the home district of Thomas Foley, Democratic Speaker of the House, it is by no means a liberal bastion. Residents support school prayer and family values, and they're laissez-faire on environmental concerns, except when the issue is nuclear waste. Living so close to the leaky Hanford nuclear weapons facilities, who can blame them?

| *Lower-middle-class commercial center* | *Predominantly white families and couples* | *Some college educations* | *Jobs in farming, forestry, and mining* |
|---|---|---|---|

**Key Demographics**

| | | | |
|---|---|---|---|
| Total Population: | 876,623 | Primary Ages of Adults: | 25–44 |
| Median Household Income: | $26,452 | Median Home Value: | $60,462 |

# Springfield, Massachusetts

## What's Hot          What's Not

| What's Hot | What's Not |
|---|---|
| Gourmet cooking, videos, the arts, lotteries | Junk mail, baking, the Bible, convertibles |
| Skiing, golf, exercise, tennis, walking | Gardening, target shooting, hunting, fishing |
| Stereos, toaster ovens, CD players, woks | Microwaves, PCs, RVs, chain saws, sofa beds |
| "Primetime Live," "Golden Girls," "Cheers" | Morning news, "Dinosaurs," "Santa Barbara" |
| Rock, rap, heavy metal, talk radio | Classical, country, folk, rhythm & blues |
| *Parade, Working Mother, Life, Sports Illustrated* | *House Beautiful, Playboy, Essence, Outdoor Life* |
| Fish, salad, spaghetti sauce, canned fruit | Mexican food, sausage, beef stew, corn on the cob |
| Milk, domestic beer, imported wine, orange juice | Tea, powdered drinks, decaf coffee, diet soda |
| Hyundais, Eagles, Plymouths, Peugeots, Ford Tempos | Volvos, Infinitis, BMWs, Mercedes-Benz 300s |
| Savings bonds, interest checking, money orders | Mutual funds, Keoghs, precious metals, stocks |
| Moderates, military cutbacks, buying American | Conservatives, legalizing drugs, less government |

THINK OF SPRINGFIELD, MASS., as a bygone town that's made some concessions to the future. Its aging textile mills and recently launched high-tech firms cumulatively result in a healthy middle-class lifestyle. Thanks to three symphony orchestras and a half-dozen art museums, residents attend cultural events at rates far above the national average. With several colleges nearby, recent graduates pursue a shared interest in travel, photography, and politics. Springfield is the birthplace of basketball, and locals watch a lot of professional teams on TV. But the mix of blue- and white-collar workers creates political ambiguity. Folks around here may describe themselves as moderates, but they're the insular sort who hate big government, defense spending, and even foreign products.

| *Middle-class industrial city* | *Predominantly white singles* | *College educations* | *Service, transportation, and manufacturing jobs* |
|---|---|---|---|

**Key Demographics**

| | | | |
|---|---|---|---|
| Total Population: | 675,907 | Primary Ages of Adults: | 25–44 |
| Median Household Income: | $36,044 | Median Home Value: | $136,821 |

# Springfield, Missouri

### What's Hot

Crafts, sewing, rodeos, veterans, the Bible
Fishing, gardening, woodworking, knitting
Charcoal grills, power tools, mobile homes
"Wheel of Fortune," "Miss America," "Blossom"
Country, gospel, heavy metal, religious radio
*Country Living, True Story, Sports Afield*
Bacon, baked beans, biscuits, American cheese
Cocoa, tomato juice, powdered drinks, milk
Mercurys, Pontiacs, Chryslers, Dodge trucks
Medical insurance, personal loans, securities
Conservatives, school prayer, pro-lifers

### What's Not

Foreign travel, fashion, theme parks, plays
Tennis, skiing, bicycling, jogging, bowling
Radar detectors, CD players, 35mm cameras
"Letterman," "Honeymooners," "Doogie Howser"
Rap, modern rock, soft rock, classical
*Bon Appetit, Essence, Mademoiselle, Esquire*
Canned tuna, rice cakes, rye bread, yogurt
Imported beer, skim milk, cocktails, ale
Hondas, Mazdas, Acuras, Cadillacs, VW vans
Annuities, savings bonds, stocks, mutual funds
Liberals, ozone depletion, gun control

HERE'S SOMETHING OF AN ODDITY: a booming market without bright city lights, white-collar industry, or cosmopolitan allure. In fact, Springfield, Mo., is one of the Midwest's fastest-growing areas precisely because it offers residents quiet mountains, dam-made lakes, and some of the nation's best traditional country music at the clubs in nearby Bransom. As the Gateway to the Ozarks, Springfield offers locals, many of whom are retirees, plenty of opportunity to pursue outdoor sports like camping, fishing, hunting, and boating. They also have the time to enjoy domestic activities like woodworking, sewing, and needlecraft. This is no place for visitors with interests in art, theater, or the latest foreign films. Indeed, the pleasures of Springfield are old-fashioned and Old South: bacon and biscuits, rodeos and religious fundamentalism.

| Lower-middle-class retirement resort | Predominantly white couples | High school educations | Craft, construction, and farm jobs |
| --- | --- | --- | --- |

## Key Demographics

| | | | |
| --- | --- | --- | --- |
| Total Population: | 850,985 | Primary Ages of Adults: | 55+ |
| Median Household Income: | $22,761 | Median Home Value: | $52,375 |

# Springfield-Decatur-Champaign, Illinois

### What's Hot

Clubs, books, cable TV, adult-ed courses
Swimming, bicycling, woodworking, gardening
Microwaves, Tupperware, tillers, motorcycles
NCAA basketball, "Major Dad," "Blossom"
Classic rock, country, '40s–'60s pop, folk
*Redbook, Popular Science, National Geographic*
Ham, canned soup, cheese, popcorn, dried fruit
Vegetable juice, draft beer, lemon-lime soda
Olds 88s, Subaru Loyales, Chevy Luminas
Education loans, CDs, first mortgages
Moderates, privacy rights, school sex ed

### What's Not

Gourmet cooking, travel, theater, skiing, RVs
Tennis, racquetball, jogging, exercise, sailing
CD players, PCs, sofa beds, convertibles
"Family Feud," "Geraldo," "Beverly Hills, 90210"
Classical, jazz, rhythm & blues, gospel
*Inc., Architectural Digest, Psychology Today*
TV dinners, canned chicken, rye, cookies
Milk, wine, imported beer, orange juice
Nissan Maximas, Peugeot 405s, BMW 318s
Homeowners insurance, precious metals, bonds
Liberals, death penalty, legalizing drugs

TALK ABOUT A HODGEPODGE: this tri-city market in Illinois is composed of a state capital (Springfield), a college town (Champaign), and a factory city (Decatur). The result is a hard-to-pin-down lifestyle where residents tend to behave occasionally like other middle-class communities — going to shopping malls, taking adult-education courses, and belonging to a variety of clubs — and at other times like working-class towns with little affection for fashion, fine art, or travel. Many locals share a fondness for outdoor sports, such as camping, boating, hunting, and golf. With the nearest big city, Chicago, more than 100 miles away, residents are more likely to make do with closer-to-home entertainment such as state fairs and fraternal lodge parties. And while everyone claims some connection with the area's most famous son, Republican President Abraham Lincoln, this is a moderate-Democratic area, where big government remains popular for helping local farmers.

| Middle-class state capital and farm region | Predominantly white singles | High school educations | Farm, education, and transportation jobs |
| --- | --- | --- | --- |

## Key Demographics

| | | | |
| --- | --- | --- | --- |
| Total Population: | 937,222 | Primary Ages of Adults: | 25–44 |
| Median Household Income: | $29,378 | Median Home Value: | $52,718 |

# St. Joseph, Missouri

| What's Hot | What's Not |
|---|---|
| Collectibles, veterans programs, grandchildren | Dancing, movies, casinos, health clubs, travel |
| Bowling, walking, fishing, hunting, knitting | Jogging, exercise, skiing, tennis, bicycling |
| Cable TV, charcoal grills, recliners, tillers | Toaster ovens, PCs, CD players, VCRs |
| CNN, USA, "Unsolved Mysteries," "Full House" | "Joan Rivers," "Married with Children," "Cops" |
| Country, heavy metal, adult contemporary | Jazz, rhythm & blues, heavy metal, rap |
| *Field & Stream, Ladies' Home Journal, Parents* | *Smithsonian, GQ, Ebony, Fortune, Gourmet* |
| Beef stew, American cheese, dried fruit, Jell-O | Fast food, canned chicken, rice cakes, waffles |
| Tomato juice, powdered drinks, tea, milk | Light beer, orange juice, wine, skim milk |
| Chevrolets, Buicks, Oldsmobiles, Dodge Daytonas | Acuras, Jaguars, Saabs, Audis, Infiniti M30s |
| Medical insurance, CDs, personal loans | Stocks, savings bonds, precious metals, IRAs |
| Moderates, privacy rights, pro-lifers | Liberals, consumerism, school sex ed |

ONCE THE HOME OF the Pony Express, St. Joseph still retains some of the Old West flavor in the above-average popularity of horseback riding, rodeos, and target shooting. But St. Joe today is mostly known as a manufacturing town for chemicals, processed food, and beer. The local blue-collar workers are into fishing, hunting, and bowling. With a high concentration of retirees, locals have popularized sedentary domestic activities like sewing, knitting, and working crossword puzzles. For exercise, they're big on walking through the many local parks and maintaining the numerous Romanesque homes. This is the nation's top market for collectibles, and activities like gardening and woodworking aren't far behind. In contrast to its former reputation as an 18th-century party town — attracting the likes of Buffalo Bill Cody and Jesse James — St. Joseph now is a more sedate community where residents express relatively little interest in dancing or designer fashions. Opinion polls confirm that locals have virtually no interest in keeping up with new styles.

| *Lower-middle-class manufacturing city* | *Predominantly white couples and singles* | *High school educations* | *Farm, transportation, and craft jobs* |
|---|---|---|---|

**Key Demographics**

| | | | |
|---|---|---|---|
| Total Population: | 118,815 | Primary Ages of Adults: | 55+ |
| Median Household Income: | $23,833 | Median Home Value: | $40,319 |

# St. Louis, Missouri

| What's Hot | What's Not |
|---|---|
| Home improvement, bowling, lotteries, unions | Art, gourmet cooking, movies, health clubs, cats |
| Swimming, golf, gardening, fishing, woodworking | Jogging, skiing, sailing, racquetball, hiking |
| Video games, VCRs, food processors, Tupperware | CD players, microwaves, cable TV, RVs |
| "Nightline," "Another World," "Dinosaurs" | "In Living Color," "Murphy Brown," "Rescue 911" |
| Folk, '40s–'60s pop, golden oldies, radio baseball | Rap, gospel, classical, jazz, modern rock |
| *Colonial Homes, Popular Mechanics, Redbook* | *Business Week, Photography, Self, Vanity Fair* |
| Beef, BBQ sauce, canned fruit, rye, popcorn, Trix | Health food, chili, corn on the cob, croissants |
| Powdered drinks, vegetable juice, Cold Duck | Herbal tea, imported beer, wine, milk |
| Chryslers, Lincolns, Cadillacs, Dodge Shadows | VWs, Mazdas, Acuras, Toyota Passeos |
| Stocks, savings bonds, first mortgages, loans | Annuities, Keoghs, term insurance, securities |
| Moderates, endangered animals, school prayer | Liberals, legalizing drugs, military cutbacks |

LOCATED NEAR THE NATION'S geographic midpoint, St. Louis seems to straddle the nation's varied sensibilities, a blend of big-city and small-town ways. This is a market where residents are more likely than average Americans to read *Popular Science* as well as the *Star*, invest in stocks as well as lottery tickets, and drive luxury Cadillacs as well as modest Dodge Shadows. With a varied economy based on beer, banking, machinery, and defense, residents have the time and middle-class incomes to enjoy domestic travel, weekend golfing, and fishing trips. But while the city has an impressive collection of museums and trendy restaurants, locals have relatively little interest in fine art, theater, and classical music. They're keener on local attractions, such as the National Bowling Hall of Fame and the Anheuser-Busch plant (world's largest brewery). In St. Louis, heaven is a night of beer and bowling.

| *Middle-class commercial metropolis* | *Predominantly white families and singles* | *High school educations* | *Service, transportation, and craft jobs* |
|---|---|---|---|

**Key Demographics**

| | | | |
|---|---|---|---|
| Total Population: | 2,955,782 | Primary Ages of Adults: | 25–44 |
| Median Household Income: | $33,541 | Median Home Value: | $71,267 |

# Syracuse, New York

## What's Hot / What's Not

| What's Hot | What's Not |
|---|---|
| Home furnishing, golf, books, videos, cats | Theater, casinos, wrestling, vitamins, junk mail |
| Bowling, boating, skiing, camping, woodworking | Sailing, racquetball, exercise, sewing |
| PCs, food processors, lawn furniture, microwaves | CD players, sofa beds, stereos, auto tools |
| "Northern Exposure," "Roseanne," "20/20" | "Murder, She Wrote," "Hard Copy" |
| Middle-of-the-road, golden oldies, folk, classic rock | Classical, jazz, rhythm & blues, gospel |
| *1001 Home Ideas, Parade, Field & Stream, TV Guide* | *Time, Working Woman, Consumer's Digest, Forbes* |
| Beef, macaroni, pizza, pretzels, pudding | Chili, canned chicken, rice, frozen yogurt |
| Skim milk, powdered drinks, light beer, vodka | Brandy, scotch, lemon-lime soda, spring water |
| Subarus, Dodges, Oldsmobiles, Pontiac Sunbirds | Acuras, Ferraris, BMWs, Cadillac Sevilles |
| Loans, savings accounts, CDs, Sears cards | Stocks, Keoghs, bonds, investment property |
| Moderates, ozone depletion, military cutbacks | Liberals, gun control, gay rights |

SYRACUSE IS SOMETHING of a classic: an Average American city with median incomes and home values, and ages hovering around the nation's midpoint. With the presence of Syracuse University, a number of industrial jobs, and several large high-tech firms, area lifestyles tend to be youthful and upscale. Residents are more likely than the general population to be into books and videos, as well as to express an interest in art, politics, and literature. And yet, locals are also involved in a number of leisure sports that reflect working-class lifestyles: Syracuse is a prime market for golf, boating, and bowling. When it comes to domestic pursuits, area residents mirror the tastes of average Americans in their fondness for sewing, crafts, dieting, crossword puzzles, and middle-of-the-road music. And no one should be surprised how Syracuse voters describe themselves politically: moderates, of course.

| *Middle-class manufacturing center* | *Predominantly white singles and families* | *High school educations* | *Craft and service jobs* |
|---|---|---|---|

## Key Demographics

| | | | |
|---|---|---|---|
| Total Population: | 1,080,506 | Primary Ages of Adults: | 25–44 |
| Median Household Income: | $33,091 | Median Home Value: | $81,246 |

# Tallahassee, Florida–Thomasville, Georgia

## What's Hot / What's Not

| What's Hot | What's Not |
|---|---|
| Home furnishing, college sports, pets, junk mail | Movies, theme parks, casinos, car repair, unions |
| Walking, fishing, hunting, gardening | Skiing, golf, bowling, swimming, coin collecting |
| Cable TV, mobile homes, charcoal grills, tillers | Food processors, CD players, home gyms, cameras |
| "Family Feud," "American Gladiators," "Cosby" | "Siskel & Ebert," "Face the Nation," "Joan Rivers" |
| Rhythm & blues, rap, gospel, urban contemporary | Contemporary pop, jazz, modern rock, golden oldies |
| *Southern Living, Ebony, Outdoor Life, Cycle World* | *Money, Stereo Review, Cosmopolitan, Tennis* |
| Beef stew, biscuits, spaghetti, doughnuts, grits | Take-out, cheese, raisin bread, waffles, yogurt |
| Tea, powdered drinks, milk, cola, orange juice | Tomato juice, cocktails, ground coffee, light beer |
| Isuzus, Nissan Stanzas, Cadillac Broughams | Ferraris, Peugeot 405s, Mercedes-Benz 560s |
| Medical insurance, money orders, personal loans | Annuities, savings bonds, mutual funds, Keoghs |
| Conservatives, pro-lifers, less government | Moderates, school sex ed, endangered animals |

DESPITE BEING THE state capital of one of the nation's largest states, Tallahassee remains, like Thomasville across the Florida-Georgia border, an overgrown farmer's market. Residents are conservative Bible-belters who care about keeping up their homes, listen to religious radio, and enjoy domestic activities like sewing and woodworking at high rates. The rural portrait would be complete except that two huge universities — Florida State and Florida A&M — give this market a collegiate feel. Residents are big on self-help activities, signing up for career-oriented seminars, pursuing graduate degrees, and watching college sports on television. Still, this is the land of Dixie when it comes to politics, a place where locals support family values and the pro-life movement, while opposing gays, drugs, and many environmental concerns.

| *Lower-middle-class farm and government area* | *Racially diverse singles* | *Less than high school educations* | *Jobs in farming, manufacturing, and services* |
|---|---|---|---|

## Key Demographics

| | | | |
|---|---|---|---|
| Total Population: | 552,213 | Primary Ages of Adults: | 25–44 |
| Median Household Income: | $26,478 | Median Home Value: | $63,726 |

# Tampa–St. Petersburg, Florida

## What's Hot

Gourmet cooking, bus travel, TV sports, clubs
Swimming, boating, bicycling, walking
Cable TV, microwaves, recliners, crossword puzzles
"Love Connection," "Nightline," "Evening Shade"
Gospel, '40s–'60s pop, easy listening, talk radio
*Gourmet, Weight Watchers, Prevention, Health*
Dried fruit, canned vegetables, oat bran, crackers
Tomato juice, tea, decaf coffee, scotch
Cadillacs, Lincolns, Jaguars, Mercedes-Benz 350s
Medicare, CDs, precious metals, bonds, gold cards
Moderates, school prayer, legalizing drugs

## What's Not

Rodeos, rock concerts, movies, health clubs
Camping, hunting, jogging, skiing, exercise
Lawn mowers, VCRs, PCs, charcoal barbecues
"Letterman," "Seinfeld," "Fresh Prince"
Rhythm & blues, modern rock, contemporary pop
*Mademoiselle, Family Handyman, Business Week*
Macaroni, frozen pizza, snack cakes, Pop Tarts
Imported wine and beer, lemon-lime soda, Tab
Saabs, Subarus, Audis, Alfa Romeo 164s
IRAs, credit lines, savings bonds, term insurance
Liberals, gun control, nuclear waste disposal

SOME COMMUNITIES SEEM easiest to describe by what they're not: For instance, Tampa–St. Petersburg is not a cosmopolitan market filled with nightclubs, museums, or chichi boutiques; it's not a wilderness resort offering camping, hiking, or hunting; nor is it a child-rearing sprawl where locals are into theme parks and backyard barbecuing. No, this Gulf Coast area is mostly a retirement haven (despite Tampa's role as a business city), where half of all household heads are over 53 years old. The most popular sports are walking, bicycling, and boating — not to mention just watching others engage in sports on television. Although the median income of all households is modest at around $29,000, the elderly locals have managed to accumulate assets and can afford to travel abroad, frequent gourmet restaurants, and buy luxury cars; Cadillacs and Lincolns are the most popular new-car nameplates. Once declared the healthiest place in America — and the setting for the movie *Cocoon* — St. Petersburg is, not surprisingly, one of the nation's best markets for vitamins, health foods, and publications like *Prevention* and *Health*.

| Lower-middle-class metropolis | Predominantly white singles and couples | High school educations | Jobs in health care and services |
|---|---|---|---|

| **Key Demographics** | | | |
|---|---|---|---|
| Total Population: | 3,017,044 | Primary Ages of Adults: | 65+ |
| Median Household Income: | $29,096 | Median Home Value: | $76,750 |

# Terre Haute, Indiana

## What's Hot

Veterans groups, motorcycles, grandchildren, pets
Gardening, bowling, fishing, hunting, sewing
Power tools, video games, collectibles, RVs
Morning news, "Young & Restless," "Current Affair"
Country, middle-of-the-road, gospel, golden oldies
*Redbook, Country Living, Outdoor Life, Parents*
Ham, baked beans, American cheese, pies, nuts
Cocoa, ground coffee, powdered drinks, skim milk
Oldsmobiles, Pontiacs, Buicks, Dodge Spirits
Medical insurance, personal loans, CDs
Moderates, family values, death penalty

## What's Not

Dancing, the arts, fashion, health clubs, casinos
Racquetball, tennis, skiing, exercise, jogging
PCs, VCRs, home gyms, convertibles, CD players
"Joan Rivers," "Married with Children"
Jazz, folk, rap, rhythm & blues, soft rock
*Financial World, Vanity Fair, Car & Driver*
Canned chicken, Italian bread, chocolates
Herbal tea, brandy, scotch, vodka, wine, milk
Acuras, Porsches, Lexuses, VW Cabriolets
Mutual funds, IRAs, annuities, precious metals
Liberals, military cutbacks, gay rights

IT'S EARLY TO BED and early to rise in Terre Haute. In this blue-collar community, three of the top-rated TV shows are morning news programs from the three networks, followed by a number of daytime soaps enjoyed by the high concentration of retirees and homemakers. By contrast, this is no place for night owls: residents are less likely than the general population to enjoy movies, plays, dance clubs, or late-night TV shows. And while Terre Haute is popularly known as the home of Indiana State University, the relatively small percentage of students have only a marginal effect on this market. More important are the 44 percent of all adults who are over 55 years old, who make this a prime area for crafts, collectibles, needlecraft, and crossword puzzles. Like many political districts in Indiana, Terre Haute is filled with right-of-center moderates who oppose environmentalists, consumer advocates, and gay rights activists.

| Lower-middle-class commercial center | Predominantly white singles and couples | High school educations | Farm, craft, and transportation jobs |
|---|---|---|---|

| **Key Demographics** | | | |
|---|---|---|---|
| Total Population: | 414,948 | Primary Ages of Adults: | 55+ |
| Median Household Income: | $24,997 | Median Home Value: | $39,425 |

# Toledo, Ohio

## What's Hot | What's Not

| What's Hot | What's Not |
|---|---|
| Mall shopping, TV sports, theme parks, unions | Plays, rock concerts, foreign travel, fashion |
| Bowling, bicycling, boating, golf, knitting | Exercise, jogging, skiing, racquetball, walking |
| Radar detectors, video games, cameras, crafts | CD players, microwaves, toaster ovens, stereos |
| Indianapolis 500, "Coach," Super Bowl | "Jeopardy," "Donahue," "Doogie Howser," "Loving" |
| Golden oldies, adult contemporary, country | Jazz, classical, urban contemporary, gospel |
| *Home Mechanix, Field & Stream, Family Circle* | *Time, Scientific American, Harper's Bazaar* |
| Frozen pizzas, french fries, rye bread, pudding | Chili, rice, canned chicken, sweet rolls, yogurt |
| Vegetable juice, cocktails, ground coffee | Orange juice, wine, imported beer, herbal tea |
| Chevy Cavaliers, Pontiac Sunbirds, Dodge Spirits | Mitsubishi Sigmas, Toyota Supras, Infiniti M30s |
| Life insurance, CDs, first mortgages, auto loans | Stocks, bonds, investment property, mutual funds |
| Moderates, toxic waste, military cutbacks | Liberals, gun control, oil drilling |

THE AUTO INDUSTRY helped turn Toledo into an industrial powerhouse — that is, until the oil crisis of the '70s. Since then, Toledo has recast itself with nonfactory jobs, although it's never quite reclaimed the stable, middle-class status of the boom years. Like the James Rouse Portside Festival Marketplace that went belly-up in 1990, consumer patterns here reflect an American Dream gone bust. Surveys show that residents enjoy no "good-life" activities at above-average rates: not fashion, the arts, or gourmet cooking. Locals don't have the incomes to get into high-tech electronics, such as computers, CD players, and camcorders. Toledo is still a strong market for sports like bowling, golf, and fishing. And area folks still enjoy domestic activities like woodworking, sewing, and gardening. But when they want to refurbish their homes, they do it themselves. And after they've had their made-in-USA cars a few years, they fix them up rather than trade them in on new models. Toledo is no place to open a new dealership for luxury imports.

| Lower-middle-class industrial city | Predominantly white families and singles | High school educations | Jobs in manufacturing, crafts, and transportation |
|---|---|---|---|

## Key Demographics

| | | | |
|---|---|---|---|
| Total Population: | 1,105,583 | Primary Ages of Adults: | 25–44 |
| Median Household Income: | $32,380 | Median Home Value: | $61,970 |

# Topeka, Kansas

## What's Hot | What's Not

| What's Hot | What's Not |
|---|---|
| State fairs, dancing, baking, car repair | Politics, health food, movies, gourmet cooking |
| Horseback riding, fishing, hunting, knitting | Camping, boating, skiing, tennis, bowling |
| Power tools, food processors, crafts, tillers | PCs, CD players, weights, convertibles |
| "Major Dad," "Full House," "Designing Women" | "Primetime Live," "Sisters," "Cops," "Simpsons" |
| Country, '40s–'60s pop, soft rock, folk, gospel | Jazz, rhythm & blues, classical, rap |
| *Outdoor Life, Woman's Day, Reader's Digest* | *Glamour, Photography, Food & Wine, Fortune* |
| Mexican food, canned vegetables, pudding, nuts | Cold cuts, canned tuna, rice, raisin bread |
| Powdered drinks, light beer, diet soda, skim milk | Spring water, wine, imported beer, orange juice |
| Subarus, Buicks, Oldsmobiles, Dodge Dynastys | Volvos, Saturns, Peugeots, Alfa Romeo 164s |
| Medical insurance, home-improvement loans, CDs | Homeowners insurance, stocks, Keoghs, IRAs |
| Conservatives, family values, privacy rights | Liberals, consumerism, gun control |

AS A MARKET, Kansas's state capital owes more to the surrounding farmlands than the downtown capitol building. More blue-collar than white-collar, residents here are less likely than average Americans to express an interest in politics, technology, or the arts; they attend movies, plays, and concerts — whether it's rock or classical music — at below-average rates. Nor are they big on foreign travel, gourmet cooking, or designer fashions. Located halfway between the college towns of Lawrence and Manhattan, Topeka seems to have abdicated any literary pretensions. While residents take adult education courses at above-average rates, they have low rates for buying books, reading newspapers, or subscribing to arts or political magazines. Like nearby farmers, these Kansans get their information on sunrise TV news shows.

| Middle-class industrial state capital | Predominantly white singles and couples | High school educations | Farm, transportation, and service jobs |
|---|---|---|---|

## Key Demographics

| | | | |
|---|---|---|---|
| Total Population: | 417,470 | Primary Ages of Adults: | 25–44 |
| Median Household Income: | $28,188 | Median Home Value: | $53,212 |

# Traverse City–Cadillac, Michigan

## What's Hot

Home workshops, boating, mobile homes, crafts
Skiing, hunting, camping, fishing, knitting
Lawn furniture, recliners, Tupperware, RVs
"Price Is Right," "Guiding Light," "Cheers"
Country, adult contemporary, golden oldies
*Mother Earth News, McCall's, Home Mechanix*
Baked beans, American cheese, canned fruit
Cocoa, ground coffee, tea, powdered drinks
Oldsmobiles, Pontiacs, Cadillac Broughams
Medical insurance, investment property, CDs
Moderates, nuclear waste, pro-lifers

## What's Not

Fashion, fine art, travel, books, lotteries
Jogging, sailing, exercise, tennis, racquetball
Cable TV, toaster ovens, PCs, CD players
"Dinosaurs," "Blossom," "David Brinkley"
Soft rock, rhythm & blues, classical, rap
*Ebony, Sunset, New Yorker, Cosmopolitan*
TV dinners, canned hash, croissants, waffles
Diet Coke, Heineken, imported wine, milk
VWs, Audis, Volvos, Mazda RX-7s
Stocks, mutual funds, annuities, IRAs
Liberals, ozone depletion, endangered animals

ONE OF THE PREMIERE resort areas in Michigan, the Traverse City–Cadillac market is considered a sporting paradise to many tourists across the Midwest. There are few communities boasting a higher percentage of residents into hunting, fishing, skiing, and boating. The smooth-sand beaches, cherry orchards, and national forests attract RVs throughout the summer months as well as year-round retirees who are big on knitting, crafts, and crossword puzzles. Although residents have only modest incomes — they're twice as likely as average Americans to live in mobile homes — they do believe in being financially protected. This is a prime market for medical, life, and disability insurance.

| *Lower-middle-class resort area* | *Predominantly white couples* | *High school educations* | *Farm, transportation, and craft jobs* |
|---|---|---|---|

## Key Demographics

Total Population: 497,142
Median Household Income: $25,016
Primary Ages of Adults: 55+
Median Home Value: $52,789

# Tucson, Arizona

## What's Hot

Books, dancing, travel, the arts, health food
Camping, exercise, jogging, bicycling, walking
Home gyms, CD players, PCs, 35mm cameras
"Simpsons," "Letterman," "Face the Nation"
Rock, classical, middle-of-the-road, heavy metal
*Shape, Scientific American, People, Barron's*
Mexican food, chicken, cheese, sweet rolls
Imported beer, domestic wine, herbal tea
Porsches, Saabs, Audis, VWs, Nissan 300ZXs
Interest checking, bonds, mutual funds, CDs
Liberals, abortion rights, wilderness protection

## What's Not

Home decorating, gourmet cooking, wrestling
Boating, skiing, fishing, hunting, tennis
Recliners, chain saws, power tools, tillers
"Sally," "Hard Copy," "Designing Women"
Gospel, country, rhythm & blues, religious radio
*Prevention, Popular Mechanics, 1001 Home Ideas*
Hot dogs, canned hash, sausage, Twinkies
Powdered drinks, orange juice, lemon-lime soda
Pontiacs, Oldsmobiles, Chevrolets, Ford Probes
First mortgages, personal loans, money orders
Conservatives, gay rights, school sex ed

A MIX OF COLLEGE STUDENTS and retirees helps Tucson appear to live beyond its means. Despite lower-middle-class incomes, residents share the consuming patterns of upscale yuppies. They travel, invest in stocks, see movies, and buy computers at high rates. And the University of Arizona also attracts a literate crowd, making Tucson one of the nation's top markets for reading books as well as such magazines as the *New Yorker, Architectural Digest*, and *Smithsonian*. The dry, sunny weather and desert landscape also lure tourists and health fans who come for the camping, hiking, and touring by RV. Republican gerrymandering turned most of this downscale area Democrat, leaving affluent conservatives in other districts. Yet this is still an area of moderate views where supporting environmental issues is almost a given but backing gay rights is not.

| *Lower-middle-class college and retirement town* | *Ethnically diverse singles and couples* | *Some college educations* | *Jobs in recreation, business, and services* |
|---|---|---|---|

## Key Demographics

Total Population: 841,955
Median Household Income: $27,689
Primary Ages of Adults: 25–44
Median Home Value: $81,599

# Tulsa, Oklahoma

| What's Hot | What's Not |
|---|---|
| Baking, rodeos, fast food, crafts, the Bible | Dancing, fashion, travel, movies, book clubs |
| Fishing, hunting, sewing, gardening, camping | Skiing, walking, bicycling, golf, racquetball |
| Grills, video games, power tools, recliners | Home gyms, toaster ovens, PCs, CD players |
| "Coach," "Am.'s Funniest Home Videos," "Cops" | "Wonder Years," "Married with Children," "Nightline" |
| Country, religious, heavy metal, ethnic radio | Jazz, comedy, rhythm & blues, modern rock |
| *Health, Family Handyman, Field & Stream* | *GQ, Business Week, Food & Wine, Ebony, Shape* |
| Beef, pork & beans, chili, crackers, pie, nuts | Chicken, canned tuna, French bread, Häagen-Dazs |
| Ground coffee, tomato juice, diet soda, Kool-Aid | Cocktails, wine, imported beer, ale |
| Dodge Daytonas, Pontiac Grand Ams, Chevy Berettas | Peugeot 405s, Volvo 740s, Hyundai Sonatas |
| Personal loans, life insurance, Medicare | IRAs, mutual funds, precious metals, gold cards |
| Conservatives, school prayer, family values | Liberals, gun control, legalizing drugs |

YOU CAN THANK the citizens of Tulsa for the McRib sandwich. As a midsize city with age demographics close to the national average, Tulsa is often used as a test market for new products, especially fast food because of the above-average rate of commuters in the area. Tulsa was once an oil boomtown and cultural center, but hard times have emptied the downtown area, and some nifty Art Deco architecture can't hide the fact that residents today live like working-class Bible-Belters. Indeed, religion is taken seriously in a town where Oral Roberts built his church headquarters — not to mention a college and hospital — and the local *Tulsa Press* runs a regular feature on church news called "Pew View." Locals pursue rustic pleasures like fishing, camping, and hunting in the woods and lakes of the nearby Ozarks. Inside their homes, woodworking, sewing, and needlework are popular. One of the nation's more conservative cities — it has consistently voted for Republican presidential candidates for five decades — residents back school prayer, family values, and free markets. Around here, multinational oil corporations are not considered the enemy.

| *Lower-middle-class midsize city* | *Ethnically diverse couples and families* | *Some college educations* | *Jobs in farming, transportation, and crafts* |
|---|---|---|---|

## Key Demographics

| Total Population: | 1,186,701 | Primary Ages of Adults: | 35–54 |
|---|---|---|---|
| Median Household Income: | $26,462 | Median Home Value: | $55,233 |

# Tuscaloosa, Alabama

| What's Hot | What's Not |
|---|---|
| Job seminars, cable TV, book clubs, junk mail | Health clubs, casinos, the arts, unions, golf |
| Camping, fishing, target shooting, water skiing | Snow skiing, bowling, bicycling, weight training |
| Rifles, Tupperware, video games, gardening tools | CD players, power tools, VCRs, 35mm cameras |
| USA Cable, "Current Affair," "In Living Color" | "60 Minutes," "America's Most Wanted," "Letterman" |
| Gospel, urban contemporary, religious radio | Easy listening, classical, jazz, all-news radio |
| *Essence, Southern Living, Sports Afield, Us* | *Newsweek, Travel & Leisure, Tennis, Forbes* |
| Beef stew, canned vegetables, pizza, doughnuts | Beef, canned tuna, cheese, pumpernickel, Jell-O |
| Tea, milk, orange juice, cola, cocoa | Spring water, wine, beer, skim milk, Tab |
| Chevrolets, Isuzus, Mazda 626s, Eagle Summits | Porsches, Sterlings, Acura NSXs, Audi 100/200s |
| Medical insurance, home improvement loans | Annuities, CDs, interest checking, Keoghs |
| Conservatives, less government, death penalty | Moderates, gay rights, military cutbacks |

HOW DO YOU EXPLAIN a market where attending job seminars and state fairs are both at above-average rates? In the case of Tuscaloosa, residents happen to live in a college town (the University of Alabama being the indigenous campus) in the heart of the Deep South. Consuming patterns are somewhat divided between student interests — like college sports, video games, and high-tech electronics — and those of older, blue-collar residents, who still appreciate the age-old pursuits of hunting, fishing, and listening to gospel music. Together, residents share a fondness for serious couch potatoism: they rank second in the nation for enjoying cable TV and watching TV in general — no doubt, they tune in to every game played by the powerhouse Crimson Tide teams. But the town's citizenry is divided another way: more than one-quarter of the residents are African American, and there's little racial mixing outside public places. The popularity of the Democratic Party notwithstanding, though, in this area there runs a strong conservative streak.

| *Lower-middle-class college town* | *Racially mixed singles* | *College educations* | *Service, craft, and manufacturing jobs* |
|---|---|---|---|

## Key Demographics

| Total Population: | 158,268 | Primary Ages of Adults: | 18–34 |
|---|---|---|---|
| Median Household Income: | $26,015 | Median Home Value: | $66,150 |

# Twin Falls, Idaho

| What's Hot | What's Not |
|---|---|
| Antiques, casinos, books, photography, pets, RVs | Politics, fashion, frequent flying, dieting |
| Camping, bicycling, skiing, gardening | Jogging, tennis, boating, bowling, exercise |
| Camcorders, chain saws, recliners, motorcycles | PCs, cable TV, VCRs, radar detectors |
| Evening news, "Coach," "Family Matters" | HBO, "General Hospital," "Star Trek" |
| Country, golden oldies, adult contemporary | Modern rock, urban contemporary, classical |
| *Outdoor Life, Ladies' Home Journal, Cycle World* | *Self, Money, Rolling Stone, New Yorker* |
| Pork & beans, biscuits, dried fruit, ice cream | Pasta, canned hash, waffles, rye, cookies |
| Decaf coffee, powdered drinks, light beer | Ale, imported wine, tea, milk, diet soda |
| Dodge pickups, Chevy Luminas, Oldsmobile 98s | Suzuki Sidekicks, Acura Legends, Jaguar XJSs |
| Investment property, medical insurance, auto loans | Savings accounts, bonds, securities, Visa cards |
| Moderates, school prayer, death penalty | Liberals, endangered animals, ocean dumping |

THIS IS POTATO COUNTRY, a small town in the center of Idaho's agricultural region, where residents are three times as likely as average Americans to work on farms and twice as likely to live in mobile homes. Accordingly, consuming patterns reflect a resourceful populace. This is one of the nation's best markets for hunting, fishing, and gardening. With Idaho's northern wilderness areas only a short drive away, citizens have also made Twin Falls one of America's hotbeds for camping and snow skiing as well as for owning recreational vehicles and motorcycles. The arrival of urban migrants, drawn to the country lifestyle and traditional family values, has also meant an increase in the popularity of books, photography, and antiques. Most of all, the convergence of farms, wilderness, and small-town living has made Twin Falls a place where locals take pride in their homes and domestic activities — and a prime market for pets. Both cats and dogs no doubt pull their weight on the farm.

| *Lower-middle-class farm town* | *Predominantly white couples and families* | *Some college educations* | *Jobs in farming, construction, and transportation* |
|---|---|---|---|

### Key Demographics

| | | | |
|---|---|---|---|
| Total Population: | 88,182 | Primary Ages of Adults: | 35–54 |
| Median Household Income: | $24,392 | Median Home Value: | $49,776 |

# Tyler-Longview-Jacksonville, Texas

| What's Hot | What's Not |
|---|---|
| Veterans groups, car repair, roses, baking | Photography, the arts, travel, gourmet cooking |
| Walking, hunting, fishing, gardening, sewing | Bicycling, bowling, skiing, exercise, tennis |
| Cable TV, video games, microwaves, recliners | Food processors, PCs, CD players, 35mm cameras |
| Game shows, "Fresh Prince," "Cheers," "Sally" | "Letterman," "Face the Nation," "Empty Nest" |
| Gospel, country, heavy metal, urban contemporary | Modern rock, easy listening, jazz, classical |
| *National Enquirer, McCall's, Seventeen, TV Guide* | *Sports Illustrated, Changing Times, USA Today* |
| Chili, biscuits, canned vegetables, pizza, doughnuts | Fish, TV dinners, frozen yogurt, raisin bread |
| Tea, cocoa, milk, orange juice, cola, diet soda | Wine, skim milk, draft and domestic beer, ale |
| Chryslers, Dodges, Isuzus, Nissan Stanzas | Infinitis, Alfa Romeos, Acuras, Lexus LS400s |
| Money orders, whole life insurance, loans | Investment property, annuities, bonds, IRAs |
| Conservatives, less government, privacy rights | Liberals, gay rights, oil pollution |

AT ONE TIME back in the '30s, the land around Tyler was considered the richest oil ground in the nation. Millionaires sprang forth from their wildcat strikes. Today, many of the residents still work for oil-based industries, but the predominant lifestyle is working-class. In this part of Texas, folks are into rodeos, chewing tobacco, and country music at rates far above the national average. Thanks to the presence of local nurseries that grow roses for the national market, even the lowliest yards of Tyler explode each year with vibrant roses — which helps explain why gardening and walking are so popular among residents. With more than one-quarter of all household heads over 65 years old, this is an area with rightist leanings. The local congressman, Ralph Hall, has one of the most conservative records of any Democrat and was one of two Democrats to support expelling Barney Frank on ethics charges in 1990.

| *Lower-middle-class oil towns* | *Racially diverse couples* | *Some college educations* | *Mining, manufacturing, and transportation jobs* |
|---|---|---|---|

### Key Demographics

| | | | |
|---|---|---|---|
| Total Population: | 559,711 | Primary Ages of Adults: | 55+ |
| Median Household Income: | $25,040 | Median Home Value: | $54,355 |

# Utica, New York

## What's Hot | What's Not

| What's Hot | What's Not |
|---|---|
| Collectibles, unions, lotteries, puzzles, RVs | Foreign travel, movies, photography, casinos |
| Bowling, skiing, camping, woodworking | Tennis, exercise, jogging, racquetball, hiking |
| Lawn furniture, grills, 126/110 cameras, cable TV | PCs, VCRs, CD players, microwaves, stereos |
| "Evening Shade," "Classic Concentration," "Coach" | "Hard Copy," "I Love Lucy," "Siskel & Ebert" |
| Adult contemporary, classic rock, country | Gospel, '40s–'60s pop, modern rock, rhythm & blues |
| *Working Mother, Home Mechanix, Prevention, Star* | *Scientific American, Architectural Digest, Vogue* |
| Hot dogs, cold cuts, pasta, frozen potatoes, Trix | Chili, corn on the cob, canned chicken, grits |
| Tomato juice, tea, cocoa, ground coffee | Herbal tea, cocktails, imported beer, vodka |
| Plymouth Acclaims, Chevy Luminas, Mercury Topazes | VW Corrados, Audi 80/90s, Nissan 300ZXs, BMW 325s |
| Christmas clubs, whole life insurance, loans | Mutual funds, annuities, precious metals, bonds |
| Moderates, buying American, school prayer | Liberals, consumerism, gun control |

UTICA IS NO LONGER the thriving factory town it once was, but it still gets by manufacturing tools, textiles, and electronic equipment. The area's aging population, nearly 30 percent of which are over 65 years old, has comfortable lifestyles, thanks to sports facilities ranging from a minor-league baseball park to a harness racetrack. In fact, Utica citizens are more likely than average Americans to go to the track and bowling alley. As in other communities with a large number of seniors, activities like walking, coin collecting, and working crossword puzzles are all popular. The high school–educated residents show little passion for the arts, gourmet cooking, or foreign travel. But they do like to socialize at the local American Legion or during a weekend camping trip in their recreational vehicle. And they haven't forgotten their factory roots: when it comes to cars, beer, and cheese, this is made-in-America country.

| *Lower-middle-class manufacturing city* | *Predominantly white singles* | *High school educations* | *Service and transportation jobs* |
|---|---|---|---|

### Key Demographics

| | | | |
|---|---|---|---|
| Total Population: | 282,466 | Primary Ages of Adults: | 55+ |
| Median Household Income: | $28,276 | Median Home Value: | $74,235 |

---

# Waco-Temple-Bryan, Texas

## What's Hot | What's Not

| What's Hot | What's Not |
|---|---|
| Veterans groups, science fiction, wrestling, pets | Dancing, casinos, movies, health clubs, books |
| Jogging, horseback riding, hunting, fishing | Skiing, racquetball, boating, bowling, camping |
| Cable TV, auto tools, microwaves, mobile homes | Food processors, Tupperware, VCRs, 35mm cameras |
| TV sports, "Fresh Prince," "Nightline," "Sally" | "Hard Copy," "Wonder Years," "Letterman," "Loving" |
| Gospel, urban contemporary, country, heavy metal | Modern rock, soft rock, classical, jazz, pop |
| *Outdoor Life, True Story, Jet, Woman's World* | *Barron's, New Yorker, Psychology Today, Time* |
| Ham, beef stew, American cheese, biscuits, candy | Shellfish, canned chicken, pretzels, rye, yogurt |
| Powdered drinks, lemon-lime soda, light beer | Cocktails, spring water, domestic wine, Diet Coke |
| Pontiac Firebirds, Chevy Camaros, Jeep Cherokees | Acura Integras, Porsche 911s, Dodge Ram 50s |
| Medical insurance, loans, money orders, Medicare | Mutual funds, homeowners insurance, Keoghs, bonds |
| Conservatives, less government, school prayer | Moderates, gun control, military cutbacks |

IT WILL LIKELY BE some years before Americans stop associating Waco with the Branch Davidian compound, which was the site of one of the largest and most senseless mass killings in U.S. history. But some of the passions that gave rise to that tragedy continue to thrive here: a fondness for guns, fundamentalist religion, and don't-tread-on-me individualism. With the concentration of young singles in the area, due partly to the presence of Baylor University and the army's nearby Fort Hood, activities like jogging, watching TV sports, and listening to heavy metal music are popular. The Waco-Temple-Bryan market is also one of the best in the nation for veterans clubs and programs. Downscale incomes limit local interest in such "good-life" activities as the arts, fashion, travel, and gourmet cooking. But folks take their politics seriously. Once a Democratic stronghold — Governor Ann Richards is a Waco native — the local congressional district voted for George Bush in 1988 and has moved further to the right in recent years.

| *Lower-middle-class commercial cities* | *Racially and ethnically diverse singles* | *Some college educations* | *Jobs in education, manufacturing, and services* |
|---|---|---|---|

### Key Demographics

| | | | |
|---|---|---|---|
| Total Population: | 709,573 | Primary Ages of Adults: | 18–34 |
| Median Household Income: | $24,589 | Median Home Value: | $56,809 |

# Washington, D.C.

| What's Hot | What's Not |
|---|---|
| Politics, foreign travel, books, the arts | Crafts, casinos, mobile homes, sweepstakes, cats |
| Exercise, tennis, jogging, bicycling, skiing | Bowling, hunting, camping, fishing, sewing |
| PCs, woks, faxes, calculators, home gyms | Tillers, 126/110 cameras, recliners, microwaves |
| "In Living Color," "Letterman," "Meet the Press" | "Love Connection," "Major Dad," "Current Affair" |
| Classical, urban contemporary, folk, rock, jazz | Golden oldies, country, religious radio |
| *New Yorker, Money, Ebony, Smithsonian* | *Field & Stream, Soap Opera Digest, Star* |
| Bagels, fish, salad, cheese, yogurt, popcorn | Sausage, pork & beans, biscuits, doughnuts, Fritos |
| Wine, spring water, imported beer, scotch, rum | Powdered drinks, milk, lemon-lime soda, cocoa |
| Acuras, Hondas, Infinitis, BMWs, Saabs, Volvos | Pontiacs, Chevrolets, Oldsmobiles, Chryslers |
| Gold cards, stocks, mutual funds, bonds, Keoghs | Life insurance, first mortgages, money orders |
| Liberals, environmental concerns, consumerism | Moderates, death penalty, pro-lifers |

THE NATION'S CAPITAL is the kind of company town where the workers are button-down bureaucrats and the boss is a free-spending Uncle Sam. Washington residents stand near the top when it comes to brains (nearly two out of three have gone to college), bucks (half of all households earn more than $50,000 a year), and workaholics (there are more two-career couples here than anywhere else). And it ranks among the nation's best markets for interest in politics, computers, the arts, and foreign travel. With young singles drawn to the dozen area colleges and high-glamour, low-pay Capitol Hill jobs, Washington is also a haven for the athletic-minded, with high rates for exercise, jogging, tennis, and downhill skiing. Despite problems typical of most urban cores — crime, drug abuse, and illiteracy — the market takes its character from its affluent suburbs, where residents splurge on half-million-dollar-plus homes (three times the U.S. average) and drive luxury cars by BMW, Ferrari, and Mercedes-Benz. Politically, the area is a liberal stronghold, where environmentalists and consumer advocates are considered heroes. Socially, this is a conservative town, where, according to interior designers, the most requested piece of bedroom furniture is a good reading lamp.

| *Affluent metropolitan sprawl* | *Racially diverse singles* | *College educations* | *Jobs in business, education, and public administration* |
|---|---|---|---|

| **Key Demographics** | Total Population: | 4,911,402 | Primary Ages of Adults: | 25–44 |
|---|---|---|---|---|
| | Median Household Income: | $50,424 | Median Home Value: | $165,118 |

# Watertown-Carthage, New York

| What's Hot | What's Not |
|---|---|
| Home workshops, baking, recliners, cable TV | Movies, health clubs, business trips, lotteries |
| Bowling, boating, skiing, camping, walking | Swimming, hiking, bicycling, tennis, exercise |
| Tupperware, lawn mowers, 126/110 cameras | Toaster ovens, microwaves, PCs, stereos |
| "Evening Shade," "Regis & Kathie Lee," "Coach" | "Donahue," "Doogie Howser," "Wonder Years" |
| Country, adult contemporary, golden oldies | Modern rock, easy listening, urban contemporary |
| *Ladies' Home Journal, Family Handyman, Parents* | *Rolling Stone, Working Woman, GQ, Fortune* |
| Ham, nuts, pizza, canned fruit, sweet rolls | Canned hash, corn on the cob, French bread |
| Tomato juice, ground coffee, tea, Kool-Aid | Wine, malt liquor, ale, imported beer, Diet Coke |
| Mercurys, Buicks, Pontiacs, Dodges, Oldsmobiles | Porsches, Volvos, Alfa Romeos, Jaguars, BMWs |
| Medical insurance, home-improvement loans, CDs | Mutual funds, bonds, Keoghs, annuities |
| Moderates, family values, toxic waste disposal | Liberals, gay rights, military cutbacks |

MORE THAN A CENTURY AGO, Frank Woolworth launched the country's first discount retail chain from his home in Watertown. Today's residents, most of whom are working-class families with modest lifestyles, would certainly feel at home strolling the aisles of a Woolworth's. In this market, composed of a couple of small manufacturing cities surrounded by farms, locals consider the arts, designer clothes, and gourmet cooking expendable luxuries. They're do-it-yourselfers who work on their cars, do their own home improvements, and borrow their way to middle-class comfort. When it comes to sports, residents are into beer-based pursuits, such as bowling, boating, and fishing. For media, their tastes lean toward television — especially prime-time comedies and talk shows — as well as domestic magazines. With their proximity to the Canadian border, local malls draw "international" shoppers and boost the tourist trade. But area residents don't do much in the way of reciprocating. Their idea of fun is staying home and turning their houses into proletarian castles equipped with a full set of Tupperware and a massive bowling trophy display.

| *Lower-middle-class commercial cities* | *Predominantly white singles and families* | *High school educations* | *Jobs in farming, transportation, and crafts* |
|---|---|---|---|

| **Key Demographics** | Total Population: | 259,272 | Primary Ages of Adults: | 25–44 |
|---|---|---|---|---|
| | Median Household Income: | $28,193 | Median Home Value: | $54,786 |

# Wausau-Rhinelander, Wisconsin

| What's Hot | What's Not |
|---|---|
| Home workshops, bowling, adult-ed courses | Foreign travel, rock concerts, theater, lotteries |
| Fishing, hunting, camping, boating, gardening | Tennis, exercise, jogging, weight training |
| Microwaves, Tupperware, RVs, motorcycles, tools | PCs, VCRs, tape recorders, video games, stereos |
| TV baseball, "Wheel of Fortune," "Full House" | "Wonder Years," "All My Children," "Hard Copy" |
| Heavy metal, country, gospel, '40s–'60s pop | Rap, modern rock, rhythm & blues, classical |
| *Redbook, Country Living, Popular Mechanics* | *Newsweek, Cosmopolitan, Bon Appetit, Forbes* |
| Ham, beef stew, canned soup, pizza, pudding | Take-out, rice, canned chicken, English muffins |
| Cocoa, tomato juice, Cold Duck, light beer | Herbal tea, imported wine, orange juice, vodka |
| Chevy Celebritys, Dodge Spirits, Subaru Justys | VW Golfs, Mercedes-Benz 190s, Toyota MR2s |
| Medical and life insurance, CDs, auto loans | IRAs, stocks, mutual funds, savings bonds |
| Conservatives, pro-lifers, death penalty | Liberals, gun control, endangered animals |

TIMBERLANDS AND FARMS first attracted settlers to these central Wisconsin towns. But today Wausau-Rhinelander residents stay for the jobs in paper mills, small factories, or the local Wausau insurance company. The woods and lakes are still around, however, making this one of the nation's best markets for fishing, hunting, skiing, and camping. And like other aging blue-collar communities, this one eschews an interest in art, film, and theater for more domestic pursuits, such as needlework, crafts, and gardening. With more than 40 percent of all household heads over 55, the prime age group for do-it-yourselfers, this is "honey-do" country (as in "honey, do this, honey, do that"). Wausau-Rhinelander is the nation's second-best market for home workshops and one of the top for installing your own carpeting, spark plugs, and thermal windows. With all that hard work, it's no wonder that recliners are so hot in the area: the better to rest those weary backs with a beer in hand, a ball game on the TV.

| *Lower-middle-class trade centers* | *Predominantly white couples* | *High school educations* | *Jobs in forestry, transportation, and crafts* |
|---|---|---|---|

| **Key Demographics** | | | |
|---|---|---|---|
| Total Population: | 450,083 | Primary Ages of Adults: | 55+ |
| Median Household Income: | $28,888 | Median Home Value: | $54,389 |

# West Palm Beach–Ft. Pierce–Vero Beach, Florida

| What's Hot | What's Not |
|---|---|
| Frequent flying, stocks, politics, clubs, the arts | Crafts, gardening, baking, car repair, pets |
| Tennis, golf, bicycling, boating, skiing | Camping, bowling, hunting, jogging, fishing |
| Microwaves, cable TV, convertibles, books | Lawn mowers, calculators, video games |
| "Nightline," "Meet the Press," British Open | "Fresh Prince," "Roseanne," "Simpsons" |
| Classical, folk, easy listening, news-talk radio | Rap, rhythm & blues, gospel, heavy metal |
| *Sunset, Travel & Leisure, Gourmet, Forbes* | *Sports Afield, Parents, Ebony, Star, Us* |
| Health food, rye, dried fruit, oatmeal, cheese | Bacon, spaghetti, white bread, snack cakes |
| Domestic wine, cocktails, skim milk, diet soda | Milk, tea, powdered drinks, lemon-lime soda |
| Rolls-Royces, Jaguars, Mercedes-Benzes, Cadillacs | Chevrolets, Plymouths, Pontiacs, Eagles |
| Mutual funds, CDs, bonds, Keoghs, gold cards | Personal loans, money orders, whole life insurance |
| Conservatives, less government, military cutbacks | Moderates, ozone depletion, gay rights |

DON'T BE FOOLED by the median income and home value of this seemingly middle-class market. By virtue of the unbridled affluence of Palm Beach, playground for the Kennedys, British royalty, and tennis aces, this area has "hoity-toity" written all over it. It's one of the nation's best markets for gourmet cooking, stock investing, and frequent flying, as well as sports like tennis, boating, and golf — not to mention croquet and polo. Motorists get around in some of the costliest motor vehicles in the world; they're nearly three times as likely as average Americans to own Rolls-Royces, Jaguars, and Mercedes-Benzes. The area's collection of educated retirees — half of all residents are over 55 — are big on current affairs, crossword puzzles, and financial publications. And even the presence of downscale minorities working in service jobs cannot turn this into an acceptable market for staples like powdered drinks, processed food, and power tools. As for the local political streak, the maxim holds that the more you have to conserve, the more conservative you become. These cranky folks dislike government, gays, and environmental advocates.

| *Middle-class* | *Predominantly white couples* | *College educations* | *Jobs in health, finance, and recreation* |
|---|---|---|---|

| **Key Demographics** | | | |
|---|---|---|---|
| Total Population: | 1,328,834 | Primary Ages of Adults: | 65+ |
| Median Household Income: | $36,433 | Median Home Value: | $104,466 |

# Wheeling, West Virginia–Steubenville, Ohio

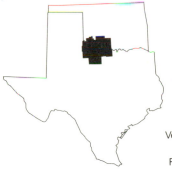

| What's Hot | What's Not |
|---|---|
| Pro wrestling, crossword puzzles, car repair, dogs | Movies, concerts, health clubs, travel, fashion |
| Gardening, bowling, woodworking, fishing, hunting | Jogging, skiing, sailing, racquetball, tennis |
| Radar detectors, cable TV, Tupperware, powerboats | CD players, smoke detectors, 35mm cameras |
| Soaps, "Regis & Kathie Lee," "Evening Shade" | "Doogie Howser," "Honeymooners," "Letterman" |
| Heavy metal, adult contemporary, golden oldies | Rhythm & blues, classical, rap, classic rock |
| *Prevention, Home Mechanix, Family Circle* | *People, Omni, Vanity Fair, Business Week* |
| Pork & beans, frozen potatoes, biscuits, doughnuts | TV dinners, chili, corn on the cob, raisin bread |
| Vegetable juice, cola, powdered drinks, skim milk | Herbal tea, imported wine and beer, Tab |
| Chevy Luminas, Buick Centurys, Dodge Omnis | Acura Vigors, Porsche 940s, BMW 5s, Volvo 780s |
| Whole life insurance, loans, savings accounts | IRAs, annuities, stocks, precious metals |
| Moderates, toxic waste disposal, death penalty | Liberals, gun control, endangered animals |

IN THIS REGION, once one of the wealthiest coal areas in the country, the collapse of coal prices in the 1980s has led to steep population declines. Today, Wheeling-Steubenville is a working-class market where residents toil in factories and wind down in the rugged wilderness; fishing and hunting are the most popular outdoor activities. Inside mobile homes and houses built more than thirty years ago, residents enjoy collecting coins, making crafts, and working crossword puzzles. Outside of bowling, there's not much nightlife hereabouts, and locals exhibit relatively little interest in movies, concerts, and arts events. Like most of West Virginia, this has been a Democratic area since John L. Lewis first organized the coal miners. But nowadays, local politicians reflect a centrist streak, favoring the pro-life movement, opposing wildlife conservation, and worrying about toxic waste, though not enough to hassle local oil and gas industries for fear of losing precious jobs.

| *Lower-middle-class manufacturing cities* | *Predominantly white singles and families* | *High school educations* | *Jobs in manufacturing, mining, and transportation* |
|---|---|---|---|

| **Key Demographics** | Total Population: | 401,457 | Primary Ages of Adults: | 55+ |
|---|---|---|---|---|
| | Median Household Income: | $23,688 | Median Home Value: | $44,923 |

# Wichita Falls, Texas–Lawton, Oklahoma

| What's Hot | What's Not |
|---|---|
| Veterans groups, baking, state fairs | Theater, books, art, gourmet cooking, lotteries |
| Camping, fishing, hunting, sewing, gardening | Tennis, skiing, golf, weight training, bowling |
| Video games, cable TV, 126/110 cameras, tillers | PCs, VCRs, 35mm cameras, CD players, stereos |
| "Sally," "Evening Shade," "Unsolved Mysteries" | "Seinfeld," "Honeymooners," "Dinosaurs," "Hard Copy" |
| Country, gospel, heavy metal, religious radio | Classical, modern rock, rap, pop vocal, jazz |
| *Outdoor Life, Southern Living, Redbook, Star* | *Consumer's Digest, Mademoiselle, Inc., Essence* |
| Ham, pork & beans, chili, crackers, canned fruit | Chicken, pasta, sour cream, waffles, yogurt |
| Vegetable juice, Pepsi-Cola, powdered drinks, milk | Malt liquor, wine, fruit juice, cocktails |
| Buicks, Subarus, Chryslers, Pontiac 6000s | Sterlings, Acuras, Porsches, Mercedes-Benz 190s |
| First mortgages, medical insurance, money orders | Credit cards, stocks, money-market accounts |
| Conservatives, pro-lifers, less government | Liberals, oil pollution, nuclear waste |

THE ONCE RAGING FALLS have long since vanished from Wichita Falls, along with a lot of the affluence that made this a prosperous cow and oil boomtown. Today, these twin cities have a diverse economic base composed of ranching, mining, and industry, and residents have comfortable if lower-middle-class lifestyles. These are folks who spend their free time pursuing activities much like their grandparents did: hunting, fishing, sewing, and gardening are all enjoyed at above-average rates. With Sheppard Air Force Base nearby, Wichita Falls–Lawton is one of the nation's best markets for veterans programs as well as motorcycles. Despite the local symphony and art center, this is no place to settle if you're interested in cultural events, fine arts, or classical music; all have comparatively little support among locals. Fact is, many residents just can't sit still long enough to enjoy a symphony. This is one of the nation's best markets for undertaking home-improvement projects, repairing cars, and acting out of faith. Reading the Bible and entering sweepstakes are popular pastimes.

| *Lower-middle-class farm market* | *Predominantly white singles and couples* | *High school educations* | *Jobs in farming, crafts, and transportation* |
|---|---|---|---|

| **Key Demographics** | Total Population: | 422,388 | Primary Ages of Adults: | 25–44 |
|---|---|---|---|---|
| | Median Household Income: | $24,518 | Median Home Value: | $46,098 |

# Wichita-Hutchinson, Kansas

## What's Hot | What's Not

| What's Hot | What's Not |
|---|---|
| Clubs, adult-ed courses, rodeos, crafts, RVs | Foreign travel, movies, book clubs, casinos |
| Fishing, hunting, gardening, sewing, bowling | Jogging, swimming, racquetball, sailing |
| Cable TV, food processors, power tools | PCs, CD players, toaster ovens, sofa beds |
| "Am.'s Funniest People," CNN, "20/20" | "Married with Children," "Star Trek," "Blossom" |
| Middle-of-the-road, golden oldies, radio baseball | Jazz, rhythm & blues, modern rock, classical |
| *Mother Earth News, Reader's Digest, Flying* | *Esquire, Vogue, Tennis, House & Garden, GQ* |
| Beef, pork & beans, canned vegetables, popcorn | Take-out, canned tuna, pancakes, rice |
| Skim milk, light beer, ground coffee, Countrytime | Cola, brandy, scotch, imported wine, tea |
| Olds 98s, Mercury Grand Marquises, Chevy K2500s | Peugeot 405s, Volvo 240s, Toyota Previas |
| Medical insurance, auto loans, mutual funds | IRAs, bonds, precious metals, AmEx cards |
| Moderates, privacy rights, family values | Liberals, consumerism, ozone depletion |

ONE OF THE LARGEST metro areas on the Great Plains, Wichita-Hutchinson was born a cow town, evolved into a farming center, and now is one of the nation's premier aircraft producers. As such, marketing surveys find a little something for everyone. Residents are into country clubs and adult education courses as well as rodeos and chewing tobacco. They're just as likely to drive around in a dusty pickup (Chevy K2500s and Dodge 350s are popular) as a luxury sedan (Ford Crown Victorias and Oldsmobile 98s get high marks). Although there's relatively little fascination for the usual urban cultural activities like film, theater, and the arts, this is not a wholly unsophisticated area. Upwardly striving locals are more likely than average Americans to invest in mutual funds and real estate, watch CNN and the Learning Channel, and read publications like *National Geographic* and *Popular Science* — status publications in the Midwest. In terms of politics, however, the liberalism of coastal cities has yet to reach this hinterland market.

| *Lower-middle-class commercial center* | *Predominantly white couples and families* | *Some college educations* | *Jobs in transportation, crafts, and farming* |
|---|---|---|---|

**Key Demographics**

| | | | |
|---|---|---|---|
| Total Population: | 1,119,940 | Primary Ages of Adults: | 25–44 |
| Median Household Income: | $28,860 | Median Home Value: | $50,095 |

# Wilkes-Barre–Scranton, Pennsylvania

## What's Hot | What's Not

| What's Hot | What's Not |
|---|---|
| Mall shopping, home workshops, cable TV, unions | The arts, fashion, frequent flying, health food |
| Walking, hunting, woodworking, gardening | Exercise, golf, tennis, skiing, bicycling |
| Lawn furniture, collectibles, Tupperware, recliners | CD players, 35mm cameras, PCs, books |
| "Santa Barbara," "Coach," "Murder, She Wrote" | "In Living Color," "Doogie Howser," "Brinkley" |
| Country, adult contemporary, easy listening | Soft rock, urban contemporary, jazz, news radio |
| *TV Guide, Woman's World, Home Mechanix, Star* | *Scientific American, Working Woman, New Yorker* |
| Cold cuts, pasta, corn chips, pizza, doughnuts | Take-out, chili, rice, raisin bread, jam |
| Cola, cocoa, tea, milk, orange juice | Light beer, fruit juice, wine, malt liquor |
| Pontiacs, Dodges, Oldsmobiles, Ford Tempos | Saabs, Audis, Acuras, Jaguars, Lexus SC3s |
| Loans, life insurance, savings bonds, CDs | Annuities, mutual funds, Keoghs, gold cards |
| Moderates, military cutbacks, school sex ed | Liberals, abortion rights, gun control |

ONCE THE WORLD'S biggest coal-producing region, Wilkes-Barre–Scranton has been in a slow decline for most of the past 75 years. Wages have dropped since the union mines gave way to nonunion textile mills in the 1970s, and the population is aging, with more than half of all household heads over the age of 52. Unlike seniors who move to active retirement communities for golf and tennis in the Sunbelt, those who've stayed behind here in Pennsylvania enjoy quieter pursuits: coin collecting, walking, working crossword puzzles, and sewing — all are enjoyed at high rates. Having a well-stocked home workshop is considered status, the better to make crafts and toys for your grandchildren. The European immigrants who once flocked to this area used to vote as a Democratic union bloc, but time has made the market economically liberal while socially conservative. Abortion and gay rights are opposed, while government spending — especially for the home district — is supported.

| *Lower-middle-class industrial cities* | *Predominantly white singles and couples* | *High school educations* | *Jobs in transportation, mining, and manufacturing* |
|---|---|---|---|

**Key Demographics**

| | | | |
|---|---|---|---|
| Total Population: | 1,401,095 | Primary Ages of Adults: | 55+ |
| Median Household Income: | $27,505 | Median Home Value: | $63,845 |

# Wilmington, North Carolina

## What's Hot

Home furnishing, bus travel, junk mail
Swimming, hunting, bicycling, walking
Cable TV, video games, VCRs, chain saws
"Price Is Right," "Sally," "Fresh Prince"
Rap, gospel, country, religious radio
*Ebony, Country Living, National Enquirer*
Seafood, fried chicken, aerosol cheese
Malt liquor, cola, diet soda, powdered drinks
Nissan Stanzas, Buick Roadmasters, Mazda 929s
Medical insurance, loans, term insurance
Conservatives, less government, family values

## What's Not

Clubs, movies, casinos, plane travel, dancing
Tennis, exercise, weight training, racquetball
Food processors, radar detectors, PCs, CD players
"Saturday Night Live," "Wonder Years," "Letterman"
Rock, classical, jazz, middle-of-the-road
*Money, Self, Discover, Architectural Digest*
Fresh vegetables, cheese, rice cakes, Wheaties
Wine, imported beer, cocktails, Diet Slice
Mercedes-Benz 560s, Acura Integras, Saab 9000s
Interest checking, Keoghs, bonds, mutual funds
Liberals, gay rights, ozone depletion

THE LARGEST CITY along North Carolina's coast, Wilmington has a down-home lifestyle carved out of a peculiar past. The economic base has been linked to tobacco for more than two centuries, and the local population is a racial mix of whites, African Americans, and Native Americans. Today, the nearby military installations at Camp Lejeune and Fort Bragg make this a military-friendly market where veterans programs and conservative politics are popular. This is a city for walkers who can take in the sights among the restored mansions in the historic district, the plantation gardens outside of town, and the sandy beaches along the coast. But the predominantly downscale economy produces a market known more for mobile homes, pickup trucks, country music, and chewing tobacco. One standout passion is fast food.

| *Lower-middle-class port city* | *Racially diverse singles and couples* | *Less than high school educations* | *Jobs in transportation and manufacturing* |
| --- | --- | --- | --- |

| **Key Demographics** | Total Population: | 401,733 | Primary Ages of Adults: | 35–54 |
| --- | --- | --- | --- | --- |
| | Median Household Income: | $25,670 | Median Home Value: | $63,972 |

# Yakima-Pasco-Richland-Kennewick, Washington

## What's Hot

Videos, baking, car repair, crafts, pets, RVs
Camping, fishing, boating, skiing, gardening
Power tools, 126/110 cameras, video games, VCRs
"Price Is Right," "Evening Shade," "Nightline"
Country, adult contemporary, golden oldies
*Outdoor Life, Ladies' Home Journal, Cycle World*
Ham, Mexican food, canned soup, pizza, ice cream
Skim milk, powdered drinks, light beer, tea
Subarus, Chryslers, Chevy Geos, Dodge Rams
Medical insurance, credit lines, mutual funds
Moderates, toxic waste disposal, less government

## What's Not

Lotteries, dancing, health clubs, politics
Exercise, jogging, golf, racquetball, tennis
Radar detectors, toaster ovens, CD players
"General Hospital," "Seinfeld," "Fresh Prince"
Jazz, classical, easy listening, soft rock
*Food & Wine, House Beautiful, Life, Inc., Jet*
TV dinners, rice, spaghetti sauce, doughnuts
Cola, malt liquor, imported beer, wine
VWs, Acuras, Hondas, Toyota Landcruisers
Keoghs, term insurance, stocks, bonds, IRAs
Liberals, legalizing drugs, endangered animals

THIS IS AN AREA of contrasts, of lush fruit farms in the Yakima Valley, and stark, lunar landscapes around the area's largest employer, the Hanford nuclear manufacturing facilities. Accordingly, consumer tastes are somewhat muddled. Like other rural communities in the Northwest, this market is hot for outdoor sports: skiing, camping, fishing, and hunting are all enjoyed at high rates. Yet residents also are more likely than average Americans to pursue domestic activities like sewing, woodworking, knitting, and gardening. A high concentration of downscale Hispanics — typically fruit-pickers hired to work the orchards and vineyards — makes this a relatively weak market for designer fashion. One outgrowth of these influences is a schizo political sensibility, where residents worry about nuclear waste, yet rail against the government for threatening to close Hanford due to its toxic leaks.

| *Lower-middle-class agricultural towns* | *Ethnically diverse couples and families* | *Some college educations* | *Jobs in farming, crafts, and construction* |
| --- | --- | --- | --- |

| **Key Demographics** | Total Population: | 502,392 | Primary Ages of Adults: | 25–44 |
| --- | --- | --- | --- | --- |
| | Median Household Income: | $27,384 | Median Home Value: | $60,728 |

# Youngstown, Ohio

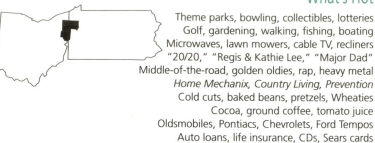

| What's Hot | What's Not |
|---|---|
| Theme parks, bowling, collectibles, lotteries | Clubs, rodeos, concerts, books, adult-ed courses |
| Golf, gardening, walking, fishing, boating | Tennis, sailing, bicycling, jogging, skiing |
| Microwaves, lawn mowers, cable TV, recliners | CD players, PCs, food processors, toaster ovens |
| "20/20," "Regis & Kathie Lee," "Major Dad" | "In Living Color," "Hard Copy, "Siskel & Ebert" |
| Middle-of-the-road, golden oldies, rap, heavy metal | Rhythm & blues, folk, soft rock, jazz |
| *Home Mechanix, Country Living, Prevention* | *Mademoiselle, Harper's Bazaar, American Photo* |
| Cold cuts, baked beans, pretzels, Wheaties | Chili, canned chicken, rice cakes, grits |
| Cocoa, ground coffee, tomato juice | Ale, beer, wine, vodka, rum, herbal tea |
| Oldsmobiles, Pontiacs, Chevrolets, Ford Tempos | Acuras, Audis, Mercedes-Benzes, BMW 6/7s |
| Auto loans, life insurance, CDs, Sears cards | Annuities, stocks, mutual funds, AmEx cards |
| Moderates, buying American, death penalty | Liberals, ocean dumping, gun control |

YOUNGSTOWN'S STORY is like that of many once-thriving steel towns that have fallen on tough times. With the factories closed and young people leaving in droves for other towns and more opportunities, the population is dwindling, becoming more downscale, and aging. Half of all residents are over 51 years old, and the lifestyles reflect as much: locals would rather walk than run, watch TV than go out to a movie, relax in a recliner than take a drive in the country. And like other blue-collar towns, Youngstown has a passion for bowling; in one survey of 60 lifestyle activities, bowling was the most popular. It's one of the few vestiges of Youngstown's past — a group-oriented world when unionized workers stoked the steel furnaces. Today, the unions have lost their muscle, and the sense of belonging has left town. Membership in fraternal orders, veterans clubs, and business groups all occur at rates below the national average.

| *Lower-middle-class industrial city* | *Predominantly white couples and singles* | *High school educations* | *Jobs in transportation, manufacturing, and crafts* |
|---|---|---|---|

## Key Demographics

| | | | |
|---|---|---|---|
| Total Population: | 725,265 | Primary Ages of Adults: | 55+ |
| Median Household Income: | $27,056 | Median Home Value: | $50,219 |

# Zanesville, Ohio

| What's Hot | What's Not |
|---|---|
| Mobile homes, mall shopping, crafts, pro wrestling | Movies, junk mail, casinos, foreign travel |
| Bowling, golf, hunting, sewing, woodworking | Jogging, sailing, skiing, weight training |
| Chain saws, lawn furniture, tillers, cable TV | PCs, 35mm cameras, stereos, woks |
| Soaps, "Coach," "Roseanne," "Wheel of Fortune" | "Full House," "Donahue," "Wonder Years" |
| Country, heavy metal, golden oldies, religious radio | Rap, modern rock, rhythm & blues, classical |
| *Field & Stream, 1001 Home Ideas, Reader's Digest* | *Newsweek, Working Woman, Vogue, Gourmet* |
| Sausage, frozen potatoes, croissants, candy | TV dinners, canned chicken, corn on the cob |
| Cola, fruit juice, decaf coffee, cocoa | Imported wine and beer, scotch, rum, ale |
| Dodge trucks, Chevy Luminas, Dodge Daytonas | Jeep Cherokees, Volvo 940s, Acura Legends |
| Life insurance, loans, CDs, savings accounts | Interest checking, bonds, brokerage accounts |
| Moderates, privacy rights, nuclear waste disposal | Liberals, family values, legalizing drugs |

ZANESVILLE IS OHIO'S VERSION of an Appalachian community, a poor and rugged area where 40 percent of all adults earn under $20,000 a year. Mobile homes, trucks, and motorcycles are omnipresent. Hunting, fishing, and target shooting are the popular sports. In this relatively isolated community, television provides much of the evening entertainment: this is one of the nation's top markets for watching cable TV — especially sports, soaps, and game shows. And a big night out means going bowling or to a distant mall. While political surveys find Zanesville residents to be middle-of-the-roaders, they're more apathetic than anything else. This is one of the nation's five worst markets when ranking interest in politics and current affairs. And their indifference toward world affairs is also reflected in their dislike of things foreign, including imported foods, cars, and high-tech electronics.

| *Lower-middle-class trade center* | *Predominantly white couples and families* | *High school educations* | *Jobs in mining, transportation, and manufacturing* |
|---|---|---|---|

## Key Demographics

| | | | |
|---|---|---|---|
| Total Population: | 82,768 | Primary Ages of Adults: | 55+ |
| Median Household Income: | $26,054 | Median Home Value: | $50,028 |

# Alaska (not in any ADI)

| What's Hot | What's Not |
|---|---|
| Skiing, plane travel, movies, books, baking | Bus travel, religious clubs, all-news radio |
| Hiking, boating, camping, woodworking, jogging | Gardening, target shooting, horse racing |
| Food processors, musical instruments, radios | Microwaves, tillers, carpeting, domestic cars |
| "Saturday Night Live," "Seinfeld," "Murphy Brown" | Soaps, "Sally," "Fresh Prince," "Current Affair" |
| Easy listening, jazz, rock, country, folk | Gospel, rhythm & blues, rap, urban contemporary |
| *Smithsonian, Money, Skiing, National Geographic* | *Weight Watchers, Life, Vogue, National Enquirer* |
| Chili, fish, yogurt, dried fruit, oat bran, bacon | Beef stew, cookies, corn on the cob, Lucky Charms |
| Ground coffee, vegetable juice, spring water | Malt liquor, orange juice, cola, ale, Diet RC |
| Subaru Legacys, Mitsubishi 3000GTs, Toyota Previas | Ford Tempos, Buick Skylarks, Chevy Astros |
| Mutual funds, annuities, stocks, IRAs, Keoghs | Money orders, mail-order life insurance |
| Liberals, consumerism, abortion and gay rights | Moderates, less government, oil drilling |

ONLY A HALF-MILLION PEOPLE live in this state roughly twice the size of Texas, but their affluence more than makes up for the scarcity of consumers. The median income of residents, many of whom work for the government, is $43,925, thanks partly to proceeds from the oil pipeline that abolished the state's income tax and provides each resident with an annual dividend check of $1,000. On average, Alaskans are likely to invest in mutual funds and stocks, own imported cars and electronic equipment, and enjoy books and movies. The state's expansive wilderness makes this a prime market for skiing, hiking, boating, and camping. And with more than half of the state's residents living in Anchorage, Alaskan media tastes are similar to any other city in the lower 48: jazz, "Saturday Night Live," and *Smithsonian* magazine are all popular in this market. But Alaskans still pride themselves on being free-spirited risk-takers, and their political concerns are a striking melange. Despite being surrounded by wilderness, they're pro-development even to the point of supporting big government projects and the oil industry — the *Valdez* oil spill notwithstanding.

| *Affluent frontier market* | *Ethnically diverse couples and families* | *College educations* | *Jobs in education, mining, and public administration* |
|---|---|---|---|

**Key Demographics**

| | | | |
|---|---|---|---|
| Total Population: | 595,714 | Primary Ages of Adults: | 25–44 |
| Median Household Income: | $44,968 | Median Home Value: | $99,210 |

# Hawaii (not in any ADI)

| What's Hot | What's Not |
|---|---|
| Dancing, foreign travel, clubs, boating, books | Home improvements, rodeos, tobacco, pest control |
| Tennis, sailing, hiking, racquetball, golf | Pro wrestling, horseback riding, knitting |
| Woks, charcoal grills, PCs, faxes, cable TV | 126/110 cameras, carpeting, compact pickups |
| "Letterman," "Simpsons," "Star Trek" | Soaps, "NBC Boxing Tour," "Sally," "Major Dad" |
| Modern rock, classical, jazz, contemporary pop | Adult contemporary, rap, gospel, rhythm & blues |
| *Harper's Bazaar, Sports Illustrated, Time* | *True Story, Ebony, Outdoor Life, Seventeen* |
| Fish, canned chicken, rye, popcorn, chocolates | Cold cuts, pizza, pasta, peanut butter, pies |
| Cocktails, ground coffee, scotch, wine, beer | Tea, malt liquor, powdered drinks, cocoa |
| Acura Integras, Nissan 300ZXs, Mazda MPVs | Eagle Summits, Dodge Dynastys, Chevy Cavaliers |
| Homeowners insurance, mutual funds, annuities | Medicare, securities, medical insurance |
| Liberals, family values, ozone depletion | Moderates, toxic waste disposal, gun control |

THE LAND OF DIAMOND HEAD, Don Ho, and "Just Maui-ed" vacations is also one of the nation's most affluent markets, with a whopping median home value of $262,631, caused in part by land-hungry Asian buyers. The state's tourism-based economy has created a vacation mecca for visitors but made life tough for many of the local service workers who often must share tiny studio apartments. Fortunately, away from the commercial strips in Waikiki, there's still plenty of pristine beauty for all residents to feel rich while they enjoy swimming, hiking, fishing, and camping. Those Hawaiian residents who are upscale in the traditional sense have made this a strong market for "good-life" activities, including foreign travel, local nightlife, luxury cars, and high-tech electronics. With a diverse population that's one-third Caucasian, one-third Japanese, and one-sixth Filipino, residents are into clubs and tolerance on cultural issues; the state's voters support abortion and gay rights and, of course, concern about environmental issues. A popular bumper sticker reads "Hawaii — just another lousy day in paradise," and most residents want to keep it that way.

| *Affluent tourist center* | *Ethnically diverse couples and families* | *College educations* | *Recreation, service, and government jobs* |
|---|---|---|---|

**Key Demographics**

| | | | |
|---|---|---|---|
| Total Population: | 1,174,796 | Primary Ages of Adults: | 25–44 |
| Median Household Income: | $43,512 | Median Home Value: | $262,631 |

# THE
# Ratings Chart

**KEY**
- ■ High
- ◼ (half) Above average
- ◼ (half) Below average
- □ Low

**MARKET**

## Food

Columns: Croissants · White Bread · Pizza · Nuts · Beef · Instant Mashed Potatoes · Ben & Jerry's Ice Cream · Weight Watchers Frozen Dessert · Oat Bran · Bacon · Bagels · Twinkies · Apples · Oranges · TV Dinners · Fast Food

## Drink

Columns: Lemon-Lime Soda · Herbal Tea · Ground Coffee · Red Wine · White Wine · Budweiser · Coors · Miller

| Market |
|--------|
| Abilene-Sweetwater, TX |
| Albany, GA |
| Albany et al., NY |
| Albuquerque, NM |
| Alexandria, LA |
| Alpena, MI |
| Amarillo, TX |
| Anniston, AL |
| Ardmore-Ada, OK |
| Atlanta, GA |
| Augusta, GA |
| Austin, TX |
| Bakersfield, CA |
| Baltimore, MD |
| Bangor, ME |
| Baton Rouge, LA |
| Beaumont-Port Arthur, TX |
| Bend, OR |
| Billings-Hardin, MT |
| Biloxi et al., MS |
| Binghamton, NY |
| Birmingham, AL |
| Bluefield et al., WV |
| Boise, ID |
| Boston, MA |
| Bowling Green, KY |
| Bristol et al., TN-VA |
| Buffalo, NY |
| Burlington et al., VT-NY |
| Butte, MT |
| Casper-Riverton, WY |
| Cedar Rapids et al., IA |
| Charleston, SC |
| Charleston et al., WV |
| Charlotte, NC |
| Charlottesville, VA |
| Chattanooga, TN |
| Cheyenne et al., WY-NE |
| Chicago, IL |
| Chico-Redding, CA |
| Cincinnati, OH |
| Clarksburg-Weston, WV |

*Note: Variations between product ratings and maps featuring two topics may occur due to different calculation methods.*

| Leisure | | | | | | | | | | | Home | | | | | | | | | | | | | Personal | | | | | | | |
|---|---|---|---|---|---|---|---|---|---|---|---|---|---|---|---|---|---|---|---|---|---|---|---|---|---|---|---|---|---|---|---|
| Books | Television | Theme Parks | Shopping Malls | State Fairs | Fraternal Orders | Movies | Video Rentals | Baking from Scratch | Stocks | Lottery Tickets | Recliners | Woks | Power Tools | Personal Computers | Tupperware | Cats | Dogs | Mobile Homes | Junk Mail | Home Fax Machines | Boom Boxes | Plush Dolls/Animals | Nintendo | Condoms | Headache Remedies | Obsession for Men | Old Spice | Pregnancy-Test Kits | Cigarettes | Dental Floss | Mouthwash |

The Ratings Chart • 205

**KEY**    **INTEREST**
- ■ High
- ◧ Above average
- ◨ Below average
- □ Low

## Food

## Drink

**MARKET**

Food columns: Croissants · White Bread · Pizza · Nuts · Beef · Instant Mashed Potatoes · Ben & Jerry's Ice Cream · Weight Watchers Frozen Dessert · Oat Bran · Bacon · Bagels · Twinkies · Apples · Oranges · TV Dinners · Fast Food

Drink columns: Lemon-Lime Soda · Herbal Tea · Ground Coffee · Red Wine · White Wine · Budweiser · Coors · Miller

| Market |
|--------|
| Cleveland, OH |
| Colorado Springs et al., CO |
| Columbia, SC |
| Columbia et al., MO |
| Columbus, GA |
| Columbus, OH |
| Columbus-Tupelo, MS |
| Corpus Christi, TX |
| Dallas-Ft. Worth, TX |
| Davenport et al., IA-IL |
| Dayton, OH |
| Denver, CO |
| Des Moines, IA |
| Detroit, MI |
| Dothan, AL |
| Duluth-Superior, MN-WI |
| El Centro-Yuma, CA-AZ |
| El Paso, TX |
| Elmira, NY |
| Erie, PA |
| Eugene, OR |
| Eureka, CA |
| Evansville, IN |
| Fargo, ND |
| Flagstaff, AZ |
| Flint-Saginaw et al., MI |
| Florence et al., SC |
| Fresno-Visalia, CA |
| Ft. Myers-Naples, FL |
| Ft. Smith, AR |
| Ft. Wayne, IN |
| Gainesville, FL |
| Grand Junction et al., CO |
| Grand Rapids et al., MI |
| Great Falls, MT |
| Green Bay-Appleton, WI |
| Greensboro et al., NC |
| Greenville et al., NC |
| Greenville et al., SC-NC |
| Greenwood-Greenville, MS |
| Hagerstown, MD |
| Harrisburg et al., PA |

| Leisure | Home | Personal |
|---------|------|----------|
| Books, Television, Theme Parks, Shopping Malls, State Fairs, Fraternal Orders, Movies, Video Rentals, Baking from Scratch, Stocks, Lottery Tickets | Recliners, Woks, Power Tools, Personal Computers, Tupperware, Cats, Dogs, Mobile Homes, Junk Mail, Home Fax Machines, Boom Boxes, Plush Dolls/Animals, Nintendo | Condoms, Headache Remedies, Obsession for Men, Old Spice, Pregnancy-Test Kits, Cigarettes, Dental Floss, Mouthwash |

KEY — INTEREST

■ *High*
⬒ *Above average*
⬓ *Below average*
□ *Low*

## Food

| MARKET | Croissants | White Bread | Pizza | Nuts | Beef | Instant Mashed Potatoes | Ben & Jerry's Ice Cream | Weight Watchers Frozen Dessert | Oat Bran | Bacon | Bagels | Twinkies | Apples | Oranges | TV Dinners | Fast Food |
|---|---|---|---|---|---|---|---|---|---|---|---|---|---|---|---|---|
| Harrisonburg, VA | □ | □ | ■ | ⬒ | ⬒ | ■ | □ | □ | □ | ■ | □ | ■ | □ | □ | ⬓ | ⬓ |
| Hartford-New Haven, CT | ⬒ | ⬒ | □ | ⬒ | ⬒ | □ | ⬒ | ■ | ■ | ⬓ | ■ | □ | ■ | ■ | ⬓ | ⬓ |
| Helena, MT | ⬓ | □ | ■ | ■ | ■ | ⬓ | □ | ■ | ■ | ■ | ⬓ | ⬓ | ■ | ⬓ | ■ | ■ |
| Houston, TX | ■ | ⬒ | ⬒ | ⬓ | ⬓ | ⬓ | ⬒ | ⬒ | ⬒ | ⬓ | ⬒ | ⬓ | ⬒ | ⬒ | ⬒ | ■ |
| Huntsville et al., AL | □ | □ | ⬒ | ⬓ | ⬓ | ■ | □ | □ | □ | ■ | □ | ■ | □ | □ | ⬓ | ⬒ |
| Idaho Falls et al., ID | □ | □ | ■ | ■ | ■ | ⬒ | □ | □ | ■ | ■ | □ | ■ | ■ | ⬓ | ■ | □ |
| Indianapolis, IN | ⬓ | ⬓ | ⬒ | ■ | ■ | ⬒ | ⬓ | □ | ⬓ | ⬒ | ⬓ | ■ | ⬒ | ⬓ | ■ | ■ |
| Jackson, MS | □ | □ | ⬓ | □ | □ | ■ | □ | ⬓ | □ | ■ | □ | ■ | □ | □ | □ | ⬒ |
| Jackson, TN | □ | □ | ⬓ | □ | □ | ■ | □ | □ | □ | ■ | □ | ■ | □ | □ | □ | ⬓ |
| Jacksonville, FL | ⬓ | ⬓ | ⬒ | ⬒ | ⬒ | ⬒ | ⬓ | ⬓ | □ | ⬒ | ⬓ | ⬒ | □ | □ | ⬒ | ■ |
| Johnstown-Altoona, PA | □ | □ | ■ | ■ | ■ | ■ | □ | □ | □ | ■ | □ | ■ | ⬓ | □ | ■ | ⬓ |
| Jonesboro, AR | □ | □ | ■ | □ | ⬓ | ■ | □ | □ | □ | ■ | □ | ■ | □ | □ | □ | □ |
| Joplin-Pittsburg, MO-KS | □ | □ | ■ | ⬒ | ■ | ■ | □ | □ | □ | ■ | □ | ■ | □ | □ | ⬒ | □ |
| Kansas City, MO-KS | ⬒ | ⬒ | ⬒ | ⬒ | ⬒ | ⬓ | ⬓ | ⬓ | ⬒ | ⬓ | ⬒ | ⬒ | ⬒ | ⬒ | ⬒ | ⬒ |
| Knoxville, TN | □ | □ | ■ | ⬓ | ⬒ | ■ | □ | □ | □ | ■ | □ | ■ | □ | □ | ⬓ | □ |
| La Crosse-Eau Claire, WI | □ | ⬓ | ■ | ■ | ■ | ⬒ | □ | □ | ⬓ | ■ | □ | ■ | ■ | ⬓ | ⬒ | □ |
| Lafayette, IN | ⬓ | ⬓ | ■ | ■ | ■ | ⬓ | ⬒ | □ | ■ | ⬒ | ⬒ | ⬒ | ■ | ⬒ | ■ | ■ |
| Lafayette, LA | □ | □ | ⬒ | ⬓ | ⬓ | ■ | □ | ⬓ | □ | ■ | □ | ■ | □ | □ | □ | ⬒ |
| Lake Charles, LA | □ | □ | ⬓ | ⬒ | ⬒ | ■ | □ | □ | □ | ■ | □ | ■ | □ | □ | ⬓ | ⬒ |
| Lansing, MI | ⬓ | ⬓ | ⬒ | ■ | ■ | ⬒ | ⬓ | □ | ⬓ | ⬒ | ⬒ | ⬒ | ⬒ | ⬒ | ■ | ■ |
| Laredo, TX | ⬓ | ■ | ■ | □ | □ | ■ | □ | ⬒ | □ | ⬒ | □ | ■ | □ | □ | □ | ⬓ |
| Las Vegas, NV | ■ | ⬒ | ⬒ | ⬒ | ⬒ | □ | ⬒ | ⬒ | ⬒ | □ | ■ | ⬓ | ⬒ | ■ | ■ | ■ |
| Laurel-Hattiesburg, MS | □ | □ | ⬓ | □ | □ | ■ | □ | □ | □ | ■ | □ | ■ | □ | □ | □ | □ |
| Lexington, KY | □ | □ | ■ | □ | ⬓ | ■ | □ | □ | □ | ■ | □ | ■ | □ | □ | □ | □ |
| Lima, OH | □ | ⬓ | ⬒ | ■ | ■ | ■ | □ | □ | ⬓ | ■ | ⬓ | ■ | ⬒ | ⬓ | ■ | ■ |
| Lincoln et al., NE | □ | ⬓ | ■ | ■ | ■ | ⬒ | □ | □ | ⬒ | ■ | □ | ■ | ■ | ⬓ | ⬒ | □ |
| Little Rock, AR | □ | □ | ⬒ | ⬓ | ⬓ | ■ | □ | □ | □ | ■ | □ | ■ | □ | □ | ⬓ | □ |
| Los Angeles, CA | ■ | ■ | ⬓ | □ | □ | □ | ■ | ⬒ | ■ | □ | ■ | □ | ⬒ | ■ | ⬓ | ⬓ |
| Louisville, KY | □ | ⬓ | ⬓ | ⬓ | ⬒ | ■ | □ | □ | □ | ⬒ | ⬓ | ■ | □ | □ | ⬒ | ⬒ |
| Lubbock, TX | □ | ⬓ | ■ | ⬒ | ■ | ⬒ | □ | □ | ⬓ | ■ | □ | ■ | ⬓ | □ | ⬒ | ⬓ |
| Macon, GA | □ | □ | ⬓ | □ | □ | ■ | □ | ⬒ | □ | ■ | □ | ■ | □ | □ | □ | ■ |
| Madison, WI | ⬓ | ⬓ | ■ | ■ | ■ | ⬓ | ⬓ | □ | ■ | ⬒ | ⬓ | ⬒ | ■ | ⬒ | ■ | ⬒ |
| Mankato, MN | □ | ⬓ | ■ | ■ | ■ | ⬒ | □ | □ | ■ | ■ | □ | ■ | ■ | ⬓ | ■ | □ |
| Marquette, MI | □ | □ | ■ | ■ | ■ | ■ | □ | □ | ⬓ | ■ | □ | ■ | □ | □ | ⬒ | □ |
| McAllen et al., TX | □ | □ | ■ | □ | ⬒ | ■ | □ | ⬓ | □ | ■ | □ | ■ | □ | □ | □ | □ |
| Medford, OR | ⬓ | □ | ■ | ■ | ■ | ⬒ | □ | ⬓ | ■ | ■ | □ | ⬒ | ■ | ⬓ | ■ | □ |
| Memphis, TN | ⬓ | ⬓ | ⬓ | □ | □ | ■ | ⬓ | ⬓ | □ | ⬒ | □ | ■ | □ | □ | □ | ⬓ |
| Meridian, MS | □ | □ | ⬓ | □ | □ | ■ | □ | □ | □ | ■ | □ | ■ | □ | □ | □ | □ |
| Miami-Ft. Lauderdale, FL | ■ | ■ | □ | □ | □ | □ | ■ | ⬓ | ■ | □ | ■ | □ | ⬓ | ⬓ | ⬓ | □ |
| Milwaukee, WI | ⬓ | ⬒ | □ | ⬒ | ■ | ⬓ | ⬓ | ⬓ | ⬓ | ⬓ | ⬒ | ⬓ | ⬒ | ■ | ⬒ | ⬒ |
| Minneapolis-St. Paul, MN | ⬒ | ⬓ | ⬒ | ■ | ■ | ⬓ | ⬓ | ⬓ | ⬒ | ⬒ | ⬒ | ⬓ | ■ | ■ | ■ | ⬒ |
| Minot-Bismarck et al., ND | □ | □ | ■ | ■ | ■ | ⬒ | □ | □ | ⬓ | ■ | □ | ■ | ■ | ⬓ | ⬒ | □ |

## Drink

| MARKET | Lemon-Lime Soda | Herbal Tea | Ground Coffee | Red Wine | White Wine | Budweiser | Coors | Miller |
|---|---|---|---|---|---|---|---|---|
| Harrisonburg, VA | ⬓ | □ | ■ | □ | □ | □ | □ | □ |
| Hartford-New Haven, CT | □ | ⬒ | ⬒ | ⬒ | ⬒ | ⬓ | ⬒ | ■ |
| Helena, MT | □ | ■ | ■ | ⬓ | ⬓ | □ | ⬒ | □ |
| Houston, TX | ■ | ■ | ⬓ | ⬒ | ⬒ | ■ | ■ | ■ |
| Huntsville et al., AL | □ | □ | ⬒ | □ | □ | □ | □ | □ |
| Idaho Falls et al., ID | ⬓ | ⬒ | ■ | □ | ⬓ | □ | ⬓ | □ |
| Indianapolis, IN | ⬒ | ⬒ | ■ | ⬓ | ⬓ | □ | ⬓ | ⬒ |
| Jackson, MS | ■ | □ | □ | □ | □ | ⬒ | □ | □ |
| Jackson, TN | ⬒ | □ | ⬓ | □ | □ | □ | □ | □ |
| Jacksonville, FL | ⬓ | ⬓ | ⬓ | ⬓ | ⬓ | ⬓ | ⬓ | ⬓ |
| Johnstown-Altoona, PA | ⬒ | □ | ■ | □ | □ | □ | □ | ⬓ |
| Jonesboro, AR | ■ | □ | ■ | □ | □ | □ | □ | □ |
| Joplin-Pittsburg, MO-KS | ⬒ | □ | ■ | □ | □ | □ | □ | □ |
| Kansas City, MO-KS | ⬒ | ⬒ | ⬒ | ⬒ | ⬒ | ⬒ | ⬒ | ⬒ |
| Knoxville, TN | □ | □ | ⬒ | □ | □ | □ | □ | □ |
| La Crosse-Eau Claire, WI | ■ | □ | ■ | □ | □ | □ | □ | □ |
| Lafayette, IN | ■ | ■ | ■ | ⬒ | ⬒ | ■ | ⬒ | ■ |
| Lafayette, LA | ■ | □ | ⬓ | □ | □ | ⬓ | □ | □ |
| Lake Charles, LA | ⬒ | □ | ⬓ | □ | □ | □ | □ | □ |
| Lansing, MI | ■ | ■ | ■ | ⬓ | ⬓ | ⬓ | ⬒ | ■ |
| Laredo, TX | ■ | □ | □ | ⬓ | □ | ⬒ | ⬒ | □ |
| Las Vegas, NV | ■ | ■ | ⬓ | ⬒ | ⬒ | ■ | ■ | ■ |
| Laurel-Hattiesburg, MS | ■ | □ | □ | □ | □ | ⬓ | □ | □ |
| Lexington, KY | ■ | □ | ⬒ | □ | □ | □ | □ | □ |
| Lima, OH | ■ | □ | ■ | □ | ⬓ | □ | □ | ⬓ |
| Lincoln et al., NE | ⬒ | ⬓ | ■ | □ | □ | □ | □ | □ |
| Little Rock, AR | ■ | □ | ⬓ | □ | □ | □ | □ | □ |
| Los Angeles, CA | ⬓ | ■ | □ | ■ | ■ | ■ | ■ | ■ |
| Louisville, KY | ⬒ | □ | ⬒ | ⬓ | □ | □ | ⬓ | ⬓ |
| Lubbock, TX | ■ | ⬓ | ■ | □ | ⬓ | ⬒ | ⬓ | □ |
| Macon, GA | ■ | □ | □ | □ | □ | ⬒ | □ | □ |
| Madison, WI | ■ | ⬒ | ■ | ⬓ | ⬓ | ⬓ | ⬒ | ⬒ |
| Mankato, MN | ■ | ⬓ | ■ | □ | □ | ⬓ | ⬓ | ⬓ |
| Marquette, MI | ■ | □ | ■ | □ | □ | ⬓ | □ | □ |
| McAllen et al., TX | ■ | □ | ⬒ | □ | □ | □ | □ | □ |
| Medford, OR | ■ | ⬓ | ■ | □ | □ | □ | □ | □ |
| Memphis, TN | ■ | □ | □ | ⬓ | □ | ⬒ | ⬓ | □ |
| Meridian, MS | ■ | □ | □ | □ | □ | ⬓ | □ | □ |
| Miami-Ft. Lauderdale, FL | □ | ⬒ | □ | ⬒ | ⬒ | ■ | ■ | ⬒ |
| Milwaukee, WI | ⬓ | ⬓ | ⬒ | ⬒ | ⬒ | ⬓ | ⬓ | ■ |
| Minneapolis-St. Paul, MN | ⬒ | ⬒ | ■ | ⬒ | ⬒ | ⬓ | ⬒ | ⬒ |
| Minot-Bismarck et al., ND | ⬒ | □ | ■ | □ | □ | □ | □ | □ |

| Books | Television | Theme Parks | Shopping Malls | State Fairs | Fraternal Orders | Movies | Video Rentals | Baking from Scratch | Stocks | Lottery Tickets |
|---|---|---|---|---|---|---|---|---|---|---|

| Recliners | Woks | Power Tools | Personal Computers | Tupperware | Cats | Dogs | Mobile Homes | Junk Mail | Home Fax Machines | Boom Boxes | Plush Dolls/Animals | Nintendo |
|---|---|---|---|---|---|---|---|---|---|---|---|---|

| Condoms | Headache Remedies | Obsession for Men | Old Spice | Pregnancy-Test Kits | Cigarettes | Dental Floss | Mouthwash |
|---|---|---|---|---|---|---|---|

**KEY**  **INTEREST**

- ■ High
- ▬ Above average
- ▭ Below average
- ☐ Low

## Food

## Drink

**MARKET**

Food columns: Croissants, White Bread, Pizza, Nuts, Beef, Instant Mashed Potatoes, Ben & Jerry's Ice Cream, Weight Watchers Frozen Dessert, Oat Bran, Bacon, Bagels, Twinkies, Apples, Oranges, TV Dinners, Fast Food

Drink columns: Lemon-Lime Soda, Herbal Tea, Ground Coffee, Red Wine, White Wine, Budweiser, Coors, Miller

| MARKET |
| --- |
| Missoula, MT |
| Mobile-Pensacola, AL-FL |
| Monroe-El Dorado, LA-AR |
| Montgomery-Selma, AL |
| Nashville, TN |
| New Orleans, LA |
| New York, NY |
| Norfolk et al., VA |
| North Platte, NE |
| Odessa-Midland, TX |
| Oklahoma City, OK |
| Omaha, NE |
| Orlando et al., FL |
| Ottumwa et al., IA-MO |
| Paducah et al., KY-MO-IL |
| Palm Springs, CA |
| Panama City, FL |
| Parkersburg, WV |
| Peoria-Bloomington, IL |
| Philadelphia, PA |
| Phoenix, AZ |
| Pittsburgh, PA |
| Portland, OR |
| Portland et al., ME |
| Presque Isle, ME |
| Providence et al., RI-MA |
| Quincy-Hannibal, IL-MO |
| Raleigh-Durham, NC |
| Rapid City, SD |
| Reno, NV |
| Richmond, VA |
| Roanoke-Lynchburg, VA |
| Rochester, NY |
| Rochester et al., MN-IA |
| Rockford, IL |
| Sacramento-Stockton, CA |
| Salinas-Monterey, CA |
| Salisbury, MD |
| Salt Lake City, UT |
| San Angelo, TX |
| San Antonio-Victoria, TX |
| San Diego, CA |

## Leisure

Books · Television · Theme Parks · Shopping Malls · State Fairs · Fraternal Orders · Movies · Video Rentals · Baking from Scratch · Stocks · Lottery Tickets

## Home

Recliners · Woks · Power Tools · Personal Computers · Tupperware · Cats · Dogs · Mobile Homes · Junk Mail · Home Fax Machines · Boom Boxes · Plush Dolls/Animals · Nintendo

## Personal

Condoms · Headache Remedies · Obsession for Men · Old Spice · Pregnancy-Test Kits · Cigarettes · Dental Floss · Mouthwash

**KEY**
- ■ High
- ◩ Above average
- ◪ Below average
- ☐ Low

**INTEREST**

## Food

Croissants · White Bread · Pizza · Nuts · Beef · Instant Mashed Potatoes · Ben & Jerry's Ice Cream · Weight Watchers Frozen Dessert · Oat Bran · Bacon · Bagels · Twinkies · Apples · Oranges · TV Dinners · Fast Food

## Drink

Lemon-Lime Soda · Herbal Tea · Ground Coffee · Red Wine · White Wine · Budweiser · Coors · Miller

**MARKET**

- San Francisco et al., CA
- Santa Barbara et al., CA
- Sarasota, FL
- Savannah, GA
- Seattle-Tacoma, WA
- Shreveport et al., LA-TX
- Sioux City, IA
- Sioux Falls-Mitchell, SD
- South Bend-Elkhart, IN
- Spokane, WA
- Springfield, MA
- Springfield, MO
- Springfield et al., IL
- St. Joseph, MO
- St. Louis, MO
- Syracuse, NY
- Tallahassee et al., FL-GA
- Tampa-St. Petersburg, FL
- Terre Haute, IN
- Toledo, OH
- Topeka, KS
- Traverse City et al., MI
- Tucson, AZ
- Tulsa, OK
- Tuscaloosa, AL
- Twin Falls, ID
- Tyler-Longview et al., TX
- Utica, NY
- Waco-Temple-Bryan, TX
- Washington, DC
- Watertown-Carthage, NY
- Wausau-Rhinelander, WI
- W. Palm Beach et al., FL
- Wheeling et al., WV-OH
- Wichita Falls et al., TX-OK
- Wichita-Hutchinson, KS
- Wilkes-Barre et al., PA
- Wilmington, NC
- Yakima et al., WA
- Youngstown, OH
- Zanesville, OH
- AK area not in any ADI
- HI area not in any ADI

## Leisure

| Books | Television | Theme Parks | Shopping Malls | State Fairs | Fraternal Orders | Movies | Video Rentals | Baking from Scratch | Stocks | Lottery Tickets |
|---|---|---|---|---|---|---|---|---|---|---|

## Home

| Recliners | Woks | Power Tools | Personal Computers | Tupperware | Cats | Dogs | Mobile Homes | Junk Mail | Home Fax Machines | Boom Boxes | Plush Dolls/Animals | Nintendo |
|---|---|---|---|---|---|---|---|---|---|---|---|---|

## Personal

| Condoms | Headache Remedies | Obsession for Men | Old Spice | Pregnancy-Test Kits | Cigarettes | Dental Floss | Mouthwash |
|---|---|---|---|---|---|---|---|

**KEY — INTEREST**
- ■ High
- ◼ Above average
- ◾ Below average
- ☐ Low

## Sports

Jogging · Hunting · Sailing · Powerboating · Playing Golf · Home Gyms · Camping · Playing Racquetball · Bowling · Watching Pro Baseball · Watching Pro Football · Watching Pro Basketball · Watching College Basketball

## Cars

Japanese Vehicles · American Vehicles · BMWs · Cadillacs · Ford Escorts · Volvos · Muscle Cars · Sport/Utility Vehicles · Light Trucks · Used Cars

## TV

"The Simpsons" · "A Current Affair" · C-SPAN · "Oprah" · "Donahue"

**MARKET**

- Abilene-Sweetwater, TX
- Albany, GA
- Albany et al., NY
- Albuquerque, NM
- Alexandria, LA
- Alpena, MI
- Amarillo, TX
- Anniston, AL
- Ardmore-Ada, OK
- Atlanta, GA
- Augusta, GA
- Austin, TX
- Bakersfield, CA
- Baltimore, MD
- Bangor, ME
- Baton Rouge, LA
- Beaumont-Port Arthur, TX
- Bend, OR
- Billings-Hardin, MT
- Biloxi et al., MS
- Binghamton, NY
- Birmingham, AL
- Bluefield et al., WV
- Boise, ID
- Boston, MA
- Bowling Green, KY
- Bristol et al., TN-VA
- Buffalo, NY
- Burlington et al., VT-NY
- Butte, MT
- Casper-Riverton, WY
- Cedar Rapids et al., IA
- Charleston, SC
- Charleston et al., WV
- Charlotte, NC
- Charlottesville, VA
- Chattanooga, TN
- Cheyenne et al., WY-NE
- Chicago, IL
- Chico-Redding, CA
- Cincinnati, OH
- Clarksburg-Weston, WV

**TV cont.:** "Saturday Night Live" · "Am. Funniest Home Videos" · "Roseanne" · Daytime Soap Operas · MTV · "Cops"

**Music:** Classical Music · Country Music · Classic Rock · Folk Music · Jazz · Rap · Modern Rock · Heavy Metal · Gospel Music

**Periodicals:** New Yorker · National Enquirer · Gourmet · Family Circle · Vanity Fair · USA Today · Playboy

**Issues:** Liberal Politics · Conservative Politics · Moderate Politics · Anti-Abortion · Gay Rights · Privacy Rights · Charging · Saving · Green Consuming · Ozone Depletion · Endangered Animals · Death Penalty · School Prayer · Legalizing Drugs

**KEY**  **INTEREST**

- ■ High
- ◼ Above average
- ◾ Below average
- ☐ Low

## Sports | Cars | TV

**MARKET**

Column headers — Sports: Jogging, Hunting, Sailing, Powerboating, Playing Golf, Home Gyms, Camping, Playing Racquetball, Bowling, Watching Pro Baseball, Watching Pro Football, Watching Pro Basketball, Watching College Basketball

Cars: Japanese Vehicles, American Vehicles, BMWs, Cadillacs, Ford Escorts, Volvos, Muscle Cars, Sport/Utility Vehicles, Light Trucks, Used Cars

TV: "The Simpsons", "A Current Affair", C-SPAN, "Oprah", "Donahue"

| Market |
| --- |
| Cleveland, OH |
| Colorado Springs et al., CO |
| Columbia, SC |
| Columbia et al., MO |
| Columbus, GA |
| Columbus, OH |
| Columbus-Tupelo, MS |
| Corpus Christi, TX |
| Dallas-Ft. Worth, TX |
| Davenport et al., IA-IL |
| Dayton, OH |
| Denver, CO |
| Des Moines, IA |
| Detroit, MI |
| Dothan, AL |
| Duluth-Superior, MN-WI |
| El Centro-Yuma, CA-AZ |
| El Paso, TX |
| Elmira, NY |
| Erie, PA |
| Eugene, OR |
| Eureka, CA |
| Evansville, IN |
| Fargo, ND |
| Flagstaff, AZ |
| Flint-Saginaw et al., MI |
| Florence et al., SC |
| Fresno-Visalia, CA |
| Ft. Myers-Naples, FL |
| Ft. Smith, AR |
| Ft. Wayne, IN |
| Gainesville, FL |
| Grand Junction et al., CO |
| Grand Rapids et al., MI |
| Great Falls, MT |
| Green Bay-Appleton, WI |
| Greensboro et al., NC |
| Greenville et al., NC |
| Greenville et al., SC-NC |
| Greenwood-Greenville, MS |
| Hagerstown, MD |
| Harrisburg et al., PA |

## TV cont.

"Saturday Night Live" | "Am. Funniest Home Videos" | "Roseanne" | Daytime Soap Operas | MTV | "Cops"

## Music

Classical Music | Country Music | Classic Rock | Folk Music | Jazz | Rap | Modern Rock | Heavy Metal | Gospel Music

## Periodicals

New Yorker | National Enquirer | Gourmet | Family Circle | Vanity Fair | USA Today | Playboy

## Issues

Liberal Politics | Conservative Politics | Moderate Politics | Anti-Abortion | Gay Rights | Privacy Rights | Charging | Saving | Green Consuming | Ozone Depletion | Endangered Animals | Death Penalty | School Prayer | Legalizing Drugs

**KEY — INTEREST**
- ■ High
- ◨ Above average
- ◧ Below average
- □ Low

| MARKET | Sports — Jogging | Hunting | Sailing | Powerboating | Playing Golf | Home Gyms | Camping | Playing Racquetball | Bowling | Watching Pro Baseball | Watching Pro Football | Watching Pro Basketball | Watching College Basketball | Cars — Japanese Vehicles | American Vehicles | BMWs | Cadillacs | Ford Escorts | Volvos | Muscle Cars | Sport/Utility Vehicles | Light Trucks | Used Cars | TV — "The Simpsons" | "A Current Affair" | C-SPAN | "Oprah" | "Donahue" |
|---|---|---|---|---|---|---|---|---|---|---|---|---|---|---|---|---|---|---|---|---|---|---|---|---|---|---|---|---|
| Harrisonburg, VA | □ | ■ | □ | ◧ | □ | □ | ■ | □ | □ | □ | □ | □ | ◧ | □ | ◧ | □ | □ | □ | □ | ■ | ■ | ■ | ■ | □ | ◧ | ◧ | ◧ | ◧ |
| Hartford-New Haven, CT | ◧ | ◧ | ◧ | ◧ | ■ | ◧ | ◧ | ■ | ◧ | ■ | ◧ | ◧ | ◧ | ■ | ◧ | ◧ | ◧ | ◧ | ■ | ◧ | ◧ | ◧ | ◧ | ◧ | ◧ | ◧ | ◧ | ◧ |
| Helena, MT | ◧ | ■ | ◧ | ◧ | ■ | ◧ | ■ | ◧ | ◧ | ◧ | ◧ | ◧ | ◧ | ◧ | ◧ | ◧ | ◧ | ◧ | ◧ | ◧ | ■ | ■ | ■ | ◧ | ◧ | ◧ | □ | □ |
| Houston, TX | ■ | ◧ | ◧ | ◧ | ◧ | ◧ | ◧ | ◧ | ■ | ◧ | ◧ | ◧ | ◧ | ◧ | ◧ | ◧ | ◧ | ◧ | ◧ | ◧ | ◧ | ◧ | ◧ | ■ | □ | ◧ | ◧ | ◧ |
| Huntsville et al., AL | □ | ◧ | □ | ◧ | ◧ | □ | ◧ | □ | □ | □ | ◧ | ◧ | ◧ | □ | ◧ | □ | ◧ | □ | □ | ◧ | ◧ | ■ | ◧ | ◧ | ◧ | ◧ | ◧ | ◧ |
| Idaho Falls et al., ID | □ | ■ | □ | ◧ | ◧ | ◧ | ■ | ◧ | ◧ | ◧ | ◧ | ◧ | ◧ | ◧ | ◧ | □ | □ | □ | □ | ◧ | ■ | ■ | ◧ | ◧ | □ | ◧ | □ | □ |
| Indianapolis, IN | ◧ | ◧ | ◧ | ◧ | ◧ | ◧ | ◧ | ◧ | ◧ | ◧ | ◧ | ■ | ■ | ◧ | ◧ | ◧ | ◧ | ◧ | ◧ | ◧ | ◧ | ◧ | ◧ | ◧ | ◧ | □ | ◧ | ◧ |
| Jackson, MS | □ | ◧ | □ | □ | □ | □ | □ | □ | □ | □ | ◧ | ◧ | □ | □ | ■ | □ | ◧ | □ | □ | ◧ | ◧ | ■ | ◧ | ◧ | ◧ | ◧ | ■ | □ |
| Jackson, TN | □ | ■ | □ | ◧ | □ | □ | □ | □ | □ | □ | ◧ | □ | □ | □ | ◧ | □ | ◧ | □ | □ | ■ | ◧ | ■ | ■ | □ | ◧ | □ | ◧ | □ |
| Jacksonville, FL | ◧ | ◧ | ◧ | ◧ | ◧ | ◧ | ◧ | ◧ | ◧ | ◧ | ◧ | ◧ | ◧ | ◧ | ◧ | ◧ | ◧ | ◧ | ◧ | ◧ | ◧ | ◧ | ◧ | ■ | ◧ | ■ | ◧ | ◧ |
| Johnstown-Altoona, PA | □ | ◧ | □ | ◧ | □ | ◧ | ◧ | □ | ■ | ◧ | ■ | ◧ | ◧ | □ | ◧ | □ | ◧ | □ | □ | ◧ | ◧ | ◧ | ■ | ◧ | ◧ | □ | ◧ | □ |
| Jonesboro, AR | □ | ■ | □ | □ | □ | □ | □ | □ | □ | □ | □ | □ | □ | □ | ◧ | □ | ◧ | □ | □ | ◧ | ◧ | ◧ | ◧ | ◧ | □ | □ | ◧ | □ |
| Joplin-Pittsburg, MO-KS | □ | ■ | □ | ◧ | ◧ | □ | ◧ | □ | ◧ | □ | □ | □ | ◧ | □ | ◧ | □ | ◧ | □ | □ | ◧ | ◧ | ◧ | ■ | ◧ | ◧ | □ | ◧ | □ |
| Kansas City, MO-KS | ■ | ◧ | ◧ | ◧ | ◧ | ◧ | ◧ | ◧ | ◧ | ◧ | ◧ | ◧ | ◧ | ◧ | ◧ | ◧ | ◧ | ◧ | ◧ | ◧ | ◧ | ◧ | ◧ | ◧ | ◧ | ◧ | ◧ | ◧ |
| Knoxville, TN | □ | ◧ | □ | ◧ | □ | □ | ◧ | □ | □ | □ | □ | ◧ | ■ | □ | ◧ | □ | ◧ | □ | □ | ■ | ◧ | ■ | ■ | □ | ◧ | □ | ◧ | ◧ |
| La Crosse-Eau Claire, WI | □ | ■ | □ | ◧ | ◧ | ◧ | ◧ | ◧ | ■ | ◧ | ■ | □ | ◧ | □ | ◧ | □ | □ | □ | □ | ◧ | ◧ | ■ | ◧ | □ | ◧ | □ | ■ | ◧ |
| Lafayette, IN | ■ | ◧ | ◧ | ◧ | ◧ | ◧ | ◧ | ◧ | ◧ | ◧ | ◧ | ◧ | ■ | ◧ | ◧ | ◧ | ◧ | ◧ | ◧ | ◧ | ◧ | ◧ | ◧ | ◧ | □ | ◧ | □ | □ |
| Lafayette, LA | □ | ◧ | □ | ◧ | □ | □ | □ | □ | ◧ | □ | □ | ◧ | □ | □ | ◧ | □ | ◧ | □ | □ | ◧ | ◧ | ■ | ◧ | ◧ | □ | ◧ | □ | □ |
| Lake Charles, LA | □ | ◧ | □ | ◧ | □ | ◧ | □ | □ | ◧ | □ | ◧ | ◧ | ◧ | □ | ◧ | □ | ◧ | □ | □ | ◧ | ◧ | ■ | ■ | ◧ | ◧ | □ | ■ | □ |
| Lansing, MI | ◧ | ◧ | ◧ | ◧ | ◧ | ◧ | ◧ | ◧ | ◧ | ◧ | ◧ | ◧ | ◧ | ◧ | ◧ | ◧ | ◧ | ◧ | ◧ | ◧ | ◧ | ◧ | ◧ | ◧ | ◧ | □ | ◧ | ◧ |
| Laredo, TX | □ | □ | □ | □ | □ | □ | □ | □ | □ | □ | □ | □ | □ | □ | ◧ | □ | □ | □ | □ | □ | ◧ | ◧ | ■ | □ | ◧ | □ | ◧ | ■ |
| Las Vegas, NV | ■ | ◧ | ◧ | ◧ | ■ | ◧ | ■ | ◧ | ◧ | ■ | ◧ | ◧ | ◧ | ■ | ◧ | ◧ | ◧ | ◧ | ◧ | ◧ | ◧ | ◧ | ◧ | ◧ | ◧ | ◧ | ◧ | ◧ |
| Laurel-Hattiesburg, MS | □ | ■ | □ | ◧ | □ | □ | □ | □ | □ | □ | □ | ◧ | □ | □ | ◧ | □ | ■ | □ | □ | ◧ | ◧ | ■ | ◧ | □ | ◧ | □ | □ | □ |
| Lexington, KY | ◧ | ■ | □ | □ | □ | □ | □ | □ | □ | □ | □ | ◧ | ■ | □ | ◧ | □ | ◧ | □ | □ | ◧ | ◧ | ◧ | ◧ | ◧ | ◧ | □ | ◧ | □ |
| Lima, OH | □ | ◧ | ■ | ◧ | ◧ | ◧ | ◧ | □ | ◧ | ■ | ◧ | ■ | ◧ | □ | ◧ | □ | ◧ | □ | □ | ◧ | ◧ | ◧ | ■ | ◧ | ◧ | □ | ◧ | ◧ |
| Lincoln et al., NE | ◧ | ◧ | ◧ | ◧ | ■ | ◧ | ◧ | ◧ | ◧ | ◧ | ■ | ◧ | ■ | □ | ◧ | □ | ◧ | □ | □ | ◧ | ◧ | ◧ | ■ | ◧ | □ | ◧ | ◧ | □ |
| Little Rock, AR | □ | ◧ | □ | ◧ | □ | ◧ | ◧ | □ | ◧ | ◧ | ◧ | ◧ | ◧ | □ | ◧ | □ | ◧ | □ | □ | ◧ | ◧ | ◧ | ■ | ◧ | ◧ | □ | ◧ | ◧ |
| Los Angeles, CA | ■ | □ | ◧ | ◧ | ◧ | ◧ | ◧ | ◧ | □ | ◧ | ◧ | ◧ | ◧ | ■ | □ | ◧ | ◧ | ◧ | ◧ | ◧ | ◧ | □ | □ | ◧ | □ | ◧ | ◧ | □ |
| Louisville, KY | □ | ◧ | □ | ◧ | ◧ | □ | ◧ | □ | ◧ | ◧ | ◧ | ◧ | ■ | □ | ◧ | □ | ◧ | □ | □ | ■ | ◧ | ◧ | ◧ | □ | ■ | □ | ◧ | ◧ |
| Lubbock, TX | ◧ | ■ | □ | □ | ◧ | □ | □ | □ | ◧ | □ | ◧ | ◧ | ◧ | □ | ◧ | □ | ◧ | □ | □ | ◧ | ◧ | ■ | ◧ | ◧ | ◧ | □ | □ | □ |
| Macon, GA | □ | ◧ | □ | ◧ | □ | □ | □ | □ | □ | □ | ◧ | ◧ | □ | ◧ | ◧ | □ | ◧ | □ | □ | ■ | ■ | ◧ | ◧ | □ | ◧ | □ | ◧ | □ |
| Madison, WI | ◧ | ◧ | ◧ | ◧ | ◧ | ◧ | ◧ | ◧ | ◧ | ◧ | ◧ | ◧ | ◧ | ◧ | ◧ | ◧ | ◧ | ◧ | ◧ | ◧ | ◧ | ◧ | □ | ◧ | □ | ◧ | ◧ | □ |
| Mankato, MN | ◧ | ■ | ◧ | ◧ | ◧ | ◧ | ◧ | ◧ | ◧ | ◧ | ◧ | □ | ◧ | □ | ◧ | □ | ◧ | □ | □ | ◧ | ◧ | ■ | ◧ | □ | □ | □ | □ | □ |
| Marquette, MI | ◧ | ■ | ◧ | ◧ | □ | ◧ | ◧ | □ | ■ | □ | ◧ | □ | ◧ | □ | ◧ | □ | □ | □ | □ | ◧ | ■ | ■ | ◧ | □ | ◧ | □ | ◧ | □ |
| McAllen et al., TX | □ | □ | □ | □ | ◧ | □ | ◧ | □ | □ | □ | □ | □ | □ | □ | ◧ | □ | ◧ | □ | □ | ◧ | ◧ | ◧ | ◧ | ◧ | ◧ | ◧ | ◧ | ◧ |
| Medford, OR | □ | ◧ | □ | ◧ | ◧ | □ | ■ | ◧ | □ | ◧ | ◧ | □ | ◧ | ◧ | ◧ | ◧ | □ | ◧ | ◧ | ◧ | ■ | ■ | ◧ | ◧ | ◧ | □ | □ | □ |
| Memphis, TN | □ | ◧ | ■ | □ | □ | □ | □ | □ | □ | □ | ◧ | ◧ | ◧ | □ | ◧ | □ | ◧ | □ | □ | ◧ | ◧ | ◧ | ◧ | ◧ | ◧ | □ | ■ | □ |
| Meridian, MS | □ | ■ | □ | ◧ | □ | □ | □ | □ | □ | □ | □ | □ | ◧ | □ | ◧ | □ | ◧ | □ | ■ | ■ | ■ | ◧ | □ | □ | ◧ | □ | ◧ | □ |
| Miami-Ft. Lauderdale, FL | ◧ | □ | ◧ | ◧ | ◧ | ◧ | □ | ◧ | ◧ | ◧ | ◧ | ◧ | □ | ◧ | □ | ◧ | ◧ | □ | ◧ | □ | □ | □ | □ | ■ | ■ | □ | ■ | ■ |
| Milwaukee, WI | ◧ | ◧ | ◧ | ◧ | ◧ | ◧ | ◧ | ◧ | ◧ | ◧ | ◧ | ◧ | ◧ | ◧ | ◧ | ◧ | ◧ | ◧ | ◧ | ◧ | ◧ | ◧ | ◧ | ◧ | ◧ | ◧ | ◧ | ◧ |
| Minneapolis-St. Paul, MN | ◧ | ◧ | ◧ | ◧ | ◧ | ◧ | ◧ | ◧ | ◧ | ◧ | ◧ | ◧ | ◧ | ◧ | ◧ | ◧ | ◧ | ◧ | ◧ | ◧ | ◧ | ◧ | ◧ | ◧ | □ | ◧ | ◧ | □ |
| Minot-Bismarck et al., ND | □ | ■ | □ | ◧ | ◧ | □ | ◧ | □ | ◧ | □ | ◧ | □ | ◧ | □ | ◧ | □ | □ | □ | □ | ◧ | ■ | ■ | ◧ | ◧ | ◧ | □ | ◧ | □ |

**TV cont.**
- "Saturday Night Live"
- "Am. Funniest Home Videos"
- "Roseanne"
- Daytime Soap Operas
- MTV
- "Cops"

**Music**
- Classical Music
- Country Music
- Classic Rock
- Folk Music
- Jazz
- Rap
- Modern Rock
- Heavy Metal
- Gospel Music

**Periodicals**
- New Yorker
- National Enquirer
- Gourmet
- Family Circle
- Vanity Fair
- USA Today
- Playboy

**Issues**
- Liberal Politics
- Conservative Politics
- Moderate Politics
- Anti-Abortion
- Gay Rights
- Privacy Rights
- Charging
- Saving
- Green Consuming
- Ozone Depletion
- Endangered Animals
- Death Penalty
- School Prayer
- Legalizing Drugs

**KEY — INTEREST**

- ■ High
- ▬ Above average
- ▬ Below average
- ☐ Low

## Categories

**Sports** | **Cars** | **TV**

### Sports columns
Jogging, Hunting, Sailing, Powerboating, Playing Golf, Home Gyms, Camping, Playing Racquetball, Bowling, Watching Pro Baseball, Watching Pro Football, Watching Pro Basketball, Watching College Basketball

### Cars columns
Japanese Vehicles, American Vehicles, BMWs, Cadillacs, Ford Escorts, Volvos, Muscle Cars, Sport/Utility Vehicles, Light Trucks, Used Cars

### TV columns
"The Simpsons", "A Current Affair", C-SPAN, "Oprah", "Donahue"

### MARKET

- Missoula, MT
- Mobile-Pensacola, AL-FL
- Monroe-El Dorado, LA-AR
- Montgomery-Selma, AL
- Nashville, TN
- New Orleans, LA
- New York, NY
- Norfolk et al., VA
- North Platte, NE
- Odessa-Midland, TX
- Oklahoma City, OK
- Omaha, NE
- Orlando et al., FL
- Ottumwa et al., IA-MO
- Paducah et al., KY-MO-IL
- Palm Springs, CA
- Panama City, FL
- Parkersburg, WV
- Peoria-Bloomington, IL
- Philadelphia, PA
- Phoenix, AZ
- Pittsburgh, PA
- Portland, OR
- Portland et al., ME
- Presque Isle, ME
- Providence et al., RI-MA
- Quincy-Hannibal, IL-MO
- Raleigh-Durham, NC
- Rapid City, SD
- Reno, NV
- Richmond, VA
- Roanoke-Lynchburg, VA
- Rochester, NY
- Rochester et al., MN-IA
- Rockford, IL
- Sacramento-Stockton, CA
- Salinas-Monterey, CA
- Salisbury, MD
- Salt Lake City, UT
- San Angelo, TX
- San Antonio-Victoria, TX
- San Diego, CA

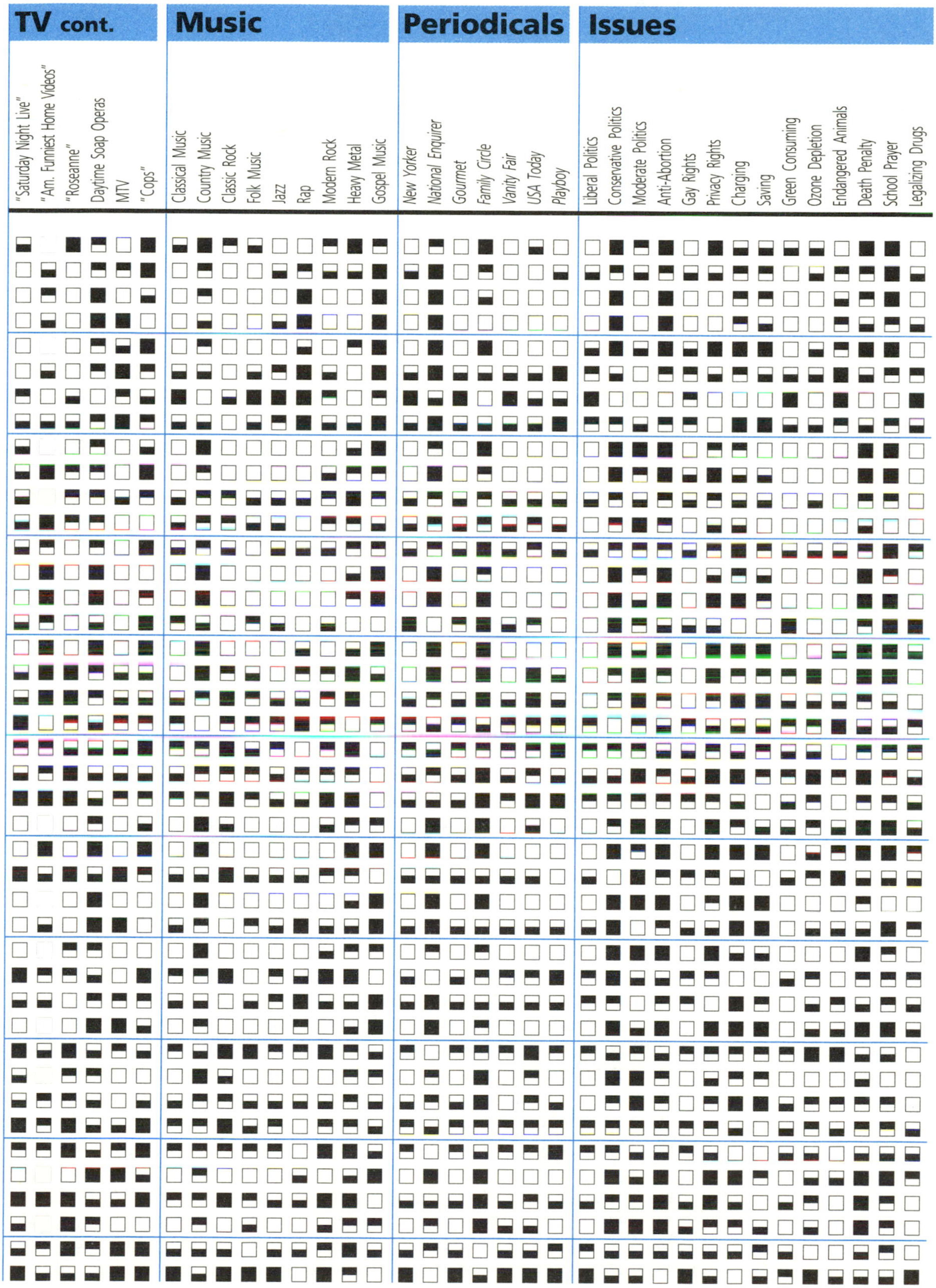

## TV cont. | Music | Periodicals | Issues

**TV cont.**
- "Saturday Night Live"
- "Am. Funniest Home Videos"
- "Roseanne"
- Daytime Soap Operas
- MTV
- "Cops"

**Music**
- Classical Music
- Country Music
- Classic Rock
- Folk Music
- Jazz
- Rap
- Modern Rock
- Heavy Metal
- Gospel Music

**Periodicals**
- New Yorker
- National Enquirer
- Gourmet
- Family Circle
- Vanity Fair
- USA Today
- Playboy

**Issues**
- Liberal Politics
- Conservative Politics
- Moderate Politics
- Anti-Abortion
- Gay Rights
- Privacy Rights
- Charging
- Saving
- Green Consuming
- Ozone Depletion
- Endangered Animals
- Death Penalty
- School Prayer
- Legalizing Drugs

**KEY**  **INTEREST**

- ■ High
- ◩ Above average
- ◪ Below average
- ☐ Low

## Sports

Jogging · Hunting · Sailing · Powerboating · Playing Golf · Home Gyms · Camping · Playing Racquetball · Bowling · Watching Pro Baseball · Watching Pro Football · Watching Pro Basketball · Watching College Basketball

## Cars

Japanese Vehicles · American Vehicles · BMWs · Cadillacs · Ford Escorts · Volvos · Muscle Cars · Sport/Utility Vehicles · Light Trucks · Used Cars

## TV

"The Simpsons" · "A Current Affair" · C-SPAN · "Oprah" · "Donahue"

**MARKET**

- San Francisco et al., CA
- Santa Barbara et al., CA
- Sarasota, FL
- Savannah, GA
- Seattle-Tacoma, WA
- Shreveport et al., LA-TX
- Sioux City, IA
- Sioux Falls-Mitchell, SD
- South Bend-Elkhart, IN
- Spokane, WA
- Springfield, MA
- Springfield, MO
- Springfield et al., IL
- St. Joseph, MO
- St. Louis, MO
- Syracuse, NY
- Tallahassee et al., FL
- Tampa-St. Petersburg, FL
- Terre Haute, IN
- Toledo, OH
- Topeka, KS
- Traverse City et al., MI
- Tucson, AZ
- Tulsa, OK
- Tuscaloosa, AL
- Twin Falls, ID
- Tyler-Longview et al., TX
- Utica, NY
- Waco-Temple-Bryan, TX
- Washington, DC
- Watertown-Carthage, NY
- Wausau-Rhinelander, WI
- W. Palm Beach et al., FL
- Wheeling et al., WV-OH
- Wichita Falls et al., TX
- Wichita-Hutchinson, KS
- Wilkes-Barre et al., PA
- Wilmington, NC
- Yakima et al., WA
- Youngstown, OH
- Zanesville, OH
- AK area not in any ADI
- HI area not in any ADI

# TV cont.　Music　Periodicals　Issues

**TV cont.**
- "Saturday Night Live"
- "Am. Funniest Home Videos"
- "Roseanne"
- Daytime Soap Operas
- MTV
- "Cops"

**Music**
- Classical Music
- Country Music
- Classic Rock
- Folk Music
- Jazz
- Rap
- Modern Rock
- Heavy Metal
- Gospel Music

**Periodicals**
- New Yorker
- National Enquirer
- Gourmet
- Family Circle
- Vanity Fair
- USA Today
- Playboy

**Issues**
- Liberal Politics
- Conservative Politics
- Moderate Politics
- Anti-Abortion
- Gay Rights
- Privacy Rights
- Charging
- Saving
- Green Consuming
- Ozone Depletion
- Endangered Animals
- Death Penalty
- School Prayer
- Legalizing Drugs

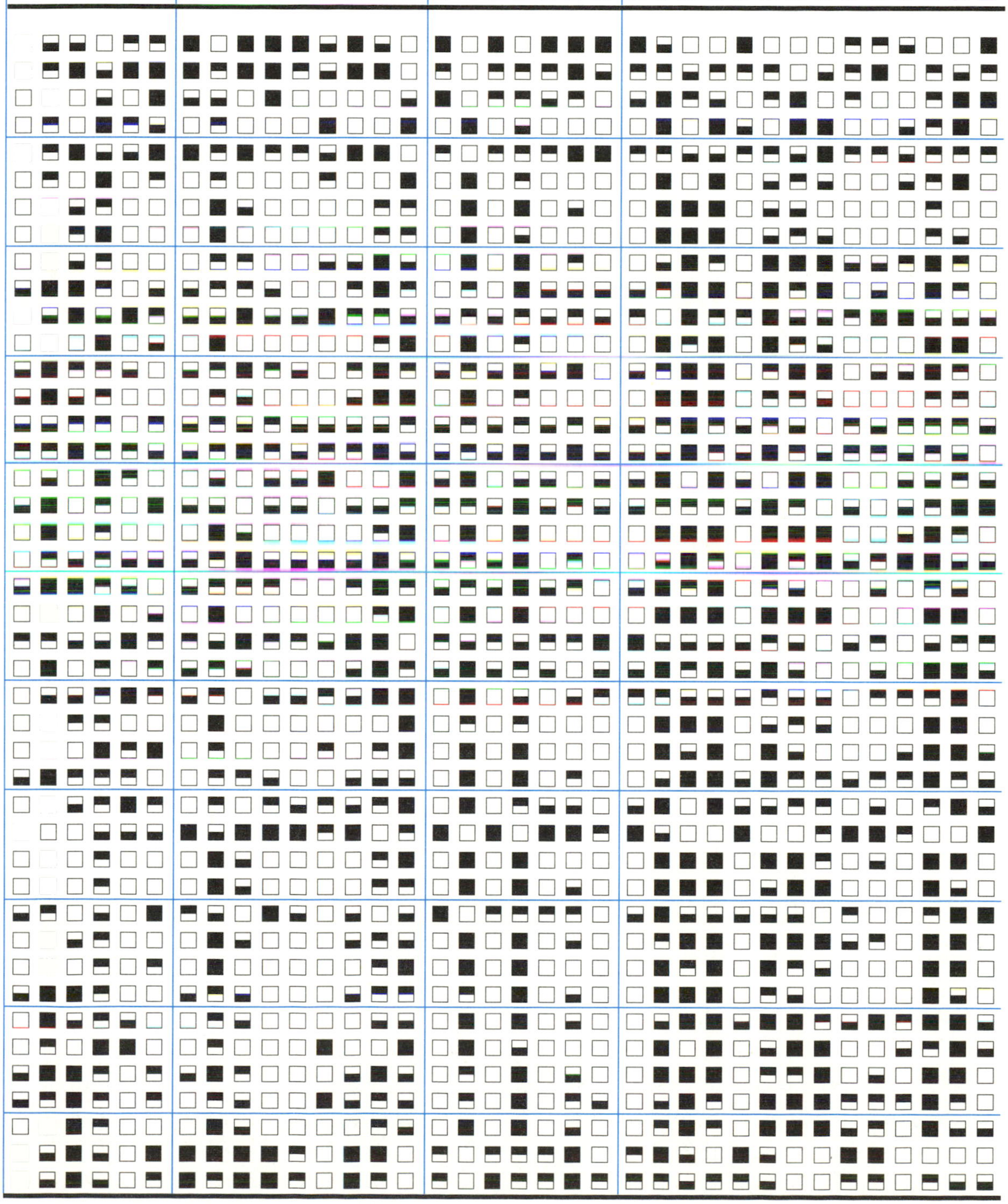

# Acknowledgments

CREATING a book like this involves many people, and I am indebted to them all for their enthusiasm and expertise. First, my thanks to Claritas Inc., for providing me with the access to staffers and databases that made this book possible. I am especially grateful to three individuals: Kathleen Dugan, my data angel, for her time, patience, and sharp eye developing the maps and market profiles; Ron Cohen, for solving the book's technical challenges and for being so generous with his marketing insights and friendship; and ace communications director Mike Reinemer, who provided crucial support and much-needed wit throughout the course of the project. Many other Claritas staffers were especially helpful at critical times, among them Mike Mancini, Rose Bacon, Emily Eelkema, Begona Lathbury, Tim Evans, Sandra Adams-Watson, Blair Zucker, Dave Miller, Terry Pittman, Fran Laura, John Kaminski, Patrise Henkel, Michelle Andreas, Jan Pitts, Andy Paul, Nancy Deck, and Gary Hill.

This book also benefited from the talents of Barbara Werden, who created the book's design; Bill Succolosky, who helped produce the maps and legends; Ellen Barry and Jennifer Edwards, who worked diligently as library researchers; and my agent, Elaine Markson, who is always fantastic. One person in particular deserves special praise: Catherine Crawford, my editor at Little, Brown, provided encouragement and guidance from the project's inception, as well as smart and sensitive editing after the copy was completed; working with her has been an unexpected pleasure.

I am also grateful to my family and friends for their sustenance and inspiration: my father, Sidney Weiss, has always been my role model for curiosity, intensity, and humor; my mother-in-law, Matilda Helfenbein, remains a source of warmth and strength; and my sisters and their families — the Franks, Morgensterns, Lusmans, and Mondsheins — are unfailingly supportive. I cannot adequately express my appreciation to my wife, Phyllis Stanger, for her love, understanding, and daily cheer. Our children, Elizabeth and Jonathan, deserve a note of recognition for managing to delight and distract at the same time. And, once again, my heartfelt gratitude to Christine Zylbert, my editor extraordinaire, who continues to contribute her advice, lucidity, energy, and brilliance for the betterment of all my projects; I cherish our working relationship as much as our friendship.

Finally, my thanks to America's consumers and their wondrous passion for everything from Chia pets to chardonnay that provides the grist for my mill.